T0374211

THE
RENEWAL
OF
ISLAM'S
WORLD ORDER

THE ROLL OF ISLAM IN THE
TWENTY- FIRST CENTURY

MUNAWAR SABIR

To my mother and father,
who set me on to the straight path of Allah.
And to my teachers who set me onto the path of knowledge,
a mountain of humankind's wisdom piled over thousands of
years. Men and women receive knowledge and wisdom through
the grace and mercy of Allah, adding up their insights and
understanding to this mountain of wisdom. The mountain
thus continues to rise and soar. They guided me, and I strode
up this mountain and drank from its streams the wisdom of
thousands of sages to quench my thirst for their knowledge.
To my wife, Eva,
whose curiosity and questioning inspired
me to the search for the truth.
And to my children—Shamma, Sarah, Roxanna, and Laila—
who will one day light the path of future generations
in the tradition of their forefathers.

CONTENTS

ACKNOWLEDGMENTS

Many years ago, I became conscious of recurring references in the Koran to a covenant between Allah and His believers. I wished to have an understanding of the terms of the covenant; my search and inquiries did not shed any more light on the subject. Little has been written on the subject of the covenant in Islam. I began my long journey in the quest of the covenant between Allah and the believers, and for over thirty years, I made mental and written observations on the subject, which had resulted in this book.

Knowledge is a mountain of humankind's wisdom piled over thousands of years. Men and women receive knowledge and wisdom through the grace and mercy of Allah, adding up their insights and understanding to this mountain of wisdom. The mountain thus continues to rise and soar. I strode this mountain and drank from its streams the wisdom of thousands of sages to quench my thirst for their knowledge.

Thirty-five years ago, I came across the book *The Covenant in the Qur'an* written by Abd al Karim Biazer that redirected my search to the source itself—the Koran. It was in the Koran that I found the answers to my search. And the search had resulted in this work. I discovered that the remedy to the ills of modern-day Islam lie in pages of the holy book.

Over the years, I have found wisdom in thousands of sages, some of whom I have mentioned and others not. They have all knowingly and unknowingly contributed to my miniscule understanding of the signs of Allah and of the divine wisdom. I wish to thank them all. May Allah bless all men and women of understanding who do beautiful works in the path of Allah and His creation.

I am touched and honored by the generous and encouraging message written by the great Muslim scholar and statesman of our time Dr. Mahathir bin Mohamad. May Allah bless him for his incredible leadership of the *ummah*.

I used the English translations of the Holy Koran of Abdullah Yusuf Ali, Hashim Amir Ali, Marmaduke Pickthall, and N. J. Dawood. I found *A Concordance of the Qur'an* by Hanna E. Kassis most useful in deciphering the Arabic text of the Koran.

In my search of the covenant of Allah, I found the monumental work of Sachiko Murata and William Chittick, *The Vision of Islam*, tremendously helpful. It should be an essential reading for everyone seeking the knowledge of the fundamentals of Islam.

I wish to acknowledge the love, understanding, and the patience of my wife, Eva, and my daughters, Shamma, Sarah, Roxanna, and Laila, when for many hours, months, and years I was holed up in my study.

Finally, I wish to thank Hala Elgammal and Shamma Sabir for their helpful suggestions in formatting and editing of this text.

Munawar Sabir

MESSAGE

I would like to commend this thesis of Dr. Munawar Sabir on the covenant of Islam (i.e., the agreement or undertaking by Muslims to fulfill their duties in return for the many blessings Allah promises the believers). Dr Munawar has chosen seventy-five verses of the Koran, thirty-seven of which begin with *O! Ye who believe* to illustrate the covenants that a Muslim enters into. I find Dr. Munawar's arguments very well grounded and persuasive. It is yet another attempt to clear the confusion in the minds of Muslims over the present state of Islam and the *ummah*. We cannot say that the oppression and humiliation of the Muslims is preordained by Allah. We are taught and we know that all that is good that happens to us is from Allah and that all that is bad is from ourselves. If we are in the parlous state that we are now, it must be because of us—because we are not following the teachings of Islam, or as Dr. Munawar put it, we are not keeping to our covenants.

Historically, we know that when the ignorant Arab tribes embraced Islam, they were almost immediately successful, being able to set up a great civilization that lasted 1,300 years, to give themselves as Muslims a place in the world arena, and to gain respect from all quarters for themselves and for Islam. If today Muslims are looked down on and oppressed, it must be because of us, our failure to regard and practice Islam as a way of life, as *ad-deen*. We must therefore relook at the Koran and its teachings to see where we have gone wrong and, having done this, to make the necessary corrections in our understanding and practice of Islam.

I hope, in doing this, we will not end up in the creation of yet another Muslim sect that will only divide and weaken us. The one religion of Islam has become hundreds of different religions, each claiming to be the true Islam because of the different interpretations of the teachings of the Koran and the Hadith. We do not need yet another interpretation and another sect. But we cannot deny that there is a need to return to the fundamental teachings of the Koran so that we can overcome the confusion that has resulted in the breakup of the Muslim *ummah* and in Muslims killing Muslims.

I pray and hope that this thesis by Dr. Munawar will not divide us again but will lead to a greater understanding of the teachings of Islam and a reunification of the Muslim *ummah*. Let us downplay our differences and seek common grounds so that we can at least say that all Muslims are brothers. Inshallah, with the restoration of our brotherhood, we can once again be able to protect ourselves in this world and gain merit for the next world.

Dr. Mahathir bin Mohamad

INTRODUCTION

Long time ago, mankind was unaware of God, the Creator of the universe. The Creator God, Allah, sent sages and wise men to every community to inform humans about God and His creation. The wise men taught the humans of the obligations of humankind to their Creator and to His creation. Islam is the continuation of the message of Allah that *Nabi* Ibrahim began to spread in Babylon in the fog of time. Ibrahim, who had lived in the mists of time on the banks of the Euphrates River, believed in one God who created the universe and everything in it. Ibrahim taught that God sustains every object, living and nonliving. He placed his trust in the universal God, Allah. He faithfully obeyed Allah's commandments and did Allah's bidding. On one momentous occasion, Ibrahim was prepared to offer his most beloved son, Ishmael, in sacrifice at Allah's bidding. As it turned out, Allah was only testing Abraham's faith, and the child was miraculously saved by an angel. This test of faith became the foundation of belief for mankind for all times to come.

Those who unquestioningly followed Ibrahim, submitted their *self* to Allah, and put their trust in Him became the believers, the *Muslims*. Muslims are those people who bow down and submit their self to the Creator and do the Creator's bidding. With time, *Nabi* Ibrahim's life story became an oral folklore; and by the time it came to be written in testaments, it had changed a whole lot. Other prophets thousands in number followed Ibrahim, giving the same message as Ibrahim did to all mankind: submit yourselves to the Lord, your Maker; believe in Him and place your trust in Him always. In return for this unconditional surrender to God, the believers are promised peace, security, and well-being in this world and the hereafter.

Submission to God sealed a *covenant* between God, Allah, and His believers. Some communities forgot the message, and the messenger became their lord and master. In their minds, the Lord became their tribal deity to be worshipped at an altar or in a shrine. Thus, their god became their tribal and personal savior. Priesthood took over the guardianship of their god and began to prescribe dogma and creed for the worshippers to obey. Both the gods and the devotees came to be the subject of creed and dogma crafted by rabbis, priests, and pundits of the temples, churches, and synagogues.

Communion with Allah: The twenty-first century is the time of awakening for the Muslims. The last two hundred years of stupor and decadence in Islamic societies was also the time for assimilation and rejuvenation. In their decadence, the Muslim rulers revealed their true colors to the believers, who grew in their knowledge of Allah and His commandments. In this period of adversity, believers not only gained their knowledge and faith in Allah but also grew in numbers and strength. Believers of Allah had not only grown within Islam but also increased in numbers and strength within other religions. This century of enlightenment and awakening is also the century of decadence and evil. An increasing number of people turned off by flagrant evil and falsehood of this period turned to Allah, wishing to know Him and to receive His *nur* in their hearts. The more they sought Allah, the more things were revealed to them through the Koran and their faith.

At the time of the birth of *Nabi* Muhammad, people in general were ignorant and illiterate. Every living being connects to its source of sustenance, be it the mother, the earth and the sun, or ultimately the Creator. The innate human yearning, the *fitra*, is for the thoughts of the Creator. Even though early thoughts link the child to the heavens, the clouds, the stars, and the sun, eventually, the child turns to the thoughts of God. Despite the innate thoughts of God, early environment and culture decides the structure of the faith, but the innate spirituality in the human persists. In the present-day culture of hierarchy of priests, man-made dogma and creed has overpowered the innate spirituality of the modern humans.

Tawhid: The Koran laid the foundation of the idea of one universal God, and from this fount arose all that is known and all that will ever be known. The Koran laid the foundation of the knowledge of one universal Allah for the believers in the first twelve years of Blessed Muhammad's prophecy, and it took another ten years to establish the precepts of truth, justice, covenant, equality, good, and evil. The Koran laid out these principles with clarity for all times to come.

In the sixth-century Arabia, at the time of the birth of the blessed *nabi*, the Arabian Peninsula was steeped in ignorance, superstition, spirit, and idol worship. There was no concept of one universal God. The people did not possess the know-how to grasp the concepts and precepts of knowledge of the unity and *taqwa* of Allah and the criterion to distinguish between good and evil, *husna* and *Fahasha*. The distinction between good and evil was fuzzy.

In the Mediterranean world, the one God was a tribal deity of the Jews, and the God of Christians was accessible to the human through the creed of Trinity, in which God had incarnated into the human Jesus and Jesus into the divine God. The blessed *nabi* Muhammad taught that everything in the universe originates from the one and only reality of Allah and that man's ultimate salvation rests with the recognition of his total dependence on Him. This entails conscious submission to the will and the law of Allah. Muhammad, the *rasul* and the *nabi* of Allah, received the revelation of the word from Allah. Allah commanded Muhammad to spread the word to the whole mankind.

Today we believe that the universal God is the center of the belief among followers of all the three monotheistic religions—Judaism, Christianity, and Islam. Nothing could be farther from the truth; for the Jews, God continues to be a tribal deity with his favorite children, and those who call themselves Christians can only access God through His favorite son, Jesus. Yet God the Creator of the universe is the God of every particle and organism that was ever created. God, Allah, through the act and sustenance of His creation, is connected to each particle, cell, and soul. Thus, God is within reach of every bit of His creation. *Islam*, the surrender of one's whole self to God, is a way of life, a *din*, in the straight path to Allah.

The Covenant with Allah: There is an implicit assumption in the Koran that there exists an agreement between Allah and His creation portrayed as a *covenant*, a mutual understanding in which Allah proposes a system of regulations for the guidance of humans. This guidance is presented in the form of commandments to be accepted and implemented by people. Allah then makes a promise of what He will do in the event of the human's willingness to abide by these commands and when the human regulates his life according to them. The concept of promise is clearly conditional on human obedience and submission, Islam. The *covenant of Allah* symbolizes the relationship between Allah and the human; the human becomes His steward, vicegerent, or custodian on the earth through submission and obedience to His will (Islam) as expressed in His commands and is able to take advantage of Allah's promises and favors.

The commandments of Allah addressed to the believers (men and women) are the fundamental values of the covenant between Him and the human, which become obligatory to the human when the fire of love for Allah is kindled in his heart and when he submits to His will and becomes His servant (believer) and steward on the earth. The covenant of Allah forms the basis of the practice of the *din*. The principles of the *din* written down, proclaimed, and stored on a shelf do not have any merit. It is only the practice of the principles that brings the *din* to life. It is the practice of the *din* that unites the believer to Allah and, through Him, to other believers.

The believer has to understand his obligations to his *din*. To believe is to obey the covenant. Those who do not obey the covenant of Allah are not His believers. Islam, the *din*, is a divine call that stems from Allah's *wahiy* through the blessed *nabi* Muhammad. Allah's *wahiy* is the word from Allah, and it constitutes the Koran. The blessed *nabi* Muhammad was the walking Koran when he carried Allah's word in his heart. The Koran, the word from Allah through *wahiy*, is the divine commandment.

The word from Allah and the *wahiy* cannot be confused with human calls and systems. The prophets convey Allah's word. Prophets, as humans, also speak their own minds. The blessed *nabi* of Allah, Muhammad, was careful not to mix his own words with those of Allah. The blessed *nabi* said:

> I am no more than a man; when I order you anything respecting religion, receive it, and when I tell you anything about the affairs of the world, and then I am nothing but a man.

xix

No human has the prerogative to speak on behalf of Allah. Priests, imams, scholars, bishops, popes, and ayatollahs are all men; some are more knowledgeable than others. None, however, can represent Allah. They can represent their personal views on the meaning of scriptures; their opinions remain within the human domain.

A believer, a man or a woman, connects with Allah upon submission, and then Allah is their hearts, and He is with them. Allah proposes a covenant, and the believer pledges on this covenant with their submission to Him. Allah speaks to the believers in *seventy-five verses* of the Koran in a clear, lucid language and tells them all that are lawful, and declared to be so, and what is forbidden and unlawful. And Allah calls on His believers with the words *O you who Believe* and commands them to acts of faith and goodness in the seventy-five verses of the Koran.

Obedience of every such command is *jihad*. A person is taught to obey the precepts of Allah's law in the Koran. Allah proclaims His law in the covenant to the believers in a simple, lucid language. Allah addresses the believers in the Koran and shows them the right way to follow Him. The observance of the covenant of Allah is the total belief system based on unity of one's personality with Allah in total awareness and His *taqwa* and with observance of all the *thirty-seven* commandments of the covenant. This communion is not only with Allah but also through Him with other believers and with rest of Allah's creation, both alive and inanimate. The phrase *amilu al saalihaat*, "to do good, to perform wholesome deeds," refers to those who persist in striving to set things right, who restore harmony, peace, justice, and balance to the whole humanity. The believer, man and woman, is then guided by Allah and His *nabi* through the covenant to show compassion, to be merciful and forgive others, to be just, to protect the weak, to defend the oppressed, to be generous and charitable, to be truthful, to seek knowledge and wisdom, to be kind, to be peaceful, to love others, and to perform beautiful deeds. This is Islam.

In this communion between Allah and His believer, there are no priests, no imams, no scholars, nor any ulema. The believer does not need a book nor a university degree to know God. The believer does not need to know whether her folded hands should be above or below her navel or his pant legs should reach above or below his ankles. In the believer's communion with Allah, it does not matter if the prayers are led by a blind man or a lame woman so long as the person leading is with *taqwa* of Allah. The believer, man or woman, reaches out to Allah in sincerity and bows down to Him in submission. Allah blesses him or her, the believer praises Allah, and He draws him or her closer. The believer asks for mercy, and Allah touches His devotee in love. The believer asks of forgiveness, and Allah pours His mercy on him or her. The believer loves Allah, and in return, Allah promises the believer *Jannat*. When Allah bestows on the believer divine mercy, grace, and guidance, why would a believer burden him- or herself with the baggage of human systems? Systems made up of laws, creed, and dogma fashioned by men?

Allah speaks to those men and women who believe in Him and guides them to the *din* of goodness, truth, unity, brotherhood, and justice. This guidance from Allah is summarized in the seventy-five verses of the Koran, where Allah speaks to those who have submitted to Him and guides them to a way of life. Upon submission to the will of Allah, the believer affirms his covenant with Him by pledging to live his life in accordance with Allah's *din*. Allah is the only reality, and it is through this reality that everything in the universe exists. Allah sustains and protects all that He has created. Everything that Allah has created is connected to Him through this act of creation.

Allah sustains and protects His creation when they praise and thank Him for His beneficence. And Allah reassures His believers that He is aware of all that is hidden and all that is manifest. To Allah belongs all that is in the heavens and on the earth.

Allah is the *Rahman*, the Most Gracious, and the *Rahim*, the Most Merciful. All of Allah's creatures, in the heavens and on earth, praise and glorify Him with His most beautiful names. Allah is the Lord of everything that has ever existed or will ever exist. He alone is worthy of praise and worship. Joining anything in worship with Him is *shirk*, which upsets the human's relationship with Allah. Allah reminds His faithful:

> Believe in Allah, His Messenger, the Book that He has sent to His Messenger and the Scriptures that He sent to the messengers before him. And those who deny Allah, His Angels, His Books, His Messengers, and the Day of Judgment have gone astray.

Allah also says,

> Verily, this is My Way leading straight, follow it, follow not other paths for they will separate you from My path.
> Verily those who pledge their allegiance unto you, (O Muhammad) pledge it unto none but Allah; the Hand of Allah is over their hands. Thereafter whosoever breaks his Covenant does so to the harm of his own soul, and whosoever fulfils his Covenant with Allah, Allah will grant him an immense Reward. (Al-Fath 48:10, Koran)

On the journey in this world, the human is presented with Allah's covenant as his guide, *taqwa* of Allah as his shield against evil, and *furqan*, the criterion to distinguish between good and evil as Allah's compass to the straight path of righteousness. If the human accepts the path of Allah and follows His covenant as his guide, *taqwa of Allah* as his shield against evil, and *furqan*—Allah's compass to the straight path—he becomes a believer and among the righteous. The way to righteousness is through Allah's guidance in the Koran and in the covenant of Allah. Every little bit of devotion makes the *nur* of Allah glow in the heart till the believer is connected with Him and begins to follow His path.

This communion between the believer and Allah becomes exclusive. Submission establishes the link between the believer and Allah. The believer asks, and Allah gives. The believer loves Allah, and Allah loves him in return. The believer asks for the straight path, and Allah shows him the way. The believer praises Allah, and Allah showers His mercy and grace on him. The believer remembers Allah, and Allah responds to those who praise Him, thank Him, and ask of Him.

Allah's *din* is divine. Allah is *haqq*, and all truth emanates from Him. The Koran is Allah's word on the earth and the expression of *haqq*. *Haqq* is the reality and the truth; *batil* refers to something that is imaginary or false. When humans add dogma and creed to Allah's *din*, it is not *haqq*. In matters of *din*, what is not absolute truth is not *haqq*. What is not *haqq* is *batil*, false or fabricated. What is not truthful cannot be a witness over Allah's word and *din*. Therefore, all human additions to the *din* of Allah do not constitute the truth. Therefore, every human fabrication to the *din* after the completion of *wahiy* is *batil*, falsehood.

> Allah is the Light of the heavens and the earth. The parable of His Light is as if there were a Niche and within it a Lamp: The Lamp enclosed in Glass; the glass as it were a brilliant star: lit from a blessed Tree, an Olive, neither of the East nor of the West, whose Oil is well-nigh luminous, though fire

scarce touched it: Light upon Light! Allah doth guide whom
He will to His Light: Allah doth set forth Parables for men:
and Allah doth know all things. (Lit is such a light) in houses,
which Allah hath permitted to be raised to honor; for the
celebration, in them, of His name: in them is He glorified in
the mornings and in the evenings, (again and again). (An-
Nur 24:35–36, Koran)

Allah created His beings with love, and He nurtures His creation
with love. His light illuminates the hearts of those who love Him,
place their trust in Him, and submit to Him. Once their heart is open
to Allah in submission, Allah's *nur* glows in the niche of the believers'
heart where the divine light, spirit, and wisdom of Allah shines in the
human. The glow of the spirit and wisdom shines with the brilliance
of a star—the star lit from the divine wisdom, the tree of knowledge,
the knowledge of Allah's signs. Allah is within those who believe.
The believer's self, his *nafs*, is aglow with Allah's radiance—light
upon light. The dwellings where Allah is praised and glorified in the
mornings and in the evenings are aglow with Allah's *nur* and His
knowledge.

When the human is stripped of his raiment, the veils of skin,
flesh, bones, viscera, and circulating fluids that are left over are
nothing but his soul, his self, the *nafs*. Removal of the veils of *self-
admiration, self-image, and pride*; wiping away covers of makeup and
couture; removal of masks and marks of social status; and stripping
scars and warps of years of greed and gluttony expose a tiny particle,
the *nuqta*, that represents the *nafs* of the human. This self is perhaps
no greater than a little dot, the *nuqta*. The combined *nafs* of the entire
human race, all of the *nuqtas* combined, will perhaps not fill a small
cup. Yet the ego of the human race through this minuteness of pride

and arrogance has controlled the destiny of Allah's creation for thousands of years.

The *nafs*, unlike the Freudian ego, is capable of both good and evil. The *nuqta*, the *nafs* magnified a million times, reveals a shiny disk, the mirror of the soul. The property, the *fitra* of the *nafs*, is to shine as a mirror with Allah's *nur*. When the human walks the path of Allah in taqwa of Him with the knowledge that Allah is with him, watching him and guiding him, Allah's *nur* shines on the *nafs*, keeping it pure and safe. Once the heart is open to Allah in submission, Allah's *nur* glows in the niche of the believer's heart, where the divine light, spirit, and wisdom of Allah shine in the human. For those who believe, Allah is within. The believer's self is aglow with Allah's radiance— light upon light. However, when the human's *desires, cravings,* and *ego* overpower his love and obedience for Allah, the shiny mirror of the *nafs* becomes obscured by the smoke of his desires, and he loses sight of the *nur* of Allah; and in this darkness, the human trips into error and decadence.

The effort required in keeping focused on Allah's *nur* and *taqwa* of Allah is jihad. And this jihad is the obedience of Allah's commandments when Allah calls on His believers with the words *O you who believe* and commands them to do acts of faith and goodness in the seventy-five verses of the Koran. Obedience of every such command is jihad. The expression *in the path of Allah*, of course, is the path of right conduct that Allah has set down in the Koran. Jihad is simply the complement to Islam, the surrender to the will of Allah.

The surrender takes place in Allah's will, and it is His will that people should struggle in His path. Hence, submission and surrender to Allah's will demands a struggle in His path. Submission to Allah's command requires the believers to struggle against all negative tendencies in their self, their *nafs*. Salat, zakat, fasting, and hajj are all struggles in the path of Allah. The greatest obstacles that people face in submitting themselves to Allah are their *desires and cravings* for the temptations of this world.

It is the *nafs* that directs intentions and actions of the human to the good and the bad. *Nafs* is the seat of the qualities of self-admiration, arrogance, and pride; hard-heartedness; suppression of Allah's love; pointing to faults of others; lying, gossiping, cheating, backbiting, envy, and jealousy; criticism of others; self-praise; bitterness; covetousness of the belongings of others even when one possesses something that is better; lack of contentment, constant complaining, lack of gratitude, and blindness to one's blessings; wishing for increase without effort; selfishness, greed, and covetousness that knows no bounds; love of control and love of self and its desires; hatred for those who criticize, even if it is for one's own good; love for those who praise, even if it is in hypocrisy; rejection of advice and counsel; and the habit of talking about oneself.

The same *nafs*, on the other hand, has a good side. When the human heart is open to Allah's *nur*, the human becomes aware of Allah's presence with him, and all his actions become governed by *taqwa* of Allah. The human becomes a believer, and all his intention and action is guided by Allah's presence in him. Islam, the submission to Allah, is a relationship between Allah and His believers. The *din* of Allah is an all-encompassing and highly personal type of relationship in which Allah's *nur* (light) resides in the believer's heart. The believer is conscious of Allah's closeness and mercy. The believer obeys, trusts, and loves Allah, who in return loves those who love Him and perform beautiful deeds.

Allah has granted knowledge and the wisdom of *furqan* and *taqwa* to the believers who have opened their hearts and minds to Him. The human has been granted the freedom of choice in doing what is wholesome and beautiful or what is corrupt or ugly. This knowledge reminds the human of the scales of Allah's justice; the two hands of Allah, His mercy and His wrath, are reflected in the human domain, where people have been appointed Allah's vicegerents. Deeds of goodness and wholesomeness are associated with Allah's mercy, wholesomeness, paradise, and what is beautiful. Evil and corruption is rewarded with Allah's wrath, hell, and what is ugly.

In the *nafs*, *taqwa* of Allah drives away the human's cravings for wealth and his inclination toward disobedience of Allah's commandments. *Taqwa* of Allah drives away the unwholesome qualities of arrogance and pride; lying, gossiping, cheating, backbiting, envy, and jealousy; self-praise and bitterness; covetousness of the belongings of others, ingratitude, and blindness to one's blessings; selfishness, greed, and covetousness; love of control; and love of self.

Obedience to the commandments of the covenant of Allah brings the believer closer to Him. By establishing regular salat, giving zakat, fasting, and traveling for the pilgrimage to the Kaaba, the believer holds on to Allah. Through this relationship with Allah, he becomes conscious of Allah's closeness and knows with certainty that Allah is aware of his intentions and actions. The believer is conscious that Allah is his *mawla*, the Protector. The believer is in *taqwa* of Allah.

The Communion of Believers: The believer's communion with Allah leads him to a communion with his fellow believers. In this relationship, the believers hold on to one another and to the rope that Allah has stretched to them. This rope is His covenant. The covenant of Allah thus becomes obligatory to each believer. The unity of Allah is *tawhid*, the unity of the believer with Allah is the *iman*, and the unity of believers makes the *ummah*. The unity of the *ummah* with Allah and the unity of the believers with one another is the foremost commandment of Allah.

Unity: Allah has ordained unity among the believers. Allah says to them, *"Hold fast, all together, the Rope, which Allah stretches out for you, and be not divided among yourselves."* When all the believers hold on to the rope that Allah casts to the believers, each believer connects not only to Allah but also, through His mercy, to every believer. The rope of Allah saves them from the turbulent waters of evil and falsehood. Allah's rope is His covenant that every believer hangs on to, and this covenant connects the believers through unity, goodness, and truth. *Thus, there is a communion of each believer with Allah and, through Him, among all the believers.* Allah tells the believers,

Let there arise out of you a band of people inviting to all that is good, enjoining what is right, and forbidding that is wrong. They are the ones to attain happiness.

Upon his submission to Allah, the believer has His mercy and protection, and Allah's hand is on the believer's hands. Upon rejecting evil, the believer grasps Allah's handhold that never breaks. Allah expels all evil out of those who abstain from all that is forbidden.

Allah holds Believer's hand firstly upon his submission and then again Allah grasps the Believer's hand when the Believer rejects all evil. In this condition of submission, faith, and performance of wholesome deeds the Believers form a community that has Allah's protection and guidance.

In His call to unity of the believers, Allah says to them:

Be not like those who are divided amongst themselves and fall into disputations after receiving clear signs: for them is a dreadful penalty.

For those who lose their way and fight, Allah shows them a way to resolve their differences:

> If two parties among the Believers fall into a quarrel, make peace between them: but if one of them transgresses beyond bounds against the other, then fight you all against the one who transgresses until he complies with the Command of Allah; but if he complies, then make peace between them with justice, and fairness: for Allah loves those who are fair and just.
>
> The Believers are but a single Brotherhood: so make peace and reconciliation between your two brothers; and fear Allah, that ye may receive Mercy. Persevere in patience and constancy; vie in such perseverance; strengthen each other; and be in taqwa of Allah, fear Allah that you may prosper.

Believers in communion with other believers form a living *ummah*. This *ummah* is akin to a beehive, the community of honeybees. Thousands of bees work together in harmony to maintain the integrity and concord of their bee community. Bees work in cooperation and build their hive of a preordained design of hexagonal units to maintain the required environment within bee nurseries to raise their young. In cohesion and unity, they gather and store honey and make wax for the good of all. When threatened, the bees swarm altogether, prepared to fight unto death, to protect their bee community from intruders. All their activity is intended for the mutual benefit, survival, and prosperity of their bee community. No single bee is seen to rebel for its own selfish reasons, for enrichment or aggrandizement of self.

Muslims are ordained to act with the same unity of purpose, in the way of Allah, for the mutual benefit of the *ummah*. Allah bequeathed to the honeybees, in His mercy, a genetic cipher that guides their conduct that nurtures their hive and pollinates Allah's garden. Upon the human, Allah has bestowed the freedom of choice, whereby he may choose to do well or follow his cravings to do evil. He has the choice to do good for his kin, his community, and humanity or to let his greed and craving of the *nafs* satisfy his desires. For those who submit to Allah and has faith in Him, the Koran is their guide. The Koran ordains unity and actions for the common good from the believers. Those who forsake the *ummah* to satisfy their lust and cravings, like kings and politicians of Islam, have also forsaken their Allah and their *din*.

The communion of individual believers with Allah and with one another translates into an *ummah* in which the critical mass of goodness on the earth outweighs evil. In this union, the Real is supreme, and His writ is ultimate. With Allah's *nur* in every heart and in every hearth, there is *haqq* (truth) on the earth, and peace will reign. People will share their substance; there will be no want and therefore no greed. Wars will be abolished. Ultimately, there will be no religion as there will be no priests. The human will be with his Allah and Allah with His creation.

THE NEW ISLAMIC CENTURY

The new Islamic century, the fifteenth century hijra, began on November 19, 1979. It will end in November 2076. The believers woke up from their deep despair at the turn of the fourteenth century hijra, conscious of their responsibilities to Allah, to their community, and to Allah's creation. The nineteenth and twentieth centuries of the Common Era were disastrous for Islam and its believers. For the disasters of the last two hundred years, Muslims universally have continued to blame everyone except themselves for their situation they are in.

Muslims are the authors of their own demise. By deposing the sultan and the caliph Abdulhamid on the twenty-seventh of April 1909, the Young Turks—a party of Westernized Turks, Jews, and Christians indoctrinated in Western political thought and Masonic intrigue—effectively put an end to the Islamic sovereignty over Muslim lands after a continuous tradition of thirteen hundred years. Ottoman sultans were not the perfect rulers; according to the covenant of the Koran, their station did represent the unity of the *ummah*, and they were a beacon of light to which the Muslims of India, Indonesia, and Africa looked at in their own fight for freedom. Sultan-Caliph Abdulhamid—a linguist, poet, astute statesman, devout Muslim, and patriot—endeavored to transform the Ottoman Empire into a modern industrial, commercial, and militarily strong nation. He succeeded in paying off the country's debts, embarked on the modernization of the educational system, and modernized the military. Another fifty years of peace and tranquility would have transformed the Muslim nation. That was not to be. Alas, what he could not combat was the coalition of traitors within and the enemies without. The appearance of four people in his office on the twenty-seventh of April 1909—an Arab, a Turk, a Jew, and a Christian—who came to remove him from power was a premonition of the dismemberment of the Islamic world with the treachery of Arabs and Turks in collusion with Jews and Christians. The caliphate effectively came to an end with the fall of Abdulhamid.

The handover of the of Islamic sovereignty and the socioeconomic future of the Middle East to the capitalistic European civilization and Euro-Christianity for the next one hundred years was presided over by two families. One family carried out its treason under the guise of its descent from the blessed *nabi*. The second one harvested the plunder of oil wealth under the banner of the Koran and *shahadah*.

The people who caused the division and subjugation of Islam are motivated by their cravings for power and hunger for wealth. The believers were prewarned; the Koran speaks of them thus:

> They have made their oaths a screen for their misdeeds, thus they obstruct men from the Path of Allah: truly evil are their deeds. That is because they believed, then they rejected Faith: so, a seal was set on their hearts: therefore, they understand not. When you look at them, their exteriors please thee; and when they speak, you listen to their words. They are as worthless as rotten pieces of timber propped up, unable to stand on their own. They think that every cry is against them. They are the enemies, so, beware of them. The curse of

Allah is on them! How are they deluded away from the Truth! (Munafiqun 63:4, Koran)

It is not only the Koran that makes the believers aware of the tricks of such people. Jesus spoke of them in these terms:

Beware of false prophets, which come to you in sheep's clothing, but inwardly they are ravenous. You shall know them by their fruits. Do men gather grapes of thorns, or figs of thistles? Even so every good tree brings forth good fruit, but a corrupt tree brings forth evil fruit. "A good tree cannot bring forth evil fruit; neither can a corrupt tree bring forth good fruit." Every tree that brings forth bad fruit is hewn down and cast into the fire. Therefore, by their fruits shall you know them.

PAX ISLAMICA

But Allah does call
To the Abode of Peace: Dar es Salaam
He does guide whom He pleases
To a way that is straight.
—Yunus 10:25, Koran

Dar es Salaam is the abode of peace that Allah has promised to His righteous servants who follow His straight path. Dar es Salaam is the home of the *ummah*, which extends in the east from the Muslim populations of the Philippines to the Atlantic coast of Africa; and in the north, its domains extend from the Muslim population of Russia to those of Indonesia to the south. Every place with a majority of Muslims constitutes the domain of Islam, the abode of peace. Believers within and outside the domain of Islam have the right to the citizenship of the Dar es Salaam and shall enjoy all the benefits and obligations that go with it. Every home and place of worship of believers everywhere on the earth constitute a piece of the Dar es Salaam. There is neither a border nor frontiers in the Dar es Salaam.

Through obedience of the covenant of Allah, the *ummah* is, at this point, ready to roll over artificial borders and barriers dividing the Dar es Salaam and to assume its executive sovereignty over the land of Islam. The *ummah* is prepared to establish the covenant of Allah in the governance of its communities through peace, justice, consultation, and consensus of the community.

The greatest miracle of Islam is the revelation and preservation of the divine word, the Koran. The next greatest miracle is survival and continuing expansion of the *ummah* through centuries of tyrannical and turbulent sultanic and colonial rule. In spite of the alien systems of governments of sultans and dictators founded on self-aggrandizement and personal power, the common people and the community of Islam have continued to receive nurturing and spiritual enlightenment through love of Allah and His blessed *nabi*. Holy men, sages, Sufis, and other humble religious teachers have continued to nurture the love of Allah in the heart of the people. They have sought to teach and preach *taqwa* and the knowledge of Allah in humility and sincerity.

Insignificant raindrops fall on parched land singly and disappear forever; the same raindrops coalesce in strength to form little streams and then little rivulets and join together to become mighty rivers flowing farther, dropping into powerful and majestic waterfalls, yet again joining other rivers, lakes, and more hill torrents to end up in mighty oceans ever increasing in size, in length, in depth, and in power, at all times obedient to the will of Allah. An insignificant human without faith is like a drop of water on parched land. Yet the same human, a believer strengthened by his covenant with Allah, joins others with the covenant to form a little community that, in communion with Allah and in unity, becomes the *ummah* of believers around the world, a powerful united people witnessing over other nations, with Allah and His prophet witnessing over them. At the turn of the twenty-first century, there are more believers than ever in the history of mankind. These believers of Allah are in Islam and in other religions. It is the obligation of every Muslim to commune with every believer of Allah in the brotherhood of the people of *haqq*.

The house of Islam, the Dar es Salaam, is spread over territories whose boundaries were demarcated by the colonial West in its sweep of plunder of the Muslim world. In the land of the believers, there are no borders among Afghanistan, Albania, Algeria, Bahrain, Bangladesh, Benin, Bosnia, Brunei, Burkina Faso, Cameroon, Chad, Chechnya, Comoros, Djibouti, Egypt, Ethiopia, East Turkistan, Gabon, Gambia, Guinea, Guinea-Bissau, Guyana, Indonesia, Iran, Ivory Coast, Iraq, Jordan, Kashmir, Kazakhstan, Kosovo, Kuwait, Kyrgyzstan, Lebanon, Libya, Malaysia, Maldives, Mali, Mauritania, Morocco, Mindanao, Mozambique, Niger, Nigeria, Oman, Pakistan, Palestine, Qatar, Saudi Arabia, Senegal, Sierra Leone, Somalia, Sudan, Suriname, Syria, Tajikistan, Tanzania, Togo, Tunisia, Turkey, Turkmenistan, United Arab Emirates, Uzbekistan, and Yemen.

Muslim homes and mosques in Russia, China, India, Kenya, Serbia, Macedonia, and the rest of the world constitute little patches of the Dar es Salaam, where the laws of Allah are supreme. Any Muslim everywhere around the world represents the *ummah*. Every believer, through his covenant with Allah, is bound to the Dar es Salaam and to his community.

In the tempest and turmoil of the last three hundred years, the believers were swept away and blown into many nations and communities lost to one another in many oasis separated by vast deserts. Individually, the believers prospered and grew into vast families. Each nation had strengths that they could not pass on to others. The wind of adversity had obscured the pathways and connections of one nation to the other with the desert sand, while others in frailty and weakness were unable to seek help. Now the believers—fortified with the *nur*, knowledge, and signs of Allah— have overcome the adversity of separation and disconnection.

PART ONE

THE COVENANT OF ALLAH

CHAPTER ONE

ALLAH'S COVENANT: COVENANT OF THE KORAN

Allah has granted knowledge and wisdom of *furqan* and *taqwa* to believers who have opened their hearts to Him. The human has been granted the freedom of choice to do what is wholesome and beautiful or what is corrupt and ugly. It is only the human, among the creation, who has been given the knowledge to distinguish right activity, right thought, and right intention from their opposites. This knowledge reminds the human of the scales of Allah's justice; the two hands of Allah—His mercy and His wrath—are reflected in the human domain, where people have been appointed Allah's vicegerents. Deeds of goodness and wholesomeness are associated with mercy, wholesomeness, paradise, and what is beautiful. Evil and corruption is rewarded with wrath, hell, and what is ugly.

Allah's Guidance and Commandments

The covenant of Allah is enshrined in the Koran. Every believer, upon his submission to Allah, makes a compact with Allah to obey His covenant. The covenant of the blessed messenger of Allah (Yathrib) affirms the covenant of Allah and pronounces the criterion

of conduct of the *ummah* and that of the Islamic state, the Dar es
Salaam. These two covenants form just basis of the code of conduct
of each believer and their community. Together, they constitute the
constitution of the Islamic state not to be tampered with by ordinary
humans, whether they come under the guise of kings, sultans, sheikhs,
presidents, generals, or ordinary citizens.

The Covenant of Allah: The Covenant of the Koran

> Verily those who pledge their allegiance unto you, (O
> Muhammad) pledge it unto none but Allah; the Hand of
> Allah is over their hands. Thereafter whosoever breaks
> his Covenant does so to the harm of his own soul, and
> whosoever fulfils his Covenant with Allah, Allah will grant
> him an immense Reward. (Al-Fath 48:10, Koran)

There is an implicit assumption in the Koran that there exists an
agreement between Allah and His creation, portrayed as a mutual
understanding in which Allah proposes a system of regulations
for the guidance of man. This guidance is presented in the form
of commandments to be accepted and implemented by man.
Allah then makes promise of what He will do in the event of the
human's willingness to abide by these commands and regulate his
life according to them. The concept of promise is clearly conditional
on human obedience. The covenant of the Koran symbolizes the
relationship between Allah and the human; the human becomes His
steward, vicegerent, or custodian on the earth through submission
and obedience to His will (Islam) as expressed in His commands
and is able to take the advantage of Allah's promises and favors.
Allah addresses those who believe in Him directly in the seventy-five
verses of the Koran, giving them guidance, advice, and a promise of

rewards in this world and the hereafter. Those who do not believe in Him—the infidels (the *kafirun*)—are promised a place in hell forever. A similar penalty is promised to those who submit to Allah according to their word but not their deeds; such people are the hypocrites or the *Munafiqeen*. The concept of the covenant also symbolizes the relationship between man and Allah's creatures and the rest of His creation. They all share one God, one set of guidance and commandments, the same submission and obedience to Him, and the same set of expectations in accordance with His promises. They all can, therefore, trust one another since they all have similar obligations and expectations. In the view of the Koran, humans, communities, nations, and civilizations will continue in harmony and peace so long as they continue to fulfill Allah's covenant.

The Koran uses three terms for the word *covenant*:

- *'Ahd* is the more frequently used term than the other two. It means commitment obligation, responsibility, pledge, promise, oath, contract, compact, covenant, pact, and treaty agreement. It also means an era or epoch.
- *Mithaq* means "to put faith in"; it is a tie of relationship between two parties.
- *Isr* means "a firm covenant, compact, or contract that makes one liable to punishment if not fulfilled."
- The covenant in the Koran contains several articles not unlike a modern legal agreement.
  a. The names of the two parties of the covenant, the first one being Allah
  b. Reminder of Allah's favors
  c. List of commandments or conditions of the covenant
  d. Promises and rewards

e. Warnings of disobedience

f. Affirmation and witness

g. Oaths by Allah's signs and favors

h. Signs of the covenant

i. Lessons from the past

In the covenant of Allah with the believers—for instance, in Surah Al-Ma'idah—the format of the pact is illustrated clearly:

a.

In the name of Allah, Most gracious Most Merciful. O, who believe! Fulfill your obligations. (Al Ma'idah 5:1, Koran)

b.

And call in remembrance the favor of Allah unto you, and His Covenant, which He ratified with you. (Al Ma'idah 5:7, Koran)

c.

Forbidden to you are: carrion, blood, the flesh of swine, and that on which has been invoked the name of other than Allah: that which has been killed by strangling, or by a violent blow, or by a headlong fall, or by being gored to death: that which has partly eaten by a wild animal; unless you are able to slaughter it (in due form); that which is sacrificed on stone alters; forbidden is also the division of meat by raffling with arrows: that is impiety

This day those who reject faith have given up all hope of your religion: yet fear them not but fear Me. This day I have, perfected your religion for you, completed my favors upon you, and have chosen Islam as your religion. (Al Ma'idah 5:3, Koran)

d.

To those who believe and do beautiful deeds, for them there is forgiveness and a great reward. (Al Ma'idah 5:8, Koran)

e.

Those who reject faith and deny Our Signs will be companions of hellfire.

f.

And remember Allah's favor to you and His covenant with which He bound you when you said, "we hear and obey", And fear Allah. Verily Allah is all knower of the secrets of your hearts. (Al Ma'idah 5:78, Koran)

g.

This day have I perfected your religion for you, completed my favors upon you, and have chosen Islam as your religion. (Al Ma'idah 5:3, Koran).

h.

Allah took a Covenant from the Children of Israel and We appointed twelve leaders from among them. And Allah said "I am with you if you establish salaat, practice regular charity, believe in my Rasools honor and assist them, and loan to Allah a beautiful loan, Verily I will wipe out from you your evils, and admit you to Gardens with rivers flowing beneath; But if any of you after this disbelieved, he has truly wandered from the path of rectitude.

i.

Therefore, because of breach of their Covenant, We cursed them and made their hearts grow hard. They perverted words from their meaning and abandoned a good part of the message that was sent them. Thou will not cease to discover treachery from them barring a few. But bear with them and pardon them. Verily Allah loves those who are wholesome.

Moreover, from those who call themselves Christians, We took their Covenant, but they have abandoned a good part of the Message that was sent to them. Therefore, We have stirred up enmity and hatred among them until the Day of Resurrection, when Allah will inform them of their handiwork.

O People of the Book! There has come to you Our Rasool, revealing to you much that you used to hide in the Scripture and passing over much. Indeed, there has come to you from Allah a light and a plain Book:

Wherewith Allah guides all who seek His good pleasure to ways of peace and safety, and leads them out of darkness, by His Will, unto the light, guides them to a Path that is Straight. (Al Ma'idah 5:12–16, Koran)

The Commandments

The commandments of Allah addressed to the believers, men and women, are the fundamentals of the *din* of Islam. These commandments make up the covenant or the compact between Allah and His believers. The fulfillment of the covenant becomes obligatory to the human when the fire of love for Allah is kindled in his heart, and he submits to the will of Allah, becoming His servant and steward on the earth.

Say, "Come I will recite what your Lord has prohibited you from:

Join not anything in worship with Him:

Be good to your parents: kill not your children because of poverty, We provide sustenance for you and for them:

Come not near to shameful deeds (Fahasha) whether open or secret.

Take not life, which Allah hath made sacred, except by the way of justice or law: This He commands you, that you may learn wisdom.

And come not near the orphan's property, except to improve it, until he attains the age of full strength, and give full measure and full weight with justice. No burden We place on any soul but that which it can bear.

Whenever you give your word speak honestly even if a near relative is concerned:

And fulfill the Covenant of Allah. Thus, He commands you that you may remember.

Verily, this is My Way leading straight: follow it: follow not (other) paths for they will separate you from His path. This He commands you that you may remember. (Al-An'am 6:151-53, Koran)

These commandments are similar to the Ten Commandments of Moses. They emphasize tawhid and respect for parents; prohibit infanticide, taking of life, lewd acts, adultery and fornication, and embezzlement of orphan's property; stress honesty in trade; and underline a person's responsibility to be just. Allah commands humans to be righteous and to fulfill their covenant with Him.

Commandments of the Covenant of Allah in Sura Al-Baqarah (2. Medina 92)[1]

1. O you who believe! Seek help with patience, perseverance, and prayer. Allah is with those who patiently persevere. (2:153)

2. O you who believe! Eat of good things provided to you by Allah and show your gratitude in worship of Him. Forbidden to you are the carrion, blood, and flesh of swine, and on any other food on which any name besides that of Allah has been invoked. If forced by necessity, without willful disobedience or transgressing due limits, one is guilt less. Allah is Most Forgiving and Most Merciful. (2:172–73)

3. O you who believe!
The law of equality is prescribed to you in cases of murder. The free for the free, the slave for the slave, the woman for the woman. However, if any remission is made by the brethren of the slain, then grant any reasonable demand, and compensate him with handsome gratitude. This is a concession and a Mercy from your Lord. After this, whoever exceeds the limits shall be in grave penalty.
In the Law of Equality, there is a saving of life for you, O men of understanding; that you may restrain yourselves. (2:178–79)

4. O you who believe!
Fasting is prescribed to you, for a fixed number of days in the month of Ramadan as it was prescribed to those before you, that you may practice self-restraint. If you are ill, or on a journey, the prescribed number of days of fasting should be made up afterwards. For those who cannot fast because of physical hardship, should feed the poor and needy but it is better to give more out of free will. However, fasting is better. The Qur'an was revealed in the month of Ramadan, guidance to humankind for judgment between right and wrong.

---

[1] The first number is the traditional sequence number of the sura, followed the period during which the sura was revealed. The second number denotes the chronological sequence of the sura.

For everyone except those ill or on a journey, this month should spend it in fasting. Allah intends to make it easy on you so that you may complete the prescribed period of fasting and to glorify Him to express your gratitude for His Guidance. (2:183–85)

5. O you who believe!
    Enter into submission to the will of Allah, enter Islam whole-heartedly, and follow not the footsteps of Satan, for he is a sworn enemy to you! (2:208)

6. O you who believe!
    Void not your charity by boast, conceit, and insult, by reminders of your generosity like those who want their generosity to be noted by all men but they believe neither in Allah nor in the Last Day. Theirs is a parable like a hard-barren rock, on which is a little soil; on it falls heavy rain, which leaves it just a bare stone. And Allah guides not those who reject Faith.
    And the likeness of those who give generously, seeking to please Allah and to strengthen their souls, is as a garden, high and fertile where heavy rain falls on it and makes it yield a double the amount of harvest, and if it receives not heavy rain, light moisture suffices it. Allah notices whatever you do. (2:264–65)

The parable of those who spend their substance in the way of Allah is that of a grain of corn: it grows seven ears, and each ear has a hundred grains. Allah gives plentiful return to whom He pleases, Allah cares for all, and He knows all things.
Those who give generously in the cause of Allah and follow not up their gifts with reminders of their generosity or with injury, for them their reward is with their Lord; on them shall be no fear, nor shall they grieve.
Kind words and the covering of faults are better than charity followed by injury. Allah is Free of all wants and He is Most Merciful. (2:261–63)

7. O you who believe!

    Spend out of bounties of Allah in charity and wholesome deeds before the Day comes when there will be neither bargaining, friendship nor intercession. Those who reject faith are the wrongdoers.

    Allah! There is no god but He, the Ever Living, the One Who sustains and protects all that exists. No slumber can seize Him or sleep. His are all things in the heavens and on earth. Who is there can intercede in His presence except as He permits? He knows what happens to His creatures in this world and in the Hereafter. Nor shall they know the scope of His knowledge except as He wills. His Throne doth extend over the heavens and the earth, and He feels no fatigue in guarding and preserving them for He is the Most High, Most Great.

    Let there be no compulsion in religion: Truth stands out clear from Error: whoever rejects Evil and believes in Allah hath grasped the most trust worthy handhold that never breaks. And Allah hears and knows all things.

    Allah is the Wali, protector of those who have faith. From the depths of darkness, He will lead them forth into light. Of those who reject faith their Wali (protectors) are the false deities: from light, they will lead them forth into the depths of darkness. They will be Companions of the Fire, to dwell therein (forever). (2:254–57)

    Those who spend of their goods in charity by night and by day, in secret and in public, have their reward with their Lord: on them shall be no fear, nor shall they grieve. Those who devour usury will not stand except stands the one whom the Satan by his touch has driven to madness. That is because they say: "Trade is like usury", but Allah hath permitted trade and forbidden usury. Those who after receiving direction from their Lord, desist, shall be pardoned for the past; their case is for Allah to judge; but those who repeat (the offence) are Companions of the Fire; they will abide therein (forever).

    Allah will deprive usury of all blessing but will give increase for deeds of charity, for He does not love ungrateful and wicked creatures. (2:274–76)

8. O you who believe!
    Those who do wholesome deeds, establish regular prayers and regular
    charity have rewards with their Lord. On them shall be no fear, nor
    shall they grieve. (2:277)

9. O you who believe!
    Have Taqwa of Allah, fear Allah, and give up what remains of your
    demand for usury, if you are indeed believers. If you do it not, take
    notice of war from Allah and His Rasool: but if you turn back, you
    will still have your capital sums.
    Deal not unjustly, and you shall not be dealt with unjustly.
    If the debtor is in a difficulty, grant him time until it is easy for him
    to repay. But if you remit it by way of charity, that is best for you.
    (2:278–80)

10. O you who believe!
    When you make a transaction involving future obligations, write it
    down in presence of witnesses, or let a scribe write it down faithfully.
    Let the party incurring the liability dictate truthfully in the presence
    of two witnesses from among your own men and if two men are not
    available then a man and two women, so that if one of them errs then
    the other one, can remind him. If a party is mentally or physically
    or unable to dictate, let his guardian do so faithfully. The witnesses
    should not refuse when called upon to give evidence. Disregard not to
    put your contract in writing, whether it be small or large, it is more
    suitable in the eyes of Allah, more suitable as evidence, and more
    convenient to prevent doubts in the future amongst yourselves.
    But if you carry out a transaction instantaneously on the spot among
    yourselves, there is no blame on you if you do not reduce it to
    writing. But neither takes witnesses whenever you make a commercial
    contract; and let neither scribe nor the witnesses suffer harm. If you
    do such harm, it would be wickedness in you. So, fear Allah; for it is
    Allah that teaches you. And Allah is well acquainted with all things.
    If you are on a journey, and cannot find a scribe, a pledge with
    possession may serve the purpose. And if one of you deposits a thing
    on trust with another let the trustee faithfully discharge his trust and

let him fear his Lord. Conceal not evidence; for whoever conceals it, his heart is tainted with sin. And Allah knows all that you do. (2:282–83)

Commandments of the Covenant of Allah in Sura Ali 'Imran (3. Medina 93)

11. O you who believe!
If you listen to a faction among the People of the Book, (Jews and Christians) they would render you apostates after you have believed! And how could you deny Faith when you learn the Signs of Allah, and amongst you lives the Rasool? Whoever holds firmly to Allah will be shown a Way that is straight. (3:100–101)

12. O you who believe!
Be in Taqwa of Allah, fear Allah as He should be feared, and die not except in a state of Islam. And hold fast, all together, by the Rope, which Allah stretches out for you, and be not divided among yourselves; and remember with gratitude Allah's favor on you; You were enemies, and He joined your hearts in love, so that by His Grace, you became brethren and a community. You were on the brink of the pit of fire, and He saved you from it. Thus, does Allah make His Signs clear to you that you may be guided.
Let there arise out of you a band of people Inviting to all that is good, enjoining what is right, and forbidding what is wrong: they are the ones to attain happiness.
Be not like those who are divided amongst themselves and fall into disputations after receiving clear signs: for them is a dreadful penalty. (3:102–5)

13. O you who believe!
Devour not usury, doubled, and multiplied; Be in taqwa of Allah (fear Allah) that you may prosper. Fear the Fire, which is prepared for those who reject Faith; And obey Allah and the Rasool; that you may obtain mercy.

Be quick in the race for forgiveness from your Lord, and for a Garden whose measurement is that of the heavens and of the earth, prepared for the righteous.

Those who give freely whether in prosperity, or in adversity, those who restrain anger, and pardon all humans, for Allah loves those who do beautiful deeds. (3:130–34)

14. O you who believe!

    Take not into intimacy those outside your ranks: they will not fail to corrupt you. They only desire your ruin: rank hatred has already appeared from their mouths: what their hearts conceal is far worse. We have made plain to you the Signs if you have wisdom. Ah! You are those who love them, but they love you not, though you believe in the whole of the Book, when they meet you, they say, "We believe": but when they are alone, they bite off the very tips of their fingers at you in their rage. Say: "Perish in your rage; Allah knows well all the secrets of the heart."

    If all that is good befalls you, it grieves them; but if some misfortune overtakes you, they rejoice at it. But if you are constant and do right, not the least harm will their cunning do to you; for Allah compasses round about all that they do. (3:118–20)

15. O you who believe!

    If you obey the Unbelievers, (kafaru) they will drive you back on your heels, and you will turn your back to your Faith to your own loss. Allah is your protector, and He is the best of helpers. (3:149–50)

16. O you who believe!

    Be! Be not like the Unbelievers, who say of their brethren, who were traveling through the earth or engaged in fighting: "If they had stayed with us, they would not have died, or been slain." So, that Allah may make it a cause of regret in their hearts.

    It is Allah that gives Life and Death, and Allah is seer of all that you do. And if you are slain, or die, in the Way of Allah, forgiveness and mercy from Allah are far better than all they could amass. And if you die, or are slain, it is unto Allah that you are brought together. (3:156–58)

17. O you who believe! Persevere!
    Persevere in patience and constancy; vie in such perseverance;
    strengthen each other; and be in taqwa of Allah, fear Allah that you
    may prosper. (3:200)

Commandments of the Covenant of Allah in Sura An-Nisa (4. Medina, 94)

18. O you who believe!
    You are forbidden to take women against their will. Nor should you
    treat them with harshness, so that you may recant on part of the
    dower you have given them, and that is only where they have been
    guilty of open lewdness. On the contrary, live with them on a footing
    of kindness and equality. If you take a dislike to them, it may be that
    you dislike a thing, through which Allah brings about a great deal of
    good. (4:19)

19. O you who believe!
    Squander not your wealth among yourselves in egotism and conceit:
    Let there be trade and traffic amongst you with mutual goodwill nor
    kill or destroy yourselves: for verily Allah hath been Most Merciful to
    you. If any do that in rancor and injustice, soon shall We cast them
    into the fire: and easy it is for Allah. If you abstain from all the odious
    and the forbidden, Allah shall expel out of you all evil in you and
    admit you to a Gate of great honor.
    And crave not those things of what Allah has bestowed His gifts more
    freely on some than others, men are assigned what they earn and
    women that they earn. But ask Allah of His bounty. Surely, Allah is
    knower of everything. (4:29)

20. O you who believe!
    Approach not prayers with a mind befogged until you understand all
    that you utter, nor come up to prayers in a state of uncleanliness, till
    you have bathed. If you are ill, or on a journey, or when you come

from the closet or you have had sexual intercourse, and find no water, take for yourself clean sand or earth and rub your hands and face. Allah shall blot out your sins and forgive again and again. (4:43)

21. O you who believe!
Obey Allah and obey the Rasool, and those charged amongst you with authority in the settlement of your affairs. If you differ in anything among yourselves, refer it to Allah and His Rasool (The Qur'an and the Prophet's teachings). If you do believe in Allah, the last Day that is best, and the most beautiful conduct in the final determination. (4:59)

22. O you who believe!
Take your precautions, and either go forth in parties or go forth all together.
There are certainly among you men who would tarry behind; if a misfortune befalls you, they say: "Allah did favor us in that we were not present among them."
But if good fortune comes to you from Allah, they would be sure to say – as if there had never been ties of affection between you and them – "Oh! I wish I had been with them; a fine thing should I then have made of it!"
Let those fight in the cause of Allah who sell the life of this world for the Hereafter, To him who fights in the cause of Allah – whether he is slain or gets victory – soon shall We give him a reward of great (value).
And why should you not fight in the cause of Allah and of those who, being weak, are ill-treated (and oppressed)? Men, women, and children, whose cry is: "Our Lord! Rescue us from this town, whose people are oppressors; and raise for us from the one who will protect; and raise for us from the one who will help! (4:71–75)

23. O you who believe!
When you go forth in the cause of Allah be careful to discriminate and say not to the one who greets you with alaikum as salaam, "Though art not a believer".

Would you covet perishable goods of this life when there are immeasurable treasures with Allah. You were like the person who offered you salutation before Allah conferred on you His favors. Therefore, carefully investigate for Allah is well aware of all that you do. (4:94)

24. O you who believe!
Stand firm for justice as witness to Allah, be it against yourself, your parents, or your family. Whether it be against rich or poor, both are nearer to Allah than they are to you. Follow not your caprice lest you distort your testimony. If you prevaricate and evade justice Allah is well aware what you do. (4:135)

25. O you who believe!
Believe in Allah, His Rasool, and the Book, which He has sent to His Rasool and the scriptures, which He sent to those before him. Any who deny Allah, His angels, His Books, His Rasools, and the Day of Judgment has gone astray. (4:136)

26. O you who believe!
Take not infidels (Kafirun) for awliya (friends and protectors) in place of believers. Would you offer Allah a clear warrant against yourselves? (4:144)

Commandments of the Covenant of Allah in Sura Al-Ma'idah (5. Medina 95)

27. O you who believe!
Fulfill your Covenants. (5:1)

28. O you who believe!
Violate not the sanctity of the Symbols of Allah, or of the sacred month, or of the animals brought for sacrifice, nor the garlands that mark out such animals, nor the people coming to the Sacred House, seeking the bounty and good pleasure of their Lord. But when you

are clear of the Sacred Precincts and of ihram, you may hunt, and let not the enmity of those who once debarred you from the sacred place make you guilty of bearing malice. Help one another in virtue and piety but help not one another in sin and acrimony. Be in taqwa of Allah, fear Allah, for Allah is swift in reckoning. (5:2)

Forbidden to you for food is carrion, blood, flesh of swine and on which name other than of Allah has been invoked, also the strangled, the felled, the mangled or the gored and that has been sacrificed on alters; forbidden is also the division of meat by raffling with arrows: that is impiety
This day have those who reject faith (kafaru) given up all hope of compromising your faith, fear them not, but only fear Me. This day have I perfected your religion for you, bestowed on you with My blessings, and decreed Islam as your religion. (5:3)

29. O you who believe!
When you arise for salaat, purify yourself by washing your faces, your hands to the elbows, wipe your heads, and wash your feet to the ankles. If you are unclean, purify yourself. If you are ill or on a journey or you come from call of nature, or you have been in contact with women and you find no water then take for yourself clean sand or earth and rub there with your faces and hands. Allah does not wish that you should be burdened, but to make you clean, and to bestow His blessings on you, that you might be grateful. (5:6)

30. O you who believe!
Stand firmly for Allah as a witness of fair dealing. Let not the malice of people lead you to iniquity. Be just, that is next to worship. Be with taqwa of Allah, fear Allah. Allah is well aware with what you do. (5:8)

To those who believe and do deeds of righteousness, Allah has promised forgiveness and a great reward. (5:9)

31. O you who believe!
Remember Allah's blessings on you. When a people planned to stretch out their hands against you and Allah did hold back their hands from you to protect you from your enemies. Be in taqwa of Allah, fear Allah, and place your trust in Allah. (5:11)

32. O you who believe!
Be in taqwa of Allah, fear Allah. Perform Jihad and strive your utmost in Allah's Cause, and approach Him so that you may prosper. (5:35)

33. O you who believe!
Take not the Jews and the Christians as your friends and protectors (awliya). They are friends and protectors unto each other. He who amongst you turns to them is one of them. Allah does not guide those who are unjust and evil doers (zalimun). (5:51)

34. O you who believe!
If any among you turn back on his faith Allah will bring a people whom He loves and who love Him, and who are humble towards the believers, and stern towards unbelievers, who perform jihad and strive in the cause of Allah and fear not reproaches of any blamer. Such is the Grace of Allah, which He bestows on whom He wills. Allah is All Sufficient for His Creatures and all Knowing. (5:54)

35. O you who believe!
Take not for friends and protectors (awliya) those who take your religion for mockery, whether from amongst people of the book or from amongst the kafireen. Be in taqwa of Allah, fear Allah if you have faith indeed. (5:57)

36. O you who believe!
Make not unlawful the good things that Allah hath made lawful to you. Commit no excess; Allah loves not people given to excess. Eat of things, which Allah has provided for you, lawful and good. Be in taqwa of Allah, fear Allah in whom you believe. (5:87–88)

37. O you who believe!
   Forbidden to you are intoxicants and gambling, dedication of stones and divination by arrows. These are an abomination and Satan's handiwork; they hinder you from prayer and remembrance of Allah, and place enmity and hatred amongst you. Abstain from them so that you may prosper. (5:90–91)

Commandments of the Covenant of Allah in Sura Al-Anfal (8. Medina, 113)

38. O you who believe!
   When you meet the infidel's rank upon rank, in conflict never turn your backs to them. (8:15)

39. O you who believe!
   Obey Allah and His Rasool and turn not to others when you should hear him speak. Nor be like those who say: "We hear" but listen not. For the worst of creatures in the sight of Allah are those who neither listen, nor look or try to comprehend. (8:20–22)

Obey Allah and His *rasul*; hear the *rasul*'s message. And grasp with your mind and heart the truth. The truth that Allah speaks of is tawhid, *nubuwwa*, and *Ma'ad*.

Tawhid is accepting that there is no god but Allah and that He is the only One worthy of worship. As a principle of faith, tawhid explains the oneness of Allah and His creatures, including the angels connected to Him. *Nubuwwa* (prophecy) is the belief in the prophets of Allah and acceptance of their Scriptures. *Ma'ad*, the return, is to Allah the Creator.

Do not be like those who say they hear but listen not. The worst creatures in Allah's sight are those who neither listen nor look or try to comprehend and grasp the truth. Allah took the light from them, and they are left in the darkness.

40. O you who believe!
Respond to Allah and His Rasool when He calls you to that give you life. And know that Allah intervenes in the tussle between man and his heart, and it is to Allah that you shall return.
Fear treachery or oppression that afflicts not only those who perpetrate it but affects guilty and innocent alike. Know that Allah is strict in punishment. (8:24–25)

41. O you who believe!
Betray not the trust of Allah and His Rasool. Nor knowingly misappropriate things entrusted to you. (2:27)

42. O you who believe!
If you have taqwa of Allah, He will grant you a Criterion to judge between right and wrong and remove from you all misfortunes and evil and forgive your sins. Allah is the bestower of grace in abundance. (8:29)

Fight the infidel until there is no more treachery and oppression and there prevails Justice and Faith in Allah altogether and everywhere. If they cease, then Allah is seer of what they do.
If they refuse, be sure that Allah is your Protector, the Best to protect, and the Best to help. (8:39–40)

43. O you who believe!
When you meet the enemy force, stand steadfast against them, and remember the name of Allah much, so that you may be successful. And obey Allah and His Rasool, and do not dispute with one another lest you lose courage, and your strength departs and be patient. Allah is with those who patiently persevere. (8:45–46)

Commandments of the Covenant of Allah in Sura At-Tawbah (9. Medina 114)

44. O you who believe!
Take not for your protectors and friends (awliya) your kin who practice infidelity over faith. Whosoever does that will be amongst the wrong doers. (9:23)

45. O you who believe!
The Mushrikun (unbelievers) are unclean, so let them not approach the Sacred Mosque. If you fear poverty, soon Allah will enrich you, if He wills out of His bounty, for Allah is All-Knowing, All Wise. Fight those who believe not in Allah, the Last Day, nor forbid what has been forbidden by Allah and His Prophet, nor acknowledge the Religion of Truth from among the Jews and Christians until they pay jaziya in willing submission. (9:28–29)

46. O you who believe!
There are indeed many among the priests and clerics who in falsehood devour the substance of men and hinder them from the way of Allah. And there are those who bury gold and silver and spend it not in the way of Allah: announce unto them a most grievous penalty. On the Day when heat will be produced out of that wealth in the fire of Hell, and with it will be branded their foreheads, their flanks, and their backs, "This is the treasure which you buried for yourselves: taste then, the treasures which you buried!" (9:34–35)

47. O you who believe!
What ails you? When you are asked to march forwards in the Cause of Allah you cling to the earth! Do you find the life of this earth more alluring than the hereafter? But little is the enjoyment of this life as compared with the hereafter! Unless you go forwards in Allah's cause, He will punish you and put other people in your place. But Him you will not harm in the least. Allah has power over all things.
Whether you do or do not help Allah's Rasool, your leader, Allah strengthens him with His Peace and with forces that you do not see.

The words of the infidels He humbled into the dirt but Allah's word is Exalted, High. Allah is Mighty, Wise. Go forth, advance! Whether equipped well or lightly, perform jihad strive your utmost and struggle with your wealth and your persons in the cause of Allah. That is best for you, if you knew. (9:38–41)

48. O you who believe!
Be in taqwa of Allah, fear Allah, and be with those who are true in word and deed. (9:119)

49. O you who believe!
Fight the unbelievers who surround you. Let them find you firm, and know Allah is always with those who have taqwa, who are Allah –wary. (9:123)

Commandment of the Covenant of Allah in Sura Al-Hajj (22. Medina 112)

50. O you who believe!
Bow down, prostrate yourself and serve your Lord, and do wholesome deeds that you may prosper. Perform Jihad; strive to your utmost in Allah's cause as striving (jihad) is His due. He has chosen you and Allah has imposed no hardship in your endeavor to His cause. You are the inheritors of the faith of your father Abraham. He has named you Muslims of the times before and now, so that Allah's Rasool may be an example to you and that you are an example to humankind.
Establish regular Salaat, give regular charity, and hold fast to Allah. He is your Mawla, protector, the best of Protectors and the best Helper. (22:77–78)

Commandments of the Covenant of Allah in Sura An-Nur (24. Medina 110)

51. O you who believe!
    Do not follow Satan's footsteps: if any will follow the footsteps of Satan, he will command to what is shameful (Fahasha) and wrong (Munkar): and were it not for the grace of Allah and His mercy on you, not one of you would have been unblemished: but Allah does purify whom He pleases: and Allah is all Hearer and all Knower.
    Let not those among you who are blessed with grace and ample means hold back from helping their relatives, the poor, and those who have left their homes in Allah's cause. Let them forgive and overlook, do you not wish that Allah should forgive you? And Allah is Oft Forgiving, Most Merciful.
    Those who slander decent women, thoughtless but believing, are cursed in this life and in the Hereafter: for them is a grievous Penalty. (24:21–23)

52. O you who believe!
    Enter not houses other than yours until you have asked permission and invoked peace upon those in them. If you find none in the house whom you seek, enter not unless permission is granted. If you asked to leave, go back, it is best for you that makes for greater purity for you. Allah knows all that you do. (24:27)

Commandments of the Covenant of Allah in Surah Al-Ahzab (33. Medina 111)

53. O You who believe!
    Remember the Grace of Allah, bestowed upon you, when there came down hordes to overpower you: We sent against them a hurricane and forces that that you did not see: but Allah sees all that you do.
    Behold! They came on you from above you and from below you, your eyes became dim and the hearts gaped up to the throats, and you imagined various vain thoughts about Allah! (33:9)

54. O you who believe!
Celebrate the Praises of Allah often and Glorify Him in the morning and at night. It is Allah and His Angels Who send their blessings upon you, that He may lead you out of the depths of darkness into light. Allah is full of mercy to the believers! On the Day, they meet Him with the salutation: Salaam, He has prepared for them a generous Reward. O Nabi, We have set thee as a witness, a bearer of glad tidings, as a Warner and as one who invites to Allah's Grace by His leave and as an inspiration and beam of light. Give glad tidings to the believers that they shall have from Allah bounty in abundance. And obey not the command of the Unbelievers (kafireen) and the hypocrites (munafiqeen), heed not their annoyances, and put your trust in Allah, for enough is Allah as Disposer of affairs. (33:41–48)

55. Allah and His angels bless the Prophet.

O you who believe!
You should also ask for Allah's blessings and peace on the Prophet. (33:56)

56. O you who believe!
Be you not like those who tormented and insulted Moses, but Allah cleared Moses of the slander they had uttered: and he was honorable in Allah's sight.
O you who believe!
Fear Allah and speak always the truth that He may direct you to righteous deeds and forgive you your sins: he that obeys Allah and His Rasool have already attained the highest achievement.
We did indeed offer the Trust to the Heavens and the Earth and the Mountains; but they refused to undertake it, being afraid thereof: but man undertook it; he was indeed unjust and ignorant, so that Allah will punish the Hypocrites (munafiqeen), men and women, and the Unbelievers (Mushrikun), men and women, and Allah turns in Mercy to the Believers, men and women; for Allah is Oft-Forgiving, Most Merciful. (33:69–73)

Commandments of the Covenant of Allah in Sura Muhammad (47. Medina 107)

57. O you who believe!
    If you will aid (the cause of) Allah, He will aid you, and make your foothold firm. But those who reject Allah, for them is destruction, and Allah will render their deeds vain. That is because they hate the Revelation of Allah; so, He has made their deeds fruitless. Do they not travel through the earth, and see what was the end of those before them who did evil? Allah brought utter destruction on them, and similar fates await those who reject Allah.
    That is because Allah is the Protector of those who believe, but those who reject Allah have no protector. (47:7:11)

58. O you who believe!
    Obey Allah, obey the Rasool, and make not vain your deeds!
    Those who reject Allah (kafiru), and hinder men from the Path of Allah, then die rejecting Allah; Allah will not forgive them.
    Be not weak and ask for peace, while you are having an upper hand: for Allah is with you, and will never decrease the reward of your good deeds.
    The life of this world is but play and amusement: and if you believe, fear Allah, and guard against evil, He will grant you your recompense, and will not ask you (to give up) your possessions.

    If He were to ask you for all of them, and press you, you would covetously withhold, and He would bring out your entire ill wills.

    Behold, you are those invited to spend of your wealth in the Way of Allah: but among you are some that are parsimonious. But any who are miserly are so at the expense of their own souls. But Allah is free of all wants, and it is you that are needy. If you turn back (from the Path), He will substitute in your stead another people; then they would not be like you! (47:33–38)

Commandment in the Covenant of Allah in Sura Al-Hujurat (49. Medina 109)

59. O you who believe!

    Be not presumptuous and impudent before Allah and His Rasool, but fear Allah: for Allah is He Who hears and knows all things. (49:2)

60. O you who believe!

    Raise not your voices above the voice of the Prophet, nor speak aloud to him in talk, as you may speak aloud to one another, lest your deeds become vain and you perceive it not. (49:2)

61. O you who believe!

    If an impostor (fasiq) comes to you with any news, ascertain the truth, lest you harm people unsuspectingly and afterwards become full of remorse for what you have done. And know that among you is Allah's Rasool: were he, in many matters, to follow your desires, you would certainly fall into misfortune: but Allah has bestowed on you the love of iman (Faith), and has made it beautiful in your hearts, and He has made abhorrent to you disbelief, wickedness, and disobedience to Allah: such indeed are those who are the righteous (rashidun).

    This is a grace from Allah, and a favor; and Allah is All Knowing and All Wise. If two parties among the Believers fall into a quarrel, make peace between them: but if one of them transgresses beyond bounds against the other, then fight you all against the one who transgresses until he complies with the Command of Allah; but if he complies, then make peace between them with justice, and fairness: for Allah loves those who are fair and just. The Believers are but a single Brotherhood: so make peace and reconciliation between your two brothers; and fear Allah, that you may receive Mercy. (49:6–10)

62. O you who believe!

    Let not some folk among you ridicule others: it may be that they are better than you are: nor let some women mock others: it may be that the others are better than them: nor defame or revile each other by offensive names: ill-seeming is wicked name calling for the one who has believed; and those who do not desist are indeed wrong doers (zalimun). (49:11)

63. O you who believe!
Avoid suspicion, for suspicion in some cases is sin; and spy not on each other, nor speak ill of each other behind their backs. Would any of you eat the flesh of his dead brother? No, you would abhor it. Be in taqwa of Allah, fear Allah: for Allah is Forgiving, Most Merciful. O humankind!
We created you from a single pair of a male and a female, and made you into nations and tribes, that you may know each other. Verily the most honored of you in the sight of Allah is the one with taqwa of Allah, the most righteous of you. And Allah is All Knowing, All Aware. (49:12–13)

Commandment of the Covenant of Allah in Sura Al-Hadid (57. Medina 97)

64. O you who believe!
Be in Taqwa of Allah, Fear Allah, and believe in His Rasool, and He will bestow on you the double portion of His Mercy: He will provide for you a Light by which you shall walk straight in your path, and He will forgive you; for Allah is Most Forgiving, Most Merciful: That the People of the Book may know that they have no power whatever over the Grace of Allah that His Grace is entirely in His Hand, to bestow it on whomsoever He wills. For Allah is the Lord of Grace abounding. (57:28–29)

Commandment of the Covenant of Allah in Sura Al-Mujadila (58. Medina 98)

65. O you who believe!
When you hold secret counsel, do it not for iniquity and hostility, and disobedience to the Rasool; but do it for righteousness and

self-restraint; and be in taqwa of Allah, to Whom you shall be brought back.

Secret counsels are only inspired by the Satan, in order that he may cause grief to the Believers; but he cannot harm them in the least, except as Allah permits; and on Allah let, the Believers put their trust. (58:9–10)

66. O you who believe!

When you are told to make room in the assemblies, spread out and make room: ample room will Allah provide for you. And when you are told to rise up, for prayers, Jihad or other good deeds rise up: Allah will exalt in rank those of you who believe and who have been granted Knowledge. And Allah is well acquainted with all you do. (58:11)

Commandment of the Covenant of Allah in Sura Al-Hashr (59. Medina 99)

67. O you who believe!

Be in Taqwa of Allah and fear Allah and let every soul judge as to the provision he has sent forth for the morrow. Yes, be in taqwa of Allah and fear Allah: for Allah is well acquainted with all that you do.

And be not like those who forgot Allah, and He made them forget their own souls! Such are the rebellious transgressors (fasiqun)!

Not equal are the Companions of the Fire and the Companions of the Garden: it is the Companions of the Garden that will achieve felicity.

Had We sent down this Qur'an on a solid rock, verily, you would have seen it tremble and cleave asunder in deference to Allah. Such are the similitudes which We give out to men that they may reflect. He is Allah, there is no Deity but He, Knower of the hidden and manifest. He is the Rahman (the Most Gracious), the Rahim, (Most Merciful.)

He is Allah, There is no Deity but He,

The Sovereign, The Pure and The Hallowed,

Serene and Perfect,

The Custodian of Faith, the Protector, the Almighty,

The Irresistible, the Supreme,

Glory be to Allah; He is above all they associate with Him.
He is Allah, the Creator, the Sculptor, the Adorner of color and form.
To Him belong the Most Beautiful Names: whatever so is in the
heavens and on earth, Praise and Glory Him; and He is the Almighty
and All Wise. (59:18–24)

Commandments of the Covenant of Allah in Sura Al-Mumtahinah (60. Medina 100)

68. You who believe!
Take not My enemies and yours as awliya (friends and protectors),
offering them love and regard, even though they have rejected the
Truth bestowed on you. And they have driven out the Rasool and
yourselves from your homes, because you believe in Allah as your
Rabb (Lord)! You have come out to strive in My Cause and to seek
My favor, take them not as friends, holding in secret regard and
friendship for them: for I know all that you conceal and all that you
reveal. And any of you that do this has strayed from the Straight Path.
If they were to gain an upper hand over you, they would treat you as
enemies, and stretch forth their hands and their tongues against you
with evil; and they desire that you should reject the Truth. (60:1–2)

69. O you who believe!
Befriend not people who have incurred Allah's wrath. They are already
in despair of the Hereafter, just as the Unbelievers are in despair about
those in graves. (60:13)

Commandments of the Covenant of Allah in Sura As-Saf (61. Medina 101)

70. O you who believe!
Why do you promise what you do not carry out? Hateful is indeed to
Allah that you say what you do not act upon. Allah loves those who
fight in His cause in array of unison and solidarity. (61:2–4)

71. O you who believe!

Shall I guide you to a bargain that will save you from a painful torment? That you believe in Allah and His Rasool, and that you perform Jihad (strive to your utmost) in the way of Allah, with all that you own and in all earnestness: that will be best for you, if you but knew! He will forgive you your sins, and admit you to Gardens beneath which rivers flow, and to beautiful dwellings in Jannat of I (Gardens of Eternity): that is indeed the supreme blessing. And another favor will He bestow, which you will cherish; help from Allah and a speedy victory. So, give the glad tidings to the believers. (61:10–13)

72. O you who believe!

Be you helpers of Allah: as said Jesus, the son of Mary, to the Disciples, "Who will be my helpers in the work of Allah?" Said the Disciples, "We are Allah's helpers!" Then a portion of the Children of Israel believed, and a portion disbelieved: but We gave power to those who believed against their enemies, and they became the ones that prevailed. (61:14)

Commandment of the Covenant of Allah in Sura Al-Jumu'ah (62. Medina 102)

73. O you who believe!

When the call is proclaimed to prayer on Friday, the day of assembly, hasten earnestly to the Remembrance of Allah, and leave off business and everything else: that is best for you if you but knew! And when the Prayer is finished, then may you disperse through the land, and seek of the Grace of Allah: remember and praise Allah a great deal: that you may prosper. (62:9–10)

Commandment of the Covenant of Allah in Sura Al-Munafiqun (63. Medina 103)

74. O you who believe!
Let not your wealth or your children divert you from the remembrance of Allah. If any act thus, the loss is their own. And give freely, out of which We have bestowed on you, before death should come to each of you and he should say, "O my Lord! Why didst Thou not give me respite for a little while? I should then have given generously and be among the righteous. But to none does Allah give respite when his time has come; and Allah is well acquainted with all that you do. (63:9–11)

Commandment of the Covenant of Allah in Sura At-Taghabun (64. Medina 104)

75. O you who believe!
Truly, among your wives and your children are some that are contenders of your obligations: so, beware! But if you forgive them and overlook their faults, verily Allah is Most –Forgiving, Most Merciful. Your riches and your children may be but a temptation: Whereas Allah! With Him is an immense reward. So be in taqwa of Allah and fear Allah as much as you can; listen and obey; and spend in charity for the benefit of your own souls. And those saved from their own greed are the ones that prosper. If you loan to Allah a beautiful loan, He will double it for you, and He will forgive you: for Allah is both Appreciative (Shakoor) and Magnanimous (Haleem), Knower of what is hidden and what is manifest, Exalted in Might, Full of Wisdom. (64:14–18)

CHAPTER TWO

THE COVENANT OF ALLAH IN THE PRESENT TIMES: THE THIRTY-SEVEN COMMANDMENTS

The verses or *ayahs* in this chapter contain the thirty-seven commandments of Allah[2]. The essence of the Koran is in the seventy-five verses in which Allah addresses the believers directly with the words *O you who believe!* They form the core of the belief of the believer and the nucleus of his *din*. The synthesis of the three dimensions of *din* (religion)—*islam* (submission), *iman* (faith), and *ihsan* (performance of good deeds)—is what links the true believer to the divine through total submission and faith in the reality of the Creator in addition to performance of virtuous and wholesome actions of devotion and worship of the Sublime and through beautiful deeds in the service of Allah and His creation.

With this practice, the polarity between faith and actions is reversed; instead of faith being the prerequisite for practice, the

---

[2] For the *ayahs* and the sura, please refer to the thirty-seven commandments in chapter 1. In chapter 2, the *ayahs* from different suras have been combined according to the subject matter.

practice defines faith. This reversed polarity is a reminder that Islam is defined not only as a set of beliefs but also as a body of actions that reveal the inner convictions of the believer. This practice-oriented picture of Islam is dependent on the commandments of Allah in the verses of the Koran, and the traditions provide explanatory statements that act as a complement to the Koran. In this relationship, the Koran's word-centered approach to Islam in which the divine word arouses knowledge of Allah in the human consciousness, in contrast the Hadith (tradition), expresses a law-centered perspective on Islam, in which the knowledge of spiritual realities is less important than performance of appropriate actions.

1. The Covenant of Allah: Believe in Allah

He is Allah, there is no Deity but He, Knower of the hidden and the manifest. He is the Rahman the Most Gracious, the Rahim, Most Merciful.

The Sovereign, The Pure and The Hallowed, Serene and Perfect,

The Custodian of Faith, the Protector, the Almighty, the Irresistible, the Supreme,

He is Allah, the Creator, the Sculptor, the Adorner of color and form. To Him belong the Most Beautiful Names, whatever so is in the heavens and on earth, Praise and Glorify Him; and He is the Almighty and All Wise.

There is no god but He, the Ever Living, the One Who sustains and protects all that exists.

His are all things in the heavens and on earth. Who is there to intercede in His presence except as He permits?

He knows what happens to His creatures in this world and in the hereafter. Nor do His creatures know the scope of His knowledge except as He wills.

His Throne extends over the heavens and the earth, and He feels no fatigue in guarding and protecting them.

He is the Most High, Most Great.

Believe in Allah, His Messenger, and the Book that He has sent to His Messenger and the Scriptures that He sent to those before him. Any who deny Allah, His angels, His Books, His Messengers, and the Day of Judgment has gone astray. (An-Nisa 4:136, Koran)

Verily, this is My Way leading straight: follow it: follow not (other) paths for they will separate you from His path. This He commands you that you may remember. (Al-An 'am 6: 151–53, Koran)

Islam: The Arabic word *islam* means to resign oneself to or to submit oneself. In religious terminology, it means submission or surrender of oneself to Allah or to Allah's will. Allah is the only true reality, and everything else in the universe is dependent on Him for its reality and existence. Since Allah created the universe, all things in the universe are totally dependent on Allah and thus are totally "submissive" to Him. Allah, being the Creator of all things, is the *Rabb*, the Sustainer of the whole creation. Thus, God the Creator is the universal God.

The Koranic notion of religious belief (*iman*) as dependent on knowledge is actualized in the term *islam*. The term *islam* signifies the idea of surrender or submission. The type of surrender Islam requires is a deliberate, conscious, and rational act made by a person who knows with both intellectual certainty and spiritual vision that Allah, who is the subject of Koranic discourse, is the reality.

A Muslim (fem. Muslimah) is "one who submits" to the divine truth and whose relationship with God is governed by *taqwa*, the consciousness of humankind's responsibility toward its Creator. However, consciousness of God alone is not sufficient to make a person a Muslim. Neither is it enough to be merely born a Muslim or to be raised in an Islamic cultural context. The concept of *taqwa* implies that the believer has the added responsibility of acting in a way that is in accordance with three types of knowledge: *ilm al-yaqin*, *ain al-yaqin*, and *haqq al yaqin* (knowledge of certainty, eye of certainty, and the truth of certainty). The believer must endeavor at all times to maintain himself in a constant state of submission to Allah. Trusting in the divine mercy of his divine Master yet fearing Allah's wrath, the slave of Allah walks the road of life with careful steps, making his actions deliberate so that he will not stray from the straight path that Allah laid out for him. It is an all-encompassing and highly personal type of commitment that has little in common with academic understanding of Islam as a civilization or a cultural system.[3]

The universality of religious experience is an important premise of the Koran's argument against a profane or secular life. This universalism has never been more important than it is in the present when the majority of the believers do not speak Arabic. Such transcendence of culture is necessary, for the Koran is the vehicle of the word of God to overcome linguistic and cultural differences and express itself in a metalanguage that can be understood even when its original Arabic is translated into a non-Semitic language such as English, Mandarin, or Hindi.

---

[3] Vincent Cornell, "Fruit of Tree of Knowledge," in *Oxford History of Islam*, ed. John L. Esposito (Oxford University Press).

Most humans, whatever their experiences and cultural background, think in similar ways and have similar wants and needs. The Koran seeks to establish a common foundation for belief that is based on such shared perceptions and experiences. Over and over again, the Koran reminds the reader to think about the truths that lie behind the familiar or mundane things of the world, such as signs of God in nature, the practical value of virtue, and the cross-cultural validity of moral principles. The Koran, therefore, appeals to both reason and experience in determining the criterion for distinguishing between truth and falsehood.

The most important theological point made by the Koran is that there is one God, Allah, who is universal and beyond comparison, the Creator who creates and sustains both the material world and the world of human experience. All other forms of so-called truth are either false in their initial premises or contingently true only in limited situations. The recognition of this fact produces a profound effect on the human soul that it forever transforms the outlook of the believer.

Iman: Faith of Islam is based on certain knowledge, which is both a liberation and a limitation. It is liberation in the sense that certainty of divine reality allows the human spirit to expand inward, outward, and upward so that consciousness becomes three-dimensional. Nevertheless, it is also a limitation because with the knowledge of Allah comes a concomitant awareness of the limits and responsibilities imposed on a person as a created being. Unlike a secular humanist, a true Muslim believer who submits to Allah cannot delude himself by claiming that he is the sole author of his destiny as he knows that a person's fate is routinely controlled by factors beyond his control.

Ihsan: The third dimension of *din* is *ihsan*. The word *ihsan* is derived from the word *husn*, which designates the quality of being good, beautiful, virtuous, pleasing, harmonious, or wholesome. The

Koran employs the word *hasana*, from the same root as *husn*, to mean a good or a beautiful deed, for example:

> Whatever beautiful touches you, it is from Allah, and whatever ugly touches you, it is from yourself. And We have sent thee as a Rasool to instruct humanity. And enough is Allah for a witness. (An-Nisa 4:79, Koran).

> If any does beautiful deeds, the reward to him is better than his deed; but if any one does evil, the doers of evil are only punished (to the extent) of their deeds. (Al-Qasas 28:84, Koran).

> And for him who has faith and does wholesome works, his recompense shall be most beautiful. (Al-Kahf 18:88, Koran).

The word *ihsan* is a verb that means to establish or to perform what is good and beautiful. The Koran employs the word *ihsan* and its active particle *muhsin* (the one who does what is beautiful and good) in seventy verses. The Koran often designates Allah as the One who does what is beautiful, and *al-Muhsin* is one of Allah's divine names. Allah's beautiful work is the universe of galaxies, stars, sun, and moon, all in their ordained orbits, destined in their paths by Allah's mysterious forces. All are shining and luminescent with Allah's blessed light, *nur*, providing life and vigor to billions of Allah's creatures so that they may acknowledge and praise their Creator, who made this beautiful and wholesome universe.

The Koran ascribes the love of Allah in about fifteen verses. One of the emotions most strongly associated with *ihsan* is *hubb*. To have *ihsan* is to do what is beautiful. According to the Koran in five verses, Allah loves those who have *ihsan*. Allah loves them because by doing what is beautiful, they themselves have developed beautiful character traits and are worthy of Allah's love. In every Koranic verse where Allah is said to love something, the object of this love is human beings, not the human species but those human beings whose traits and activities are beautiful.

The phrase *amilu al saalihaat* (to do good, to perform wholesome deeds) refers to those who persist in striving to set things right, who restore harmony, peace, and balance. The other acts of good works recognized in the covenant of the Koran are to show humility, to be generous and charitable, to be truthful, to seek knowledge and wisdom, to be kind, to be peaceful, to love others, and to perform beautiful deeds.

Religion as practiced by followers of different faiths comprises the practice of set rituals and prayers individually or in congregation and celebrations of rituals in communal and family settings. The *din*, as envisaged in the covenant of Allah, is a three-dimensional belief system based on total submission and communion of oneself to Allah in constant awareness of Him (*taqwa* of Allah) through fulfillment of these thirty-seven commandments. This communion is not only with Allah but also, through Him, with other humans and Allah's other creation.

> Those who submit to Allah must believe in Allah, His blessed Messenger, and the Book that Allah has sent to His Messenger, the Qur'an and the Scriptures that He sent to those Prophets before him. Anyone who denies Allah, His angels, His Books, His Messengers, and the Day of Judgment has gone astray. Verily, this is Allah's Way leading straight, follow it, and do not follow other paths for they will separate you from Allah's path. Do not join any other being in worship with Allah.
>
> This He commands that you may remember.
>
> Celebrate the Praises of Allah often, and Glorify Him in the morning and in the night.

It is Allah and His Angels who send their blessings upon you, that Allah may lead you out of the depths of darkness into light. Allah is full of mercy to the believers!

On the Day they meet Him with the greeting Salaam, He has for them a generous reward.

Be quick in race to forgiveness from your Lord for He has prepared for the righteous a garden whose measurement is that of the heavens and of the earth.

Allah loves those who do beautiful deeds, those who give freely in charity whether in prosperity or in adversity, and those who restrain anger and pardon all humans. (Various ayahs of Koran)

Allah made a covenant with all the peoples of the book—the children of Israel, those who call themselves Christians, and then the Muslims as an essential observation of their religion. Those who chose to ignore their obligations to Allah therefore suffered from dire consequences.

Allah took a covenant from the Children of Israel and We appointed twelve leaders from among them. And Allah said "I am with you if you establish salaat, practice regular charity, believe in my messengers, honor and assist them and loan to Allah a beautiful loan, Verily I will wipe out from you your evils and admit you to Gardens with rivers flowing beneath. But if any of you after this disbelieved, he has truly wandered from the path of rectitude.

Therefore, because of breach of their covenant, We were annoyed with them and made their hearts grow hard. They perverted words from their meaning an abandoned a greater part of the message that was sent them. Thou will not cease to discover treachery from them barring a few. Nevertheless, bear with them and pardon them. Verily Allah loves those who are wholesome.

Moreover, We took the Covenant from those who call themselves Christians, but they have abandoned a good part of the Message that was sent to them. Therefore, We have stirred up enmity and hatred amongst them until the Day of Resurrection, when Allah will inform them of their handiwork.

O People of the Book! There has come to you Our Messenger, revealing to you much that ye used to hide in the Scripture and passing over much. Indeed, there has come to you from Allah a light and a plain Book, in which Allah guides all those who seek His good pleasure to the path of peace. He brings them out of darkness into light by His will and guides them to a straight path". (5:12–16 Al-Ma'idah, Koran)

The verses in the above surah show the importance of the Koran:

A light and plain Book from Allah where Allah guides all those who seek His good pleasure to the path of peace. He brings them out of darkness into light by His will and guides them to a straight path.

The Koran is a guide and Allah's covenant a code of conduct for all humans to trust and believe in the Creator, the one universal God, Allah. Allah will lead all those people who believe in Him to His straight path and to the path of peace. The children of Israel disobeyed Allah, and they lost His favor. As for those who call themselves Christians, Allah took their covenant, but they abandoned the central part of the message Allah sent them, to trust and believe in the Creator, the one God of the universe. Therefore, Allah had stirred up hatred and enmity among them because of their transgressions. Having split into sects and nations, they have constantly battled among themselves for the last two thousand years over doctrine, gold, wealth, and possessions. Allah has left every human ways open to His straight path through His covenant. Allah demands of the believers to fulfill His covenant by observing its thirty-seven commandments.

Therefore, a believer is the one who has submitted of his own free will to the will and command of the one universal God (*islam*), maintains his faith (*iman*) in God by being constantly aware of Allah's presence with him (taqwa), obeys the covenant of Allah in the Koran, and performs wholesome and beautiful deeds (*ihsan*) in the service of God and His creation.

Believe in Allah:

> He is Allah, there is no Deity but Him, Knower of the hidden and the manifest. He is the Rahman, the Most Gracious, the Rahim and Most Merciful.

> He is Allah, there is no Deity but He, Knower of the hidden and the manifest. He is the Rahman the Most Gracious, the Rahim, Most Merciful.

> He is Allah; there is no Deity but Him,

> The Sovereign, the Pure and the Hallowed,

> Serene and Perfect,

> The Custodian of Faith, the Protector, the Almighty,

> The Irresistible, the Supreme,

> Glory be to Allah; He is above all they associate with Him

> He is Allah, the Creator, the Sculptor, the Adorner of color and form. To Him belong the most beautiful names.

> All that is in the heavens and on earth, praise and glorify
> Him; and He is the Almighty and All-Wise. (Al-Hashr 59:1–
> 24, Koran)

Allah is the only true reality, and everything else in the universe is dependent on Him for its reality and existence. Since Allah created the universe, all things in the universe are therefore totally dependent on Allah and hence totally submitted to Him. The Koran uses the term *submission* (*islam*) and its derivatives more than seventy times; its definition, in the broadest sense, is that true religion is established by Allah alone and that everything in the universe praises and glorifies Him. All creatures simply by existing demonstrate the Creator's glory and perform acts that acknowledge Allah's mastery over them.

> Verily I am Allah. There is no god but I, so worship Me and
> perform salaat in remembrance of Me.
> (Taha 20:14, Koran)

Only Allah is worthy of worship. Those who worship other deities and associate them with Allah have fallen into *shirk*. Other gods associated with Allah by some "Muslims" and non-Muslims are their *caprice, wealth and material possessions, and power and influence over others.* Absolute power corrupts. Religious figures, royals, and dictators in Islamic countries have lost track of their mortality and settled themselves on an elevated status—"I am divine, I am real, and others cannot have the same rights as I do"—leading them to serve their own egos in place of Allah. This leads to *shirk*, loss of tawhid. Sycophancy and blind subservience of self-serving courtiers leads these dictators into actions inimical to the community of Islam. People who claim to be kings and others who become dictators with the might of arms and take life and wealth on a whim commit acts of *shirk* by misappropriating Allah's prerogative.

Acts of worship, supplication, and remembrance (*dhikr*) have a specific ritual and devotional nature in which the worshipper orients himself to Allah and obeys His commands and prohibitions. To worship is to orient one's life and existence to Allah (*Haqq*), to beseech Allah (*Rahman* and *Rahim*) for guidance and help, and to show gratitude for the blessings already received. Such humility precludes a man's superiority over others.

Allah's guidance to mankind is through divine revelation through His prophets, who were charged with the task of communicating the word of Allah. Allah's blessed *rasul* Muhammad took precautions to prevent Allah's guidance to humanity from becoming tainted with his own or with anyone else's expressions. Scholars in Iran two and a half centuries after the *nabi's* death resurrected sayings and parables attributed to the blessed *nabi* and circulated them in the Muslim world. These collections of sayings and parables attributed to the blessed *nabi* Muhammad were in the words of the narrators. Over the next one thousand years, these Hadith began to take the divine role of Allah and His *rasul* in the minds of the common man through the teachings of Muslim ulema. Only Allah is worthy of worship. Those who worship other deities and associate them with Allah have fallen into *shirk*. Those who give a divine status to the Hadith of the third century and equate them with Allah's word have also lost their way. This is *shirk*, which leads to loss of tawhid and *furqan* (Allah's guidance).

Tawhid: The oneness and reality of Allah demands that human beings recognize the greatness of Allah and the minuteness of the human—the reality of the Real and the unreality of the unreal, which places people in their correct relationship with Allah and allows them to understand that they are His servants and that they must act in

43

submission (*islam*). They must therefore recognize human failings and follow divine guidance brought by the prophets and their scriptures.

2. The Covenant of Allah: The Nabi, the Rasool

> The Nabi, the Rasool Verily, this is My Way leading straight: follow it: follow not (other) paths for they will separate you from His path. This He commands you that you may remember. (Al-An'am 151–53, Koran)

> Join not anything in worship with Him. (Al-An'am 6:151–53, Koran)

> Believe in Allah, His Messenger and the Book that He has sent to His Rasool and the Scriptures that He sent to those before him. Any who deny Allah, His angels, His Books, His Messengers, and the Day of Judgment has gone astray. (An-Nisa 4:136, Koran)

> Celebrate the Praises of Allah often and Glorify Him in the morning and at night. It is Allah and His Angels Who send their blessings upon you, that He may lead you out of the depths of darkness into light. Allah is full of mercy to the believers! On the Day they meet Him with the salutation: Salaam, He has prepared for them a generous Reward. (Al-Ahzab 33:41–48, Koran)

> O Nabi, We have sent thee as a witness, a bearer of glad tidings, as a Warner and as one who invites to Allah's Grace by His leave and as an inspiration and beacon of light.
> O Nabi, We have sent thee as a witness, a bearer of glad tidings, as a Warner and as one who invites to Allah's Grace by His leave and as an inspiration and beacon of light. Give glad tidings to the believers that they shall have from Allah bounty in abundance. Moreover, obey not the command of

the unbelievers (kafireen) and the hypocrites (munafiqeen), heed not their annoyances and put your trust in Allah, for enough is Allah as Disposer of affairs. (Al-Ahzab 33:41–48, Koran)

Believe in Allah, His Messenger and the Book that He has sent to His Rasool and the Scriptures that He sent to those before him. Any who deny Allah, His angels, His Books, His Messengers and the Day of Judgment has gone astray. (An-Nisa 4:136, Koran)

Allah—in His mercy, grace, and love of His creation—has from the beginning of time communicated with humans and taught them all that they know of His workings, His universe, and His creation. Humans have always been resistant to accepting Allah's guidance regarding worship of Allah and man's relationship with other humans in matters of truth, justice, peace, equality, and sharing of their resources. Man's ego, selfishness, and greed always have come in the way of his salvation. Allah inspired truthful men—prophets—with *taqwa* of Allah, humility, spiritual purity, and knowledge to convey His teachings and commandments to man so that he may continue to exist in the world during his short span of life in submission of Allah and in love, peace, and harmony with his fellow humans. To follow Allah's wisdom, man must first agree to submit himself to the total, unquestioning mercy and will of Allah with the knowledge that, on an appointed day, he will meet his Maker to be questioned and judged on his conduct during his life on the earth.

Those who have faith and do wholesome deeds, them we shall admit to gardens through which rivers flow. (An-Nisa 4:57, 122, Koran)

Allah will measure out good and evil, the wholesome and the corrupt things that the humans carried out in their lifetime. Humans have enough freedom to make their own choices; if they make the choice to do beautiful and wholesome deeds (*saalihaat*) motivated by faith (*iman*) and god-wariness (*taqwa*), they please Allah and bring harmony and wholesomeness to the world, resulting in peace, justice, mercy, compassion, honor, equity, well-being, freedom, and many other gifts through Allah's grace. Others choose to do evil and work with corruption (*mufsidun*), destroying the right relationship among the creation, causing hunger, disease, oppression, pollution, and other afflictions. In the universal order, corruption is the prerogative of humans, and vicegerency gives humans the freedom to work against the Creator and His creation. When humans choose wrong and corrupt actions, they displease Allah. Allah loves those who do what is beautiful, not those who do what is ugly:

> When he turns his back, he hurries about the earth to work corruption there and destroy the tillage and the stock. Allah loves not corruption. (Al-Baqarah 2:205, Koran)

> Obey Allah and His Messenger and turn not to others when you should hear him speak. For the worst of creatures in the sight of Allah are those who neither listen, nor look or try to comprehend. (Al-Anfal 8:20, Koran)

> And how could you deny Faith when you learn the Signs of Allah and amongst you lives the Messenger? Whoever holds firmly to Allah will be shown a Way that is straight. (Ali 'Imran 3:100–101, Koran)

3. The Covenant of Allah: And fulfill the Covenant of Allah.

> And fulfill the Covenant of Allah. Thus, He commands you that you may remember. (Al-An 'am 6:151–53, Koran)

> Believers! Fulfill your Covenant. (Al-Ma'idah 5:1, Koran)

> Verily those who pledge their allegiance unto you (O Muhammad), pledge it unto none but Allah; the Hand of Allah is over their hands. Thereafter whosoever breaks his Covenant, does so to the harm of his own soul and whosoever fulfils his Covenant with Allah, Allah will grant him an immense Reward. (Al-Fath 48:10, Koran)

Economics plays a significant role in the social structure of Islam, so significant that Allah did not leave the economic aspect of life to be solely determined by human intellect, experience, caprice, and lust. Allah made it subject to revelation. Thus, Muslims prosper when they follow Allah's laws and subject themselves to scarcity when they turn to the human systems. Koran promises peace and plenty to those who obey their covenant with Allah, and to those who turn away from His covenant, the Koran portends a life of need, scarcity, and want.

> "But whosoever turns away from My Message, verily for him is a life narrowed down and We shall raise him up blind on the Day of Judgment."

> And thus, do We recompense him who transgresses beyond bounds and believes not in the Signs of his Lord: and the Penalty of the Hereafter is far more grievous and more enduring.

> It is not a warning to such men (to call to mind) how many generations before them We destroyed, in whose haunts they

> (now) move? Verily, in this are Signs for men endued with
> understanding. (Taha 20:124, 127–28, Koran)

In the above *ayah* of the Koran, there is the word *ma'eeshat*, which comes from the word *ma'ashiyyat*, which is the recognized meaning of the word "economics." The consequences of the rejection of Allah's covenant and guidance are clearly portrayed: a life narrowed down or constricted is a miserable one—one of need, scarcity, unhappiness, poverty, hunger, disease, pestilence, and famine all at the same time or separately.

The Koran's covenant does not put off the realization of the fruits of obeying or ignoring Allah's guidance until after death, nor does it hide it in spiritual abstractness. Observance of the covenant makes life on the earth economically, physically, and spiritually rich and happy. Nonobservance makes it economically miserable and physically and spiritually depressing. In fact, the economic, physical, and spiritual condition of a people provides a pragmatic test of the soundness of the revealed guidance.

Furthermore, the Koran declares that the people who transgress Allah's guidance and are economically deprived in this world will also be worse off in the hereafter.

> Verily for him is a life narrowed down and We shall raise him
> up blind on the Day of Judgment.

According to the Koran, economics and the observance of the moral code of Allah's covenant goes hand in hand, and they cannot be separated from each other.

> He has created the heavens and the earth for just ends, far is
> He above having the partners they ascribe to Him!

He has created man from a sperm-drop; and behold this same (man) becomes an open disputer!

And cattle He has created for you (men): from them you derive warmth and numerous benefits and of their (meat) you eat.

And you have a sense of pride and beauty in them as you drive them home in the evening and as you lead them forth to pasture in the morning.

And they carry your heavy loads to lands that you could not (otherwise) reach except with souls distressed: for your Lord is indeed Most Kind, Most Merciful.

And (He has created) horses, mules and donkeys, for you to ride and use for show; and He has created (other) things of which you have no knowledge.

And unto Allah leads straight the Way, but there are ways that turn aside: if Allah had willed, He could have guided all of you.

It is He Who sends down rain from the sky. From it you drink and out of it (grows) the vegetation on which you feed your cattle.

With it He produces for you corn, olives, date palms, grapes and every kind of fruit: verily in this is a Sign for those who give thought.

He has made subject to you the Night and the Day; the Sun and the Moon; and the Stars are in subjection by His Command: verily in this are Signs for men who are wise.

And the things on this earth which He has multiplied in varying colors (and qualities): verily in this a Sign for men who celebrate the praises of Allah (in gratitude).

It is He Who has made the sea subject, that you may eat thereof flesh that is fresh and tender and that you may extract there from ornaments to wear and You see the ships therein that plough the waves, that you may seek (thus) of the bounty of Allah and that you may be grateful.

And He has set up on the Earth mountains standing firm, lest it should shake with you; and rivers and roads; that you may guide yourselves.

And marks and sign-posts; and by the stars (Men) guide themselves.

Is then He Who creates like one that creates not? Will you not receive admonition?

If you would count up the favors of Allah, never would you be able to number them; for Allah is Oft-Forgiving, Most Merciful. (An-Nahl 16:3–18, Koran)

Sama in the Koran signifies the universe and *ardh*, man's domain on the earth pertaining to his social and economic world. Allah is the Lord of the heavens and the earth and all that comes forth from them. The divine laws under which the universe functions so meticulously and smoothly should also apply to the economic life of man so that he might achieve a balanced, predictable, equitable, and just financial life. *Sama* is the source of Allah's benevolence to mankind and of His universal laws that govern the human subsistence and sustenance on the earth (*ardh*), controlling man's economic life in this world. Allah's kingdom over the heavens and the earth sustains man's economic life and directly affects man's conduct and his obedience to Allah's covenant.

4. The Covenant of Allah: Taqwa of Allah

The word *taqwa* means to be dutiful to Allah, to be wary of Him, to be conscious of Allah, to be pious toward Him, and to be Allah fearing. A person with *taqwa* always has Allah in mind with every action and word spoken, "as if Allah sees you and you see Him."

> Be in Taqwa of Allah and fear Allah and let every soul judge as to the provision he has sent forth for the morrow. Yes, be in Taqwa of Allah and fear Allah: for Allah is well acquainted with all that you do. (Al-Hashr 59:18–24, Koran)

> So be in Taqwa of Allah and fear Allah as much as you can; listen and obey; and spend in charity for the benefit of your own souls. And those saved from their own greed are the ones that prosper. If ye loan to Allah a beautiful loan, He will double it for you and He will forgive you: for Allah is both Appreciative (Shakoor) and Magnanimous (Haleem), Knower of what is hidden and what is manifest, Exalted in Might, Full of Wisdom. (At-Taghabun 64:14–18, Koran)

> Humankind! We created you from a single pair of a male and a female and made you into nations and tribes, that ye may know each other. Verily the most honored of you in the sight of Allah is the one with taqwa of Allah, the most righteous of you. And Allah is All Knowing, All-Aware. (Al-Hadid 57:28–29, Koran)

> Be in Taqwa of Allah, Fear Allah and believe in His Messenger and He will bestow on you the double portion of His Mercy: He will provide for you a Light by which ye shall walk straight in your path and He will forgive you; for Allah is

Most Forgiving, Most Merciful. That the People of the Book may know that they have no power whatever over the Grace of Allah, that His Grace is entirely in His Hand to bestow on whomsoever He wills. For Allah is the Lord of Grace abounding. (Al-Hadid 57:28-29,Koran)

Be in Taqwa of Allah and be with those who are true in word and deed. (At-Tawbah 9:11, Koran)

Be not presumptuous and impudent before Allah and His Messenger; be in taqwa of Allah, fear Allah: for Allah is He Who hears and knows all things. (Al-Hujurat 49:2, Koran)

The believer protects himself by always keeping Allah in view with every action and thought, ensuring that every action is in accord with Allah's way. Perform every act and utter every word as if you see Allah, and if you do not see Him, be aware that Allah not only sees your deeds but also knows your thoughts. To ensure that one is dutiful to Allah, conscious of Allah's presence, and God-fearing, the believer with every action recites:

In the name of Allah, Most Gracious, Most Merciful.

There is a distinction between two types of divine mercy. In the broader sense, mercy refers to Allah's gentleness and kindness to all His creation, for He brings into existence, nurtures, and protects it to its destination. In a narrower sense, Allah's mercy refers to the closeness to Allah that is given to those with *taqwa* in contrast to the chastisement inflicted to those who have chosen to stay distant from Him. Their distance from Allah, in itself, is chastisement because to be distant from the wholeness and harmony of the Real (truth) is to be overcome by the turmoil and chaos of the unreal (falsehood). Allah's mercy is achieved by *taqwa* of Allah, and *taqwa* itself demands both submission (*islam*) and faith (*iman*).

> My Chastisement I mete out to whomsoever I will; but My Mercy extends to all things. That Mercy I shall ordain for those who are muttaqun, those who have *Taqwa* and practice regular charity and those who believe in Our Signs.

> Those who follow the Rasool, the Nabi of the unlettered, about whom they find mentioned in the Taurat (Torah) and the Injeel (Gospel). He bids them what is just and forbids them what is evil; he allows them as lawful what is good and pure and prohibits them from what is bad and impure; he relieves them of their heavy burdens and from the fetters that are on them. So it is those who believe in him, honor him, help him and follow the Light which is sent down with him, it is they who will prosper. (Al-A'raf 7:156–57, Koran)

5. The Covenant of Allah: Worship of Allah

Bow down, prostrate yourself, and serve your Lord.

> Establish regular Salaat, give regular charity and hold fast to Allah. He is your Mawla, Protector, the best of Protectors and the best Helper. (Al-Hajj 22:77–78, Koran)

> Those who do wholesome deeds, establish regular prayers and regular charity have rewards with their Lord. On them shall be no fear, nor shall they grieve. (Al-Baqarah 2:227–80, Koran)

> Seek help with patience, perseverance and prayer. Allah is with those who patiently persevere. (Al-Baqarah 2:153, Koran)

> When you arise for salaat, purify yourself by washing your faces, your hands to the elbows, wipe your heads and wash your feet to the ankles. If you are unclean purify yourself.

Allah does not wish that you should be burdened, but to make you clean and to bestow His blessings on you, that you may be grateful. (Al-Ma'idah 5:6, Koran)

Approach not prayers with a mind befogged until you understand all that you utter, nor come up to prayers in a state of un-cleanliness, till you have bathed. (An-Nisa 4:43, Koran)

Bow down, prostrate yourself and serve your Lord and do wholesome deeds that you may prosper. Perform Jihad; strive to your utmost in Allah's cause as striving (jihad) is His due. He has chosen you and Allah has imposed no hardship in your endeavor to His cause. You are the inheritors of the faith of your father Abraham. He has named you Muslims of the times before and now, so that Allah's Rasool may be an example to you and that you are an example to humankind. (Al-Hajj 22:77-78, Koran)

When the call is proclaimed to prayer on Friday, the day of assembly, hasten earnestly to the Remembrance of Allah and leave off business and everything else: that is best for you if ye but knew! And when the Prayer is finished, then may ye disperse through the land and seek of the Grace of Allah: remember and praise Allah a great deal: that ye may prosper. (Al-Jumu'ah 62:9-10, Koran)

Koran, Allah's word, is the primary source of the believers' spiritual well-being. Recitation of the Koran imparts peace, tranquility, and closeness to Allah and also renews the believers vow to obey Allah's covenant. All believers memorize some parts of the Koran, particularly Sura Al-Fatihah and certain other verses to recite the salat. The salat is the daily renewal of the Koran in the believer, a daily rejuvenation of his or her covenant with Allah and communion with Him.

The blessed *nabi* said, "*Iman is* knowledge in the heart, a voicing with the tongue and activity with the limbs." The term *heart*, often used in the Koran, refers to a specific faculty or a spiritual organ that provides the humans *intellect* and *rationality*. Therefore, *iman* in effect means confidence in the reality and truth of things and commitment to act on the basis of the truth that they know. Thus, *iman* (faith) involves words and actions on the basis of that knowledge.

Koran is Allah's speech to the believers, and it is the foundation of everything Islamic. Thus, the humans connect with Allah by speaking to Him. The believer speaks to Allah through daily salat and supplication, *du'a*. The words are accompanied by action of the body, symbolizing subservience, respect, and humility. The salat consists of cyclic movements of standing in humility in the presence of Allah, bowing down to Him, going down in prostration in the Lord's presence, sitting in humility, reciting verses from the Koran, and praising Allah. Recitation of the Koran serves to embody it within the person reciting salat.

Allah is light (*nur*), and His word (the Koran) is His luminosity. To embody the Koran through faith and practice is to become transformed by this divine light that permeates through the believer in his closeness to Allah. Such proximity to Allah's presence gives the worshipper a "luminous presence."

6. The Covenant of Allah: Fasting Is Prescribed to You in the Month of Ramadan

> Fasting is prescribed to you, in the month of Ramadan as it was prescribed to those before you, that you may practice self-restraint. The Qur'an was revealed in the month of Ramadan, guidance to humankind for judgment between right and wrong. For everyone except those ill or on a

journey, this month should spend it in fasting. Allah intends to make it easy on you so that you may complete the prescribed period of fasting and to glorify Him to express your gratitude for His Guidance. (Al-Baqarah 2:178–79, Koran)

Fasting during Ramadan is a month of self-discipline, prayer, and remembrance of Allah. This is a month of renewal of a believer's commitment to Allah's covenant and a vow to follow His guidance. During this month, there is heightened attention to the rules of right conduct, which helps the believer follow Allah's straight path during the following year. This month is a reminder to the believers of their obligation to Allah's creatures in need of sustenance, shelter, protection, peace, and other help.

7. The Covenant of Allah: Zakat

Spend out of bounties of Allah in charity and wholesome deeds.

And the likeness of those who give generously, seeking to please Allah and to strengthen their souls, is as a garden, high and fertile where heavy rain falls on it and makes it yield a double the amount of harvest and if it receives not heavy rain, light moisture suffices it.

The parable of those who spend their substance in the way of Allah is that of a grain of corn: it grows seven ears and each ear has a hundred grains. Allah gives plentiful return to whom He pleases, Allah cares for all and He knows all things. Those who give generously in the cause of Allah and follow not up their gifts with reminders of their generosity or with injury, for them their reward is with their Lord; on them shall be no fear, nor shall they grieve. Kind words and the covering of faults are better than charity followed by injury. Allah is Free of all wants and He is Most Merciful. (Al-Baqarah 2:261–63, Koran)

Let not those among you who are blessed with grace and ample means hold back from helping their relatives, the poor and those who have left their homes in Allah's cause. Let them forgive and overlook, do you not wish that Allah should forgive you? And Allah is Oft Forgiving, Most Merciful. (An-Nur 24:21–23, Koran)

Spend out of bounties of Allah in charity and wholesome deeds before the Day comes when there will be neither bargaining, friendship nor intercession. Those who reject faith are the wrongdoers. (Al-Baqarah 2:254–57, Koran)

Void not your charity by boast, conceit and insult, by reminders of your generosity like those who want their generosity to be noted by all men but they believe neither in Allah nor in the Last Day. Theirs is a parable of a hard-barren rock, on which there is a little soil, washed by heavy rain, which leaves it just a bare stone. And Allah guides not those who reject Faith. And the likeness of those who give generously, seeking to please Allah and to strengthen their souls, is as a garden, high and fertile where heavy rain falls on it and makes it yield a double the amount of harvest and if it receives not heavy rain, light moisture suffices it. Allah notices whatever you do. (Al-Baqarah 2:264–65, Koran)

Alms are for the poor and the needy and those employed to administer the funds; for those whose hearts have been recently reconciled to the truth; for those in bondage and in debt; in the cause of Allah; and for the wayfarer: thus is it ordained by Allah and Allah is full of knowledge and wisdom. (At-Tawbah 9:60, Koran)

In the above verses, the clear indication is that a human is given bounty by Allah. In return, his obligation is to distribute the surplus to the needy after his needs have been met. The Koran specifies that the zakat be distributed to the *fuqara* (the poor who ask), *al-masakin* (the poor and the needy who don't ask), and zakat administrators (those who spread the light of Islam to those inclined, for the freedom of those in bondage, those in debt, for the cause of Allah, and for the wayfarer who treads the path for Allah's service).

In the covenant, the believer surrenders his life and belongings to Allah in return for His guidance, a place in paradise in the hereafter, and peace with prosperity in this world. Every believer, according to his or her covenant with Allah, has the obligation to extend the benefits that Allah has provided him or her to those who did not receive the same benefits. Such acts of generosity will be rewarded by Allah with a place in *Jannat* (place of peace and plenty) in the afterlife. Life of *Jannat* is to be attained in this world also, provided that the compact with Allah is adhered to. The believer is Allah's instrument who will fulfill His promise to Adam that, among his progeny,

> None will remain without food or clothes and none will suffer from heat or thirst. (Koran 20:118)

In the verses below, Allah has promised to those who believe in and obey His covenant a reward for their acts of charity; He will double the harvest of their labors, forgive their sins, and provide them His bounties, and they shall not grieve. Fear and grief arise from misfortunes, which cause anxiety, depression, and panic. Allah promises to safeguard the believers from misfortune. And those devouring usury Allah will deprive of all blessings. Obedience to Allah's covenant provides *Jannat* in the hereafter and a life of *Jannat* (peace and plenty) in this world. It also brings balance, harmony, and stability to the economic life of the world in that it meets the necessities of each person and eliminates unnecessary suffering.

> O you who believe! Give of the good things that you have honorably earned and of the fruits of the earth that We have produced for you and do not even aim at giving anything which is bad, that you would not receive yourself except with closed eyes. And know that Allah is free of all wants and worthy of all praise.
>
> The Satan threatens you with poverty and bids you to unseemly actions. Allah promises you His forgiveness and bounties. And Allah cares for all and He knows all things.
>
> He grants wisdom to whom He pleases; and those who are granted wisdom receive indeed a magnificent benefit, but none will grasp the Message but men of knowledge and understanding.
>
> And whatever you spend in charity or devotion, be sure Allah knows it all. But the wrongdoers have no helpers. (Al-Baqarah 2:267–70)

The covenant of Allah has laid down principles and guidelines for the well-being of the economic life of the believers. Obedience to these principles will bring peace, harmony, spiritual enlightenment, and economic prosperity. Disobedience means misery, ruin, and Allah's wrath.

Land and sources of production do not become the personal property of people. *Ardh* is the source of life and means of sustenance and production of food and resources and therefore must remain available to the community, the *ummah*. Every Muslim, male and female, who at the end of the year is in possession of about fifteen dollars or more in cash or articles of trade must give zakat at the minimum rate of 2.5 percent. Zakat is incumbent on all liquid, visible, movable, and immovable properties belonging to Muslims. Two and a half percent of all the liquid assets of a Muslim adult after deduction of a reasonable amount of expenses for the maintenance of the person's family and other dependents is not an excessive amount of money. Allah constantly reminds the believers to practice regular charity. Giving to the needy with love and respect out of love of Allah is a profound act of spiritual cleaning. The more one gives in wealth and in kindness, the higher is his status with Allah.

- In the united Muslim lands of the Dar es Salaam, if every adult man and woman gives minimum of *$15* in *zakat*, the total collected will amount to *$12 billion.*

- If every one of the two thousand billionaires and two million millionaires in the Islamic world contributes a minimum of 2.5 percent of their liquid wealth in the way of Allah, the total collected will be in the tune of another *$100 billion.*

- If we approach another twenty million prosperous businesspeople with liquid assets of $500,000 to pay their minimum zakat, the sum collected from them will amount to another *$250 billion.*

- The total sum thus collected amounts *$360 billion.*

- Now we appeal to the same population that, in this twenty-first century, 2.5 percent is not really enough to feed and house the large, disadvantaged population of the *ummah* and ask for 5 percent of their liquid assets. The total collected will amount to *$724 billion.* Half of this sum may then be used to feed, clothe, house, and educate the poor and needy population and the remaining half to create industries and jobs and training for the people who have not been able to exit the cycle of poverty.

- If we approach Hosni Mubarak, Muammar Khadafy, Ben Ali, Saddam Hussein, Saudi and Gulf sheikhs, and other royal Arab families of 5 percent of their $3 trillion stash, we will have another *$150 billion* annually.

- There is an estimated forty-five thousand tons of accumulated gold hoardings in the Islamic countries in the form of jewelry, gold bricks, gold bars, gold artifacts, and national treasures in museums of an estimated value of $1.8 trillion. Five percent in zakat will amount to *$85 billion* annually.

- In addition, there is a hoard of precious stones worth another $2 trillion, 5 percent of which will yield another *$100 billion* in zakat money.

The total zakat owed to the Muslim community is over *$1.1 trillion dollars annually.*

Even though the Islamic states have been milked dry by our elite and their colonial cohorts, the *ummah*—acting in accordance with Allah's covenant—shall be able to eradicate all poverty and destitution within the Dar es Salaam within *three years* with the resources from the community of believers. The remedy lies within the *ummah*, with zakat amounting to *$3.3 trillion* over three years without ever touching any of the government revenues. So why is the *ummah* so destitute? Fewer than five thousand families in the Islamic state are hoarding the wealth of the *ummah*.

Were the precepts of the covenant of Allah applied to the rest of the humanity, all poverty, depravation, and disease would disappear from the world in one year. Less than 10 percent of the world's population owns 80 percent of the world's wealth. This disparity is caused by unbridled feudalism and capitalism in man's history.

The total wealth of the world is estimated to be $300 trillion. If every human gave away 2.5 to 5.0 percent of their surplus income in zakat to eradicate poverty, disease, and hunger in the global village, *$7.5 to $15.0 trillion* will become available; half this amount can be used to eradicate, hunger, illiteracy, unemployment, and disease annually and the remaining amount to build the world's infra-structure for environmentally sustainable agriculture and industrial production to sustain mankind. In no time, the world will be a stable place with the eradication of wars, famines, epidemics, ignorance, and hunger.

The solution to the ills of humanity lies in Allah's word:

> And the likeness of those who give generously, seeking to please Allah and to strengthen their souls, is as a garden, high and fertile where heavy rain falls on it and makes it yield a double the amount of harvest and if it receives not heavy rain, light moisture suffices it.

> The parable of those who spend their substance in the way of Allah is that of a grain of corn: it grows seven ears and each ear has a hundred grains. Allah gives plentiful return to whom He pleases, Allah cares for all and He knows all things. Those who give generously in the cause of Allah and follow not up their gifts with reminders of their generosity or with injury, for them their reward is with their Lord; on them shall be no fear, nor shall they grieve.

8. The Covenant of Allah: Hajj and Proclaim the Pilgrimage to Mankind

> And proclaim the Pilgrimage to mankind; they will come to thee on foot and mounted on every kind of camel, lean

on account of journeys through deep and distant mountain highways; that they may witness the benefits provided for them and celebrate the name of Allah, through the Days Appointed, over the cattle which He has provided for them for sacrifice: then eat you thereof and feed the distressed ones in want. Then let them complete the rites prescribed for them, perform their vows and again circumambulate the Ancient House. Such is the Pilgrimage: whoever honors the sacred rites of Allah, for him it is good in the sight of his Lord. Lawful to you for food in Pilgrimage are cattle, except those mentioned to you as exceptions: but shun the abomination of idols and shun the word that is false. (Al-Hajj 22:27–30, Koran)

Violate not the sanctity of the Symbols of Allah, or of the sacred month, or of the animals brought for sacrifice, nor the garlands that mark out such animals, nor the people coming to the Sacred House, seeking the bounty and good pleasure of their Lord. Help one another in virtue and piety but help not one another in sin and acrimony. Be in Taqwa of Allah, fear Allah, for Allah is swift in reckoning. (Al-Ma'idah 5:2, Koran)

For thirteen hundred years, Muslims traveled to Mecca by foot or on horse- or camelback, taking more than a year to complete the rituals of the hajj. This slow pace helped the believer in his spiritual pursuit and his worldly quest to get acquainted with Muslims of other lands that kept the *ummah* united. The hajj since then has been seen as a grand rite of passage from this worldly life to a person's total devotion to Allah. Hajjis have been treated as models of piety and blessedness. With modern air travel, hajj has become accessible to a larger population, bringing the Islamic world closer. To the large number of children and young adults performing hajj, the rituals at the house inspire the renewal of their vows to the covenant of Allah, and they carry forward their passion to inspire others to perform the good works in the path of Allah.

9. The Covenant of Allah: Speak Always the Truth

> O you who believe! Have Taqwa of Allah, fear Allah and always speak the truth, that He may direct you to deeds of righteousness and forgive your sins: he that obeys Allah and His Rasool have already attained the highest achievement.
>
> We did indeed offer al-Amanah, the Trust to the Heavens and the Earth and the Mountains; but they shrank from the burden, being afraid of it, but man assumed it and has proved to be a tyrant and a fool, with the result that Allah has to punish the Munafiqeen, truth concealers, men and women and the Mushrikun, unbelievers, men and women and Allah turns in Mercy to the Believers, men and women; for Allah is Forgiving, Most Merciful. (Al-Ahzab 33:69–73, Koran)

To live up to the trust of Allah, the vicegerent—the human—has to distinguish between good and evil, truth and falsehood, *adl* and *zulm*. Falsehood is the abomination that corrupts the very basis of Allah's vicegerency and His covenant with the human. The Koran discredits workers of corruption, the worst among them being the *Munafiqeen*, truth concealers, the hypocrites who claim to be doing good deeds but whose inner intentions are vile and harmful to others. Good deeds and truth are motivated by faith and *taqwa*. Corruption, dishonesty, and falsehood come about when humans—Allah's vicegerents—turn away from Allah's covenant and forget the message of the prophets:

> But those who break the Covenant of Allah, after having pledged their word on it and sever that Allah has commanded

to be joined together and who work corruption on earth, on them shall be the curse and theirs is the ugly abode. (Ar-Ra'd 13:25, Koran)

10. The Covenant of Allah: *Fahasha*: Avoid Indecency, Iniquity, Abomination, Shameful Deeds, and Scandalous Acts

Allah's covenant forbids the believers from shameful deeds such as adultery, fornication, sodomy, deception, treason, lying, cheating, stealing, and murder whether in open or in secret. People who commit such deeds are not immune from other abominations against their community and humankind. A believer's life and soul are akin to a dew pond of crystal clear water from which a fountain gushes forth, pure and refreshing; in the same manner, the beautiful deeds of the believers quench the thirst of humanity and bring peace and satisfaction. Acts of indecency and shame sully the dew pond with water so foul that the believers and humanity fall prey to plague, pestilence, and diseases of the body and spirit and lose Allah's grace.

When people and the rulers of Muslim lands indulge in shameful deeds (*Fahasha*), they do indeed follow Satan's footsteps and lose *furqan*, the criterion to distinguish right from wrong. Shameful actions open the gates to the world of iniquity, where there are no inhibitions nor shame. One licentious act leads to another till all thoughts of Allah are lost in a haze of debauchery and decadence. Intoxication leads to loss of inhibitions, licentiousness, and indecent acts against oneself and others. Inequity trespasses boundaries of self-control until there are trespasses against oneself, other people, the community, the state, and above all the commandments of Allah.

When Allah's gifts and grace are deemed inadequate, there begins a struggle for the acquisition of wealth. Wealth condones *Fahasha* and facilitates the activities of lewdness, debauchery, and indecency. Under every pile of wealth lies the sweat and blood of its victims. Wealth is the engine of *Fahasha*, and wealth and power are begotten through foul means. The covenant of Allah forbids shameful deeds, dishonesty, and deceit. To sustain the incumbent royals and dictators' riches and power, the conscientious and those who fight for decency and truth are taken into custody, tortured, and imprisoned. Some simply disappear, never to be heard of again. The *Fahasha* and the powerful are not accountable to Allah, and they thrive in the company of Satan. Their acts of shame and profanity are perpetrated in the open and obvious to those who surround them in the circles of power.

> Enter into submission to the will of Allah, enter Islam whole-heartedly and follow not the footsteps of Satan, for he is a sworn enemy to you! (Al-Baqarah 2:208, Koran)

> Do not follow Satan's footsteps: if any will follow the footsteps of Satan, he will command to what is shameful (Fahasha) and wrong (Munkar): and were it not for the grace of Allah and His mercy on you, not one of you would have been unblemished: but Allah does purify whom He pleases: and Allah is all Hearer and all Knower. (An-Nur 24:21–23, Koran)

> Come not near to shameful deeds (fornication, adultery, and shameful activities) whether open or secret. (Al-An 'am 151–53, Koran)

11. The Covenant of Allah: Unity of the *Ummah*

> And hold fast, all together, by the Rope, which Allah stretches out for you and be not divided among yourselves; and remember with gratitude Allah's favor on you; you were enemies, and He joined your hearts in love, so that by His

Grace, you became brethren and a community. You were on the brink of the pit of fire, and He saved you from it. Thus, does Allah make His Signs clear to you that you may be guided.

Let there arise out of you a band of people inviting to all that is good, enjoining what is right and forbidding that is wrong. They are the ones to attain happiness.

Be not like those who are divided amongst themselves and fall into disputations after receiving clear signs: for them is a dreadful penalty. (Ali 'Imran 3:103-5, Koran)

Persevere in patience and constancy; vie in such perseverance; strengthen each other; and be in Taqwa of Allah, fear Allah that you may prosper. (Ali 'Imran 3:200, Koran)

This is a grace from Allah and a favor; and Allah is All Knowing and All Wise. If two parties among the Believers fall into a quarrel, make peace between them: but if one of them transgresses beyond bounds against the other, then fight you all against the one who transgresses until he complies with the Command of Allah; but if he complies, then make peace between them with justice and fairness: for Allah loves those who are fair and just. The Believers are but a single Brotherhood: so make peace and reconciliation between your two brothers; and fear Allah, that you may receive Mercy. (Al-Hujurat 49:6-10, Koran)

Just as the bond to Allah is indivisible, all the Believers shall stand behind the commitment of the least of them. All the Believers are bonded one to another to the exclusion of other men. (The Covenant of Muhammad)

The Divide of Islam

All Muslims are one brotherhood, one *ummah*, all servants of one Allah, the First and the Last, fulfilling His covenant, witnessed over by Allah's messenger—an *ummah* that is witness over other nations. After the peace conference at Versailles Palace, the French and the British met quietly in San Remo in Italy to carve up the former possessions of the Ottoman Empire. France was given Syria and Lebanon, Persia became a British protectorate, and Mesopotamia and Palestine came under British possession.

The map of modern Middle East was conceived by a young Englishman drunk with power and alcohol. Winston Churchill traveled to Cairo in March 1921. He and Thomas Edward Lawrence had reviewed the aspirants of the Arabian thrones at the Ship restaurant in London over dinner and, afterward, brandy and liqueurs. The two likeliest candidates were Sharif Hussein's sons Faisal and Abdullah. On March 21, 1921, the Cairo Conference opened with thirty-eight participants, out of whom thirty-six were British. Churchill wrote afterward a description of this meeting: "Lawrence suggested that Feisal be crowned head of Iraq, not only because of his personal knowledge and friendship of the individual, but also on the ground that in order to counteract the claims of rival candidates and in order to pull together the scattered elements of a backward and half civilized country it was essential that the first ruler should be an active and inspiring personality."[4]

His motion with Churchill's approval carried without dissent. Abdullah, in Lawrence's view, was "lazy and by no means dominating"; but though unfit to rule Iraq, he would be permitted

---

[4] William Manchester, *The Last Lion* (Bantam Double Day Publishing Group Ltd.), 700.

to rule over Transjordan under the watchful eye of a British high commissioner. Churchill announced his intention to appoint Abdullah in Palestine. Years later, Churchill would say, "Emir Abdullah is in Transjordania where I put him one Sunday afternoon in Jerusalem."

Zionism's hopes were honored. Sir Herbert Samuel—a Jew, Winston Churchill's cabinet colleague—was appointed high commissioner in Palestine and instructed to foster a Jewish homeland in Palestine. An Englishwoman who attended the conference remembered, "Winston going around the hotel followed by an Arab carrying a pail and a bottle of wine. When things got boring at the conference everyone would cheer when Winston came in.

On March 23, 1921, Winston Churchill, Sir Herbert Samuel, and Lawrence left Cairo Station by rail for Jerusalem. Between them, they drew the boundaries of the British-mandated territory. What was once one land for hundreds of years became Syria, Lebanon, Palestine, Iraq, Kuwait, and Hejaz. Hejaz was soon occupied with the British encouragement by Ibn Sa'ud. Israel was carved out of Palestine. Little desert domains of desert Bedouins, after treaties with Britain, became the Trucial States with further hinterland added to their territories for the exploitation and exploration of oil by the British. The Arabian Peninsula was further carved into Oman, Muscat, and the South and North Yemen.

The borders between the Muslim communities and the kingdoms of Islam are Western innovation for division, exploitation, and control of Muslim lands, the Dar es Salaam. This divide was carried out and maintained by the West with the connivance of rulers of Islam, against the commandments of the covenant between Allah and His people.

12. The Covenant of Allah: Perseverance and Patience

> O ye who believe! persevere in patience and constancy; vie in such perseverance; strengthen each other; and fear Allah; that ye may prosper.

Ṣabr, ṣābir, ṣabbār, and *ṣābara* denote the qualities of patience, steadfastness, self-restraint, forbearance, endurance, and perseverance. One of Allah's ninety-nine names is *al-Ṣabur,* the Patient. It is one who does not precipitate an act before its time but decides matters according to a specific plan and brings them to fruition in a predefined manner, neither procrastinating nor hastening the matters before their time but disposing each matter in its appropriate time according to its needs and requirements and doing all that without being subjected to a force opposing Allah's will. *Ṣabr, ṣābir, ṣabbār,* and *ṣābara* are mentioned in the Koran sixty-nine times. Allah reassures the believers:

> O Believers, be patient and vie you with patience. (3:200)

> Pray for succor to Allah and be patient. (7:128)

> Be thou patient, Allah will not leave to waste the wage of good-doers. (11:115)

> Be thou patient; Surely Allah's promise is true. (30:60)

> Bear patiently whatever may befall you. (31:17)

> So be thou patient with a sweet patience. (70:5)

> And be patient unto your Lord. (74:7)

> O Believers, seek you help in patience and prayer. (21:153)

But come sweet patience. (12:18, 83)

Surely Allah is with the is with the patient. (2:153, 249)

Allah loves the patient (3:146)

For a man and a woman to be patient (*ṣabr*), it requires endurance and discipline to affirm a rational resolve in opposing the impulses of passion or anger. It involves balancing two opposing desires. The believer has to overcome the impulse leading to rashness and haste and at the same time lean toward the delay of the act. To be patient, one has to resolve the conflict between acts of anger and rashness, on one hand, and procrastination and delay, on the other.

Lack of *ṣabr*, self-restraint, patience, and self-discipline has overwhelmed the Muslim world at the beginning of the twenty-first century. The Muslim world has been rudderless and leaderless over one hundred years and poorly led during the previous one thousand years. The result is 1.5 billion people following their own instincts for the sake of mere survival. *Ṣabr* teaches self-restraint in the matters of need and giving precedence to others over oneself in matters of need. Islam teaches that the elderly, the sick, the needy, the women, and the children take precedence in matters of care, shelter, and food and that spirituality takes precedence over one's daily needs. Consideration of the well-being of the kin, the neighbor, and the fellowman requires a thought before fulfilling one's own requirements. The state of *ṣabr* in the Muslim world is obvious when one looks at the lines at bus and rail stations. People are trampled at the holy sites. Old men, women, and the disabled are pushed and trampled during the holiest act of circumambulation around the Kaaba, at Safa and Marwah, and during the ritual stoning of the devil. The same is true in the shopping centers, down the streets, and bus stops.

The extreme desire for immediate gratification of desires and ambitions leads to small and major crimes. Lying, theft, and robbery are common acts involved in the impulse of possession of the unreachable. Military revolutions, palace coups, conspiracies, and conquests bring power to the hands of the unjust and ambitious without a capacity for hard work, honesty, and *sabr* (patience).

> Persevere in patience and constancy; vie in such perseverance; strengthen each other; and be in Taqwa of Allah, fear Allah that you may prosper. (Ali 'Imran 3:200, Koran)

13. The Covenant of Allah: Theft, Deception, Fraud, Honesty, and Justice

Betray not the trust of Allah and His messenger. Nor knowingly misappropriate wealth entrusted to you, whether on behalf of an orphan or another party. Be honest in handling property, goods, credit, confidences, and secrets of your fellow men and display integrity and honesty in using your skills and talents. Whenever you give your word, speak truthfully and justly, even if a near relative is concerned.

Similarly, the *amri minkum*—those entrusted with the administration of the affairs of the believers—should not betray the trust of Allah, the *rasul*, and the believers and knowingly misappropriate the wealth of the Muslims. The populations of the Islamic lands are akin to the orphans whose land and heritage has been forcibly sequestered by conquest, soon to be redeemed, and those who seized it will, on the appointed day, be asked to account for every grain of stolen sand and gold. The Arabian Peninsula and other Muslim lands have been the plundering fields of the royal families and their kin for one hundred years, in partnership with the *circle of evil*.

The rulers of the Arabian Peninsula and their royal relatives regularly skim the cream off the top one-third of the wealth of the *ummah* for their personal benefit. The dictators, the royals, and their circle of sycophants and cheerleaders in all Muslim nation-states have siphoned off the cream of their national wealth. Suharto, Benazir Bhutto, Nawaz Sharif, Reza Shah of Iran, Saddam Hussein, Anwar Sadat, Hosni Mubarak, Gaddhafi, Ben Ali, kings of the Arabian Peninsula, their families, and the inner circle of their regimes have plundered trillions of dollars from their nation's treasuries over their prolonged reign.

The greatest pillage and plunder in history took place systematically when the descendants of ten barefoot, camel-herding Bedouins took control of the Arabian Peninsula with the help of British money and arms. In the second half of the twentieth century, over a short period of forty-five years, they heisted $4.5 trillion. In the Arabian Peninsula, in the kingdoms of Oman, Kuwait, the United Arab Emirates, Qatar, Bahrain, and Saudi Arabia, there are now six kings and over five hundred billionaires and thousands of millionaires among this narrow circle of ten clans. Over this short period, these tent dwellers who had never been inside the four walls of a dwelling now owned hundreds of palaces in Arabia, Europe, and America.

Yet this plunder is ongoing. The total amount of petty cash taken out by the ever-increasing progeny of these Bedouin sheikhs in allowances, salaries, commissions, and expenses is so immense that their take of $50 billion annually is more than the total combined annual budget of the nation-states of Pakistan, Afghanistan, Iran, Syria, and Jordan, with a population of 250 million people. The cost of security of these "royals" (90,000 troops), personal jets, helicopters, yachts, travel, and private air terminals in Jidda, Riyadh, Dubai, and Doha is an additional $20 billion. This is going on when most Arabs and Muslims live in conditions of utter poverty and deprivation. Two fundamental terms used in the Koran are *haqq* (right and honest means of income) and *bātel* (wrongful and dishonest way of making money). The ways of making money approved by the Koran are halal, and those forbidden are haram.

Muslims the world over follow the verses about fasting in Surah Al-Baqarah 2:183–87 but very conveniently ignore the following verse (188):

> And do not devour each other's wealth dishonestly, nor use it as bait for the judges, with intent that ye may devour dishonestly and knowingly a little of (other) people's wealth.

> O you who believe! Fasting is prescribed to you as it was prescribed to those before you, that ye may (learn) self-restraint.

> (Fasting) for a fixed number of days; but if any of you is ill, or on a journey, the prescribed number (should be made up) from days later. For those who can do it (with hardship), is a ransom, the feeding of one that is indigent but he that will give more, of his own free will, it is better for him. And it is better for you that ye fast, if ye only knew.

> Ramadan is the (month) in which was sent down the Qur'an, as a guide to mankind, also Clear (Signs) for guidance and judgment (between right and wrong). So, every one of you who is present (at his home) during that month should spend it in fasting, but if anyone is ill, or on a journey, the prescribed period (should be made up) by days later. Allah intends every facility for you; He does not want to put you to difficulties. (He wants you) to complete the prescribed period and to glorify Him in that He has guided you; and perchance ye shall be grateful.

When My servants ask thee concerning Me, I am indeed close (to them): I listen to the prayer of every suppliant when he calls on Me: let them also, with a will, listen to My call and believe in Me: that they may walk in the right way.

Permitted to you, on the night of the fasts, is the approach to your wives. They are your garments and ye are their garments. Allah knows what you used to do secretly among yourselves; but He turned to you and forgave you; so now associate with them and seek what Allah hath ordained for you and eat and drink until the white thread of dawn appear to you distinct from its black thread; then complete your fast till the night appears; but do not associate with your wives while ye are in retreat in the mosques. Those are limits (set by) Allah: approach not nigh thereto. Thus, doth Allah make clear His Signs to men: that they may learn self-restraint.

And do not devour each other's wealth dishonestly, nor use it as bait for the judges, with intent that ye may devour dishonestly and knowingly a little of (other) people's wealth. (Al Baqarah 2:183–88, Koran)

There are several dishonest financial practices—cheating, bribery, stealing, embezzlement, hoarding, and swindling—but one mentioned specifically by the Koran is often overlooked. That is the one practiced by the aristocrats, clergy, clerics, and claimants of spiritual leadership all across the world:

O you who believe! There are indeed many among the leaders, priests and clerics, who in falsehood devour the substance of men and hinder (them) from the Way of Allah. And there are those who bury gold and silver and spend it not in the Way of Allah: announce unto them a most grievous penalty. (At- Tawbah 9:34, Koran)

Like the politicians and dictators, these priests and spiritual leaders deceive the unlettered masses with false doctrines and fallacies to keep them entrapped in their web to safeguard their own power over people and their wealth.

14. The Covenant of Allah: Obey Allah and His *Rasul* and Those Charged with Authority among You

> Obey Allah and obey the Messenger and those charged amongst you with authority in the settlement of your affairs. If you differ in anything among yourselves, refer it to Allah and His Rasool (The Qur'an and the Prophet's teachings). If you do believe in Allah and the last Day that is best and the most beautiful conduct in the final determination. (An-Nisa 4:43, Koran)

The Koran teaches that all affairs of individuals and the Muslim community is to be conducted through mutual consultation (*ijma*) and decisions arrived through consensus. Furthermore, the Koran proclaims consultation as the principle of governance and the method that must be applied in the administration of public affairs. The sovereignty of Islamic state belongs exclusively to Allah, whose will and command binds the community and state. The dignified designation in the Koran of the community as vicegerent of Allah on the earth makes the Muslim community, the *ummah*, a repository of the "executive sovereignty" of the Islamic state. The community as a whole, after consultation and consensus, charges people from among themselves with authority to manage its affairs (*ulil amri minkum*). Those charged with authority act in their capacity as the representative (*wakil*) of the people and are bound by the Koranic mandate to consult the community in public affairs, and consensus is the binding source of the law. The community, by consultation and in consensus, has the authority to depose any person charged with authority, including the head of state, in the event of gross violation of Allah's law.

> Those who hearken to their Lord and establish regular prayer; who (conduct) their affairs by mutual Consultation; who spend out of what We bestow on them for Sustenance; And those who, when an oppressive wrong is inflicted on them do not flinch and courageously defend themselves.(Ash-Shura 42:38-39, Koran)

Islam pursues its social objectives by reforming the person. The ritual ablution before prayer, the five daily prayers, the fasting during the month of Ramadan, and the obligatory giving of charity all encourage punctuality, self-discipline, and concern for the well-being of others. An individual is seen not just a member of the community and subservient to its will but also as a morally autonomous agent who plays a distinctive role in shaping the community's sense of direction and purpose. The Koran has attached to the individuals the duty of obedience to the government and the right of the individual to simultaneously dispute with rulers over government affairs. The individual obeys the ruler on the condition that the ruler obeys the covenant of the Koran and Allah's commandments, which are obligatory to all Muslims regardless of their status in the social hierarchy. This is reflected in the declaration of the blessed *nabi*:

> There is no obedience in transgression; obedience is only in the righteousness.

The citizen is entitled to disobey an oppressive command that is contrary to the covenant of the Koran. The blessed *nabi*, Allah's emissary, brought Allah's word to the world and disseminated it to the populations of the continents. Thus, it is essential to obey the commandments that Blessed Muhammad brought from Allah for mankind.

> O you who believe! Obey Allah and obey the Messenger and those charged with authority among you. If ye differ in anything among yourselves, refer it to Allah and His Messenger, if ye do believe in Allah and the Last Day: that is best and most suitable for final determination. (An-Nisa 4:59, Koran)

15. The Covenant of Allah: Freedom of Religion: Let There Be No Compulsion in Religion

> Let there be no compulsion in religion: Truth stands out clear from Error: whoever rejects Evil and believes in Allah hath grasped the most trustworthy handhold that never breaks. And Allah hears and knows all things. (Al-Baqarah 2:254–57, Koran)

The Koranic notion of religious belief (*iman*) is dependent on the knowledge that is actualized in practice in the term *islam*. The term *islam* signifies the idea of surrender or submission. Islam is a religion of self-surrender. Islam is the conscious and rational submission of dependent and limited human will to the absolute and omnipotent will of Allah. The type of surrender Islam requires is a deliberate, conscious, and rational act made by a person who knows with both intellectual certainty and spiritual vision that Allah, who is the subject of Koranic discourse, is the only reality.

The knower of God is a Muslim (fem. *Muslimah*), "one who submits" to the divine truth and whose relationship with God is governed by *taqwa*, the consciousness of humankind's responsibility toward its Creator. However, consciousness of God alone is not sufficient to make a person a Muslim. Neither is it enough to be merely born a Muslim or to be raised in an Islamic cultural context. The concept of *taqwa* implies that the believer has the added responsibility of acting in a way that is in accordance with the three types of knowledge, *ilm al-yaqin*, *ain al-yaqin*, and *haqq al yaqin* (knowledge of certainty, eye of certainty, and truth of certainty). The believer must endeavor at all times to maintain himself or herself in a constant state of submission to Allah. By doing so, the believer attains the honored title of "slave of Allah" (*abd* Allah, feminine: *amat* Allah), for he recognizes that all power and all agency belongs to God alone. Thus, the believer surrenders to the will of Allah. No one can compel anyone to undergo submission without his will and understanding.

16. The Covenant of Allah: *Awliya*: Allah is the *Wali*, Protector of Those Who Have Faith

> Do not take the Kafirun (infidels), Jews and Christians as your awliya.

> Waliy: O you who believe! Allah is the Waliy and the protector of the Believers. Allah commands:
> Believers not to take people outside their ranks in closeness and confidence, who in their loathing for them wish them destruction.

Allah, in His covenant, reminds the believers repeatedly:

◇ turns to them is one of them. Allah does not guide those who are unjust and evil doers (zalimun). He that from amongst the Believers turns to them is from amongst the Kafirun, Mushrikun and the zalimun.

⋄ Take not for Awliya, friends and protectors, from amongst your kin who are Kafirun.

Allah also admonishes believers:

⋄ Not to take My enemies and yours as Awliya (friends and protectors), offering them love and regard, even though they have rejected the Truth bestowed on you. You have come out to strive in My Cause and to seek My favor, take them not as friends, Not to take the Kafirun (infidels), Jews and Christians as their awliya, (friends and protectors) in place of Believers. They are friends and protectors unto each other. He who amongst Believers holding in secret regard and friendship for them, for I know full well all that you conceal and all that you reveal. And any of you that do this, has strayed from the Straight Path.

⋄ Befriend not people who have incurred Allah's wrath.

There is a recurring cycle in Islamic history of destruction and humiliation of Islam by the manipulations of the circle of evil. The story starts with a scheming Jew who spins a web, planning meticulously to amass the world's wealth, and uses the power and organization of the strongest Christian monarch by tempting him with the acquisition of a world empire and its fabulous wealth. Then meticulous planning begins; the execution of such an expedition may take several years, in which intelligence services, diplomats, and the armed services play a role, while only the top, select echelon is aware of all the moves on the chessboard. A willing victim, a weak Muslim, a *Munafiq* with a propensity for greed and lust for power endowed with overwhelming vanity and conceit is picked up, trained, and slowly eased into a position of power to be used at the opportune moment.

Ottoman Empire

The plan to destabilize the Ottoman Empire was hatched by the Jewish Rothschild cousins in Berlin, Paris, and London. Each branch of the family collaborated with their favorite governments in each city. The German chancellor von Bethmann-Hollweg, a Jew, and a Rothschild cousin won the day, and the Kaiser began to make overtures to the Young Turks and assisted their revolution against the sultan. Enver Pasha was the Turkish *Munafiq* who joined the circle of evil— the *Yahudi, Salibi,* and *Munafiq* coalition. Talat, Cemal, and Enver *presided* over the dissolution of the Ottoman Empire, subjugating the Middle East to the West for the next one hundred years.

State of Israel

The history of the creation of the state of Israel tells us that Theodor Herzl and Chaim Weizmann were the founding fathers of Israel. The hidden hand that helped create the Jewish state is seldom mentioned.

The actual creators of Israel were a group of English and Jewish conspirators in the British cabinet. David Lloyd George appointed Alfred Milner, a Jew, to his war cabinet in 1916 as secretary of war. After becoming the secretary of war, he brought in Leo Amery, another Jew, albeit a secret one, as secretary of the war cabinet. Milner had close contacts with the Rothschilds; in 1912, he had helped Natty Rothschild unify the divided Jewish community of London under one spiritual head, Chief Rabbi Joseph Herman Hertz.[5]

---

[5] Niall Ferguson, *The House of Rothschild* (Penguin Books), 259.

Another Jew, a cabinet minister, Herbert Samuel, convinced the cabinet in 1915—when Palestine was still a Turkish possession—that Palestine should become a British protectorate, "into which the scattered Jews in time swarm back from all quarters of the globe, in due course obtain home rule and form a Jewish Commonwealth like that of Canada and Australia." Lord Walter Rothschild, as the leader of the British Jews, twisted the ears of the prime minister Lloyd George and his foreign secretary for a declaration about Palestine. Lloyd George had previously served as the legal counsel for the British Zionist Federation. Balfour suggested that "they submit a declaration for the cabinet to consider." The declaration was written by Milner and revised several times. The final version was drafted by Leo Amery, which read,

> His Majesty's Government view with favor the establishment in Palestine a national home for the Jewish people and will use their best endeavors to facilitate the achievement of this object, it being clearly understood that nothing shall be done which may prejudice the civil and religious rights of existing non-Jewish communities in Palestine, or the rights and political status enjoyed in any other country.

This declaration was approved by the British cabinet and was addressed to Lord Walter Rothschild and signed by the foreign secretary Balfour. The Balfour Declaration—as this Jewish Magna Carta came to be known, the document that gave the illegitimate birth to the state of Israel—was written by Lord Alfred Milner, a Jew, revised and finalized by Leo Amery, another Jew, at the behest of and addressed to Lord Walter Rothschild, the leader of the Jews in London, for the purpose of the creation of a Jewish state in the name of the British government on a land that did not belong to either the Jews or the British. In fact, this was an agreement among a group of conspiring *Yahudi-Salibi* conspirators belonging to a secret organization that had a long history of fraud and extortion to grab the world's wealth.

In this case, the plotters made a full circle in their relationship. Lord George Joachim Goschen, a German Jew, patronized Alfred Milner, another German Jew, and brought him into the English establishment and introduced him to the Rothschilds. Milner, in turn, brought Leo Amery, a secret Jew, into the war cabinet; and together, they wrote the Balfour Declaration for the Lord Rothschild. To complete the circle, George Goschen's daughter Phyllis Evelyn Goschen married Francis Cecil Balfour, Foreign Secretary Balfour's son, on August 31, 1920.

Herbert Samuel was appointed overseer of Palestine to guide and control King Abdullah of Jordan to facilitate the Jewish migration to Palestine. Arthur Hirtzel, a Jew, was appointed as head of the British India Office, which also controlled the British governance of Iraq and Arabia. Hirtzel, at that time, expressed the need for Ibn Sa'ud to establish himself in Mecca. Rufus Isaacs, Lord Reading, another Jew, was appointed as the British viceroy of India. Isaacs directed the British policy in Iraq, Palestine, and Arabia. He used 'Abd al-'Aziz to remove Sharif Hussein's son Ali from Hejaz. He had a free hand in Arabia and Iraq. He used British Indian troops to quell uprisings in Iraq. Isaacs also facilitated the massacres and repression in At Ta'if, Bureida, and Huda by providing 'Abd al-'Aziz with money, artillery, rifles, ammunition, training, and transport.

From this time onward, Zionists were considered an ally of the British government, and every help and assistance was forthcoming from each government department. Space was provided for the

Zionists in Mark Sykes's office with liaison to each government department. The British government provided financial, communication, and travel facilities to those working in the Zionist office. Mark Sykes, who had negotiated the Sykes-Picot Agreement giving Syria to the French, was now working for the Zionists, offering them a part of the same territory.

Partition of the Land of Islam in the Middle East

To complete the circle of evil, Sharif Hussein and his sons—hungry for power, fame, and gold—were the willing recruits of the British to destabilize the Ottoman Empire and carve out a Jewish state in Palestine. Hussein led a revolt against his caliph, sultan, country, and coreligionists under the protection of an alien, *kafir*, colonial, expansionist power under the full knowledge that parts of the Islamic state—including Syria, Lebanon, Palestine, and Iraq—would pass from Islamic rule to an economic and colonial serfdom of a non-Muslim, *kafir* power. While the British set out to expedite the war against the Turks, they also began to lay the groundwork for an indirect postwar British political control of Arabia.

June 1916 was a historical moment when, for the first time in the history of Islam since the Battle of Badr in the first year of hijra, combined forces of the *kafireen* and *Munafiqeen* and British and Hussein's armies attacked the city of the *nabi* of Islam, though unsuccessfully; this attack introduced the combined evil dominion of the *Mutaffifeen*, *kafireen*, and *Munafiqeen* over the heartlands of Islam for the century to come.

For his treachery, Sharif Hussein received his first reward in gold sovereigns in March 1916, a shipment amounting to £53,000, three months before he announced his revolt. Commencing on August

8, 1916, the official allowance was set at £125,000 a month, a sum that was frequently exceeded on Hussein's demand; for example, in November 1916, £375,000 in gold sovereigns was dispatched to Hussein by the British for hajj expenses. The payments were broken down into five categories representing the four armies under the command of Hussein's sons and an allotment for the upkeep of the mosque at Kaaba and for hajj facilities as well as for the operation of Hussein's government in Mecca and Jeddah. Forty thousand pounds was allotted to Faisal, £30,000 to Abdullah, £20,000 each for Ali and Zeid, and £15,000 for expenses at Mecca and Jeddah.

The year 1916 must have been the lowest point in the history of Islam, when it was surrounded by powerful enemies around the world; and inside, it was being destroyed by self-serving traitors at the very heart of the faith, the Kaaba. For the first time in the history of Islam, the very upkeep of the holy mosque of Mecca and the Kaaba and hajj expenses were being paid for by the *kafireen*, at the behest of the *Munafiqeen*, under the claim of their lineage to the holy prophet. While claiming the bloodline, they forgot the teachings of the Koran and the example of the prophet.

'Abd al-'Aziz was picked as a willing tool by British scouts in around 1902 and was kept on a short leash with small handouts to keep him available and above starvation level. 'Abd al-'Aziz set out to conquer Arabia with the financial and military assistance of the British. Sir Percy Cox, a British resident in the Persian Gulf, wrote, "With Ibn-Saud in Hasa (the Gulf Coast of Arabia) our position is very much strengthened." Percy Cox openly encouraged Ibn Sa'ud to attack the remaining territory of the Ibn Rashids to divert them from reinforcing Turkish troops against the British. Ibn Sa'ud had constant British financial aid, arms, and advisers, initially William Shakespeare and Percy Cox and later Harry St. John Philby.

After they helped him master eastern Arabia in 1917, the British found another use for Ibn Sa'ud. In 1924, Hussein declared himself caliph of Islam without the consent of the British. Ibn Sa'ud, with British encouragement, started his thrust to Hejaz; although the British ostensibly cut off the arms supplies to both sides, they continued to supply small but crucial amounts of money and arms to Ibn Sa'ud and his merciless Ikhwan. Some of the military equipment used by Ibn Sa'ud was expensive and could only have been obtained from the British and used with the help of British instructors. At the time, statements by British officials did point to the British hand in Ibn Sa'ud's attack on Mecca. Arthur Hirtzel—a Jew, head of the British India Office at that time—expressed the need for Ibn Sa'ud to establish himself in Mecca. The British viceroy of India at that time, another Jew, Rufus Isaacs, Lord Reading, directed the British policy in Arabia. He used 'Abd al-'Aziz to remove Sharif Hussein's son Ali from Hejaz.

Ibn Sa'ud afforded Britain the comfort of keeping the Arabs and Muslims divided and protected its commercial and political interests, which opposed a unified Muslim state. Sharif Hussein and his sons Faisal and Abdullah continued to be clients and servants of the British. For a few thousand pounds and personal glory, they and their descendants, Faisal, Abdullah, Hussein, and Abdullah sold the honor of Islam for the next one hundred years. 'Abd al-'Aziz's sons inherited their father's debauchery and treason against Islam for their personal gain.

Treason runs deep in the veins of the descendants of Sharif Hussein and 'Abd al-'Aziz. They are *Munafiqeen* who have taken their *awliya* from among the *kafireen*. According to the covenant, they are of the *kafireen*. This circle of evil, the coalition of the *Yahudi, Salibi,* and *Munafiqeen* triumphed over Islam for over one hundred years. The

Jewish money in London, New York, Berlin, and Paris collaborated with the Christian powers of Europe and America and the *Munafiqeen*—Enver Pasha, Cemal Pasha, Talat Pasha, Sharif Hussein and sons, and Ibn Sa'ud and sons—to defeat the Islamic Empire and fragment it into scores of impoverished mini-client-states for political and economic exploitation by the *Yahudi, Salibi, Munafiq* coalition.

Egypt and the Slavery in Palestine

Anwar Sadat and the Egyptian Army won partial victory over the Jewish state of Israel in 1973. The victory made Sadat a hero in the eyes of many Arabs—if not equal to, then almost comparable to the great Arab hero Gamal Abdel Nasser. Puffed up by success and sycophancy from the likes of Henry Kissinger, Sadat forgot his own roots and began to take advice and comfort from Kissinger and Israeli lobbyists in Washington. Against the advice of his closest advisers and the leaders of other Arab countries, Sadat offered himself as a servant and a tool of the circle of evil, the *Yahudi-Salibi* confederation. He made a trip to Israel and addressed the Knesset, the Israeli Parliament. Under American tutelage and patronage, he abandoned his Arab allies, negotiated, and signed a peace treaty with many secret appendices with Israel at the expense of the Palestinians, Syrians, and Muslims in general.

As a consequence, all Palestine and the Golan Heights are under Israeli occupation. The Arabs are disunited and in disarray. Sadat sold the Egyptian sovereignty, the Islamic nation, and the holy Islamic places in Jerusalem for three billion dollars a year. Sadat took Jews and Christians as *awliya* and willfully disobeyed the covenant that every Muslim has pledged to obey. He also disobeyed the provisions of the covenant of Yathrib and the blessed *nabi's* teaching:

> Just as the bond to Allah is indivisible, all the believers shall stand behind the commitment of the least of them. All believers are bonded one to another to the exclusion of other men.

> This Pax Islamica is one and indivisible. No believer shall enter a separate peace without all other believers whenever there is fighting in the cause of God but will do so only on the basis of equality and justice to all others. In every expedition for the cause of God we undertake, all parties to the covenant shall fight shoulder to shoulder as one man. All believers shall avenge the blood of one another when anyone falls fighting in the cause of God.

Once again, the *Yahudi-Salibi* ingenuity used a *Munafiq* to grow the seeds of discord in the Islamic world.

The Ruin of Iraq

Saddam Hussein replaced al-Bakr as President of Iraq in July 1979. The bloodbath that followed eliminated all potential opposition to him. Saddam was now the master of Iraq with no one around him daring to question his actions. Two actions that he initiated led the Islamic community to disastrous disunity and debt. He attacked fellow Muslims, Iran in 1980 and Kuwait in 1990.

The Iran-Iraq War turned out to be a battle between two egomaniac personalities with a Messiah complex, neither of them willing to call a truce to the hostilities. The result was emaciation and bleeding of both countries to near bankruptcy. The Iraqi troops launched a full-scale invasion of Iran on September 22, 1980. France supplied high-tech weapons to Iraq, and the Soviet Union was Iraq's largest weapon supplier. Israel provided arms to Iran, hoping to bleed both the nations by prolonging the war. At least ten nations sold arms to both the warring nations to profit from the conflict. The United States followed a more duplicitous policy toward both warring parties to prolong the war and cause maximum damage to both.

The Iran-Iraq War was not between good and evil. Islam forbids fighting among the Muslims, murder, and taking of life unless it is in the cause of justice. Saddam Hussein launched a murderous war to regain a few square miles of territory that his country had relinquished freely in the 1975 border negotiations. There were one and a half million Muslim casualties in this senseless fraternal war. The war ended in a ceasefire that essentially left prewar borders unchanged. The Covenant of Allah not only forbids such an internecine war but also provides a mechanism for dispute resolution.

Instead of condemning the aggressor, the Arab states sided with Saddam Hussein, providing him with funds for further bloodletting. Saddam Hussein used banned chemical weapons against fellow Muslims, Iranians, and Kurds. The eight-year-long war exhausted both countries. Primary responsibility for the prolonged bloodletting must rest with the governments of the two countries, the ruthless military regime of Saddam Hussein and the ruthless clerical regime of Ayatollah Khomeini in Iran. Whatever his religious convictions were, Khomeini had no qualms about sending his followers, including young boys, to their deaths for his own greater glory. This callous disregard for human life was no less characteristic of Saddam Hussein. Saudi Arabia gave $25.7 billion and Kuwait $10 billion to Iraq to fuel the war and the killings. Saddam also owed the Soviets, the USA, and Europe $40 billion for the purchase of arms. The cost of war to the Iranians was even greater. The world community sold arms for eight and a half years and watched the bloodletting. The USA sold arms and information to both sides to prolong the war strategically and to profit and gain influence and bases in Gulf countries. Ayatollah Khomeini, in particular, was a hypocrite in dealing with Israel in secret when his public pronouncements were venomously anti-Israel.

Iran, Iraq, and all the Arab states of the Persian Gulf took the Western countries, the Soviet Union, and Israel as their *awliya*, in contradiction to the commandments of the covenant. The ayatollah and his clerics should have known and understood their obligations to Allah and to their people as spelled out in Allah's covenant. The uncontrolled Arab-Iranian hostility left a deep, festering wound in the body of the nation of Islam. The West made gains by setting up permanent bases in Saudi Arabia, Oman, the United Arab Emirates, Bahrain, Qatar, and Kuwait. This is the land that Muhammad, the blessed *rasul* of Allah, freed from infidels, only to be handed over to infidels by the *Munafiqeen*.

After the Kuwait war, at the invitation of King Fahd, the USA has continued to maintain large operational army and air force bases and command and control facilities that enable them to monitor air and sea traffic and civilian and military communications in the Middle East. Bahrain became the headquarters of a US naval fleet. The Middle East, at the beginning of the twenty-first century, is under the absolute military and economic control of the USA and NATO. The circle of evil—the *Yahudi*, *Salibi*, and *Munafiqeen*—continue to dominate the lives of Muslims.

17. The Covenant of Allah: Jihad: Fight the Infidel Until There Is No More Treachery and Oppression

> Fight the infidel until there is no more treachery and oppression and there prevails Justice and Faith in Allah altogether and everywhere. If they cease, then Allah is seer of what they do. If they refuse, be sure that Allah is your

Protector, the Best to protect and the Best to help. And why should you not fight in the cause of Allah and for those men, women, and children, who are weak, abused and oppressed, those who beseech their Lord to deliver protectors and helpers.

The Koranic use of the term *jihad* means "struggle." The Koran commonly uses the verb along with the expression *in the path of Allah.* The path of Allah, of course, is the path of right conduct that Allah has set down in the Koran. Jihad is simply the complement to *islam*, the surrender to the will of Allah. The surrender takes place in Allah's will, which people struggle with in His path. Hence, submission and surrender to Allah's will demands struggle in His path. Submission to Allah's command requires the believers to struggle against all negative tendencies in themselves and in the society that draw them away from Allah's path. Salat, zakat, fasting, and hajj are all struggles in the path of Allah. The greatest obstacles that people face in submitting themselves to Allah are their laziness, lack of imagination, and currents of contemporary opinion. These weaknesses and events carry them along without resisting. It takes an enormous struggle to submit to an authority that breaks one's likes and dislikes of current trends and pressures of society to conform to the crowd.

The jihad, which is normally a daily struggle within oneself against temptations and evil, will sometimes take an outward form against the enemies of Islam. Such a war is permitted strictly in the path of Allah in today's contemporary world to enforce truth, justice, and freedom.

And why should you not fight in the cause of Allah and for those men, women and children, who are weak, abused and oppressed, those who beseech their Lord to deliver them from their oppressors and those who ask Allah to send for them protectors and helpers. (An-Nisa 4:71–75, Koran)

The oft-repeated phrase in the Koran to proclaim jihad is to fight *fitnah*, tyranny, and oppression. Yet most of the wars in the Muslim world were civil wars, with Muslims killing Muslims for the sake of territory, wealth, and power.

Life is a chain of emotions, intentions, and actions. Before each deed, the human stops to intend an action. Each intention is the product of an emotion that acts on the human's self, the *nafs*. The *nafs* may intend to act on its animal instincts of craving and lust, or in situations where the self is sufficiently refined with *taqwa* of Allah, the human will follow His path as commanded by the covenant. The self is in a continuous battle whether to follow its base cravings or to perform wholesome deeds. Such ongoing fluctuation of intent between the base and the honorable is stressful. Such stress leads to anxiety, anger, and depression, which in the end will cause an emotional turmoil and breakdown. When the human intends to do his deeds with the knowledge that Allah is with him, that Allah is aware of his intent, and that Allah guides him to the right objective and action, there is peace and satisfaction.

When the believer is in *taqwa* of Allah, the *nur* of Allah cleans his *nafs* and aids him in obeying His covenant. Jihad is this struggle that prepares the believer in following and obeying Allah's commandments without question. Jihad is the struggle of the human from the path of ignorance to the path of Allah. The human hears Allah's call amid the noise and commotion of the world and, through the eye of his soul, lets the *nur* of Allah into the niche of his heart. Allah's call is about obedience, goodness, and selflessness. The human bows down his head on the earth in submission to his Lord and in humility. The Lord guides, and the believer follows; the believer has faith in Allah, and Allah holds his hand. Allah shows His believer the way to goodness, and the believer performs wholesome deeds. The *nur* of Allah glows in the believer's heart, and the believer accepts Allah in his heart.

This communion between the believer and Allah becomes exclusive. Submission establishes a link between the believer and Allah. Allah commands, and the believer follows. The believer asks, and Allah gives. The believer loves Allah, and Allah loves him in return. The believer asks for the straight path, and Allah shows him the way. The believer praises Allah, and Allah showers His mercy and grace upon him. The believer remembers Allah, and Allah responds to those who praise Him.

The *nafs*, unlike the Freudian ego, is capable of both good and bad. The *nuqta* of the *nafs*, when magnified a million times, becomes visible as a shiny disk, a mirror. The inherent nature (*fitra*) of the *nafs* is to shine like a mirror with Allah's *nur*. When the human walks the path of Allah in *taqwa* of Him with the knowledge that Allah is with him, watching him and guiding him, Allah's *nur* shines on the *nafs*, keeping it pure and safe. However, when the human's desires, cravings, and ego overpower his love and obedience of Allah, the shiny mirror of his *nafs* becomes obscured by the dirt and smoke of his desires, and he loses sight of the *nur* of Allah and trips into error and decadence.

The effort required to keep focusing on Allah's *nur* and *taqwa* of Him is the inner jihad. And this jihad is obedience to Allah's commandments when He calls on His believers with the words *O you who Believe* and commands them to do acts of faith and goodness in the *seventy-five* verses of the Koran. Obedience to every such command is jihad. Jihad is the struggle to fulfill the commandments of Allah in the covenant. *Taqwa* of Allah shines His light (*nur*) into core of the human, in the self (*nafs*), that clears the smoke of evil and temptation from the *nafs*, allowing the human to follow God.

Once the believer has purified himself with Allah's *nur*, he has prepared himself for the external jihad. When the believer has purified his own *nafs* and soul with submission to Allah (*islam*) and faith (*iman*) in the only reality, the Lord, and by performing wholesome deeds in the name of Allah, he is ready for the outer struggle for his *din*, to fight the *fitnah* of tyranny and oppression.

The blessed *nabi* of Allah wrote the following covenant in the first year of hijra in Medina. This is the essential constitution of the whole *ummah*. This is a covenant given by Muhammad to the believers.

1. They constitute one Ummah to the exclusion of all other men.
2. The believers shall leave none of their members in destitution without giving him in kindness that he needs by the way of his liberty.
3. No believer shall slay a believer in retaliation for an unbeliever, nor shall he assist an unbeliever against a believer.
4. All believers shall rise as one man against anyone who seeks to commit injustice, aggression, crime, or spread mutual enmity amongst the Muslims even if such a person is their kin.
5. Just as the bond to Allah is indivisible, all the believers shall stand behind the commitment of the least of them. All believers are bonded one to another to the exclusion of other men.
6. This Pax Islamica is one and indivisible. No believer shall enter a separate peace without all other believers whenever there is fighting in the cause of God but will do so only on the basis of equality and justice to all others. In every expedition for the cause of God we undertake, all parties to the covenant shall fight shoulder to shoulder as one man. All believers shall avenge the blood of one another when anyone falls fighting in the Way of Allah.
    The pious believers follow the best and the most upright guidance. Whoever is convicted of killing a believer deliberatively but without righteous cause shall be liable to the relatives of the killed. Until the

latter are satisfied, the killer shall be subject to retaliation by each and every believer.

Allah speaks to the believers about the struggle in His way:

Fight in the cause of Allah those who fight you, but do not transgress limits; for Allah loves not transgressors.

And slay them wherever you catch them and turn them out from where they have turned you out; for Fitnah, tumult and oppression are worse than slaughter; but fight them not at the Sacred Mosque, unless they fight you there first; but if they fight you, slay them. Such is the reward of those who suppress faith.

But if they cease, Allah is Oft-Forgiving, Most Merciful.

And fight them on until there is no more Fitnah, tumult or oppression and there prevail justice and faith in Allah; but if they cease, let there be no hostility except to those who practice oppression. (Al-Baqarah 2:190–93, Koran)

And why should you not fight in the cause of Allah and for those men, women and children, who are weak, abused and oppressed, those who beseech their Lord to deliver them from their oppressors and those who ask Allah to send for them protectors and helpers.

Those who believe fight in the cause of Allah and those who reject Faith fight in the cause of Evil: so fight you against the friends of Satan: feeble indeed is the cunning of Satan. (An-Nisa 4:75–76, Koran)

And slacken not in following up the enemy; if you are suffering hardships, they are suffering similar hardships; but you have hope from Allah, while they have none. And Allah is full of Knowledge and Wisdom. (An-Nisa 4:104, Koran)

If Allah helps you none can overcome you: if He forsakes you, who is there, after that, that can help you? In Allah, then, let Believers put their trust (Ali 'Imran 3; 160, Koran)

We did indeed send, before you Rasools to their respective peoples, with Clear Signs: To those who transgressed, We meted out Retribution: and as a right those who earned from us, We helped those who believed. (Ar-Rum 30:47, Koran)

Here is a declaration to the human, a guidance and advice to those who live in awareness, Taqwa of Allah!

So, lose not hope nor shall you despair, for you shall achieve supremacy, if you are true in Faith.

If you have suffered a setback, verily a setback has been there for the other party too. We make such days of adversity go around amongst the humans so that Allah may distinguish those who believe and choose His witnesses from amongst them. And Allah loves not the evil doers.

Allah's objective is to distinguish the True Believers from those who reject Faith. (Ali 'Imran 3:138–41, Koran)

Wars and slaughter are abhorrent to Allah. Allah says:

If anyone slew a person, unless it is in retribution for murder or for spreading mischief, fasaad in the land it would be as if he slew the whole people. And if anyone saved a life, it would be as if he saved the life of the whole people. Take not life, which Allah has made sacred, except by the way of justice or law. This He commands you, that you may learn wisdom.

And then Allah declares to the Believers that *fitnah*, treachery, and oppression are worse than slaughter and the taking of life. They are so vile and repugnant to Allah that He commands the believers to fight those who assail them and inflict oppression:

> And slay them wherever you catch them and turn them out from where they have turned you out; for Fitnah, tyranny and oppression are worse than slaughter; And fight them on until there is no more Fitnah, tumult or oppression and there prevail justice and faith in Allah; but if they cease, let there be no hostility except to those who practice'. oppression. (Al-Baqarah 2:190–93, Koran)

Allah's command to fight *fitnah*, however, is conditional:

> If the oppressors cease, let there be no further hostility except to those who practice oppression. Do not transgress limits. Allah does not love transgressors. (Al-Baqarah 2:190–93, Koran)
>
> When the Believers fight against Fitnah and oppression, they fight in the cause of Allah. Those who reject faith in Allah, they fight in the cause of evil. (An-Nisa 4:75–76, Koran)

18. The Covenant of Allah: *Fitnah*, Tyranny, and Oppression Are So Vile and Repugnant That Allah Commands the Believers to Fight Those Who Assail Them

Fitnah: Allah has granted each believer the freedom to practice his or her *din* in accordance with his or her beliefs since, in Islam, there is no compulsion in matters of religion; the right to life, which includes mental, physical, and emotional well-being; the right to intellectual endeavors, acquisition of knowledge, and education; the right to make a living; and the right to free speech and action to enjoin good and forbid evil. In enjoying his freedoms, a person should ensure that his activities do not impinge on the similar rights of others. Oppression and tyranny—which deprives a believer, a community of believers, or their nation (the *ummah*) of their God-given rights and freedom—is *fitnah* as described in the Koran. The tyrants and oppressors cannot belong to the fellowship of Allah, of His Covenant, nor of the blessed *nabi* of Allah.

In the above *ayahs*, Allah commands the believers to fight such infidels until there is no more *fitnah*, treachery, and oppression and until there prevails justice and faith in Allah everywhere. He orders them to slay them wherever they catch them and turn them out from where they have turned them out, for *fitnah*, tumult, and oppression are worse than slaughter. Allah has forbidden the taking of life. "Take not life, which Allah has made sacred, except by the way of justice or law." *Fitnah*, tyranny, and oppression are so vile and repugnant that Allah commands the believers to fight those who assail them and inflict oppression. "Go forth, advance! Whether equipped well or lightly, perform *jihad* strive your utmost and struggle with your wealth and your persons in the cause of Allah." Allah loves those who fight for His cause in unison and solidarity. *Fitnah*, tyranny, and oppression not only afflict those who perpetrate it but also affect everyone, guilty and innocent alike. Allah's command to fight *fitnah* is conditional however: if the oppressors cease, let there be no further hostility except to those who practice *fitnah*. Do not transgress limits. Allah does not love transgressors.

In the twenty-first century, weakness, poverty, disunity, and fragmentation of the *ummah* arise from lack of appreciation of the immense understanding and knowledge in the Koran. Muslims look at the word of Allah but do not see it. They listen to the word but do not hear it. Allah's *nur* (His light) is with them, but they do not let it enter their hearts. The mirror of their *nafs* is covered with the smoke of their greed and craving of worldly wealth. They cannot see Allah's *nur* through the smoky darkness in their heart. *Fitnah*, treachery, and oppression are by-products of darkened hearts, causing blindness to the *nur* of Allah. Without His *nur*, there cannot be *taqwa* of Allah; and in the absence of the consciousness of the reality of Allah, the darkened soul is open to the evil of Satan.

Muslim societies have been plagued by *fitnah* and oppression since the death of the blessed *nabi*. In Muslim countries, *fitnah* is the result of the combination of internal and external forces. Although the perpetrators of *fitnah* often proclaim Allah as their Savior, their actions always belie their faith in Him.

Most believers do not know that when the blessed Muhammad died, every believer inherited the Koran, Allah's covenant, His *din*, and the Dar es Salaam. Every believer became the successor, inheritor, and custodian of the blessed *nabi*'s legacy till the end of time. Consequently, in the twenty-first century, majority of believers are unaware of their rights granted by Allah. They are unaware that Allah commands them to fight the *fitnah* of tyranny and oppression perpetrated by their self-appointed rulers, kings, military dictators, and infidel *awliya*, the Euro-Christian patrons.

Internal *Fitnah*: Hundreds of years of rule of sultans and later of the Western colonial masters produced three unique sources of internal *fitnah* that rules the roost in the Muslim societies of our day.

1. *Priesthood.* There is no priesthood in Islam; the believer has a highly personal and exclusive relationship with Allah. Such relationship does not permit the intervention of another human being. When the blessed Muhammad was taken up by Allah, the priests and clerics of Islam assumed the legacy of the pagan priesthood and began to speak on behalf of Allah. Through distortion and misrepresentation of the word

of Allah and the pronouncements of His *nabi*, over the last fourteen hundred years, the priests and imams of Islam have created divisions and schisms in Islam to generate hundreds of self-righteous sects and subsects among the Muslims. Each sect is the enemy of the other. Every group has the dagger in the back of the other. This gradually smoldering *fitnah* of the priesthood is slowly consuming the body of the *ummah*.

2. *Mercenary armies of Islam.* The blessed *nabi* said,

> All believers shall rise as one man against anyone who seeks to commit injustice, aggression, crime, or spread mutual enmity amongst the Muslims. All believers are bonded one to another to the exclusion of other men. The believers shall leave none of their members in destitution without giving him in kindness that he needs by the way of his liberty.

However, this fight for unity, equality, and justice did not occur in the lands of Islam; the army of God and of Islam did not arise to fight in the cause of Allah to defend against *fitnah*, tyranny, and oppression and to seek retribution against injustice. The absolute loyalty of the army of Islam is to God, the Koran, and the *ummah*. The army of Islam defends the believers, their faith, their land, their wealth, and their honor and fights only against *fitnah* for truth and justice. In case of injury to the believers, their faith, their land, their wealth, and their honor, the believers are obliged to exact retribution. No believer shall side with an unbeliever against a believer. Whosoever is convicted of killing a believer without a righteous cause shall be liable to the relatives of the killed. The killers shall be subject to retaliation by each believer until the relatives of the victim are satisfied with the retribution.

Had the Muslim communities stood united as one to avenge the blood of every fallen Muslim and rejected a separate peace with the pagans without all the Muslims participating in it, there would have been no *fitnah* and massacres in Algeria, Palestine, India, Afghanistan, Iraq, Bosnia, Chechnya, Kosovo, and Darfur. This unity demands revenge, retribution, and reprisal for every act of murder and injury in Dayr Yasin, Sabra, Shatila, Srebrenica, Janin, Sarajevo, Fallujah, Kosovo, Chechnya, Gujarat, Kashmir, Iraq, Guantanamo Bay, and Abu Ghraib. Had the Muslims stood up for one another and fought those who perpetrated the *fitnah*, they would not have been groveling in the dustheap of humanity today.

Contrary to the stipulations of the covenant of Allah, the present six-million-man mercenary armies of Muslim states serve to bolster illegal regimes of *Munafiqeen, the* traitors to the cause of Islam. Instead of relieving the believers of *fitnah* and oppression, they cause them. They are the source of dichotomy and division in Islam; they are the defenders of the foreign hegemony over Islam. The armies of the sultans of the previous centuries and the rulers of modern times are the perpetrators of *fitnah* and the enemies of Islam. They are the defenders of the borders created by the Western colonial powers that divide Islam today. They are the *fitnah*.

3. *Rulers of Islam.* Islam is a religion of voluntary submission of a human to the will of Allah after a considered conviction that Allah is the only reality and that everything else springs out of that reality. Allah has given every human the freedom of choice to submit or not to His will. There is no compulsion in matters of the *din*. And yet there are humans who, by force of arms, compel other humans to submit to their will. They demand obedience through imprisonment, torture, and murder. Every Muslim state in this day is a police state. Every Muslim ruler abuses his authority to plunder and debase the

lands of Islam. Every Muslim state today is the source of *fitnah* that is eating into the heart and the soul of Islam.

The External *Fitnah* of the Circle of Evil: Two hundred years ago, the circle of evil began its control of the world's wealth through conspiracy, subterfuge, and secrecy by undermining the stability of countries through war, strife, and discord and by weakening governments through creation of confusion in financial markets. The Western armies and intelligence services are the foot soldiers of the circle of evil, and the rulers of both the East and the West are their pawns and puppets to be manipulated at will to control the power and wealth of the world. The circle of evil is the external *fitnah* whose intent is to destroy Islam. It has always been its intention to corrupt, divide, and control the wealth of the Islamic land through the manipulation of its rulers, who were initially placed in positions of power by the circle with the help of the Western armies, intelligence, and diplomacy.

The weakness of the mercenary armies of the modern Islamic states clearly arises from the nonfulfillment of Allah's injunctions in the covenant. Faith in Allah's promise and power, unity of the *ummah*, justice, and the struggle to end *fitnah* and tyranny are essential actions ordained in the covenant. When a believer reneges on his covenant with Allah, he only does it to the detriment to his own soul. However, such an action on the part of the community and its appointed leaders leads to the undermining, enslavement, and impoverishment of the whole Islamic community for many generations. The regimes of the imperial families of the Arabian Peninsula, Jordan, Brunei, and Morocco and the imperial occupation governments of Hosni Mubarak of Egypt and the generals of Pakistan are supported by the external *fitnah*—the British, US, and NATO armed forces, intelligence, and diplomatic services—in opposition to the aspirations of their own people. In return, these regimes provide services to the circle of evil to subvert, undermine, and weaken the neighboring Islamic and Arab countries of Iran, Afghanistan, Iraq, Syria, Libya, Algeria, Sudan, and Mauritania. The *ummah* is saddled with the curse and the *fitnah* of the priesthood, the mercenary armies of Muslim states, their corrupt rulers, and the foreign masters of their rulers.

Imagine a country with the largest land base, with coasts rimmed by thousands of miles of blue oceans, and with a vast number of rivers flowing from hundreds of snowcapped mountains through its deserts, grasslands, fertile valleys, and plains into rich deltas, lakes, and oceans bursting with marine life and other resources—a land blessed by Allah with resources never equaled in history, peopled with a devout, hardworking population with the knowledge of how to utilize such resources in the service of Allah and His creatures. Again, see in your mind's eye an army, the largest in history of mankind, keeping this land, its borders and resources, its oceans and skies, and its people and wealth secure from marauders who have traditionally raided other lands for their resources. These defense forces compose of an army of six million men in about 300 infantry and mechanized divisions equipped with 30,000 tanks and armored vehicles, an air force of 3,580 aircraft of varying models, and a naval force equipped with 230 coastal and oceangoing ships equipped with armaments bought from the West and Russia. There are also 60 submarines in the armada. These armed forces are also equipped with short- and medium-range missiles tipped with about sixty nuclear bombs. The country has a budding arms-manufacturing industry producing low- and medium-technology arms. The annual budget of the combined forces is $150 billion, of which $50 billion annually goes to Western countries to purchase their discarded and obsolete weaponry. The West then uses these funds to refurbish its own arsenal with the latest, high-tech weapons.

You might have guessed that we are talking about the combined might of the Islamic world at the onset of the twenty-first century. This army has never won any battle of significance since the war for the Gallipoli Peninsula about a century ago. These armed forces have not defended in any significant manner the Islamic world since the disintegration of the Ottoman Empire. The wars of independence of Islamic lands from the colonial rule in India, Iran, Iraq, Syria, Egypt, Morocco, and Algeria were fought by the masses with civil disobedience and guerrilla warfare. The state-organized armies of Islam have failed to safeguard the freedom of the people of Palestine, Iraq, Kashmir, Sinkiang, Iraq, Kosovo, Bosnia, Mindanao, Chechnya, and Russia.

What went wrong? The Muslim army of the twentieth and the twenty-first centuries has its guns pointed toward its own people, whereas the external borders of Islam are guarded and patrolled by the naval fleets of America and Europe. The Muslim state armies should be fighting the treachery and oppression by enemies of Allah and Islam—the *kafaru*, *mushrikun*, *Munafiqeen*, and *zalimun*, who have usurped and plundered resources of the believers for the last two hundred years. Instead, the Muslim armies and security services are themselves the source of oppression and treachery to the *momineen*, resisting tyranny of the circle of evil of the *Munafiqun* and the *Mutaffifeen*. The clear examples are the armed and security forces of Reza Shah Pahlavi, the mullahs of Iran, Saddam Hussein of Iraq, the Taliban, the Pakistani governments, the Saudi family, Suharto, Syria, Anwar Sadat, Hosni Mubarak, Gaddhafi, the Algerian military, and Morocco's royalty.

This is a clear testimony that the believers of the covenant of Allah and those who control the so-called armies of Islam have not surrendered to the will of Allah and do not strive in His path. The obligations assigned to the individual believer in the covenant of Allah are the same for the community of Islam and for the leaders whom the believers appoint to look after and to protect their individual and communal interests. The covenant is specific in pointing out the responsibilities of the individual, the community, and its appointed leaders.

Jihad is the internal struggle of the believer to cleanse oneself of the temptations of the evil that surrounds him or her. It is also a constant external struggle to rid the community of the treachery and oppression by the enemy of the covenant and *din*. The enemy may be obvious, visible, and easily overpowered. The web of intrigues and conspiracies of the *kafaru*, *mushrikun*, *Munafiqeen*, and *zalimun* is hard to detect and overcome. The deception may come from familiar people working from within the community for the circle of evil whose motive is to tempt you away from Allah's path and also take control of your land and wealth, enslaving you in the process. The following four principles should guide the believers in their striving for Allah's cause.

1. *Faith in Allah's covenant and promise.* Join not anything in worship with Him. Allah is the *Waliy* (Friend and Defender) of the believers who obey His covenant. Allah promises His strength and power (*al-qawiyy al-Aziz*) to aid the believer and promises victory in his striving for Allah's *din*. Therefore, the believer shall maintain his faith in Allah's promise always. Trust in Allah's promise endows the believer with the greatest strength from Allah's might in his determination to struggle and fight for Allah's cause. All strength belongs to Allah. All physical,

worldly, political, and cosmic strength is nothing before the infinite strength of Allah.

Allah is the All-powerful the Almighty, Al-qawiyy al-Aziz. (Hud 11:66, Koran)

There is no Power except in Allah. (Al-Kahf 18:39, Koran)

Verily it is I and My Messengers who will be victorious Verily Allah is All-powerful, All-mighty. (Al-Mujadila 58:21, Koran)

2. *Unity.* The believers constitute one *ummah* to the exclusion of all other men. Just as the bond with Allah is indivisible, all believers shall stand in commitment with the least of them. All believers are bonded to one another to the exclusion of other men. The believers shall leave none of their members in destitution and give them in kindness and liberty what they need. The pious believers follow the best and the most upright guidance of Allah's covenant.

3. *Jihad.* All believers shall rise as one against anyone who seeks to commit injustice, aggression, or crime or spread mutual enmity among the Muslims. This Pax Islamica is one and indivisible. No believer shall enter a separate peace without all other believers whenever there is fighting in the cause of Allah but will do so only on the basis of equality and justice to all others. In every expedition for the cause of Allah, all parties to the covenant shall fight shoulder to shoulder as one man. All believers shall avenge the blood of one another when anyone falls while fighting for the cause of Allah.

4. *Murder.* No believer shall slay a believer in retaliation for an unbeliever, nor shall he assist an unbeliever against a believer.

Whoever is convicted of killing a believer deliberately but without righteous cause shall be liable to the relatives of the killed. Until the latter are satisfied, the killer shall be subject to retaliation by each and every believer.

5. *Justice.* Justice (*'adl*) is a divine attribute defined as "putting in the right place." The opposite of *'adl* is *zulm*, which in Koranic terms means "wrongdoing." Wrongdoing is a human attribute defined as "putting things in the wrong place." *Zulm* (wrongdoing) is one of the common terms used in the Koran to refer to the negative acts employed by human beings. Wrongdoing is the opposite of justice, putting everything in its right place, and every act of humans as prescribed by Allah. Wrongdoing is to put things where they do not belong. Hence, wrongdoing is injustice, for example, associating others with Allah; others do not belong in the place for the divine. It is to place false words in place of the truth and to put someone else's property in place of your own. Other examples are taking a life against the divine commandments, replacing people's liberty with oppression, waging war instead of peace, and usurping people's right to govern themselves. The Koran repeatedly stigmatizes men of wrongdoing.

The Koran, when it points out who is harmed by injustice and wrongdoing, always mentions the word *nafs* (self). People cannot harm Allah. By being unjust or by putting things in the wrong place, people harm themselves. They distort their own natures, and they lead themselves astray. Who can one wrong? It is impossible to wrong or do injustice against Allah since all things are His creatures and do His work. Hence, wrongdoing and injustice is an activity against people and Allah's creation. Allah had prescribed His covenant to the humans for the good of human beings. People, tribes, and nations are being helped since Allah leads them into accord, harmony, and justice, which in turn create peace in the world. Allah has laid out all the basic principles for justice in His covenant for the humans to live in harmony. Those who refuse to follow His commandments are therefore ungrateful and hence *kafirs*. Thus, they are wrongdoers (*zalimun*) and only harm themselves. Therefore, there can be no jihad unless it is for justice and against wrongdoing.

There is a clear reason for the glaring weakness of the state-run armies of the Muslim nation-states. The Muslim states are governed by self-appointed kings, dictators, and politicians who are divorced from their *din* and their people. They belong to and serve the interests of the circle of evil.

> Make careful preparations and take precautions. Then go forth in groups or all together to the endeavor.
> There amongst you is he who will linger behind, if misfortune befalls you he will say, "Allah did favor him as he was not with you." When good fortune comes to you from Allah, he would wish that he had been with you.
>
> Those who swap the life of this world for the hereafter let them fight in the cause of Allah. Whosoever fights in the cause of Allah, whether he is slain or he is victorious, there is a great award for him from Allah.
>
> And why should you not fight in the cause of Allah and for those men, women and children, who are weak, abused and oppressed, those who beseech their Lord to deliver them from their oppressors and those who ask Allah to send for them protectors and helpers.(An-Nisa 4:71–75, Koran)
>
> Remember Allah's blessings on you. When a people planned to stretch out their hands against you and Allah did hold back

their hands from you to protect you from your enemies. Be in taqwa of Allah, fear Allah and place your trust in Allah. (Al-Ma'idah 5:11, Koran)

Be in taqwa of Allah, fear Allah. Perform Jihad and strive your utmost in Allah's Cause and approach Him so that you may prosper. (Al-Ma'idah 3:35, Koran)

If any among you turn back on his faith Allah will bring a people whom He loves and who love Him and who are humble towards the believers and stern towards unbelievers, who perform jihad and strive in the cause of Allah and fear not reproaches of any blamer. Such is the Grace of Allah that He bestows on whom He wills. Allah is All-Sufficient for His Creatures and all Knowing. (Al-Ma'idah 5:54, Koran)

When you meet the infidels rank upon rank, in conflict never turn your backs to them. (Al-Anfal 8:15, Koran)

Respond to Allah and His Rasool when He calls you to that gives you life. And know that Allah intervenes in the tussle between man and his heart, and it is to Allah that you shall return. Fear treachery or oppression that afflicts not only those who perpetrate it but affects guilty and innocent alike. Know that Allah is strict in punishment. (Al-Anfal 8:24–25, Koran)

Fight the infidel until there is no more treachery and oppression and there prevails Justice and Faith in Allah altogether and everywhere. If they cease, then Allah is seer of what they do. If they refuse, be sure that Allah is your Protector, the Best to protect and the Best to help. (Al-Anfal 8:39–40, Koran)

When you meet the enemy force, stand steadfast against them, and remember the name of Allah much, so that you may be successful. And obey Allah and His Messenger and do not dispute with one another lest you lose courage, and your strength departs and be patient. Allah is with those who patiently persevere. (Al-Anfal 8:45–46, Koran)

Whether you do or do not help Allah's Messenger, your leader, Allah strengthens him with His Peace and with forces that you do not see. The words of the infidels He humbled into the dirt, but Allah's word is Exalted, High. Allah is Mighty, Wise. Go forth, advance! Whether equipped well or lightly, perform jihad strive your utmost and struggle with your wealth and your persons in the cause of Allah. That is best for you, if you knew. (At-Tawbah 9:38–41, Koran)

Fight the unbelievers who surround you. Let them find you firm and know Allah is always with those who have taqwa, who are Allah-wary. (At-Tawbah 9:123, Koran)

Remember the Grace of Allah, bestowed upon you, when there came down hordes to overpower you: We sent against them a hurricane and forces that that you did not see: but Allah sees all that ye do.
Behold! They came on you from above you and from below you, your eyes became dim and the hearts gaped up to the throats and you imagined various vain thoughts about Allah! (Al-Ahzab 33:9, Koran)

If you will aid (the cause of) Allah, He will aid you and make your foothold firm. But those who reject Allah, for them is destruction and Allah will render their deeds vain. That is because they hate the Revelation of Allah; so, He has made their deeds fruitless. Do they not travel through the earth and see what was the end of those before their times, who did evil? Allah brought utter destruction on them and similar fates await those who reject Allah. That is because Allah is the Protector of those who believe, but those who reject Allah have no protector. (Muhammad 47:7–11, Koran)

Be not weak and ask for peace, while you are having an upper hand: for Allah is with you and will never decrease the reward of your good deeds.

The life of this world is but play and amusement: and if ye believe, fear Allah and guard against evil, He will grant you your recompense and will not ask you (to give up) your possessions.

Behold, you are those invited to spend of your wealth in the Way of Allah: but among you are some that are parsimonious. But any who are miserly are so at the expense of their own souls. But Allah is free of all wants and it is ye that are needy. If ye turn back (from the Path), He will substitute in your stead another people; then they would not be like you! (Muhammad 47:33–38, Koran)

When ye are told to make room in the assemblies, spread out and make room: ample room will Allah provide for you. And when ye are told to rise up, for prayers, Jihad or other good deeds rise up: Allah will exalt in rank those of you who believe and who have been granted Knowledge. And Allah is well acquainted with all you do. (Al-Mujadila 58:11, Koran).

Why do you promise what you do not carry out? Hateful is indeed to Allah that you say what you do not act upon. Allah loves those who fight in His cause in array of unison and solidarity. (As-Saf 61:2–4, Koran)

Shall I guide you to a bargain that will save you from a painful torment? That you believe in Allah and His Messenger and that you perform Jihad (strive to your utmost) in the way of Allah, with all that you own and in all earnestness: that will be best for you, if you but knew! He will forgive you your sins and admit you to Gardens beneath which rivers flow and to beautiful dwellings in Jannat of adn (Gardens of Eternity):

that is indeed the supreme blessing. And another favor will He bestow, which you will cherish; help from Allah and a speedy victory. So, give the glad tidings to the believers. (As-Saf 61:10–13, Koran)

19. The Covenant of Allah: Forgiveness: Be Quick in the Race for Forgiveness from Your Lord, Restrain Anger, and Pardon All Humans

O you who believe! Be quick in the race for forgiveness from your Lord. Those who give freely whether in prosperity, or in adversity, those who restrain anger and pardon all humans, for Allah loves those who do beautiful deeds. Fear the Fire, which is prepared for those who reject Faith; And obey Allah and the Messenger; that ye may obtain mercy. Be quick in the race for forgiveness from your Lord and for a Garden whose measurement is that of the heavens and of the earth, prepared for the righteous.

Those who give freely whether in prosperity, or in adversity, those who restrain anger and pardon all humans, for Allah loves those who do beautiful deeds. (Ali 'Imran 3:130–34, Koran)

Amongst Allah's names are *Ar Rahman,* the Beneficent, *Ar Rahim,* the Merciful and *Al Ghafoor,* the Forgiving. His Mercy overtakes His punishment and anger.

Say: "O my Servants who have transgressed against their souls! Despair not of the Mercy of Allah: for Allah forgives all sins: for He is Oft-Forgiving, Most Merciful.

Every human action in daily life reaches back into the divine reality that everything in the universe is governed by tawhid, yet Allah has granted humans a freedom of choice, which can upset the balance in the creation, the balance of justice, and the balance of atmospheric elements and lead to environmental pollution, destruction of animal species, and destruction of populations, cities, and agriculture through human actions. The covenant tells people why they should be Allah's servants and explains which path they should follow to become His vicegerents. It makes it clear that human activity is deeply rooted in the Real, and this has everlasting repercussions in this world and in the hereafter.

The wholesome (*salihun*) are the ones who live in harmony with the Real (*Haqq*) and establish wholesomeness (*saalihaat*) through their words and deeds throughout the world. In contrast, the corrupt (*mufsidun*) destroy the proper balance and relationship with Allah and His creation. *Fasid* means "corrupt, evil, wrong."

> When he turns his back, he hurries about the earth to work corruption there and destroy the tillage and the stock. Allah loves not corruption. (Al-Baqarah 2:205, Koran)

Allah loves doing what is beautiful. Because of His love for those who do the beautiful, He brings them near to Himself, and His nearness is called Allah's mercy:

> Work not corruption in this world after it has made wholesome and call upon Allah in fear and hope. Surely the mercy of Allah is near to those who do what is beautiful. (Al-A'raf 7:56, Koran)

To err is human. Allah is most forgiving to those who have erred and repented. Above all, Allah's mercy knows no bounds. The Koran and the teaching of the blessed *nabi* guide those who seek the path of Allah. Allah says:

O my Servants who have transgressed against their souls! Despair not of the Mercy of Allah: for Allah forgives all sins: for He is Oft-Forgiving, Most Merciful.

Turn you to your Lord (in repentance) and bow to His (Will) before the Penalty comes on you: after that ye shall not be helped. (Az-Zumar 39:53, Koran)

Allah, in His mercy, has laid down guidelines for punishment of the transgressors. For transgressors and sinners, there is Allah's wrath in this world and the next. If they repent, however, Allah forgives them. The Koran constantly emphasizes repentance and reform of a person and Allah's mercy and grace. Allah's mercy knows no bounds. Justice (*'adl*) is a divine attribute defined as "putting every object in the right place." When the transgressor repents, mends his ways, and does not repeat the wrongdoing, evil has been replaced with good. Allah bestows His mercy.

The community's obligation is to pardon and help educate and reform an individual. Allah advises every human to restrain from anger and resentment. Anger is a smoldering volcano quietly burning the human from the inside, robbing his tranquility and peace. Forgiving others restores peace and brings nearness to Allah. For the unrepentant transgressor, the penalty is prescribed in the Koran. Never is the gate to Allah's mercy closed. The key to this gate is repentance and a walk in Allah's path.

20. The Covenant of Allah: If Anyone Slew a Person, It Would Be as If He Slew the Whole People

If anyone slew a person, unless it be for punishment for murder or for spreading mischief in the land, it would be as if he slew the whole people: and if anyone saved a life, it would be as if he saved the life of all the people.

Life is sacred. Allah forbids the taking of life unless it is by the way of justice (jihad against tyranny and oppression) or when ordained by the law of equality or punishment for murder, where the Koran recommends clemency. As the covenant forbids the believers and the community of Islam to take a life and murder, the same injunction applies to the ruler or the *amri minkum* appointed by the believers. War against Muslims and others for acquisition of territory and wealth is forbidden, and anyone waging such a war blatantly disobeys Allah's covenant and is not of the believers. Persecution, punishment, imprisonment, and murder of the citizens of the Islamic state who strive for the cause of Allah is a heinous crime. Rulers and their bureaucracy responsible for such crimes are unfit to discharge their responsibility and liable for punishment for their crime according to the law of the Koran.

If anyone slew a person – unless it be for murder or for spreading mischief in the land – it would be as if he slew the whole people: and if anyone saved a life, it would be as if he saved the life of the whole people. (Al-Ma'idah 5:32, Koran)

Take not life, which Allah hath made sacred, except by the way of justice or law: This He commands you, that you may learn wisdom. (Al-An'am :151–153, Koran)

21. The Covenant of Allah: Usury and Hoarding of Wealth: Devour Not Usury, Doubled, and Multiplied; Be in *Taqwa* of Allah (Fear Allah) That Ye May Prosper

Forbidden is the practice of usury to the Muslims. Also forbidden is making money from money. Money in its present form is only a medium of exchange, a way of defining the value of an item, but in itself has no value and therefore should not give rise to more money by earning interest through deposit in a bank or loaning it to someone else. The human endeavor, initiative, and risk involved in a productive venture are much more important than the money used to finance it. Money deposited in a bank or hoarded is potential capital rather than capital. Money becomes capital only when it is invested in a venture. Accordingly, money loaned to a business is regarded as a debt and is not capital; and as such, it is not entitled to any return, such as interest.

Muslims are encouraged to spend (purchase necessities or spend in the way of Allah) or invest their money and are discouraged from keeping their money idle. Hoarding money is unacceptable. Allah's commandments in His covenant with the believers in the following three *ayahs* exhort Muslims to (a) spend in charity after their needs are met, (b) devour not in usury, and (c) hoard not gold and silver.

> They ask thee how much they are to spend (in charity); say: "What is beyond your needs." Thus, doth Allah make clear to you His Signs: in order that ye may consider. (Al-Baqarah 2:222, Koran)

> Allah will deprive usury of all blessing but will give increase for deeds of charity; for He loves not creatures ungrateful and wicked. (Al-Baqarah 2:275–76, Koran)

And there are those who hoard gold and silver and spend it not in the Way of Allah: announce unto them a most grievous penalty. (Al-A'raf 9:34, Koran)

Gharar (uncertainty, risk, or speculation) is forbidden. Any transaction entered into should be free from uncertainty, risk, and speculation. The parties cannot predetermine a granted profit, and this does not allow an undertaking from the borrower or the customer to repay the borrowed principal, plus an amount to consider inflation. Therefore, options and futures are regarded as un-Islamic; so are foreign exchange transactions because rates are determined by interest differentials.

An Islamic government is forbidden to lend or borrow money from institutions such as international banks, the World Bank, or the International Monetary Fund on interest as both usury and interest are expressly forbidden. Banking based on fiat money is also forbidden. The value of money is diluted by the creation of new money out of nothing; the property rights of savers and those who have been promised future payments, such as pensioners, are violated. This is stealing. The trappings of the money and banking system have been compared to that of a cult; only those who profit from it understand its inner workings. They work hard to keep it that way. The central banks print notes adorned with signatures, seals, and pictures of a president or that of a queen; counterfeiters are severely punished; governments pay their expenses with them; and populations are forced to accept them. They are printed like newspapers in such vast quantity, representing an equal worth to all the treasures of this world, all the resources above and under the ground, all assets of populations, and their work and labor to fabricate every item that has ever been manufactured. And yet these notes cost nothing to make.

In truth, this has been the greatest hoax, the worst crime against humanity, a swindle of proportions never seen by humanity before.

As we have found, the Koran forbids usury, gambling, speculation, and hoarding of gold and silver. The Koran does advocate trade; spending on good things in life, kith, and kin; and giving wealth for the cause of Allah. The modern economic system is entirely alien to the teachings of the Koran and full of pitfalls and trappings laid down by Satan. The Dar es Salaam has slid downhill, submerged into the quicksand of make-believe economy. Every successful businessman and trader is forced to operate in the pagan, sinful system of economy. Here is the solution for a successful economic system as laid down in the covenant of the Koran:

1. Elimination of usury and interest in Dar es Salaam.

2. Elimination of fiat money and of banking based on money created out of nothing with a printing press. There will be no more creation and lending of capital nine times that of the bank deposits. It is dishonest and forbidden because it is based on institutionalized theft, supported by the state and international institutions.

3. Creation of a single currency for the united Islamic state, such as gold dinars and silver dirhams based on the measures established by Umar ibn al-Khattab, the second caliph. A currency bureau, an arm of the state of Dar es Salaam, will supervise the minting and circulation of the currency.

4. Drastic changes to Dar es Salaam's trading relations with the rest of the world. All goods utilized within the state—whether industrial, agricultural, manufactured, or raw—will be produced within the country so that the *ummah* is self-sufficient and independent of foreign trading systems. The

goods for export—oil, minerals, raw and manufactured goods—shall be sold against gold and gold-based currency as well as barter. Paper and printed money will not be acceptable. Pricing for international trade will use an index of equal value to human labor internationally.

Those that spend of their goods in charity by night and by day, in secret and in public, have their reward with their Lord: on them shall be no fear, nor shall they grieve.

Those who devour usury will not stand except stands the one whom the Satan by his touch has driven to madness. That is because they say: "Trade is like usury," but Allah hath permitted trade and forbidden usury. Those who after receiving direction from their Lord, desist, shall be pardoned for the past; their case is for Allah to judge; but those who repeat (the offence) are Companions of the Fire; they will abide therein (forever).

Allah will deprive usury of all blessing but will give increase for deeds of charity; for He does not love ungrateful and wicked creatures. (Al-Baqarah 2:274–76, Koran)

Those who believe and perform wholesome deeds, establish regular prayers and regular charity have rewards with their Lord. On them shall be no fear, nor shall they grieve.
Fear Allah and give up what remains of your demand for usury if you are indeed believers. If you do it not, take notice of war from Allah and His Messenger: but if you turn back, you will still have your capital sums.

Deal not unjustly and ye shall not be dealt with unjustly.

If the debtor is in a difficulty, grant him time until it is easy for him to repay. But if ye remit it by way of charity, that is best for you. (Al-Baqarah 2:277–80, Koran)

Devour not usury, doubled, and multiplied; Be in taqwa of Allah (fear Allah) that ye may prosper.
Fear the Fire, which is prepared for those who reject Faith; and obey Allah and the Messenger; that ye may obtain mercy.

Be quick in the race for forgiveness from your Lord and for a Garden whose measurement is that of the heavens and of the earth, prepared for the righteous.

Those who give freely whether in prosperity, or in adversity; those who restrain anger and pardon all humans; for Allah loves those who do beautiful deeds (Al-Muhsinun). (Ali 'Imran 3:130–34, Koran)

There are indeed many among the priests and clerics who in falsehood devour the substance of men and hinder them from the way of Allah. And there are those who bury gold and silver and spend it not in the way of Allah: announce unto them a most grievous penalty.

On the Day when heat will be produced out of that wealth in the fire of Hell and with it will be branded their foreheads, their flanks and their backs, "This is the treasure which you buried for yourselves: taste then, the treasures which you buried!" (At-Tawbah 9:34–35, Koran)

22. The Covenant of Allah: Be Good to Your Parents; Allah Forbids Infanticide and Abortion

The Koran repeatedly commands the believers to do what is beautiful to be brought under the sway of Allah's gentle, merciful, and beautiful names. Human qualities gain their reality from the most beautiful divine qualities. When humans turn to Allah, their beautiful qualities become indistinguishable from Allah's own.

> To Allah belongs all that is in the heavens and on earth; so that He rewards those who do ugly, according for what they have done, and He rewards those who do beautiful with the most beautiful. (An-Najm 53:31, Koran)

The first beautiful act that believers perform after tawhid is to do what is beautiful and do good to their parents, those who brought them into existence. It is parents who provide means that Allah employs in creating people, nurturing, educating, and making them beautiful and God fearing. Allah takes credit for His creation, which is the requirement of tawhid. Allah expects his creatures to act appropriately toward His intermediaries of creation. Only in this manner can humans expect other creatures, including their own children, to act beautifully toward them.

Respect and care for the parents is the fundamental act in the Islamic society to maintain the cohesion of the family structure. The family is the underlying unit of the community that forms the support group for children, adults, the elderly, the relatives, the neighborhood, the kin, and the communal structure around the mosque and schools.

Infanticide and its modern version, abortion, and the taking of life of both humans and animals are forbidden by the Koran. Allah has made life sacred. And avoid *Fahasha*, the shameful deeds that set the human down a slippery slope of the ugly and evil.

> Worship none but Allah; treat with kindness your parents and kindred and orphans and those in need; speak fair to the people; be steadfast in prayer; And practice regular charity. (Al-Baqarah 2:82, Koran)

> Say: "Come, I will rehearse what Allah hath (really) prohibited you from": join not anything as equal with Him; be good to your parents; kill not your children on a plea of want - We provide sustenance for you and for them - come not nigh to

shameful deeds, whether open or secret; take not life, which Allah hath made sacred, except by way of justice and law: thus doth He command you, that ye may learn wisdom. (Al-An' am 6:151, Koran)

Take not with Allah another object of worship; or thou wilt sit in disgrace and destitution Thy Lord hath decreed that ye worship none but Him and that ye be kind to parents. Whether one or both of them attain old age in thy life, say not to them a word of contempt, nor repel them, but address them in terms of honor. And out of kindness, lower to them the wing of humility and say: "My Lord! Bestow on them thy Mercy even as they cherished me in childhood." (Al-Isra 17:22, 24, Koran)

We have enjoined on man kindness to his parents: in pain did his mother bear him and in pain did she give him birth. The carrying of the (child) to his weaning is (a period of) thirty months. At length, when he reaches the age of full strength and attains forty years, he says: "O my Lord! grant me that I may be grateful for Thy favor which Thou hast bestowed upon me and upon both my parents and that I may work righteousness such as Thou may approve; and be gracious to me in my issue. Truly have I turned to Thee and truly do I bow (to Thee) in Islam." (Al-Ahqaf 46:15, Koran)

23. The Covenant of Allah: Women and Equality

You are forbidden to take women against their will. Nor should you treat them with harshness, on the contrary treat them with them on a footing of equality kindness and honor.

Fifty percent of the population of the believers, the women, has been excluded from the mainstream Islam by the mullahs, jurist-scholars, and the Hadith scholars against the commandments of the

Koran. Women were regarded as inferior beings in most pre-Islamic cultures, including among the Arabs, Persians, Greeks, and Romans as well as the Hindus. Their status was not any higher among the Turkish and the Mongol tribes of Central Asia. In Judaism, women were forbidden from the inner sanctuary of the temple; and in the early Pauline Christianity, their position was relegated to the entrance of or outside the church at prayer time.

Islam brought dignity and grace to the status of women—the mothers, wives, and daughters. Women had their rights established and their social status elevated as equal to that of men. They attended prayer services at the Prophet's Mosque; they held regular and frequent discourse with the *nabi* of Allah on religious, women's, and family issues. They participated in battles alongside their men. Women worked outside their homes. The first person to convert to Islam, Khadijah, was a successful international trader and owned an import and export business, dealing goods from India, Persia, Africa, Yemen, and the Byzantine Empire. She employed several men to assist her in her business. Other women memorized the Koran and taught other Muslims. A'ishah gave regular talks and discourses on religious matters. Other women led the ritual prayers and *dhikr-e-Allah* gatherings.

The ulema and other followers of the *Hadith collections* over the last one thousand years have totally excluded women from congregation prayers, businesses, public and social affairs, and most importantly education. The Muslim communities have betrayed Allah and His *rasul* concerning their obligations to the women—their mothers, wives, sisters, and daughters. Allah's covenant provides equality to every individual within the community, both men and women. Allah has elevated the rank and dignity of the children of Adam, both men and women, with special favors above that of most of His creation, including the angels. The dignity and favors promised by Allah include six special values: faith, life, intellect (education), property, lineage, and freedom of speech and action.

Equality of Men and Women: The Koran addresses men and women who submit to Allah, who believe, who are devout, who speak the truth, who are righteous, who are humble, who are charitable, who fast and deny themselves, who guard their chastity, and who remember Allah and promises them a great reward and forgiveness for their transgressions. In this address, Allah treats men and women equitably with the promise of a similar reward for their good acts. In Allah's eyes, all men and women who do good deeds carry an equal favor with Him.

Allah admonishes believing men and women to lower their gaze and guard their chastity. Allah is well acquainted with what men did. Allah also admonishes women to dress modestly and not display their adornments outside their immediate family environment. Allah commands believers, men and women, to turn *all together* toward Allah so that they may prosper. This can happen only when the believers, men and women, turn to Allah collectively as a community in a mosque as was customary during the lifetime of the *nabi* of Allah.

According to the Koran, men and women are autonomous and answerable to Allah for their own deeds and actions, and only they as individuals are rewarded or punished for their deeds. In a community, men as a group or the state has no authority from the Koran to enforce any restrictions on the freedom of righteous and believing women. To every man and woman, Allah has bestowed rights to *faith, life, intellect, property, education, and freedom of action and speech*. The authority of a ruler who denies these basic freedoms to men or to women is openly disputable. A person obeys the ruler on the condition that the ruler obeys the Koran and Allah's covenant.

For men and women who surrender unto Allah,

For men and women who believe,

For men and women who are devout

For men and women who speak the truth,

For men and women who persevere in righteousness,

For men and women who are humble,

For men and women who are charitable,

For men and women who fast and deny them selves

For men and women who guard their chastity,

For men and women who remember Allah much,

For them Allah has forgiveness and a great reward.

Say to the

Believing men that they should lower their gaze and guard their modesty:

That will make for greater purity for them:

And Allah is acquainted with all that they do.

And say to the

Believing women that they should lower their gaze and guard their modesty.

That they should not display their adornments except what is ordinarily obvious,

That they should draw a veil over

Their bosom and not display their adornments.

(Except to the immediate family)

And that they should not strike their feet

In order to draw attention

To their hidden adornments.

and O you Believers!

Turn ye all together Toward Allah that ye may prosper.

The believer's men and women are protectors one of another.

They enjoin what is just and forbid what is evil.

They observe regular prayers, practice regular charity and obey Allah and His messenger.

On them will Allah pour His mercy, for Allah is exalted in power, wise.

O you who believe! Guard your souls,

If you follow [right] guidance,
No hurt can come to you from those who stray.
The goal of you all is to Allah,
It is He who will show you the truth of all that ye do.

The Koran, as in the sura above, addresses men and women equally, subjecting them together to similar obligations of submission to Allah, regular prayer, giving in charity, modesty in dress and behavior, righteousness, humility, chastity, worship, truthfulness, remembrance of Allah, and being kind and just. Allah blessed mankind (*insan*), both men and women, with dignity, justice, and equality. He promised them the same rewards and gave them the same obligations. *Be steadfast in prayer and practice regular charity* is an ongoing and repetitive theme in the Koran. Allah calls those who believe, both men and women, to hasten to the congregation prayer on Friday, the day of assembly.

O ye who believe! (Men and women) When the call is proclaimed to prayer on Friday (the Day of Assembly), hasten earnestly to the Remembrance of Allah and leave off business (and traffic): that is best for you if ye but knew!

and when the Prayer is finished, then may ye disperse through the land and seek of the Bounty of Allah: and celebrate the Praises of Allah often (and without stint): that ye may prosper. (Al-Mumtahanah 62:9–10, Koran)

Women attended obligatory prayers, *jum'ah* prayers, and Eid prayers in the Prophet's Mosque. Whenever the apostle of Allah finished his prayers with *Taslim*, the women would get up first, and he would stay in his place for a while before getting up. The purpose of staying was that the women might leave before the men who had finished their prayer.

Soon after the *nabi* died, there occurred an enormous expansion of the Islamic domain. Women, for a while, enjoyed their newly won freedom and dignity given by Islam and proclaimed by the blessed *nabi* Muhammad. Soon afterward, the Arabs reached an unprecedented level of prosperity and began to accumulate large harems of wives, concubines, and female slaves and servants. These women were increasingly confined to their quarters and not allowed to go out unchaperoned. Subsequently, the architecture of the Middle East dwellings changed to suit the new circumstances. The courtyard of the house had high walls, and the only entrance was where the master of the house sat. The master of the harem was so jealous of the chastity of his women that he only employed eunuchs as his servants and guards at his house. The institution of eunuchs was a peculiar Middle Eastern practice related to the institution of the harems of the elite.

The trampling of women's rights was and is a betrayal of the blessed *nabi* Muhammad's emancipation of women. As more Arabs, Romans, Persians, Hindus, Turks, and Mongols embraced Islam, they brought with them their peculiar bias against women and female infants. The Islamic emancipation of women was ignored; women were confined within their houses, covered head to foot in cloth, denied spiritual growth, and denied access to education and to places of worship. Shamefully, the scholars and the ulema encouraged this state of affairs. Women were gradually discouraged from praying in the mosque and were excluded from congregational worship. Thus, the Muslims for centuries have betrayed the *nabi* of Allah and disobeyed Allah's covenant.

Pre-Islamic Arab and other cultures regarded women as their chattel and possession. Abduction and rape of opponents' women was a favored pastime of those victorious in battle to humiliate the vanquished. Thus, the birth of a female child was regarded as a matter of shame, which led to the practice of infanticide. This practice was forbidden earlier on during the prophet's mission. However, the primordial masculine instinct resurfaced in the new Muslim. His subconscious shame and embarrassment of the female in his household was sublimated into gentler and more socially acceptable alternative. As the Koran points out, he chose to retain the female child on sufferance and contempt rather than bury her in the dust. And the Koran says, *"What an evil choice they decide on!"* The shame and cultural burden in some of the Muslim societies is so intense that the female infant is buried in the coffin of yashmak (burka) in the confines of her brick house. She is not killed off physically but intellectually and spiritually by withholding the intellectual and spiritual sustenance that Allah had provided for her.

> Indeed, Lost are those who slay their children, foolishly and without knowledge and have forbidden that which Allah has provided for them and inventing lies against Allah. They have indeed gone astray and heeded no guidance. (Al-An' am 6:140, Koran)

> When news is brought to one of them, of the birth of a female child, his face darkens and he is filled with inward grief! With shame does he hide himself from his people, because of the bad news he has had! Shall he retain it on sufferance and contempt, or bury it in the dust? Ah! What an evil choice they decide on?
> (An-Nahl 16:58–59, Koran)

Women have their freedoms, bestowed by the covenant of Allah. Women can achieve their God-given equality and respect only when they stand up to men to demand equality and respect in all the spheres of life in Muslim societies. This will occur only when women have an intellectual awakening to understand and assert their rights. The dignity and favors promised by Allah include six special values: faith, life, intellect (education), property, lineage, and freedom of speech and action.

Until Muslim men do not eliminate their *fitnah* against 50 percent of believers—their mothers, wives, sisters, and daughters—they will continue to be mired in the pit of ignorance, poverty, and *Fahasha*. To arise out of the pit of decadence, they will have to swallow their ego and pride and learn to respect and honor their women. To every man and woman, Allah has bestowed equal rights to faith, life, intellect, property, education, and freedom of speech and action, enjoining what is right and forbidding what is wrong.

> You are forbidden to take women against their will. Nor should you treat them with harshness, so that you may renounce of the dower you have given them and that is only permitted where they have been guilty of open lewdness. On the contrary live with them on a footing of kindness and honor. If ye take a dislike to them it may be that you dislike a thing, through which Allah brings about a great deal of good. (An-Nisa 4:19, Koran)

> Truly, among your wives and your children are some that are contenders to your obligations so beware! If ye forgive them and overlook their faults, verily Allah is Most-Forgiving, Most Merciful. Your riches and your children may be but a temptation: Whereas Allah! With Him is an immense reward.

> So be in taqwa of Allah and fear Allah as much as you can; listen and obey; and spend in charity for the benefit of your own souls. And those saved from their own greed are the ones that prosper. If ye loan to Allah a beautiful loan, He will double it for you and He will forgive you: for Allah is both Appreciative (Shakoor) and Magnanimous (Haleem), Knower

of what is hidden and what is manifest, Exalted in Might, Full of Wisdom. (At-Taghabun 64:14–18, Koran)

Those who slander decent women, thoughtless but believing, are cursed in this life and in the Hereafter: for them is a grievous Penalty. (An-Nur 24:21–23, Koran)

23. The Covenant of Allah: Wealth: Crave Not Those Things of What Allah Has Bestowed His Gifts More Freely on Some than Others; Men Are Assigned What They Earn and Women What They Earn

Allah created the earth and then bestowed on man His favor to extract sustenance from it. He also created the sun, moon, and stars for a just equilibrium and harmony in the universe. The sun provides energy for the growth, sustenance, and well-being of humans, plants, and animals. Gradually, man began to extract more than his personal needs from the earth; and the boom of economics, trade, and commerce started, creating cycle imbalance, disharmony, wars, poverty, and injustice throughout the globe. This disharmony caused by greed not only blemished the humans but the animal life also suffered with disappearance of species. Pollution and contamination of the environment resulted from the race to accumulate and hoard the world's wealth in a few hands. Man disobeyed Allah's universal laws and Allah's covenant.

In return for all of Allah's favors, Allah commands the following:

- Justice (al-'adl). Justice, fairness, honesty, integrity, and evenhanded dealings are a prerequisite of every Muslim's conduct when dealing with others whether socially or in a business transaction.

- Doing what is good and beautiful (*al-ihsan*). This attribute includes every positive quality such as goodness, beauty, and harmony. Human beings have an obligation to do what is wholesome and beautiful in their relationship with Allah and His creatures. Provide for those near you (*qurba*) and your kith and kin. Help them with wealth, kindness, compassion, humanity, and sympathy.

Allah forbids *Fahasha*—all evil deeds, lies, false testimony, fornication, selfishness, ingratitude, greed, and false belief. One must fulfill the covenant of Allah, and whosoever does beautiful and righteous deeds will be given a new life and rewarded with greater wages by Allah.

> Allah commands justice, the doing of good and liberality to kith and kin and He forbids all shameful deeds and injustice and rebellion: He instructs you, that ye may receive admonition.
>
> Fulfill the Covenant of Allah when ye have entered into it and break not your covenants after ye have confirmed them: indeed, ye have made Allah your surety; for Allah knows all that you do. (Koran 16:90–91)
>
> Whoever works righteousness, man or woman and has Faith, verily, to him will We give a new Life, a life that is good and pure and We will bestow on such their reward according to the best their actions. (Koran 16:97)

Tawhid, the main pillar of Islam, signifies that man's economic life depends wholly on Allah's laws of the universe and that their relationship to those who believe is through the obedience to the covenant of Allah. Allah maintains in the Koran that there is no creature on the earth whose sustenance is not provided by Allah.

> No creature crawls on earth that Allah does not nourish. He knows its essential nature and its varying forms; every detail has its place in the obvious plan. (Koran 11:6)

How are the people in need provided for their sustenance and needs daily?

All wealth belongs to Allah, who bestows it on some people more than others. This wealth is given in trust, whereby the possessor is obliged to give the surplus for Allah's cause, to his kin, to the widows and orphans, and to the needy first in his community and then in the other communities around him. Wealth is to be shared so that not a single individual of the *ummah*, or indeed in the world, should go hungry or be without education and shelter.

> It is not righteousness that ye turn your faces towards East or West; but it is righteousness to believe in Allah and the Last Day and the Angels and the Book and the Messengers; to spend of your substance, out of love for Him, for your kin, for orphans, for the needy, for the wayfarer, for those who ask and for the ransom of slaves; to be steadfast in prayer and practice regular charity, to fulfill the contracts which you have made; and to be firm and patient, in pain (or suffering) and adversity and throughout all periods of panic. Such are the people of truth, the God-fearing. (Al-Baqarah 2:177, Koran)

> And when they are told, "Spend you of (the bounties) with which Allah has provided you," The Unbelievers say to those who believe: "Shall we then feed those whom, if Allah had so willed, He would have fed, Himself? Ye are in nothing but manifest error. (Koran 36:47)

Alms are for the poor and the needy and those employed to administer the funds; for those whose hearts have been (recently) reconciled (to the truth); for those in bondage and in debt; in the cause of Allah; and for the wayfarer: (thus is it) ordained by Allah and Allah is full of knowledge and wisdom. (At-Tawbah 9:60, Koran)

In the above two verses, the clear indication is that man is given bounty by Allah. In return, his obligation is to distribute the surplus after his needs have been met to the needy. The Koran specifies that the zakat should be distributed to the *fuqara* (the poor who ask), *al-masakin* (the poor and the needy who don't ask), and zakat administrators (those who spread the light of Islam to those inclined, for the freedom of those in bondage, to those in debt, for the cause of Allah, and for the wayfarer who treads the path in Allah's service).

In the covenant, the believer surrenders to Allah his life and belongings in return for His guidance, a place in paradise in the hereafter, and peace with prosperity in this world. Every believer, according to his or her covenant with Allah, has the obligation to extend the benefits that Allah has provided him or her to those who did not receive the same. Such acts of generosity will be rewarded by Allah with a place in *Jannat* (place of peace and plenty) in the afterlife. Life of *Jannat* is to be attained in this world also, provided that the compact with Allah is adhered to. The believer is Allah's instrument who will fulfill His promise to Adam that,

none will remain without food or clothes and none will suffer from heat or thirst. (Koran 20:118)

In the verses below, Allah has promised those who believe and obey His covenant that, as the reward for their acts of charity, He will double the harvest of their labors, forgive their sins, and provide them of His bounties; nor shall they have fear or grieve. Fear and grief arise from misfortunes, which cause anxiety and depression. Allah's promise, therefore, is to safeguard the believers from misfortunes. And to those devouring usury, Allah will deprive them of all blessings. Obeying of Allah's covenant provides *Jannat* in the hereafter and in this world. It also brings balance, harmony, and stability to the economic life of the world in that it meets the necessities of each person and eliminates unnecessary suffering.

> O you who believe! Do no render in vain your charity by reminders of your generosity or by injury, like him who spends his wealth to be seen of men, but he does not believe in Allah nor in the Last Day. His likeness is the likeness of a smooth rock on which is a little soil; on it falls heavy rain, which leaves it bare. They will not be able to do anything with what they have earned. And Allah does not guide the disbelieving people.

> And the likeness of those who spend their substance, seeking to please Allah and to strengthen their souls, is as a garden, high and fertile; heavy rain falls on it but makes it yield a double increase of harvest and if it receives not heavy rain, light moisture suffices it. And Allah is seer of what you do. (Al-Baqarah 2:264–65, Koran)

> O ye who believe! Give of the good things that ye have (honorably) earned and of the fruits of the earth that We have produced for you and do not even aim at getting anything which is bad, in order that out of it ye may give away something, when ye yourselves would not receive it except with closed eyes. And know that Allah is free of all wants and worthy of all praise.

The Evil One threatens you with poverty and bids you to conduct unseemly. Allah promises you His forgiveness and bounties. And Allah cares for all and He knows all things.

He grants wisdom to whom He pleases; and he to whom wisdom is granted receives indeed a benefit overflowing; but none will grasp the Message but men of understanding.

And whatever ye spend in charity or devotion, be sure Allah knows it all. But the wrongdoers have no helpers. (Al-Baqarah 2:267-70, Koran)

Those who (in charity) spend of their goods by night and by day, in secret and in public, have their reward with their Lord: on them shall be no fear, nor shall they grieve.

Those who devour usury will not stand except as stands one whom the Satan by his touch hath driven to madness. That is because they say: "Trade is like usury," but Allah hath permitted trade and forbidden usury. Those who after receiving direction from their Lord, desist, shall be pardoned for the past; their case is for Allah (to judge); but those who repeat (the offence) are Companions of the Fire; they will abide therein (forever.)

Allah will deprive usury of all blessing but will give increase for deeds of charity; for He loves not creatures ungrateful and wicked. (Al-Baqarah 2:274-76, Koran)

Economic Principles of the Covenant of Allah

The covenant of Allah in the Koran has laid down principles and guidelines for the well-being of the economic life of the believers. Obeying the principles will bring peace, harmony, spiritual enlightenment, and economic prosperity. Disobeying means misery, ruin, and Allah's wrath.

First Principle: Land and sources of production are not the personal property of individuals. *Ardh* is the source of life and means of sustenance and production of food and resources and therefore must remain available to the community, the *ummah*.

Allah created *ardh* and *sama* and has power over everything in and between them. To Allah belong the heaven and the earth and what is in between them. *Sama* in the Koran signifies the universe and *ardh* man's domain on the earth pertaining to his social and economic world. Allah is the Lord of the heavens and the earth. The divine laws under which the universe functions so meticulously and smoothly should also apply to the economic life of man so that he might achieve a balanced, predictable, equitable, and just financial life. *Sama* is the source of Allah's benevolence to mankind and of His universal laws that govern the human subsistence and sustenance on the earth, controlling man's economic life. Allah's kingdom over the heavens and the earth sustains man's economic life and directly affects man's conduct and his obedience to Allah's covenant.

Ayahs in Sura An-Nahl are explicit. Allah created the heavens and the earth for just ends—to bring peace, harmony, equilibrium, and justice to the universe. He is Allah, the One, Lord of creation. He sends water from the heavens for the sustenance of life on the earth—humans, plants, and animals. Allah sends sunshine to the earth to provide warmth and light to sustain human, plant, and animal life. Allah created the moon and the stars to create equilibrium in the universe, with every object in its intended place revolving in its fixed orbit in perfect harmony and balance. Allah has the secrets and mysteries of the heavens and the earth, the so-called sciences, and the knowledge of particles, elements, cells, mitochondria, chromosomes, gravity, and black holes, only an infinitesimal portion of which he revealed to man.

In other *ayahs* of Sura An-Nahl, Allah clearly mentions all the comforts He has provided man for the sustenance of life and for his economic well-being. Allah created cattle for humans for warmth, food, and transport and horses, mules, and donkeys for riding and to show. With the moisture from the skies, He produces for man corn, olives, date palms, grapes, and every type of fruit. Allah made good things for humans in different colors and quantities so that man can celebrate and praise Allah in gratitude. Allah made the sea subject to humans so that they may eat fresh and tender seafood, obtain beautiful ornaments from the ocean, sail their ships, and plow the oceans around the world. From the cattle, Allah produces milk, pure and wholesome to drink; and from the fruit of the date palm and vine, you get food and drink. And from the bees, there is honey of varying colors that heals ailments.

Historically, land was there for man and the beasts to roam around freely and spread through the world. Later, tribes and communities' laid claims on pieces of land they needed for their needs with some extra surrounding area for their security. At the beginning of the Islamic era, productive land and water resources were owned by tribes for the use of their clan members. After the message of the Koran was established, the clans, tribes, former kingdoms, and nations amalgamated to form the community of Islam, the *ummah*, which in principle owned the title to the land and resources with theoretical tenancy. The owner ship of land by the *ummah* began to change with the downfall of the Abbasid caliphate.

From 1040 to 1200, with the collapse of the central authority, there were many regional power struggles that allowed for the breakdown of the eastern Iranian frontiers against nomadic invasions.

Central Asian nomads searching for pasturage in the tenth, eleventh, and the twelfth centuries spilled over into the region north of the Aral Sea and into Transoxiana and Afghanistan. From contact with settled peoples, trade, and the activities of the missionaries, these Turkish peoples began to convert to Islam. Their chieftains became acquainted in the ways of agriculture, trade, city administration, and imperial conception of rule and order. Most of the useful land in the Islamic states was taken over by the Turkish chiefs and soldiers for their own use and for the advancement of their own political power.

The Seljuk decline opened the way for the third phase in the history of the region from 1150 to 1350. This was a period of further nomadic invasion from inner Asia, culminating in the devastating Mongol invasions and the establishment of Mongol regimes over most of the Middle East. With every change of the ruling class, the land and resources shifted from the peasantry to the tribal chiefs and the soldiery. To the west, the slave military forces in Egypt and Syria consolidated the Mamluk regime, with land being distributed among the new elite.

The final phase was the Timurid period, 1400–1500. The Mongol period was succeeded by new times of troubles and conquest by Timur, also known as Tamerlane. This era of repeated nomadic invasions brought demographic changes in the ethnic and religious identity of populations. A new Turkic-speaking population migrated into Transoxania, the Hindu Kush mountain range, Iran, the Caucasus, Anatolia, and Mesopotamia. Turkish settlement led to the Islamization of northeastern Iran, Armenia, and Anatolia both by settlement of newcomers and by the conversion of existing populations.

To consolidate their power, control of provinces was delegated to the family members and the nomadic chieftains. *Iqtas* lands were assigned to the military leaders. The result was usurpation of power at both the provincial and local levels, with the formation of micro regimes funded by the resources of the land and heavy taxation of the peasants.

The Ottoman cavalry were recruited from among Turkish warriors. They were not garrisoned as a regular army, but they were provided with land grants and timars (Arabic equivalent of *iqt'at*) throughout the empire. The timar holders provided local security and served in Ottoman campaigns. The timar system was based on an old-fashioned feudal pattern. The Ottomans also used the resources of the land to maintain their control over the empire and toward their new conquests. The timar holders exploited the peasants and the subject population.

The subject population belonged to a lesser order of existence. All commoners, Muslim, and non-Muslim were considered the *reava* (flocks) to be shorn in the interests of the political elite. The Ottomans operated on the principle that the subjects should serve the interests of the state; the economy was organized to ensure the flow of tax revenues, goods in kind, and the services needed by the government and the elites. The populace was systematically taxed by maintaining a record of the population, households, property, and livestock.

All the lands in the empire were owned by the ruler; some lands (*tapulu*) were on perpetual lease to the peasants who had the right to assign that right to their male descendants, and *mukatalu* lands were leased to a tax collector in return for a fixed payment for a lease. In the fifteenth century, the Ottomans had conceded to Turkish military rulers and Muslim religious rulers the ownership right to the land. In the course of the next century and a half, the sultans dispossessed the local notables and reassigned the tax rights to the timar holders appointed by the sultan. Ottoman policies were inimical to accumulation of private property. Large private fortunes were regularly confiscated by the state. The Ottoman economic policy on taxation and trade was based on fiscalism that was aimed at accumulation of as much bullion as possible in the state treasury, which was primarily used for the expenditure of running the Topkapi court and the ongoing wars in the West.

The ownership of land in the Islamic world is not owned or distributed according to the covenant of the Koran, causing the present unequal distribution of wealth, poverty, deprivation, and degradation of a large part of the Islamic society. Land, therefore, belongs to Allah, who bestowed it to man and woman, His regents on the earth. The covenant expects man to take care of the land for all of Allah's creatures—men and beasts—as well as conserve its resources for future generations. Whatever is left over after his own needs are met goes to the necessities of the rest of humanity, starting with his *qurba* (near and dear) and then his community, followed by the surrounding communities. The land does not belong to the states, governments, tribal chiefs, military, aristocracy, timars, or *iqt'at*. Land cannot be owned by individuals or families nor inherited.

Men and women live in small communities. These form a fellowship and a brotherhood that looks after its own who are in need, and such a need may be of sustenance, clothing, shelter, knowledge, well-being, spirituality, understanding, protection, justice, or simple reassurance. And such assistance is extended to the surrounding communities till it reaches the far-flung communities of the *ummah*. Each basic community owns the land in its surrounds, tilled and administered by the community as a whole for its well-being in justice and harmony according to the covenant of Allah. The Islamic economic system is based on capitalism in the production of wealth and communism in its expenditure, with the difference being that individuals are free and able to make wealth but are responsible for the needs of kith and kin and their neighbor. The state has little role in the welfare system. The land owned by the community may be assigned to individuals or may be tilled communally for the mutual benefit of the whole community, producing food, and paying for schools, hospitals, roadways, municipal services, and so. on. The community is meant to be self-sufficient economically and responsible for each and every individual's welfare, health, schooling, and old-age pensions.

Second principle: All surplus money and resources should not remain with individuals. How much is enough for one's needs? A hundred? A thousand? A hundred thousand? A million? A billion? How much is enough? After accumulation of a certain amount of money, any further hoarding becomes an act of obscenity and evil. All surplus money and resources shall be used for the benefit and uplift of the community and humanity.

> They ask thee how much they are to spend (in charity); say: "What is beyond your needs". Thus doth Allah make clear to you His Signs: in order that ye may consider. (Al-Baqarah 2:222, Koran)

Third Principle: Wealth and commodities should not be hoarded. Surplus wealth is to be spent for the needs of the community as prescribed by Allah.

> O you who believe! There are indeed many among the priests and anchorites, who in falsehood devour the substance of men and hinder (them) from the Way of Allah. And there are those who bury gold and silver and spend it not in the Way of Allah: announce unto them a most grievous penalty. (At-Tawbah 9:34, Koran)

Fourth Principle: Wealth shall be spread throughout the community, the *ummah*, and shall not be impounded, stolen, and looted by conquerors, tribes, rulers, classes, and the *Mutaffifeen* (dealers in fraud) as practiced in un-Koranic societies, Muslim and Non-Muslim.

> What Allah has bestowed on His Rasool from the people of the townships, belongs to Allah, to His Rasool and to the near of kin and orphans, the poor and the homeless, in order that it may not (merely) make a circuit between the wealthy among you. So, take what the Rasool assigns to you and deny yourselves that which he withholds from you. And fear Allah, for Allah is strict in Punishment. (Al-Hashr 59:7, Koran)

Fifth Principle: No one shall subsist on the earnings of another, and except for those who are incapacitated, everyone shall work. Everyone—man and woman—shall also contribute their labor and sweat toward community well-being.

The Koran calls the people who stint *Mutaffifeen*, those who get the full measure from others but stint when measuring for others. They lead an easy life from the earnings of others. The Koran mentions three such groups. One group consists of people who "take with an even balance and give less than what is due."

> Woe to those that deal in fraud, those who, from others exact full measure,
> But when measuring or weighing for others, give less than due.
> Do they not think that they will be called to account, on a Mighty Day,
> A Day when (all) mankind will stand before the Lord of the Worlds? (Mutaffifeen 83:1–6, Koran)

Another group comprises those who inherit money, land, and property, and they use that wealth to accumulate more and more without ever giving back to the needy. The third group gobbles up the earnings of others:

> O ye who believe! There are indeed many among the priests and clerics, who in falsehood devour the substance of men and hinder (them) from the Way of Allah. And there are those who bury gold and silver and spend it not in the Way of Allah: announce unto them a most grievous penalty. (Al-A'raf 9:34, Koran)

> Squander not your wealth among yourselves in egotism and conceit: Let there be trade and traffic amongst you with mutual goodwill nor kill or destroy yourselves: for verily Allah hath been Most Merciful to you. If any do that in rancor and injustice, soon shall We cast them into the fire: and easy it is for Allah. If you abstain from all the odious and the forbidden, Allah shall expel out of you all evil in you and admit you to a Gate of great honor.

> And crave not those things of what Allah has bestowed His gifts more freely on some than others, men are assigned what they earn and women that they earn. But ask Allah of His bounty. Surely Allah is knower of everything.

> O you who believe! Let not your riches or your children divert you from the remembrance of Allah. If any act thus, the loss is their own. And spend something (in charity) out of the substance which We have bestowed on you, before Death should come to any of you and he should say, "O my Lord! Why didst Thou not give me respite for a little while? I should then have given (largely) in charity and I should have been one of the doers of good." (Al-Munafiqun 63:9–11, Koran)

24. The Covenant of Allah: Justice and Truth

Stand firmly for Allah as a witness of fair dealing. Let not the malice of people lead you to iniquity. Be just; that is next to worship. Be with *taqwa* of Allah; fear Allah.

> O you who believe! Fear Allah and speak always the truth that He may direct you to righteous deeds and forgive you your sins: he that obeys Allah and His Rasool have already attained the highest achievement. (Al-Ahzab 33:69–73,Koran)

> Stand firm for justice as witness to Allah be it against yourself, your parents, or your family, whether it is against rich or poor, both are nearer to Allah than they are to you. Follow not your caprice lest you distort your testimony. If you prevaricate and evade justice Allah is well aware what you do. (An-Nisa 4:135, Koran)

> O you who believe! Stand firmly for Allah as a witness of fair dealing. Let not the malice of people lead you to iniquity. Be just, that is next to worship. Be with taqwa of Allah, fear Allah. Allah is well aware with what you do. (Al-Ma'idah 5:8, Koran)
> Betray not the trust of Allah and His Messenger. Nor knowingly misappropriate things entrusted to you. (Al-Anfal 8:27, Koran)

> If you have taqwa of Allah and fear Allah, He will grant you a Criterion to judge between right and wrong and remove from you all misfortunes and evil and forgive your sins. Allah is the bestower of grace in abundance. (Al-Anfal 8:29, Koran).

> Be in taqwa of Allah, fear Allah and be with those who are true in word and deed. Qur'an 9:119 Al Tawbah

Deal not unjustly and ye shall not be dealt with unjustly. (Al-Baqarah 2:277–80, Koran)

Whenever you give your word speak honestly even if a near relative is concerned.
And come not near the orphan's property, except to improve it, until he attains the age of full strength.
And give full measure and full weight with justice. No burden We place on any soul but that which it can bear. (Al-An'am 6:151–52, Koran)

If an impostor (fasiq) comes to you with any news, ascertain the truth, lest you harm people unsuspectingly and afterwards become full of remorse for what you have done. And know that amongst you is Allah's Messenger: were he in many matters to follow your desires, you would certainly fall into misfortune: but Allah has bestowed on you the love of iman (faith) and has made it beautiful in your hearts and he has made abhorrent to you disbelief, wickedness and disobedience to Allah: such indeed are those who are righteous (rashidun). (Al-Hujurat 49:6–10, Koran)

Justice (*'adl*) is a divine attribute defined as "putting in the right place." The opposite of *'adl* is *zulm*, which in Koranic terms means "wrongdoing." Wrongdoing is a human attribute defined as "putting things in the wrong place." *Zulm* is one of the common terms used in the Koran to refer to the negative acts employed by human beings. Wrongdoing is the opposite of justice. Of the 250 verses where the Koran mentions *zulm* (wrongdoing) or *zalimun* (wrongdoers), it mentions the object of wrongdoing in only twenty-five verses. In one verse, the object of wrongdoing are people:

The blame is only against those who oppress men with wrongdoing and insolently transgress beyond bounds

through the land defying right and justice: for such there will
be a Penalty grievous. (Ash-Shura 42:42, Koran)

In another verse, the object of wrongdoing and injustice is the
signs of Allah:

> The weighing that day will be true. He whose scales are heavy,
> are the prosperous. Those whose scale are light they have lost
> themselves for wronging Our Signs. (Al-A'raf 7:8–9, Koran)

Allah reveals His signs in nature and in scriptures so that the
people may be guided. By disobeying these signs, they wrong only
themselves.

In the remaining twenty-three verses in which the object of
wrongdoing is mentioned, the wrongdoers are said to only wrong
themselves.

> And We gave you the shade of clouds and sent down to you
> Manna and quails, saying: "Eat of the good things We have
> provided for you." (but they rebelled); to Us they did no
> harm, but they wronged their own souls. (Al-Baqarah 2:57,
> Al-A'raf 7:160, Koran)

> Verily Allah will not deal unjustly with humans in anything:
> it is the human who wrongs his own soul. (Yunus 10:44,
> Koran)

> And We wronged them not, but they wronged themselves.
> (Hud 11:101)

> If anyone does evil or wrongs his own soul but afterwards
> seeks Allah's forgiveness, he will find Allah Oft-Forgiving,
> Most Merciful. (An-Nisa 4:110, Koran)

The Koran admonishes:

> Deal not unjustly and you shall not be dealt with unjustly.
> (Al-Baqarah 2:278, Koran)

25. The Covenant of Allah: Knowledge

> O you who believe! Allah will exalt in rank those of you who believe and who have been granted Knowledge. Proclaim! And thy Lord is Most Bountiful, He Who taught (the use of) the Pen, Taught man that which he knew not. O my Lord! Enrich me in knowledge.

> When ye are told to make room in the assemblies, spread out and make room: ample room will Allah provide for you. And when ye are told to rise up, for prayers, Jihad or other good deeds rise up: Allah will exalt in rank those of you who believe and who have been granted Knowledge. And Allah is well acquainted with all you do. (Al-Mujadila 58:11)

> Proclaim! In the name of thy Lord and Cherisher, Who created, Created man, out of a (mere) clot of congealed blood: Proclaim! And thy Lord is Most Bountiful, He Who taught (the use of) the Pen, Taught man that which he knew not. (Iqra 96:1–5, Koran)

> And he who brings the Truth and believes therein, such are the men who do right. (Az-Zumar 39:33, Koran)

> High above all is Allah, the King, and the Truth! Be not in haste with the Qur'an before its revelation to thee is completed, but say, "O my Lord! Enrich me in knowledge." (Taha 20:114, Koran)

> Is one who worships devoutly during the hours of the night prostrating himself or standing (in adoration), who takes

heed of the Hereafter and who places his hope in the Mercy of his Lord, (like one who does not)? Say: "Are those equal, those who know and those who do not know? It is those who are endued with understanding that receive admonition. (Az-Zumar 39:9, Koran)

Knowledge of God: Humans have always looked at God in two ways:

Emotionally. It is a personal and humanized god that is tribal. This god has favorite children whom he protects and rewards over and above others. He is readily accessible in a temple, shrine, mausoleum, or mosque and has priests in attendance as intermediaries. The priest class formulates dogma, creed, and rituals to appease the god. This god is unpredictable, loving, or demanding, subject to anger and joy in accord with the deeds and sacrifices of his devotees. He has a specially trained class of helpers who acts as cheerleaders and who performs crowd control for him. These helpers include the popes, bishops, priests, ayatollahs, rabbis, imams, ulema, pundits, and various classes of religious police. Proximity to their god provides this class's power over other men and women. This source of power naturally leads to competition and often wars between the devotees. Wars fought in the name of this god leads to injustice and usurpation of the rights of others.

The priest class, scholars, and writers introduced and interjected ideas that made their god dependent on creed and dogma invented by them. Writers of the Old and New Testaments fashioned Yahweh and Jesus according to their own caprice. Muslim scholars produced Hadith and interpreted Sharia that made Allah and Muhammad subject to their own fancy. Such collective manipulations at first divided humans and then splintered communities into factions. Marriages of Henry VII fragmented the Christian Europe, and non- succession of Imam Ali split the Muslim world. These mechanizations of men interrupted the message of the God of Abraham that Moses, Jesus, and Muhammad had come to teach. In the fundamental emotional nature of humans, there is an essence of paganism under the surface that wells over in times of stress, grief, and failing belief. The signs of disbelief, mistrust, and *shirk* lie in faith in astrology, horoscope, saint worship, and amulets and in the worship of gods of wealth, power, and politics.

Intellectually. Humans wholeheartedly accept the concept of God as the Creator of everything that is. He wills, and it is. He is beyond human comprehension, and His divine systems do not conform to the human concepts, creed, and dogma. Allah, God the Creator, created the galaxies, worlds, stars, sun, moon, little atoms, protons, neutrons, and tiny particles that show the complexity of His genius, and the Lord of creation sends water from the heavens and directs sunshine to the earth to provide warmth and light to sustain human, plant, and animal life. Allah formed the sun, moon, and stars to create equilibrium in the universe, every object in its intended place revolving in its fixed orbit in perfect harmony and balance. Allah created the secrets and mysteries of the heavens and the earth, the so-called sciences, and the knowledge of particles, elements, cells, mitochondria, chromosomes, gravity, and black holes, only a minute portion of which he revealed to man. Allah clearly provided humans a mind to wonder at His infinitesimal wisdom.

Yet man is conceited and arrogant enough to believe that God is driven by man-created creed, testament, dogma, Sunna, and Sharia. Allah does not require a shrine, a temple, a tent, or a talisman to live in. His presence is everywhere. He is present in the smallest particle (*nuqta*) and in the greatest expanse. He is accessible to each and every object He has created. Every object obeys Allah's will except for the human.

The human has been given free will. The covenant of the Koran presents us with the scope of man's freedom of choice in doing what is wholesome and beautiful or what is corrupt or ugly. It reminds us of how the scales of Allah's justice, the two hands of Allah—His mercy and His wrath—are reflected in the human domain, where people have been appointed His vicegerents. Deeds of goodness and wholesomeness are associated with mercy, paradise, and the beautiful. Evil and corruption is rewarded with wrath, hell, and the ugly.

Allah the Divine is open to the most miniscule of beings. From this little particle (*nuqta*), the connection to Allah, the Cherisher and the Nourisher of the universe, extends into the vastest of expanse. Within this communion of the divine with the creation passes the Spirit of Allah into His creatures. The human lays his heart and mind open to Allah in submission to receive Allah's Spirit and guidance. In the space and the emptiness of the universe, there flow currents and whispers of wind and energy. These winds of silence, light, and sound carry the divine whisper, and in this sound is Allah's message. This message descends into the believer's receptive heart in peace, silence, and tranquility. When the angels and the Spirit descend with Allah's guidance, the eyes perceive the most beautiful divine light, the ears hear the softest tinkle of the bell, the nose smells the fragrance of a thousand gardens, and the skin feels the most tranquil of the gentle breeze. When this happens, the soul has seen nirvana. This is the knowledge of Allah.

Allah sent thousands of prophets to mankind to teach the humanity precepts and principles to His straight path of unity, truth, and goodness. Over thousands of years, these precepts and principles spread around the world through civilizations till the mankind as a whole began to comprehend the message of one universal God, the Creator of every particle and every being in the whole universe. The human listened and occasionally regressed into his inherent paganism, greed, selfishness, and egotism. Allah bestowed on the human a vicegerency on the earth, a mind, free will, and a covenant. Allah then announced that there would be no more prophets; the era of prophecy had ended. The human, in stages, had received the knowledge required to live in submission to Allah's will in peace and harmony on the earth in accordance with the divine laws, which were sent down as guidance to every community for a life of truth, justice, goodness, and peace. Such knowledge consisted of the following:

- Unity. There is one absolute Being from which all stems. The galaxies and all the living things in the universe are all connected to one another and cannot be separated from that absolute Being. Everything alive—humans, animals, plants, and microorganisms—are created by the absolute Being, all nurtured with the same organic matter, all breathing the same air. And in turn, their physical self disintegrates into the same elements that then return to the earth and the universe. In this cycle of creation and disintegration, the only one permanent is the Real, the absolute Being. All else is an illusion and a mirage. One moment you are here, and in the next, you are gone. Nothing is left behind—no riches, no honor, no ego, and no pride. What is left, however, is an account of your deeds, upon which one day you will be judged.

- Mind. The human is bestowed with a mind and free will. The mind has the ability to perceive ideas and knowledge from the divine and from the signs of Allah. The whisper of the divine, the rustle of the wind, the light of God, the fragrance of God's creation, and the sensation of the divine touch all inspire the human mind with the endless stream of ideas and knowledge. Man has been granted the ability to process his thoughts and gain knowledge with free will.

The verse of the light encompasses the totality of the message and guidance that God sent to man through His prophets. The pagan in the human confused God's message and began to worship the messenger. With the end of the era of the prophets, man has to open his heart to the light of Allah and learn to recognize the goodness of God within himself, in his own heart.

Allah speaks to each Believer in the Koran

The fundamental knowledge is the "knowledge of certainty" (*ilm al-yaqin*, Koran 102:5). This type of certitude refers to knowledge that results from the human capacity for logic and reasoning and the appraisal of what the Koran calls "clear evidence" (*bayyinat*) of Allah's presence in the world. This knowledge also comes through the study of Koran, the teachings of the prophets, and the signs of Allah. The signs of Allah encompass the whole knowledge of the creation; man's scientific and philosophical disciplines include only a miniscule fragment of this knowledge. The knowledge of certainty is rational and discursive, a point that the Koran acknowledges when it admonishes human beings to:

> Say: "Travel through the earth and see how Allah did originate creation; so will Allah produce a later creation: for Allah has power over all things. (29:20 Al-'Ankabut, Koran)

> It is He Who gives life and death and to Him (is due) the alternation of Night and Day: will ye not then understand? (Al Mu'minun 23:80, Koran)

Over time and under the influence of contemplation and spiritual practice, the knowledge of certitude may be transformed into a higher form of knowledge of Allah, which the Koran calls the "eye of certitude" (*ain al-yaqin*, Koran 102:7). This term refers to the knowledge that is acquired by spiritual intelligence that believers in the East locate metaphorically in the heart. Before attaining this type of knowledge, the heart of the believer must first be "opened to Islam."

> Is one whose heart Allah has opened to Islam, so that he has received enlightenment from Allah. Woe to those whose hearts are hardened against celebrating the praises of Allah! They are manifestly wandering (in error)! (Az-Zumar 39:22, Koran)

Once opened, the heart receives knowledge as a type of divine light or illumination (*nur*) that leads the believer toward the remembrance of Allah. Just as with the knowledge of certainty, with the eye of certainty, the believer sees Allah's existence through His presence in this world. With the eye of certainty, what lead the believer to the knowledge of Allah are not the arguments to be understood by the rational intellect but by theophanic appearances (*bayyinat*) that strip away the veil of worldly phenomenon to reveal the divine reality underneath.

From the spiritual perspective, the one who perceives reality through the knowledge of Allah is a true "intellectual." Unlike the scholar, who develops his or her skills through years of formal study, the spiritual intellectual does not need book learning to understand the divine light. A spiritual intellectual can be anyone, scholarly or otherwise, whose knowledge extends both outward to take in the physical world and upward to realize his or her ultimate transcendence of the world through his or her link with the absolute. Without such a vertical dimension of spirit, the scholar's knowledge, whatever its extent may be in academic terms, is of little worth.

The third and most advanced type of knowledge builds on transcendent nature of knowledge itself. The highest level of consciousness is called the "truth of certitude" (*haqq al-yaqin*).

> But truly (Revelation) is a cause of sorrow for the Unbelievers. But verily it is Truth of assured certainty. So, glorify the name of thy Lord Most High. (Al-Haqqah 69:50–52, Koran)

It is also known as *ilm ladduni* (knowledge "by presence"). This form of knowledge partakes directly of the divine reality and leaps off directly across the synapses of human mind to transcend both cognitive reasoning and intellectual vision at the same time. The "truth of certainty" refers to a state of consciousness in which a person knows the Real through direct participation in it without resorting to logical proofs. This type of knowledge characterizes God's prophets and messengers, whose consciousness of the truth is both immediate and participatory as what it is based on comes from direct inspiration.

According to both the word of Allah as expressed in the Koran and the tradition of the blessed *nabi* Muhammad, faith in Islam has as much to do with theoretical and empirical knowledge as it does with simple belief. This multidimensional conception of knowledge comprehends a reality that lies hidden within the unique world yet can be revealed by the human mind and the vision of the spiritual intellect through the signs of Allah that are present in the world itself. In the Koran, Allah calls humanity:

So, I do call to witness what you see

And what you see not,

(This is) a Message sent down from the Lord of the Worlds.

But verily it is Truth of assured certainty. (Al-Haqqah 69:38–39, 43, 51)

The lure of abundance beguiles you, Until you reach the graves. But in the end, you will know. Soon you shall know! Nay were you to know with the knowledge of certainty. That you shall surely see the flaming fire. You shall see it with the eye of certainty. Then, you will be questioned on that Day about the pleasures you indulged in. (At-Takathur 102, 1–8)

26. The Covenant of Allah: Inviting to All That Is Good and Right and Forbidding What Is Wrong

Let there arise out of you a band of people inviting to all that is good, enjoining what is right and forbidding what is wrong: they are the ones to attain happiness. (Ali 'Imran 3:103–5, Koran)

The Koranic principle of enjoining what is good and forbidding what is evil is supportive of the moral autonomy of the person, man and woman. This principle authorizes a person to act according to his or her best judgment in situations in which his or her intervention will advance a good purpose. The following saying of the blessed *nabi* also supports individual action by a believer:

If any one of you sees an evil, let him change it by his hand and if he is unable to do that, let him change by his words and if he is still unable to do that let him denounce it in his heart, but this is the weakest form of belief.

This principle assigns to the individual an active role in the community in which he or she lives. *The Koran annunciated the principle of free speech fourteen hundred years ago.* Believing men and women are reminded that they are the best of people, a witness over other nations. Such a responsibility carries with it a moral burden of an exemplary conduct of one who submits to the divine truth and whose relationship with Allah is governed is by *taqwa*, the consciousness of humankind's responsibility toward its Creator. The believer has the responsibility of acting in accordance with the three types of knowledge—the knowledge of certitude (*ilm al–yaqin*), the eye of certitude (*ain al-yaqin*), and the truth of certitude (*haqq al-yaqin*). With that knowledge and faith, the believer is well equipped to approach others to enjoin what is right and forbid what is wrong. This moral autonomy of the individual, when bound together with the will of the community, formulates the doctrine of infallibility of the collective will of the *ummah*, which is the doctrinal basis of consensus.

27. The Covenant of Allah: Do Not Say to Another Muslim, "You Are Not a Believer."

> When you go forth in the cause of Allah be careful to discriminate and say not to the one who greets you with alaikum o salaam, "Though art not a believer". Would you covet perishable goods of this life when there are immeasurable treasures with Allah? You were like the person who offered you salutation before Allah conferred on you His favors. Therefore, carefully investigate for Allah is well aware of all that you do. (An-Nisa 4:94)

Every believer's journey into Islam cannot be the same and uniform. A lot depends on the cultural background, education, and intellectual biases of the person. The first principle of faith is tawhid, the assertion that God is one, that there is only a single worthy object of worship, Allah. All other objects of worship are false. To serve anything else is to fall into error, misguidance, and sin of *shirk*. The Koranic notion of religious belief (*iman*) as dependent on knowledge is actualized in practice in the term *islam*. The term *islam* signifies the idea of surrender or submission. Islam is a religion of self-surrender; it is the conscious and rational submission of a dependent and limited human will to the absolute and omnipotent will of Allah. The type of surrender Islam requires is a deliberate, conscious, and rational act made by a person who knows with both intellectual certainty and spiritual vision that Allah, who is the subject of Koranic discourse, is reality itself. The knower of God is a Muslim (fem. *Muslimah*), "one who submits" to the divine truth and whose relationship with God is governed by *taqwa*, the consciousness of humankind's responsibility toward its Creator.

However, consciousness of God alone is not sufficient to make a person a Muslim. Neither is it enough to be merely born a Muslim or to be raised in an Islamic cultural context. The believer must endeavor at all times to maintain himself or herself in a constant state of submission to Allah. By doing so, the believer attains the honored title of "slave of Allah" (*abd Allah*, feminine: *amat Allah*), for he recognizes that all power and agency belongs to God alone. After submission to the will of Allah, observation of the five pillars opens the way for the believer to understand *ihsan* and perform good deeds for humanity:

> Those who believe, do deeds of righteousness, and establish regular prayers and regular charity, will have their reward with their Lord: on them shall be no fear, nor shall they grieve. (Al-Baqarah 2:277, Koran)

Every individual is at a different stage of their life's journey. Only Allah is the judge and the knower of the hidden and the manifest. Only He knows what is in a person's heart.

28. The Covenant of Allah: Suspicion and Lack of Trust: Avoid Suspicion, for in Some Cases, It Is Sin, and Spy Not on nor Speak Ill of Each Other Behind One's Back

> Avoid suspicion, for suspicion in some cases is sin; and spy not on each other, nor speak ill of each other behind their backs. Would any of you eat the flesh of his dead brother? No, you would abhor it. Be in taqwa of Allah, fear Allah: for Allah is Forgiving, Most Merciful. (Al-Hujurat 49:12–13, Koran)

Allah gave humans the trust of vicegerency over the earth with the stipulation that they acknowledge Him as their Lord and worship and thank Him for His benevolence. As part of that trust, people are free to make their choices about their actions. Allah does not force them to make the correct choices without taking the trust away from them, and if He took the trust away, they no longer are humans.

With the abuse of vicegerency came selfish acquisition of wealth, land, and women. Acquisition of wealth breeds greed, covetousness, and hoarding of wealth. The prospect of loss of such acquisitions produces insecurity and constant watchfulness. Such paranoia in humans has had a forceful impact on the society of man that leads to assumptions, suspicions, and suppositions that result in quarrels among people and wars between nations, thus a breakdown of the world order. Suspicion among nations has produced expensive and intricate security and intelligence systems that use spying equipment on the ground, in the air, and in space to obtain information on other nations. People and police spy on other people; cities are full of cameras tracking the movement of citizens. Big Brother watches everyone. Mistrust and suspicion prevails over the world, suggesting sickness in society. The same insecurity in people's psyche gives rise to resentment, jealousy, anger, and mistrust, leading to feuds and social disruption.

29. The Covenant of Allah: Do Not Ridicule Other Believers or Revile Each Other with Wicked Names

> Let not some folk among you ridicule others: it may be that they are better than you are: nor let some women mock others: it may be that the others are better than them: nor defame or revile each other by offensive names: ill-seeming is wicked name calling for the one who has believed; and those who do not desist are indeed wrong doers. (Al-Hujurat 49:11, Koran)

The covenant of Allah forbids suspicion, spying on each other, backbiting, and ridiculing other believers. The heart is like a shining mirror. Troublesome deeds are like smoke that will cover the mirror; you will not be able to see yourself, and you will be veiled from the reality of Allah. To understand the reality of Allah, you have to uncover ignorance and darkness so as to see the light and the reality. Some traits of this darkness are arrogance, ego, pride, envy, vengeance, lying, gossiping, backbiting, and other unwholesome characteristics. To be rid of these evils and odious traits, one has to clean and shine the mirror of the heart. This cleansing of the heart is done by acquiring knowledge and acting upon it to fight against one's ego by ridding oneself of multiplicity of being through unity. When the heart becomes alive with the light and *nur* of unity, the eye of the clean heart will see the reality of Allah's attributes.

30. The Covenant of Allah: Secret Counsels and Pacts: Secret Counsels Are Only Inspired by Satan so That He May Cause Grief to the Believers

> When you hold secret counsel, do it not for iniquity and hostility and disobedience to the Messenger; but do it for righteousness and self-restraint; and fear Allah, to Whom ye shall be brought back.
> Secret counsels are only inspired by the Satan, in order that he may cause grief to the Believers; but he cannot harm them in the least, except as Allah permits; and on Allah let the Believers put their trust. (Al Mujadila 58:9–10, Koran)

No believer, individual, community, or ruler shall make a compact on behalf of the *ummah* or part of it in secret with the unbelievers. Islam regards secret pacts with enemies and hostile actions against one's own people as treason. When the *nabi* was in Medina, there were some people who professed Islam but at the same time conspired with the enemy, the *kafirun*, against fellow Muslims. The Koran has the following description of the fate of the *Munafiqeen*.

> Of the people there are some who say: "We believe in Allah and the Last Day;" but they do not really believe.

> Fain would they deceive Allah and those who believe, but they only deceive themselves and realize it not!

> In their hearts is a disease; and Allah has increased their disease: and grievous is the penalty they incur, because they are false to themselves.

When it is said to them: "Make not mischief on the earth,"
they say: "Why, we only want to make peace!"

Of a surety, they are the ones who make mischief, but they
realize (it) not. (Al-Baqarah 2:8–12, Koran)

Allah will throw back their mockery on them and give them
rope in their trespasses; so, they will wander like blind ones to
and fro.

These are they who have bartered guidance for error: but
their traffic is profitless and they have lost true direction.

Their similitude is that of a man who kindled a fire; when it
lighted all around him, Allah took away their light and left
them in utter darkness. So, they could not see. Deaf, dumb,
and blind, they will not return to the path. (Al-Baqarah 2:15–
18, Koran)

In our age, we have people who think that they can get the best
of both worlds by compromising their nations and Islam's interests
with the enemy. King Abdullah of Transjordan secretly met with
Zionist leaders from 1922 onward, merely a year after the creation
of Transjordan. These meetings continued during the Palestinian
disturbances in 1932 and 1936. The amity between the two conspiring
sides was so total that, in a meeting, Abdullah and the Jewish envoy
discussed ways of eliminating the mufti of Jerusalem, the leader of
Palestinians, and the enemy of both sides[6]. He secretly conspired with
Chaim Weizmann for the partition of Palestine in 1947.

Abdullah's grandson Hussein started his secret contacts with
Israeli leaders in 1957, and by 1963, meetings with the leaders became

---

[6] Avi Shlaim, *The Politics of Partition*, 203.

a regular occurrence. In 1963, Hussein made a secret visit to Tel Aviv[7]. In the period preceding 1967, Hussein performed several treasonable acts that were openly anti-Arab. In response to the creation of PLO, which wanted to replace him as the Palestinian representative, Hussein's intelligence service provided the names and location of the Palestinian fighters infiltrating and battling the Israelis[8]. Hussein did not stop here. His intelligence service also provided the Israelis information about other Arab countries[9]. From 1970 onward, there were several secret meetings between Hussein and the Israeli defense minister Moshe Dayan and with Israeli prime minister Golda Meir[10]. This extensive period of secret Jordanian Israeli cooperation produced the most treasonable act of Hussein's life, informing Israel of the impending Egyptian Syrian attack on October 1973[11].

The rulers of Islam who work against their own faith and their own people have a disease in their hearts. They make mischief on the earth against their own faith and nation in secret collusion with the enemies in return for personal gain, power, and wealth. Allah promises a grievous penalty for them because they are false to themselves and do not realize it. Every Muslim today is enslaved by an infidel international diplomatic and financial system run through a network of secretive and deceitful treaties and clauses. Every Muslim carries the burden of four monkeys that direct his daily life. The monkeys of secret international finance, diplomacy, crime, and intelligence syndicates sit on the back of every Muslim through the

---

[7] Dan Raviv and Yossi Melman, *Every Spy a Prince*, 213.

[8] Ian Black and Benny Morris, *Israel's Secret Wars*, 238.

[9] Raviv and Melman, *Every Spy*, 214.

[10] *Secret Channels*, Mohamed Heikal, 310.

[11] Morris and Black, *Israel's Secret Wars*, 265.

connivance and ignorance of Muslim rulers, mercenary armies, and religious leaders.

31. The Covenant of Allah: Intoxicants and Gambling: Forbidden to You Are Intoxicants and Gambling

Forbidden to you are intoxicants and gambling, dedication of stones and divination by arrows. These are an abomination and Satan's handiwork; they hinder you from prayer and remembrance of Allah and place enmity and hatred amongst you. Abstain from them so that you may prosper. (Al-Ma'idah 5:90–91)

Today the world is bedeviled with evils that consume people and deprive them of self-control and motivation to lead a life of purpose and usefulness for themselves, their families, and their fellow humans. The urge for immediate gratification and relief from the stresses of daily life sends people scurrying to alcohol and drugs. In the Western world, a tenth of the adult population is addicted to alcohol or drugs, and another half are habitual users of intoxicants. One in every three families carries the burden of an addicted dear one. In the Muslim world, although alcohol is the lesser substance of abuse, marijuana, cocaine, hashish, and khat use is rampant. Tobacco, a substance of extreme addiction but of mild intoxicant properties, is the weed of popular use. A fifth of the world's workforce is underproductive and disabled physically and intellectually because of intoxication and addiction.

The covenant of the Koran fourteen hundred years ago forbade humans from the use of intoxicants in an effort to save mankind from self-destruction. All forms of gambling—including lotteries, slot machines, betting, card playing, and entertainment in casinos—are all forbidden. The covenant says,

> These are an abomination and Satan's handiwork; they hinder you from prayer and remembrance of Allah and place enmity and hatred amongst you. Abstain from them so that you may prosper. (Al-Ma'idah 5:90–91)

32. The Covenant of Allah: Forbidden to You Are the Carrion, Blood, and Flesh of Swine and Any Other Food on Which Any Name Besides That of Allah Has Been Invoked

> Eat of good things provided to you by Allah and show your gratitude in worship of Him. Forbidden to you are the carrion, blood and flesh of swine and on any other food on which any name besides that of Allah has been invoked. If forced by necessity, without willful disobedience or transgressing due limits, one is guilt less. Allah is Most Forgiving and Most Merciful. (Al-Baqarah 2:172–73, Koran)

Allah, in His generosity and mercy, has permitted the believers to eat of all good things provided by Him. Expressly forbidden is to eat unclean food, which constitutes four things: carrion, blood, flesh of swine, and animals slaughtered in the name of any other than Allah.

During the last millennium, science has discovered harmful parasites and bacteria in the flesh of diseased animals, swine, and the blood of animals. Before the establishment of veterinarian and pathological sciences, the Koran had made a clear distinction between food that was clean and good and what was bad and harmful for humans.

33. The Covenant of Allah: Make Not Unlawful the Good Things That Allah Hath Made Lawful to You

> Make not unlawful the good things, which Allah hath made lawful to you. Commit no excess; Allah loves not people given to excess. Eat of things that Allah has provided for you, lawful and good. Be in taqwa of Allah, fear Allah in whom you believe. (Al-Ma'idah 5:87–88, Koran)

Allah has, in very explicit words, laid out in His covenant the acts forbidden to the believers:

1. *Shirk*: Join not anything as equal with Him. (Worship Allah and do not associate others with Him.)
2. Mistreatment of parents: Be good to your parents.
3. Infanticide and abortion: Kill not your children on a plea of want. We provide sustenance for you and for them.
4. *Fahasha*: Come not near shameful deeds, whether open or in secret.
5. Taking of life: Take not life, which Allah hath made sacred, except by way of justice and law.
6. Stealing: Come not near to the orphan's property, except to improve it, until he attains the age of full strength. The term *orphan* may also include other helpless citizens who may be subject to oppression.
7. Cheating: And give measure and weight with justice; (do not cheat) no burden do We place on any soul, but that which it can bear.
8. Lying and falsification: Whenever you speak, speak the truth, even if a near relative is concerned.
9. Violation of Allah's covenant: Fulfill the covenant of Allah: "Thus, does He command you that ye may remember. Verily,

this is My Way leading straight: follow it; follow no other paths: they will scatter you about from His Path; thus, doth He command you, that ye may be righteous" (Al-An'am 6:151–53, Koran).

10. Intoxicants.
11. Gambling.
12. Dedication of stones.
13. Divination by arrows.

These are an abomination and Satan's handiwork; they hinder you from prayer and remembrance of Allah and place enmity and hatred amongst you. Abstain from them so that you may prosper. (Al-Ma'idah 5:90–91, Koran)

14. Carrion.
15. Blood.
16. Flesh of swine.
17. "Any other food on which any name besides that of Allah has been invoked" (Al-Baqarah 2:172–73, Koran).
18. Usury (*riba*): "Devour not usury double and multiplied: Be in taqwa of Allah, that you may prosper" (Ali 'Imran 3:130, Koran).
19. Disrespect toward women: "It is not lawful for you to take women against their will, nor should you treat them with harshness. On the contrary treat then with honor and kindness" (An-Nisa 4:19, Koran).
20. Any actions that infringe on the unity of the *ummah* and the nation of Islam.

And hold fast, all together, by the Rope which Allah stretches out for you and be not divided among yourselves. You were enemies and He joined your hearts in love, so that by His Grace, you became brethren and a community. Thus, does Allah makes His Signs clear to you that you may be guided. Be not like those who are divided amongst themselves and fall into disputations after receiving clear signs; for them is a dreadful penalty.

These twenty actions have been forbidden (haram) by the covenant of Allah. At the same time, Allah commands:

> Make not unlawful the good things, which Allah hath made lawful to you. Commit no excess; Allah loves not people given to excess. Eat of things that Allah has provided for you, lawful and good. Be in taqwa of Allah, fear Allah in whom you believe. (Al-Ma'idah 5:57, Koran)

Islamic scholar-jurists frequently quote various Hadith and proclaim many aspects of the daily life of pious and observant believers as haram. Such actions include listening to music, women's education, women's role in congregational prayers, and other mundane activities such as kite flying, tourism, pursuit of Western education, and use of modern technology. Those are the personal views of the mullahs and do not have the divine sanction of the covenant between Allah and His believers.

1. **Music:** Music is part of the human soul. Every child, when happy, springs up to a melody and dance to the rhythm. When the blessed *nabi* received the revelation from Allah, at times, it appeared in the form of a tinkle or the chimes of a

bell, and the words of the revelation blossomed in Blessed Muhammad's mind. The Koran, when recited in rhythmic Arabic, produces a heavenly song of Allah's revelation. Singing Allah's *dhikr* with or without instrument or music has a powerful and profound effect on the listener's soul, which reflects divine beauty. Listening to mere wind chimes makes one aware of the divine origin of the sounds of the wind, the rustle of trees, and the sound of running water in rivers, falls, and oceans. Allah gave the human the ability to produce the most beautiful sounds in His remembrance, to celebrate life and happiness, and to enjoy Allah's other provisions to mankind.

Observation of Allah's covenant bestows peace and tranquility to the soul and hence happiness and contentment on the believer. Islam is not a religion of gloom, sorrow, and melancholia but that of celebration of Allah's blessings and of doing beautiful deeds. To show contentment, peace, harmony, happiness, and proper balance of things in life is to express *shukr*, gratitude to Allah for His mercy and grace. The human is asked to use all his senses—sight, hearing, smell, taste, and touch—to recognize Allah's truth and signs. They signify the perception of Allah's *nur* (light), resonance of the sound of Allah's harmonious music in nature, the fragrance of Allah's garden, the flavor of Allah's bounty, and the feel of Allah's creation around us. Allah does not forbid against His divine gift of harmony and song; on the contrary, He urged the recitation of the Koran in slow, rhythmic tones and the celebration and praising of Allah often, glorifying Him in the morning and at night. It is Allah and His angels who also send their blessings on the believers so "He may lead the Believers you out of the depths of darkness into light." Celebration of Allah's praises and glorifying Him means to rejoice, to be happy, and to be joyous. The word *celebrate*, therefore, has the connotation of a happy occasion, which includes song and music.

2. Confinement of believing and devout women is not a mandate of the Covenant of Allah nor it is the covering women from head to toe.

3. **Acquisition of knowledge.** Education is Allah's gift to humanity and is incumbent on every believer, man or woman. Scholars of Islam ignore the Koranic admonition:

> Make not unlawful the good things, which Allah hath made lawful to you. Commit no excess; Allah loves not people given to excess.

34. The Covenant of Allah: Contracts and Agreements: When You Make a Transaction Involving Future Obligations, Write It down in Presence of Witnesses

> When you make a transaction involving future obligations, write it down in presence of witnesses, or let a scribe write it down faithfully. Let the party incurring the liability dictate truthfully in the presence of two witnesses from among your own men and if two men are not available then a man and two women, so that if one of them errs then the other one, can remind him. Disregard not to put your contract in writing, whether it be small or large, it is more suitable in the eyes of Allah, more suitable as evidence and more convenient to prevent doubts in the future amongst yourselves. (Al-Baqarah 2:282–83, Koran)

Fourteen hundred years ago, the Koran laid out the basis of the modern legal system of written and witnessed agreements. Muslim jurists have used this *ayah* to curtail the rights of women as witnesses in the modern court system, where they consider the testimony of two women equivalent to the testimony of one man. The mullahs imply that women have an inferior memory and intellectual capacity. Although the Koran is silent on the reason for the need for two women witnesses, it is obvious that women carry the burden and the responsibilities of nurturing and taking care of their infants and families. Women are Allah's instruments of creation and the nurturer of mankind. The act of creation and nurture has precedence over worldly affairs of commerce. Women cannot neglect their divine obligation of creation to attend to the communal affairs as witnesses in the transactions of this world. The need for a second woman witness becomes necessary when one of them becomes preoccupied with her obligations of procreation and upbringing of a family.

There is abundant of scientific evidence that the intellectual capacity of both men and women is unique in their development. This uniqueness complements the intellect and memory of men and women in the functioning of mankind. This uniqueness is a gift of Allah to humankind.

The human memory is affected by the inbuilt nature and development of the brain and its environment. Adolescent brain development is different in boys and girls. Male's aged six to seventeen years display more prominent age-related reduction in gray matter (the part of the brain that allows us to think) and increases in white matter (which transfers information between distant regions) than females. These changes in brain composition are linked to developmental processes in which nerve cell connections are "pruned" in gray matter and made more efficient (myelinated) in white matter. The more dramatic changes seen in males may be related to the different effects of estrogen and testosterone on the brain[12]. Women have smaller brains than men and have smaller bodies; women have more gray matter, and men have more white matter. This finding may help explain why women are typically better than men at verbal tasks, while men are typically better than women at spatial tasks, as well as why the sexes perform equally well on intelligence tests in spite of males having larger brains[13].

Several studies have evaluated sex differences in the histology of the cerebral cortex. One study in humans detected higher neuronal density in the female cortex compared with males[14]. In contrast, other studies have shown that the number of neurons in the cerebral cortex is greater in males than in females. Studies by Rabinowicz et al. demonstrated that males have 15 percent more cortical neurons and 13 percent greater neuronal density than females[15]. Similarly, Pakkenberg et al. showed a 16 percent higher neuronal number in males, but sex differences in neuronal density were not present[16]. Although women have fewer neocortical neurons, certain anatomical and histological characteristics of female brains may allow for more extensive dendritic

---

[12] De Bellis, MD, et al., "Sex Differences in Brain Maturation during Childhood and Adolescence," *Cereb. Cortex* 11, no. 6 (2001): 552–57.

[13] R. C. Gur et al., "Sex Differences in Brain Gray and White Matter in Healthy Young Adults: Correlations with Cognitive Performance," *J. Neurosci.* 19, no, 10 (1999): 4065–72.

[14] H. Haug, "Brain Sizes, Surfaces and Neuronal Sizes of the Cortex Cerebri: A Stereological Investigation of Man and His Variability and a Comparison with Some Mammals (Primates, Whales, Marsupials, Insectivores and One Elephant)," *Am. J. Anat.* 180, no. 2 (1987): 126–42.

[15] T. Rabinowicz et al., "Gender Differences in the Human Cerebral Cortex: More Neurons in Males; More Processes in Females," *J. Child Neurol.* 14, no. 2 (1999): 98–107.

[16] B. S. Pakkenberg and H. J. Gundersen, "Neocortical Neuron Number in Humans: Effect of Sex and Age," *J. Comp. Neurol.* 384, no. 2 (1997): 312–20.

arborization and more neuronal connections among nerve cells[17]. Certain diseases that cause neuronal loss in the cerebral cortex may be more detrimental to women due to their lower number of cortical neurons compared with men[18].

The cerebellum, an area of the brain important for posture and balance, and the pons, a brain structure linked to the cerebellum that helps control consciousness, are larger in men than in women[19]. As the brain ages, the amount of tissue mass declines, and the amount of fluid increases. This effect is less severe in women than in men, suggesting that women are somewhat less vulnerable to age-related changes in mental abilities[20]–[21]. However, women are more prone to dementia than men perhaps because of the potentially greater susceptibility to loss of neurons and neuronal connections.

Language Differences: Although men and women have been shown to process some language tasks similarly, in other aspects of language processing, there are significant sex differences[22]. Imaging studies of the living brain show that in women neurons on both sides of the brain are activated when they are listening, while in men neurons on only one side of the brain are activated. Men and women

---

[17] G.M. de Courten-Myers, "The Human Cerebral Cortex: Gender Differences in Structure and Function," *J. Neuropathology Exp. Neurol.* 58, no. 3 (1999): 217–26.

[18] T. Rabinowicz et al., "Structure of the Cerebral Cortex in Men and Women," *J. Neuropathol. Exp. Neurol.* 61, no. 1 (2002): 46–57.

[19] N. Raz et al., "Age and Sex Differences in the Cerebellum and the Ventral Pons: A Prospective MR Study of Healthy Adults," *AJNR Am. J. Neuroradiology* 22, no. 6 (2001): 1161–67.

[20] R. C. Gur et al., "Gender Differences in Age Effect on Brain Atrophy Measured by Magnetic Resonance Imaging," *Proc. Natl Acad. Sci. USA* 88, no. 7 (1991): 2845–49.

[21] S. F. Witelson, "Sex Differences in Neuroanatomical Changes with Aging," *N. Engl. J. Med.* 325, no. 3 (1991): 211–12.

[22] Ibid.

appear to process single words similarly, but in the interpretation of whole sentences, women use both sides of the brain, while men use one side[23]. Boys have a higher incidence than girls of developmental language disorders, such as developmental dyslexia. Despite these differences during childhood, it is not clear whether adult women have better verbal skills than men[21].

Spatial Information Differences: Men and women process spatial information differently[24]. When negotiating a virtual reality maze, both men and women use the right hippocampus to figure out how to exit. However, men also use the left hippocampus for this task, while women do not. Women also use the right prefrontal cortex, while men do not[25]. In an imaging study, men were found to activate a distributed system of different brain regions on both sides of the brain while performing a spatial task. Women, however, activated these regions on only the right side of the brain. Women appear to rely on landmarks to navigate their environments, whereas men tend to use compass directions[26].

Memory Differences: Some functions of memory appear to be different in males and females[27]. Higher rates of blood flow in certain

---

[23] K. Kansaku and S. Kitazawa, "Imaging Studies on Sex Differences in the Lateralization of Language," *Neurosci. Res.* 41, no. 4 (2001): 333–37.

[24] J. D. Ragland et al., "Sex Differences in Brain-Behavior Relationships between Verbal Episodic Memory and Resting Regional Cerebral Blood Flow," *Neuropsychologia* 38, no. 4 (2000): 451–61.

[25] G. Gron et al., "Brain Activation during Human Navigation: Gender-Different Neural Networks as Substrate of Performance," *Nat. Neurosci.* 3, no. 4 (2000): 404–8.

[26] D. M. Saucier et al., "Are Sex Differences in Navigation Caused by Sexually Dimorphic Strategies or by Differences in the Ability to Use the Strategies?" *Behav. Neurosci.* 116, no. 3 (2002): 403–10.

[27] S. J. Duff and E. Hampson, "A Sex Difference on a Novel Spatial Working Memory Task in Humans," *Brain Cogn.* 47, no. 3 (2001): 470–93.

portions of the brain are associated with increased memory of verbal tasks in women but not in men[28]. Compared with men, women have been shown to be better at remembering faces[29]. A key part of the brain involved in processing emotionally influenced memories acts differently in men and women.

The amygdala, an almond-shaped structure found on both sides of the brain, behaves very differently in males and females while the subjects are at rest. In men, the right amygdala is more active and shows more connections with other regions of the brain. Conversely, in women, the left amygdala is more connected with other regions of the brain. In addition, the regions of the brain with which the amygdala communicates while a subject is at rest are different in men and women. These findings suggest that the brain is wired differently in men and women. In men, the right-hemisphere amygdala showed more connectivity with brain regions such as the visual cortex and the striatum. In contrast, the left amygdala in women was more connected to regions such as the insular cortex and the hypothalamus.

Many brain areas communicating with the amygdala in men are engaged with and responding to the external environment. For example, the visual cortex is responsible for vision, while the striatum coordinates motor actions. Conversely, many regions connected to the left-hemisphere amygdala in women control aspects of the environment within the body. Both the insular cortex and the hypothalamus, for example, receive strong input from the sensors inside the body.

Throughout evolution, women have had to deal with a number of internal stressors, such as childbirth, that men have not had to

---

[28] Ragland et al., "Sex Differences," 451–61.

[29] R. C. Gur et al., "Computerized Neurocognitive Scanning: I. Methodology and Validation in Healthy People," *Neuropsychopharmacology* 25, no. 5 (2001).

experience. The brain seems to have evolved to be in tune with those different stressors. One of the brain areas communicating with the amygdala in women is implicated in disorders such as depression and irritable bowel syndrome, which predominantly affect women.

The sexes use different sides of their brains to process and store long-term memories. Another study in 2002 demonstrated how a particular drug, propranolol, can block memory differently in men and women. Differences between men and women in cognitive pattern are now well established. On average, men outperform women on a variety of spatial tasks, with the largest difference occurring on tests of spatial rotation and manipulation, where an object must be identified in an altered orientation, or after certain imaginary manipulations such as folding. Men also excel at tests of mathematical reasoning, with the differences between sexes especially marked at the higher end of the distribution. Women, in contrast, are generally better able to recall the spatial layout of an array of objects, to scan perceptual arrays quickly to find matching objects, and to recall verbal material, whether word lists or meaningful paragraphs.

Some of these differences are found early in development and last throughout the life span. The sex differences in verbal memory, spatial orientation, and mathematical reasoning have been found across cultures. These differences are due to our long evolutionary history as hunter-gatherers, in which the division of labor between men and women was quite marked. Men more often traveled farther from the home base during hunting and scavenging, whereas women gathered food nearer home. In parallel with nonhuman studies, this would tend to show different navigational strategies, with men, for example, relying more on geometric cues and women more on landmark cues.

Summary: At present, when men and women have begun to perform similar tasks, each sex has certain specialization that, on the whole, complements the other sex's abilities. None is better, and none is inferior to the other. Mullahs will continue with their age-old prejudices to maintain women's lower status. Allah, in His infinitesimal wisdom, has bestowed on men and women unique strengths that complement each other for the benefit of humanity.

We digressed from the main topic of the written agreements because of an ongoing controversy in certain legal, scholastic Muslim circles about women's capacity as witnesses in the modern court system. This controversy about women's witnessing needed to be addressed in an informed and scientific manner. It is hoped that the above discussion will go a long way to contradict those mullahs who claim to be privy to Allah's intentions.

35. The Covenant of Allah: Respect Other People's Privacy: Enter Not Houses Other Than Yours until You Have Asked Permission and Invoked Peace upon Those in Them

> Enter not houses other than yours until you have asked permission and invoked peace upon those in them. If you find none in the house whom you seek enter not unless permission is granted. If you asked to leave, go back, it is best for you that makes for greater purity for you. Allah knows all that you do. (An-Nur 24:27, Koran)

The four walls of every person's home are his circle of privacy, within the confines of which he or she has freedom from intrusion by outsiders, be it the neighbor or the state. The residents of the home are protected from physical intrusion or intrusion with electronic devices. This dwelling is the basic autonomous unit of the Islamic state that amalgamates with other such units to form a community. The communities, with some complexity, join other communities to form the state. What is important is that the residents of each dwelling have their seclusion protected by the mandate of the covenant of the Koran. Importantly, each of the adult residents has a voice in the administration of the common affairs of the community. Each family is an independent, autonomous, basic unit of the *ummah*.

36. The Covenant of Allah: This Day I Have Perfected Your Religion for You

> This Day I have perfected your religion for you. We have made the (Qur'an) easy in your own tongue, that with it you may give glad tidings to the righteous and warnings to people given to contention. Therein is proclaimed every wise decree, by command from Our Presence, for We are ever sending revelations, as a Mercy from your Lord. We have explained in detail in this Qur'an, for the benefit of mankind, every kind of similitude.

> This day have those who reject faith (kafaru) given up all hope of compromising your faith, fear them not but only fear Me. This day have I perfected your religion for you, bestowed on you with My blessings and decreed Islam as your religion. (Al-Ma'idah 5:3, Koran).

> Ha Mim. By the Book that makes matters lucid; We revealed it during the blessed night, verily We are always warning against Evil. Therein is proclaimed every wise decree, by command from Our Presence, for We are ever sending revelations, as a Mercy from your Lord: for He is the hearer and knower. The Lord of the heavens and the earth and all that is in between them, if you have an assured faith. There is no god but He: it is He who gives life and death, the Lord

and Cherisher, your Lord and Lord of your forefathers. (Ad-Dukhan 44:1–8, Koran)

So, have We made the (Qur'an) easy in your own tongue, that with it you may give glad tidings to the righteous and warnings to people given to contention. But how many (countless) generations before them have We destroyed? Canst, thou find a single one of them (now) or hear (so much as) a whisper of them? (Taha 19:97, Koran)

We have explained in detail in this Qur'an, for the benefit of mankind, every kind of similitude: but man is, in most things, contentious. And what is there to keep back men from believing, now that guidance has come to them, nor from praying for forgiveness from their Lord, but that (they ask that) the ways of the ancients be repeated with them, or the Wrath be brought to them face to face? (Al-Kahf 18:54 –55, Koran)

The blessed *nabi* of Allah, Muhammad, proclaimed to the world on the mount of Arafat Allah's *wahiy* (message) on the last Friday, the ninth day of *Zul-hajj* in the tenth year of hijra (631 CE).

This day have I perfected your religion for you.

This day have those who reject faith (kafaru) given up all hope of compromising your faith, fear them not but only fear Me. This day have I perfected your religion for you, bestowed on you with My blessings and decreed Islam as your religion. (Al-Ma'idah 5:3, Koran)

On that day, the *din* of Islam was complete, and all man-made innovations after that were just novelties; anyone indulging in such innovations was making a sport of his religion. Those believers who fulfill the commandments of the Koran, Allah's covenant, are the *muttaqeen.* From that day on, men and women who obey and keep their covenant with Allah are the believers (*muttaqeen*) of Allah and the Koran, the word that Allah revealed to the blessed *nabi*, Muhammad. The believers who follow the Koran and fulfill the covenant of Allah, for them submission to Allah only suffices them. They are not Shia or Sunni nor of any other sect. They are the Believers of Allah.

The Koran establishes a universal order based on the divinely ordained values of life. Were every human to fulfill the covenant of the Koran, the world shall be at peace forever, and justice would prevail. By following the *Hadith collections* of the third century hijra, *Muslims* have relegated their faith from a divinely ordained order to a human set of values, misleading themselves and deviating others from Allah's path. According to the Koran, *iman* is not just belief but also, in fact, knowledge. *Iman* is the conviction that is based on reason and knowledge. The Koran does not recognize belief that involves blind acceptance. Islam does include acceptance of certain things that cannot be explained by perception through human senses. Our reason and thinking will compel us to recognize the existence of such things. *Iman*, according to the Koran, signifies conviction based on full mental acceptance and intellectual satisfaction. *Iman* gives a person inner contentment, a feeling of *amn* (same common root). Thus, *iman* means to believe in something and to testify to its truthfulness, to have confidence in that belief, and to bow down in obedience.

There are five fundamental facts stated in the Koran that a believer must accept: *iman* in Allah, the law of *mukafat* and the afterlife, angels (*malaika*), the revelations, and the messengers. Belief in Allah means not only to profess obedience to Him and His Covenant but also to show it in one's actions and to be always in *taqwa* of Allah. Belief in the law of *mukafat* means to have conviction that every action of the human has an inescapable consequence of reward or retribution. Angels are not the winged creatures depicted in children's literature. They are heavenly forces that carry out laws of Allah governing the universe. They bow to Allah since they follow his orders. They also bow to the humans because we are able to study, understand, and manipulate the laws of nature for the benefit of mankind. Belief in revelations and messengers implies that human intellect alone cannot safely reach the final destination without the divine guidance in the form of *wahiy*, revelation delivered by the messengers to mankind. This guidance is to whole humankind sent through many messengers. The Muslim tradition began with *Ibrahim*, our father (Abraham of the Bible). The believers have a belief system and a course of action to witness over and spread the message to mankind that began with *Ibrahim* and was completed with *Muhammad*. Whereas the message of *wahiy* is divine and universal for all human races, the message of Hadith collections of the third century are human and therefore subject to error and cannot be equated with the Koran.

37. The Covenant of Allah: Those Who Believe and Perform Beautiful Deeds Are Companions of the Garden; Therein Shall They Abide Forever

After his submission to the will and mercy of Allah, the believer is obliged to obey and fulfill the covenant he has made with Allah as part of the compact of submission and has to perform wholesome and good deeds. The covenant of the Koran is a total belief system of an individual based upon total submersion of one's personality with Allah with total awareness and *taqwa* of Him at all times through observance of the thirty-seven commandments of Allah's covenant. This communion is not only with Allah but also, through Him, with other humans and Allah's creation, both alive and inanimate. The phrase *amilu al saalihaat* (to do good, to perform wholesome deeds) refers to those who persist in striving to set things right, who restore harmony, peace, and balance. Other acts of good works recognized in the covenant of the Koran are to show compassion, to be merciful and forgive others, to be just, to protect the weak, to defend the oppressed, to be generous and charitable, to be truthful and to seek knowledge and wisdom, to be kind, to be peaceful, to love others, and to perform beautiful deeds.

> On those who believe and do good, will [Allah] Most Gracious bestow love.

There are fifty such verses in the Koran that remind the believers of the rewards of righteous deeds. The following are some of the *ayahs* in the Koran mentioning the righteous deeds.

Alladhina aaminu wa 'amilu al saalihaat.30

> But those who believe and work righteousness. They are Companions of the Garden: therein shall they abide (forever). (Al-Baqarah 2:82)

> Those who believe, do deeds of righteousness, and establish regular prayers and regular charity, will have their reward with their Lord: on them shall be no fear, nor shall they grieve. (Al-Baqarah 2:277)

---

30 Qur'an 2:25; 2:82, 277; 4:57, 122; 5:5; 7:42; 10:9; 11:23; 13:29; 14:23; 18:2, 88, 107; 19:60, 96; 20:75, 82, 112; 21:94; 22:14; 23:50, 56; 24:55; 25:70–71; 26:67; 28:80, 29:7, 9, 58; 30:15, 45; 31:8; 32:19; 34:4, 37; 38:24; 41:8; 42:22, 23, 26; 45:21, 30; 47:2, 12; 48:29; 64:9; 65:11; 84:25; 85:11; 95:6; 98:7; 103:3.

As to those who believe and work righteousness, Allah will pay them in full their reward; but Allah loves not those who do wrong (zalimeen). (Ali 'Imran 3:57)

But those who believe and do deeds of righteousness, We shall soon admit to Gardens, with rivers flowing beneath, their eternal home and therein shall they have companions pure and holy: We shall admit them to shades, cool and ever deepening. (An-Nisa 4:57)

But those who believe and do deeds of righteousness, We shall soon admit them to Gardens - with rivers flowing beneath - to dwell therein forever. Allah's promise is the truth and whose word can be truer than Allah's? (An-Nisa 4:122)

If any do deeds of righteousness, be they male or female and have faith, they will enter Heaven and not the least injustice will be done to them. (An-Nisa 4:124)

But to those who believe and do deeds of righteousness, He will give their due rewards and more, out of His bounty: but those who are disdainful and arrogant, He will not punish with a grievous penalty; nor will they find, besides Allah, any to protect or help them. (An-Nisa 4:173)

To those who believe and do deeds of righteousness hath Allah promised forgiveness and a great reward. (Al-Ma'idah 5:9)

On those who believe and do deeds of righteousness there is no blame for what they ate (in the past), when they guard themselves from evil and believe and do deeds of righteousness - (or) again, guard themselves from evil and believe, (or) again, guard themselves from evil and do good. For Allah loves those who do good. (Al-Ma'idah 5:93)

But those who believe and work righteousness - no burden do We place on any soul, but that which it can bear - they will be Companions of the Garden, therein to dwell (forever). (Al-A'raf 7:42)

To Him will be your return, of all of you. The promise of Allah is true and sure. It is He Who began the Creation and its cycle, that He may reward with justice those who believe and work righteousness; but those who reject Him will have draughts of boiling fluids and a Penalty grievous, because they did reject Him. (Yunus 10:4)

Those who believe and work righteousness, their Lord will guide them because of their Faith: beneath them will flow rivers in Gardens of Bliss. (Yunus 10:9)

But those who believe and work righteousness and humble themselves before their Lord, they will be Companions of the Garden, to dwell therein forever! (Hud 11:23)

"For those who believe, and work righteousness is every blessedness and a beautiful place of (final) return." (Ar-Ra'd 13:29)

Summary: *Islam* is concerned with everyday activities of the believer, differentiating right from wrong and guiding the individual along the correct path. It defines *sin* as "breaking the commandments of Allah" and *good works* as "following Allah's instructions and the prophet's teachings."

Iman adds a dimension to the understanding of human activity in that every human action in daily life reaches back into the divine reality that everything in the universe is governed by tawhid, yet Allah has granted humans a freedom of choice, which can upset the balance in the creation, the balance of justice, and the balance of atmospheric elements and of environmental pollution and lead to the destruction of animal species, populations, cities, and agriculture through human actions. It tells people why they should be Allah's servants and explains which path they should follow to become His vicegerents. It makes clear that human activity is deeply rooted in the Real, and this has everlasting repercussions in this world and in the hereafter.

Ihsan adds to *islam* and *iman* a focus on people's intention to perform good and wholesome deeds on the basis of awareness of Allah's presence in all things. According to the Koran, doing wholesome deeds, along with faith, will yield paradise.

> Who so does wholesome deeds, be it male or female and has faith, shall enter the garden, therein provided for without reckoning. (Ghafir 40:40, Koran)

> Those who have faith and do wholesome deeds, them we shall admit to gardens through which rivers flow. (An-Nisa 4:57, 122, Koran)

Another fifty verses in the Koran mention that people who perform beautiful deeds and have faith shall inherit the garden. The Koran uses the word *saalihaat* for beautiful and wholesome deeds and the word *salihun* for wholesome people. The root word for both *saalihaat* and *salihun* means "to be beautiful, sound, wholesome, right, proper, and good." Another word used in the Koran about thirty times is *islah*, which means "establishing wholesomeness." In modern times, the word *islah* has been used to mean "reform." The word *sulh* is used in the Koran once to mean "peace and harmony in family relationships." In modern times, the word *sulh* has come to mean "peace in the political sense." While the Koran calls the wholesome people as *salihun*, it employs the opposite, *fasid*, for the corrupt, ruined, evil, and wrong. The wholesome are the ones who live in harmony with the Real (*Haqq*) and establish wholesomeness through their words and deeds throughout the world. In contrast, the corrupt (*mufsidun*) destroy the proper balance and relationship with Allah and His creation. *Fasid* means "corrupt, evil, and wrong."

Allah measures out good and evil, the wholesome and the corrupt. Humans have enough freedom to make their own choices; if they make the choice to do beautiful and wholesome deeds (*saalihaat*) motivated by faith (*iman*) and god-wariness (*taqwa*), they please Allah and bring harmony and wholesomeness to the world, resulting in peace, justice, mercy, compassion, honor, equity, well-being, freedom, and many other gifts through Allah's grace. Others choose to do evil and work with corruption (*mufsidun*), destroying the right relationship among the creation, causing hunger, disease, oppression, pollution, and other afflictions. In the universal order, corruption is the prerogative of humans, and vicegerency gives humans the freedom to work against the Creator and His creation. Only misapplied trust can explain how moral evil can appear in the world. Modern technology, scientific advancement in weapons of mass destruction: nuclear, chemical, and biological, genetic engineering of plants, animals, and humans, and exploitation of nonrenewable resources of the earth have made destruction of the human race and all life on the planet a distinct and imminent possibility.

> Corruption has appeared on the land and in the sea because what people's hands have earned, so that He may let them taste some of their deeds, in order that they may turn back from their evils. (Ar-Rum 30:41, Koran)

When humans choose wrong and corrupt actions, they displease Allah. Allah loves those who do what is beautiful, not those who do what is ugly:

185

> When he turns his back, he hurries about the earth to work
> corruption there and destroy the tillage and the stock. Allah
> loves not corruption. (Al-Baqarah 2:205, Koran)

Allah loves doing what is beautiful, and because of His love for those who do the beautiful, He brings them near Him, and His nearness is called Allah's mercy:

> Work not corruption in this world after it has made
> wholesome and call upon Allah in fear and hope. Surely the
> mercy of Allah is near to those who do what is beautiful. (Al-
> A'raf 7:56, Koran)

The covenant of the Koran presents us the scope of the freedom of choice that humans have in doing what is wholesome and beautiful or what is corrupt or ugly. The human's role among the creation distinguishes right activity, right thought, and right intention from their opposites. It reminds us of how the scales of Allah's justice, the two hands of Allah—His mercy and His wrath—are reflected in the human domain, where people have been appointed Allah's vicegerents. Deeds of goodness and wholesomeness are associated with mercy, paradise, and the beautiful. Evil and corruption is rewarded with wrath, hell, and the ugly.

CHAPTER THREE

THE COVENANT OF ALLAH AND THE DAR ES SALAAM: FOUNDATION AND FUNDAMENTALS FOR THE MUSLIM COMMUNITY OF DAR ES SALAAM

⋄ Verily those who pledge their allegiance unto you, (O Muhammad) swear it unto none but Allah; the Hand of Allah is over their hands. Thereafter whosoever breaks his Covenant does so to the harm of his own soul, and whosoever fulfils his Covenant with Allah, Allah will grant him an immense Reward. (Al-Fath 48:10, Koran)

⋄ He is Allah, there is no Deity but He, Knower of the hidden and the manifest. He is the Rahman (the Most Gracious), the Rahim, (Most Merciful.)

He is Allah; there is no Deity but Him,
The Sovereign, the Pure and the Hallowed,
Serene and Perfect,
The Custodian of Faith, the Protector, the Almighty,
The Irresistible, the Supreme,
Glory be to Allah; He is above all they associate with Him.

He is Allah, the Creator, the Sculptor, the Adorner of color and form. To Him belong the Most Beautiful Names: whatever so is in the heavens and on earth, Praise and Glory Him; and He is the Almighty and All-Wise. (Al-Hashr 59:18–24, Koran)

⋄　Allah. There is no god but He, the ever living, and the one who sustains and protects all that exists. No slumber can seize Him or sleep. His are all things in the heavens and on earth. Who is there to intercede in His presence except as He permits?

⋄　He knows what happens to His creatures in this world and in the hereafter. Nor do they know the scope of His knowledge except as He wills.
His Throne extends over the heavens and the earth, and He feels no fatigue in guarding and protecting them.
He is the Most High, Most Great. (Al-Baqarah 2:255, Koran)

Say, "Come I will recite what your Lord has prohibited you from:
⋄　Join not anything in worship with Him:
⋄　Be good to your parents: kill not your children because of poverty, We provide sustenance for you and for them.
⋄　Come not near to shameful deeds (sins and illegal sexual activity) whether open or secret.
⋄　Take not life, which Allah hath made sacred, except by the way of justice or law: This He commands you, that you may learn wisdom.
⋄　And come not near the orphan's property, except to improve it, until he attains the age of full strength.
⋄　And give full measure and full weight with justice.
⋄　No burden we place on any soul but that which it can bear.
⋄　Whenever you give your word speak honestly even if a near relative is concerned.
⋄　And fulfill the Covenant of Allah. Thus, He commands you that you may remember.

⋄ Verily, this is My Way leading straight: follow it: follow not (other) paths for they will separate you from His path. This He commands you that you may remember.

⋄ You who believe in Allah, fulfill your Covenant with Allah.

⋄ Believe in Allah, His Messenger, and the Book that He has sent to His Messenger and the Scriptures that He sent to those before him. Any who deny Allah, His angels, His Books, His Messengers, and the Day of Judgment has gone far far astray.

⋄ Bow down, prostrate yourself and serve your Lord, and do wholesome deeds that you may prosper.

⋄ Perform Jihad; strive to your utmost in Allah's cause as striving (jihad) is His due. He has chosen you and Allah has imposed no hardship in your endeavor to His cause. You are the inheritors of the faith of your father Abraham. It is He who has named you Muslims of the times before and now, so that Allah's Messenger may be an example to you and that you are an example to mankind.

⋄ But Allah doth call to the Abode of Peace (Dar es Salaam):
He doth guide whom He pleased to a Way that is straight.

To those who do right and in abundance neither darkness nor shame shall cover their faces! They are the heirs of Paradise, they will abide therein forever.

⋄ It is not righteousness that ye turn your faces towards East or West; but it is righteousness to believe in Allah and the Last Day, and the Angels, and the Book, and the Messengers; to spend of your substance, out of love for Him, for your kin, for orphans, for the needy, for the wayfarer, for those who ask, and for the ransom of slaves; to be steadfast in prayer, and practice regular charity, to fulfill the Covenant which ye have made; and to be firm and patient, in pain (or suffering) and adversity, and throughout all periods of panic. Such are the people of truth, the God-fearing. (Al-Baqarah 2:177, Koran)

◇ Verily fellowship of yours is a single brotherhood, and I am your Lord
and Cherisher: therefore, serve me [and no other],

◇ And hold fast, all together by the rope which Allah [stretches out
for you].
And be not divided amongst yourselves.
And remember with gratitude Allah's favor on you:
For ye were enemies and He joined your hearts in love,
So that by His grace, you became brethren.

◇ Enjoining what is right and forbidding what is wrong. Let there arise
out of you a band of people, inviting all that is good,

◇ Be not like those who are divided amongst themselves,
And fall into disputations after receiving clear signs,
For them is a dreadful penalty.

◇ Ye are the best of the peoples evolved for mankind,
Enjoining what is right, forbidding what is wrong, and believing in
Allah.

◇ Thus, have we made of you an Ummah of the center?
That ye might be witness over other nations,
And the Messenger a witness over yourselves.
And we appointed the Qibla
To which thou wast used,
Only to test those who followed,
The Messenger from those
Who would turn their heels?

◇ Whoever submits his whole self to Allah, and is a doer of good,
Has grasped indeed the most trustworthy handhold,
And with Allah rests the end and decision of [all] affairs.

◇ Take not the Jews and the Christians for your friends and protectors,
They are but friends and the protectors to each other.
And he amongst you that turns to them is of them.

Verily Allah does not guide the people who are unjust.

* O you who believe!
Take not for friends and protectors those who take your religion for a mockery or sport,
Whether among those who received the scripture before you, or among those who reject faith.
But you fear Allah if you have faith.

* O you who believe!
Take not infidels (kafireen) for Awliya (friends and protectors) in place of believers. Would you offer Allah a clear warrant against yourselves? (An-Nisa 4:144, Koran)

* O you who believe!
Take not the Jews and the Christians as your friends and protectors (Awliya). They are friends and protectors unto each other. He who amongst you turns to them is one of them. Allah does not guide those who are unjust and evil doers (zalimun). (Al-Ma'idah 5:51, Koran)

* O you who believe!
Take not for friends and protectors (Awliya those who take your religion for mockery, whether from amongst people of the book or from amongst the kafireen. Be in taqwa of Allah, fear Allah if you have faith indeed (Al-Ma'idah 5:57, Koran)

Your (real) friends are Allah,
His Messenger and the Fellowship of
Believers, those who
Establish regular prayers and regular Charity.
And they bow down humbly in worship
As to those who turn.
For friendship to Allah,
His Messenger and the fellowship
Of Believers, it is

The Fellowship of Allah
That must certainly triumph

you who believe Obey Allah and obey the messenger,
In addition, those charged with Authority among you.
If ye differ in anything among yourselves, refer it
To Allah and His Messenger. If you do believe in Allah, and the last Day
That is the best, and the most suitable for the final determination.

◇ And the firmament has He raised high,
And He has setup the balance of Justice, in order that ye may not transgress due balance.
So establish weight with justice and fall not short in the balance
Of those We have created are people who direct others with truth, and dispense justice
Therewith.

◇ Those who hearken to their Lord and establish regular prayer.
Who conduct their affairs by mutual consultation?
Who spend out what we bestow on them for sustenance.
And those who when an oppressive wrong is inflicted on them, are not intimidated but defend themselves.

◇ There is no compulsion in religion:
Truth stands out clear from error,
Whoever rejects evil and believes in Allah hath grasped the most trustworthy Handhold, which never breaks.
And Allah hears and knows all things.
Allah is exalted in power, wise?

◇ For men and women who surrender unto Allah,
For men and women who believe,
For men and women who are devout
For men and women who speak the truth,
For men and women who persevere in righteousness,

For men and women who are humble,

For men and women who are charitable,

For men and women who fast and deny them selves

For men and women who guard their chastity,

For men and women who remember Allah much,

For them Allah has forgiveness and a great reward.

Say to the

Believing men that they should lower their gaze and guard their modesty:

That will make for greater purity for them:

And Allah is acquainted with all that they do.

And say to the Believing women that they should lower their gaze and guard their modesty.

That they should not display their adornments except what is ordinarily obvious,

That they should draw a veil over

Their bosom and not display their adornments.

(Except to the immediate family)

And that they should not strike their feet

In order to draw attention

To their hidden adornments.

and O ye Believers!

Turn ye all together Toward Allah that ye may prosper.

The believer's men and women are protectors one of another.

They enjoin what is just and forbid what is evil.

They observe regular prayers, practice regular charity and obey Allah and His messenger.

On them will Allah pour His mercy, for Allah is exalted in power, wise.

O ye who believe! Guard your souls,

If ye follow [right] guidance,

No hurt can come to you from those who stray.

The goal of you all is to Allah,

It is He who will show you the truth of all that ye do.

◊ Fight in the cause of Allah

Those who fight you,

But do not transgress limits:
For Allah loves not transgressors
And slay them wherever ye catch them,
And turn them out from wherever they have turned you out.
For tumult and oppression are worse than slaughter.
But fight them not at the Sacred Mosque, unless they (first) fight you there
But if they fight you, slay them.
Such is the reward of those who suppress faith.
But if they cease,
Allah is oft Forgiving, Most Merciful.
And fight them on
Until there is no more
Tyranny or oppression,
And there prevail
Justice and faith in Allah: but if they cease
Let there be no hostility,
Except to those who practice oppression.

◊ Those who devour usury will not stand except as stands one whom the Satan by his touch hath driven to madness.
That is because they say:
Trade is like usury,
But Allah hath permitted trade and forbidden usury.
Those who after receiving direction from their Lord,
Desist, shall be pardoned for the past: their case is for Allah to (judge);
But those who repeat (the offence) are the companions of fire;
They will abide therein (forever).
Allah will deprive usury of all blessing,
However, will give increase for the deeds of charity:
For He does not love those who are ungrateful and wicked.

◊ And eat not up
Your property among yourselves
For vanities, nor use it,
As a bait for judges,

With intent that you may
Eat up wrong fully and knowingly,
A some of other people's property.

⋄   you who believe! Guard your souls,
If you follow right guidance,
No hurt can come to you from those who stray.
The goal of you all is to Allah,
It is He who will show you the truth of all that you do. (Koran 2:143,
156, 177, 188, 190–92, 275–76, 278–79; 3:103–5, 110; 4:59; 5:51, 57,
105; 7:181; 9:71; 10:25–26; 21:92; 24:30–31; 31:22; 33:35; 42:38–39;
55:79)

The Covenant of Yathrib

The Covenant of the Blessed Messenger of Allah, Muhammad

In the name of Allah, the compassionate and the merciful.

a.   No believer shall slay a believer in retaliation for an unbeliever, nor
shall he assist an unbeliever against a believer. This is a covenant given
by Muhammad to the believers.
b.   They constitute one *ummah* to the exclusion of all other men.
c.   The believers shall leave none of their members in destitution without
giving him in kindness and liberty what he needs.
d.   No believer shall take as an ally a freedman of another Muslim without
the consent of his previous master. All believers shall rise as one
against anyone who seeks to commit injustice, aggression, or crime
or spread mutual enmity among the Muslims, even if such a person
is their kin.
e.   Just as the bond to Allah is indivisible, all the believers shall stand
behind the least of them in commitment. All believers are bonded to
one another to the exclusion of other men.
f.   This Pax Islamica is one and indivisible. No believer shall enter a
separate peace without all other believers whenever there is fighting
in the cause of God except on the basis of equality and justice to all

others. In every expedition for the cause of God we undertake, all parties to the covenant shall fight shoulder to shoulder as one man. All believers shall avenge the blood of one another when anyone falls while fighting in the cause of God.

g. The pious believers follow the best and the most upright guidance.

h. Whoever is convicted of killing a believer deliberatively but without righteous cause shall be liable to the relatives of the killed. Until the latter are satisfied, the killer shall be subject to retaliation by each and every believer.

i. Any Jew who follows us is entitled to our assistance and the same rights as any one of us without injustice and partisanship. As the Jews fight on the side of the believers, they shall spend their wealth equally with the believers. The Jews are an *ummah* alongside the believers. The Jews have their religion and the Muslims theirs. Both enjoy the security of their populace and clients except the unjust and the criminal among them. The unjust and the criminal destroy only himself and his family.

j. None of the Jewish tribes may go to war without the permission of Muhammad, though none may be prevented from taking revenge for a wound inflicted on them. Whosoever murders anyone will have murdered himself and the members of his family, unless it be the case of the man suffering a wrong, for God will accept his actions. The Jews shall bear their public expenses, and so will the Muslims. Each shall assist the other against any violator of this covenant. Their relationship shall be one of mutual advice and consultation and mutual assistance and charity rather than harm and aggression. Assistance is due to the party suffering an injustice, not to one perpetrating it.

k. Yathrib shall constitute a sanctuary to the parties of this covenant. Whatever the difference or dispute between the parties that remains unsolved shall be referred to God and to Muhammad. The Jews are entitled to the same rights as this covenant has granted to other parties, together with the goodness and charity of the latter. Allah is the guarantor of the piety and goodness that is embodied in this covenant. The people in this covenant come to the assistance of one another against any aggressor.

l.   Allah is the guarantor of the truth and goodwill of this covenant.
     Allah grants His protection to whosoever acts in piety, charity, and
     goodness.

The Chain of Authority

The covenant of Allah has established a simple code of conduct
for the believers to follow in their daily lives. The same conduct
applies to the community of Islam, the *ummah*, and their state.
Muslims disobey the covenant at their peril.

1. Unity

Allah addressed the believers and ordained a chain of authority
in the management of their affairs: "Obey Allah and obey the
Messenger, and those charged amongst you with authority in the
settlement of your affairs. If you differ in anything among yourselves,
refer it to Allah and His Messenger" (the Koran and the prophet's
teachings). The sovereignty of the Islamic state belongs exclusively to
Allah, whose will and command binds the community and state. The
dignified designation in the Koran of the community as vicegerent
of Allah on the earth makes the Muslim community, the *ummah*, a
repository of the "executive sovereignty" of the Islamic state.

The community as a whole, after consultation and consensus,
grants people among themselves the authority to manage its affairs
(*ulil amri minkum*). Those given authority act in their capacity as the
representative (*wakil*) of the people and are bound by the Koranic
mandate to obey Allah and the messenger in the management of the
affairs of the *ummah*. They are also bound by the Koranic mandate to
consult with the community. The community, by consultation and

in consensus, has the authority to depose any person charged with authority, including the head of state, in the event of gross violation of Allah's law. The believers will, from time to time, choose their *wakil* to manage the affairs of the Dar es Salaam. Such affairs will be administered on the basis of the commandments of Allah in accordance with His covenant.

2. Truth

Allah has ordained every believer to,

> have taqwa of Allah, fear Allah, and speak always the truth that He may direct you to righteous deeds and forgive you your sins. He that obeys Allah and His Messenger have already attained the highest achievement. (Al-Ahzab 33:69–73, Koran)

The basis of Islam is truth (*haqq*). Every believer must always speak the truth. Allah guides the truthful to His path of righteousness. Without the truth, there is no *din* and no Islam. Allah's *din* is divine. Allah is *Haqq*, and all truth emanates from Him. The Koran is Allah's word on the earth and the expression of *haqq*. *Haqq* is the reality and the truth; *batil* refers to something that is imaginary and false. Those who believe in Allah only speak the truth. When humans add dogma and creed to Allah's *din*, it is not *haqq*. In matters of *din*, what is not absolute truth is not *haqq*. What is not *haqq* is *batil* (false or fabricated). What is not truthful cannot be a witness over Allah's word and *din*. Therefore, all human additions to the *din* of Allah do not constitute the truth, and every human fabrication to the *din* after the completion of *wahiy* is *batil* (falsehood).

The truth in the believer connects to Allah through *haqq*, the essence of Allah. In the same vein, it is falsehood that destroys the relationship between the human and his Lord, and the same untruth destroys the relationship among humans. Without truth, there is no *din*, and there is no Islam. And devoid of truth, the world of humans is barren, superficial, and fake. Without truth, the Dar es Salaam cannot exist.

All human transactions—whether personal, communal, national, or international—must always be based on the foundation of *haqq*. The statecraft, diplomacy, and international relations of the kings, sultans, autocrats, and so-called democracies have—since the beginning of time—been based on deception and mendacity. It is through falsehood and systematic deceit of propaganda that the modern nation-states control their populations. Modern democracy, in effect, grants custody of nation-states to politicians whose sophistication belies their art of deception. The economy of modern nation-states is founded on falsehood, usury, and fake paper money. Justice means fairness, fairness means truth, and truth means reality. Those who expect any of the above from the adversarial system of the modern nation-states will not hear the truth. In the Islamic state, truth will triumph over falsehood; the core of human values of the Dar es Salaam is truth and justice.

3. Justice

Justice, like truth, is the pillar of Islam. Without truth and justice, there is no Islam. Submission to Allah demands *taqwa* of Allah, truthfulness, and righteous deeds. Allah says to the believers:

> O you who believe! Fear Allah and speak always the truth
> that He may direct you to righteous deeds and forgive you

your sins: he that obeys Allah and His Messenger have already attained the highest achievement. (Al-Ahzab 33:69–73, Koran)

Stand firm for justice as witness to Allah be it against yourself, your parents, or your family, whether it is against rich or poor, both are nearer to Allah than they are to you. Follow not your caprice lest you distort your testimony. If you prevaricate and evade justice Allah is well aware what you do. (An-Nisa 4:135, Koran)

O you who believe! Stand firmly for Allah as a witness of fair dealing. Let not the malice of people lead you to iniquity. Be just, that is next to worship. Be with taqwa of Allah, fear Allah. Allah is well aware with what you do. (Al-Ma'idah 5:8, Koran)

Betray not the trust of Allah and His Messenger. Nor knowingly misappropriate things entrusted to you. If you have taqwa of Allah, and fear Allah, He will grant you a Criterion to judge between right and wrong and remove from you all misfortunes and evil and forgive your sins. Allah is the bestower of grace in abundance. (Al-Anfal 8:27, 29, Koran)

Be in taqwa of Allah, fear Allah, and be with those who are true in word and deed. (At-Tawbah 9:119, Koran)

Deal not unjustly, and ye shall not be dealt with unjustly. (Al-Baqarah 2:277–80, Koran)

Whenever you give your word speak honestly even if a near relative is concerned.

And give full measure and full weight with justice. No burden We place on any soul but that which it can bear. (Al-An 'am 6:151–52, Koran)

The Koran repeatedly stigmatizes the humans of wrongdoing. When it points out who is harmed by injustice or wrongdoing (*zulm*), it always mentions the word *nafs* (self). People cannot harm Allah. By being unjust, doing wrong, or putting things in the wrong place, people harm themselves. They distort their own natures, and they lead themselves astray. Whom can one wrong? It is impossible to wrong or do injustice against Allah since all things are His creatures and do His work. Hence, wrongdoing and injustice is an activity against people and Allah's creation.

Allah has prescribed His covenant to the humans for the good of human beings. People, tribes, and nations are being helped since Allah leads them into accord, harmony, and justice, which in turn create peace in the world. Allah has laid out the principles of justice in His covenant for the humans to live in harmony. Those who refuse to follow His commandments are therefore ungrateful and hence *kafirs*. They are wrongdoers (*zalimun*) and only harm themselves. Of the 250 verses where the Koran mentions *zulm* or *zalimun*, it refers to the object of wrongdoing in only twenty-five verses. In one verse, the object of wrongdoing are *people*:

> The blame is only against those who oppress humans with wrongdoing and insolently transgress beyond bounds through the land, defying right and justice: for such there will be a Penalty grievous.
> (Ash-Shura 42:42)

Therefore, the Dar es Salaam cannot exist without justice. The unjust have not submitted to the will and the covenant of Allah. Those who oppress humans and insolently transgress bounds through defying right and justice displease Allah. They defy the will of Allah, and they are not His believers. Such *zalimun* cannot become the *awliya*, *wakil*, nor rulers of Islam.

4. *Fahasha*

Allah tells the believers not to follow the footsteps of Satan. Satan leads them to shameful deeds (*Fahasha*) and what is wrong (*Munkar*). Allah tells the believers not to approach shameful deeds in open or in secret. Whoever rejects evil and believes in Allah has His handhold that never breaks. Allah expels all evil from those who abstain from the odious and the forbidden, and He will admit them through the gate of great honor. He will grant those with *taqwa* of Allah *furqan*, the criterion and ability to judge between right and wrong. Allah will save them from them misfortunes and evil and forgive their sins.

Man has been granted the freedom to choose the wholesome and beautiful or the corrupt and ugly. The core of the human—the *nafs*, the shiny mirror of the self—is tarnished by the dirt and the smoke of the evil and the corrupt. The *taqwa* and *nur* of Allah in man's heart blows away this dirt and smoke from the mirror of the human *nafs*. Those who perform good, reject evil, and believe in Allah have grasped His handhold that will never loosen. An *ummah* of one and a half billion believers in communion with Allah, surrounded in His *nur*, is a powerful force of good that will subdue all evil and ugly from the face of the earth.

5. Let there be no compulsion in religion

Allah says to the believers, "Let there be no compulsion in religion: Truth stands out clear from Error: whoever rejects Evil and believes in Allah hath grasped the most trustworthy handhold that never breaks." *Islam* (submission) and *iman* (faith) arise out of the communion of a believer with his Maker. According to the Koran, *iman* is not just belief but also, in fact, knowledge. *Iman* is a conviction that is based on reason and knowledge. The Koran does not recognize belief that involves blind acceptance. *Islam* does include acceptance of certain things that cannot be explained by perception through human senses. Our reasoning and thinking will compel us to recognize the existence of such things. *Iman*, according to the Koran, signifies conviction based on full mental acceptance and intellectual satisfaction. *Iman* gives us inner contentment, a feeling of *amn* (same, common root). Thus, *iman* means to believe in something and to testify to its truthfulness, to have confidence in that belief, and to act in accordance with that belief.

There are five fundamental facts stated in the Koran that a believer must accept: *iman* in (1) Allah, (2) the law of *mukafat* and the afterlife, (3) angels (*malaika*), (4) the revelations, and (5) the messengers. Belief in Allah means not only to profess obedience to Him and His covenant but also to show it in one's actions and to be in *taqwa* of Allah. Belief in the law of *mukafat* means to have conviction that every action of the human has an inescapable consequence of reward or retribution. Angels are not the winged creatures depicted in children's literature. They are heavenly forces that carry out laws of Allah governing the universe. They bow to Allah since they follow his orders. They also bow to the humans because we are able to study, understand, and manipulate the laws of nature for the benefit of mankind. Belief in revelations and messengers implies that human intellect alone cannot safely reach the final destination without divine guidance in the form of *wahiy*, revelation delivered by the messengers to mankind. This guidance is to the whole humankind sent through many messengers.

The Muslim tradition began with *Ibrahim*, our father (Abraham of the Bible). The believers have a belief system and a course of action to be witness over and spread the message to mankind that began with *Nabi* Ibrahim and was completed with *Nabi* Muhammad. Whereas the message of *wahiy* is divine and universal for all human races, man-made edicts, creed, and dogma directing the believers to beliefs and actions separate the believer in his communion with God. This communion is exclusive, and in this relationship, no human can intervene. Therefore, compulsion in matters of religion is only a human fantasy. In the same manner, the message of Hadith collections of the third century is human and therefore subject to error, and so it cannot be equated with the *haqq* of the Koran. Mullahs, scholars, Wahhabi, Taliban, and the ayatollahs who compel believers to conform to their own narrow beliefs assume the rights that are only Allah's prerogative.

6. "Take not the Jews and the Christians as your friends and protectors (awliya)."

Allah reassures the believers, "Allah is the *Waliy,* protector of those who have faith. From the depths of darkness, He will lead them forth into light. Of those who reject faith their *Waliy* (protectors) are the false deities: from light, they will lead them forth into the depths of darkness."

"Take not the Jews and the Christians as your friends and protectors (*Awliya*). They are friends and protectors unto each other. He who amongst you turns to them is one of them. Allah does not guide those who are unjust and evil doers."

"Take not for friends and protectors *(Awliya)* those who take your religion for mockery, whether from amongst people of the book or from amongst the *kafireen*. Be in *taqwa* of Allah, fear Allah if you have faith indeed."

"Allah is the *Waliy* protector of those who have faith. From the depths of darkness, He will lead them forth into light."

These verses of the Koran often cause confusion among the believers, Christians, and Jews. Yet the explanation is quite simple. The Koran recognizes only one true religion—the religion of those who have submitted their self to the one universal God, have faith in that God, and perform wholesome and beautiful deeds. Allah, God, sent thousands of His messengers and *Nabiien* with a message to humankind. Some of the messengers are named in the Koran, while others are not obvious to us. Millions of people subscribe to the teachings of these messengers; although they may on the surface be followers of Islam, Hinduism, Buddhism, teachings of Confucius, Christianity, and Judaism, they have submitted their self to one universal God, the Creator. They do His bidding as taught by the messengers, and they perform beautiful and wholesome deeds in the service of Allah's creation. Such people are the believers of God, Allah, and they are *Muslims* according to the Koran.

And there are millions of people who call themselves Muslims, Christians, Jews, and others who have not submitted their self to God, their Maker; they do not have the same faith in the one universal God. Such people do not have the *nur* of Allah in their hearts; they create evil and mischief on the earth. Such people cause wars, murder whole populations, steal from nations, and profit from famines and destitution. Such are the people Allah warns us about. They should not be taken as *awliya* by the believers.

It is not only the Koran that makes the believers aware of the tricks of such people. Jesus spoke of them in these terms:

Beware of false prophets, which come to you in sheep's clothing, but inwardly they are ravenous. You shall know them by their fruits. Do men gather grapes of thorns, or figs of thistles? Even so every good tree brings forth good fruit, but a corrupt tree brings forth evil fruit. "A good tree cannot bring forth evil fruit; neither can a corrupt tree bring forth good fruit." Every tree that brings forth bad fruit is hewn down and cast into the fire. Therefore, by their fruits shall you know them?

The Koran says:

They have made their oaths a screen for their misdeeds, thus they obstruct men from the Path of Allah: truly evil are their deeds. That is because they believed, then they rejected Faith: so, a seal was set on their hearts: therefore, they understand not. When you look at them, their exteriors please thee; and when they speak, you listen to their words. They are as worthless as rotten pieces of timber propped up, unable to stand on their own. They think that every cry is against them. They are the enemies; so beware of them. The curse of Allah be on them! How are they deluded away from the Truth! (Al-Munafiqun 63:4.

It should become absolutely clear to Muslims that the present world situation is the continuation of the Council of Clermont in 1095 CE, when Pope Urban declared a crusade against Islam, a war till the destruction of Islam. There are powerful forces in the Christian West that, for the first time in history, are not threatened by the barbarians or by any other force among themselves. The Christian West is united in NATO and the European Economic Union. The threats to Islam have been ongoing since the beginning of the Crusades and are now being renewed daily very subtly. In this battle, every component of the modern civilization has been harnessed against Islam: intelligence services, armed forces, diplomacy, economics and communications, and organizations such as the United Nations, the World Bank, the IMF, and the World Trade Organization.

The unwritten plan of the fundamentalist Christian, Jewish, and banking/oil interests work in cohesion to weaken and degrade the Islamic state and its military and economic infrastructure in such a way that Muslims countries will continue to be client states under American and NATO hegemony and to live in ongoing poverty and degradation under the despotic rule of incompetent, dishonest, and self-serving kings and dictators. Muslim and Arab states will be further divided into ministates so they can never be united to present a coherent, united front to the West. Iraq will break down into three fragments—Shiite, Sunni, and Kurdish. Saudi Arabia will be divided into the eastern Shia oil sheikhdom and a western Sunni religious kingdom centered on Mecca and Medina. Afghanistan will break down into Pashtun and Farsi components. Iran and Turkey will be forced to give up their Kurdish territories. Israel will absorb the West Bank and Gaza and expel Palestinians to Jordan, which will come to be called a Palestinian state. Sunni Iraq will become the Hashemite Kingdom. Sudan will become the desert Arab republic in the north and oil-rich Christian in the south. Punjab and Sind in Pakistan will be absorbed into India. Baloch and Pathan areas of Pakistan will join their brethren in Afghanistan. India will further break down into several countries. Indonesia will similarly disintegrate into several states.

The wealth of all the new ministates will be administered by United Nations to be controlled by America and Europe. This is the plan of the *Yahudi-Salibi* think tanks funded by secret and faceless people and corporations. Several complete groups of *Yahudi* and *Salibi* planners have been embedded in the higher offices of the United States, Britain, Australia, and European governments. They have been carefully and successfully planted into the NATO headquarters, the United Nations, the World Bank, and the IMF. The best-known example of a complete takeover of the planning for the Iraq War is in the Pentagon, the National Security Council, and the Office of the Vice President of the United States by the agents of the Israeli government and its security apparatus. After several years of covert operation in Washington, this group has sufficient backing that it is emboldened to come out in the open.

The covert and the obvious planning of the *Yahudi-Salibi* conspirators is thorough and detailed. Their agents speak Arabic, Farsi, Turkish, and Urdu fluently. They have been carefully planted in the diplomatic corps, intelligence services, armed forces, NGOs, various aid groups, commercial enterprises, airlines, shipping, and tourism services. Their function is to gather intelligence and to recruit corrupt and willing agents in the Muslim states to enhance the goals of the conspirators. A believer aware of his history has to pause and consider the effort and treasure that goes into such planning. This planning is not only worldwide but also dates back to the year 1095 CE, when Pope Urban called on his followers to destroy Islam. The expenditure on war against Islam since the 9/11 plot spent in the name of homeland security, covert and military action in Muslim countries, and war in Afghanistan and Iraq has totaled over a trillion dollars. Such worldwide planning, coordination, and financing could not possibly occur without an office, a full-fledged headquarters with staff and a head. Somewhere in this wide world, perhaps in Europe, in a stately home with boulevards and well-manicured gardens, there are secret headquarters with a man in charge over the vast apparatus that controls the world's wealth and wants to manipulate it in perpetuity. He has constant contact with his minions, executing the policy set forth by the stakeholders, Zionism and Euro-Christianity, who meet in secrecy.

Efforts by the believers to achieve unity and prosperity continue to be defeated. The average Muslim just cannot understand why the *ummah*'s efforts never come to fruition. As already mentioned, covert plans to defeat the believers' efforts toward unity are constantly formulated, discussed, and implemented. An article on the subject written by Rowan Scarborough appeared in the *Washington Times* on February 20, 2006, that points to the intentions of the world's greatest military power. Though the article talks of a long war on terrorism, Osama bin Laden's religious ideology, and extremism, the underlying objective of the plan is to fight a long war against Islam. The covenant of Allah specifies each believer's obligation to the cause of Allah and to the unity of the believers. The Western Euro-Christian civilization, however, has yet to achieve the objectives of the one-thousand-year-old crusade called by Pope Urban in 1095 CE to destroy Islam.

The United States Joint Chiefs of Staff planners have produced a twenty-seven-page briefing on the war on terror that seeks to explain how to win the "long war" against the Muslims. The report states that, in this war, Islamic extremists may be supported by twelve million Muslims worldwide. Military planners worry that al-Qaeda could win if the "traditional allies prefer accommodation." The "traditional allies" reference is to the traditional traitors of Islam in Egypt, Saudi Arabia, UAE, Kuwait, Jordan, Oman, Qatar, and Pakistan. Al-Qaeda leader Osama bin Laden, the document states, "is absolutely committed to his cause. His religious ideology successfully attracts recruits. He has sufficient population base from which to protract the conflict. ... Even support of 1 percent of the

Muslim population would equate to over 12 million 'enemies.'" The unclassified production, titled "Fighting the Long War—Military Strategy for the War on Terrorism," is a component of the Pentagon's ongoing campaign to explain that a lengthy struggle requires patience from the American people and Congress.

It holds the 1930s as an example of how not to respond to extremism, noting Europe's appeasement of German dictator Adolf Hitler. "The consequences of inaction" in the 1930s are, the briefing says, "Lives lost: 300,000; 70 million worldwide. ... War expenditures: $3.1 trillion ... 38 percent of GDP per year. (The Pentagon today is spending 3.8 percent of US GDP.) US reconstruction expenditures: $90 billion over four years."

The briefing was prepared for Rear Adm. William D. Sullivan, vice director for strategic plans and policy within the Joint Staff, which is under Marine Corps general Peter Pace, Joint Chiefs of Staff chairman. Admiral Sullivan used it to deliver a lecture in January to a national security study group at Mississippi State University. "It is an effort, when asked, to explain why we are doing what we are doing from a military perspective to fight the long war," said US Air Force major Almarah Belk, spokeswoman for General Pace. The same core information is used in briefings by other speakers to explain this protracted planned war.

The Bush administration's effort to explain Iraq and the broader war includes more than briefings. Defense Secretary Donald H. Rumsfeld was in New York, talking to the Council on Foreign Relations, and General Pace addressed the National Press Club in the district. At the same time, President Bush was in Tampa, Florida, speaking on the war.

Bin Laden, the Joint Staff paper says, wants to "expand the Muslim empire to historical significance." And Iraq "has become the focus of the enemy's effort. If they win in Iraq, they have a base from which to expand their terror. ... Extremists now have an Emirate in Iraq that serves as a base of operations from which they can revive the Caliphate [Islamic rule]. ... Baghdad becomes the capital of the Caliphate. The revived Caliphate now turns its attention to the destruction of Israel."

Admiral Sullivan's briefing contains a map that shows the bin Laden–style caliphate conquering North and East Africa, the entire Middle East, and Central and South Asia. This dire scenario can only happen if the United States is defeated in Iraq and Afghanistan.

"The United States cannot be defeated militarily," the briefing says, "the enemy knows this. But consider ... terror attacks weaken the world economy. Continued casualties weaken national resolve. Traditional allies prefer accommodation." The enemy has "inherent weaknesses," including "no military capacity to expand their fight beyond terrorist tactics."

Although it is similar to the Cold War, the war on terror has a distinction. This twenty-seven-page briefing clearly states, "Marginalizing an ideology requires patience and promoting reform from within. We cannot discredit all of Islam as we did with communism."

The document says, "It is a divine religion. We can only discredit the violent extremist."[31] Clearly, any believer reading this briefing will understand that any reference to bin Laden, extremists, and terrorism really points to mainline Islam and the dangers posed to the *ummah*.

In this game, on one side of the chessboard are men with an attention span going back a thousand years to the Council of Clermont in 1095 CE, when Pope Urban declared a crusade to destroy

---

[31] Rowan Scarborough, "Military Plots a 'Long War' on Terror," *Washington Times*, February 20, 2006.

Islam. Their commitment and passion are fueled by a thousand years of pent-up hatred stored in Europe's political and ecumenical history. The ideologues are intellectuals with accumulated knowledge and information of Islamic history, the fault lines of the Muslim psyche. The players are in full control of the economics and the mercenary armed forces of the Muslim states. They are backed by wealth, intelligence services, and the absolute military power of the West. At their beck and call are all the major players in the world of Islam. These "Muslim" *Munafiqeen* have been bribed, bought, or intimidated into subservience and service. Most of them are the descendants of the first-generation *Munafiqeen* that helped the West dismember the Ottoman Empire and establish Western control of Iran, Afghanistan, and Muslim India.

On the other side of the chessboard are the Muslim and Arab rulers whose attention span is constricted to one day at a time, devoted to staying in power and holding on to their ill-gotten wealth. In some, the attention span flickers from one alcoholic binge to the next, while others like Ibn Sa'ud attended to matters of state and Islam during brief intervals between his activities in bed, servicing a whole host of wives, concubines, and slave girls. Kings, sheikhs, and presidents are virtually unaware of the demands of their *din* regarding their obligation to the *ummah*. Those in charge are oblivious to the dangers that lie ahead that will destroy their nations and their *din*. They are insensitive to the requirements of statecraft necessary to protect the world of Islam from plots against it. In most cases, Muslim rulers themselves are part of the conspiracy to destroy Islam. They form part of the circle of evil—the circle of the *Yahudi*, *Salibi*, and *Munafiq* coalition out to destroy Islam.

The uninformed politico-military generals are confident that their parade ground skills are adequate to run the business of state and the *din* all across the Islamic world through Indonesia, Bangladesh, Pakistan, Afghanistan, Iraq, Syria, Turkey, Egypt, Libya, Algeria, and a host of West African countries. This curse of Islam has played havoc with the world of believers. The generals puff around in their fancy bemedaled uniforms like peacocks trying to dazzle their subjects with their shiny buttons. Islam has lost in this war time and again during the last two hundred years and will continue to do so unless the Muslims begin to take heed of the covenant and learn from their history. Allah addresses the believers repeatedly to emphasize the importance of unity among them. Allah repeatedly admonishes them not to take pagans, Christians, and Jews as their *awliya* in place of believers.

7. Jihad

Life is a chain of emotions, intentions, and actions. Before each deed, the human stops to intend an action. Each intention is the product of an emotion that acts on the human's self, the *nafs*. The *nafs* may intend its actions on its animal instincts of craving and lust, or in situations where the human self is sufficiently refined with *taqwa* of Allah, the human will follow the path of Allah as commanded by the covenant. The human's self is in a continuous battle whether to follow its base cravings or to perform wholesome deeds. Such ongoing fluctuation of intent between the base and the honorable is stressful. Such stress leads to anxiety, anger, and depression, which in the end will cause an emotional breakdown. When the human intends his deeds with the knowledge that Allah is with him, that Allah is aware of his intent, and that Allah guides him to the right objective and action, there is peace and satisfaction. When the believer is in *taqwa* of Allah, His *nur* cleans his *nafs* and aids him to obey the covenant of Allah.

Jihad is the struggle that prepares the believer to follow and obey Allah's commandments without question. Jihad is the struggle of man from the path of ignorance to the path of Allah. The human hears Allah's call through the noise and the commotion of the world and, through the eye of his soul, lets the *nur* of Allah into the niche of his heart. Allah's call is obedience, goodness, and selflessness. The human bows down his head in humility on the earth in submission to his Lord. The Lord guides, and the believer follows. The believer has faith in Allah, and Allah holds his hand. Allah shows His believer the way to goodness, and the believer performs wholesome deeds. The *nur* of Allah glows in the believer's heart, and the believer accepts Allah in his heart.

This communion between the believer and Allah becomes exclusive. Submission establishes a link between the believer and Allah. Allah commands, and the believer follow. The believer asks, and Allah gives. The believer loves Allah, and Allah loves him in return. The believer asks for the straight path, and Allah shows him the way. The believer praises Allah, and Allah showers His mercy and grace on him. The believer remembers Allah, and Allah responds to those who praise Him.

The *nafs*, unlike the Freudian ego, is capable of both good and bad. The *nuqta* of the *nafs*, when magnified a million times, becomes visible as a shiny disk, a mirror. The inherent nature, the *fitra*, of the *nafs* is to shine like a mirror with Allah's *nur*. When the human walks the path of Allah in *taqwa* of Him with the knowledge that Allah is with him, watching him and guiding him, Allah's *nur* shines on the *nafs*, keeping it pure and safe. However, when the human's *desires*, *cravings*, and *ego* overpower his love and obedience for Allah, the shiny mirror of his *nafs* becomes obscured by the dirt and smoke of his desires, and he loses sight of the *nur* of Allah and trips into error and decadence.

The effort required to keep focused on Allah's *nur* and *taqwa* of Allah is the inner jihad. And this jihad is the obedience of Allah's commandments when He calls on His Believers with the words *O you who Believe* and commands them to do acts of faith and goodness in the seventy-five verses of the Koran. Obedience to every such command is jihad. The expression *in the path of Allah*, of course, is the path of right conduct that Allah has set down in the Koran. Jihad is simply the complement to *islam*, the surrender to the will of Allah. And it is Allah's will that people struggle with in His path. Hence, submission and surrender to Allah's will demands struggle in His path. Submission to Allah's command requires the believers to struggle against the negative tendencies in themselves and in society that draw them away from Allah's path. Salat, zakat, fasting, and hajj are all struggles in the path of Allah. The greatest obstacles that people face in submitting themselves to Allah are their desires and cravings for the temptations of this world.

Jihad is the struggle to observe the commandments of Allah in the covenant. The *taqwa* of Allah shines the *light of Allah*, His *nur*, into core of man, the self, that clears the smoke of evil and temptation from the *nafs*, allowing man to follow God. Once the believer has purified his self with Allah's *nur*, he has prepared himself for the outer jihad. When the believer has purified his own *nafs* and soul with submission to Allah (*islam*) and faith (*iman*) in the only reality, the Lord, and by performance of wholesome deeds in the name of Allah, he is ready for the outer struggle for his *din*.

The blessed *nabi* of Allah wrote the following covenant in the first year of hijra in Medina. This is the essential constitution for all the believers:

1. This is a covenant given by Muhammad to the believers.

2. They constitute one *ummah* to the exclusion of all other men.

3. The believers shall leave none of their members in destitution without giving him in kindness and liberty what he needs.

4. No believer shall slay a believer in retaliation for an unbeliever, nor shall he assist an unbeliever against a believer.

5. All believers shall rise as one against anyone who seeks to commit injustice, aggression, or crime or spread mutual enmity among the Muslims, even if such a person is their kin.

6. Just as the bond to Allah is indivisible, all the believers shall stand behind the least of them in commitment. All believers are bonded to one another to the exclusion of other men.

7. This Pax Islamica is one and indivisible. No believer shall enter a separate peace without all other believers whenever there is fighting in the cause of God except on the basis of equality and justice to all others. In every expedition for the cause of God we undertake, all parties to the covenant shall fight shoulder to shoulder as one man. All believers shall avenge the blood of one another when anyone falls fighting in the cause of God.

8. The pious believers follow the best and the most upright guidance. Whoever is convicted of killing a believer deliberatively but without righteous cause shall be liable to the relatives of the killed. Until the latter are satisfied, the killer shall be subject to retaliation by each and every believer.

Allah speaks to the believers thus about the struggle for jihad,

⋄ Fight in the cause of Allah those who fight you, but do not transgress limits; for Allah loves not transgressors.

⋄ And slay them wherever you catch them and turn them out from where they have turned you out; for *fitnah*, tumult and oppression are worse than slaughter; but fight them not at the Sacred Mosque, unless they fight you there first ; but if they fight you, slay them. Such is the reward of those who suppress faith.

⋄ But if they cease, Allah is Oft-Forgiving, Most Merciful.

⋄ And fight them on until there is no more *fitnah*, tumult, or oppression, and there prevail justice and faith in Allah; but if they cease, let there be no hostility except to those who practice oppression (Al-Baqarah. 2:190–93, Koran)

⋄ And why should you not fight in the cause of Allah, and for those men, women and children, who are weak, abused and oppressed, those who beseech their Lord to deliver them from their oppressors, and those who ask Allah to send for them protectors and helpers.

⋄ Those who believe, fight in the cause of Allah, and those who reject Faith fight in the cause of Evil: so, fight you against the friends of Satan: feeble indeed is the cunning of Satan. (An-Nisa 4:75–76, Koran)

⋄ And slacken not in following up the enemy; if ye are suffering hardships, they are suffering similar hardships; but you have hope from Allah, while they have none. And Allah is full of Knowledge and Wisdom. (An-Nisa 4:104, Koran)

If Allah helps you none can overcome you: if He forsakes you, who is there, after that, that can help you? In Allah, then, let Believers put their trust. (Ali 'Imran 3: 160, Koran)

We did indeed send, before you Messengers to their respective peoples, with Clear Signs: To those who transgressed, We meted out Retribution: and as a right those who earned from us, We helped those who believed. (Ar-Rum 30:47, Koran)

◇ Here is a declaration to the human, a guidance and advice to those who live in awareness, Taqwa, of Allah!

◇ So lose not hope nor shall you despair, for you shall achieve supremacy, if you are true in Faith.

◇ If you have suffered a setback, verily a setback has been there for the other party too. We make such days of adversity go around amongst the humans so that Allah may distinguish those who believe and choose His witnesses from amongst them. And Allah loves not the evil doers.

◇ Allah's objective is to distinguish the True Believers from those who reject Faith. (Ali 'Imran 3:138–41, Koran)

Wars and slaughter are abhorrent to Allah. Allah says, "If anyone slew a person, unless it is in retribution for murder or for spreading mischief, *fasaad*, in the land, it would be as if he slew the whole people. And if anyone saved a life, it would be as if he saved the life of the whole people. Take not life, which Allah has made sacred, except by the way of justice or law. This He commands you, that you may learn wisdom."

And then Allah declares to the believers that *fitnah*, treachery, and oppression are worse than slaughter. They are so vile and repugnant to Allah that He commands the believers to fight those who assail them and inflict oppression until there is no more *fitnah*, tumult, or oppression and until there prevails justice and faith in Allah. Allah's command to fight *fitnah*, however, is conditional. Allah commands that if the oppressors cease, let there be no further hostility except to those who practice oppression. Do not transgress limits. Allah does not love transgressors. When the believers fight against *fitnah* and oppression, they fight for the cause of Allah. Those who reject faith in Allah fight for the cause of evil.

If you suffer hardships, your enemy suffers the same. You have hope and trust in Allah, while the enemy has none. If Allah helps you, none can overcome you; if Allah forsakes you, who is there, then, to help you? Let the believers, then, put their trust in Allah.

Here is a proclamation from Allah to man who live in *taqwa* of Allah. It is a guidance and advice from Him.

> So, lose not hope nor shall you despair, for you shall achieve supremacy, if you are true in Faith.

In the struggle in the cause of Allah against *fitnah*, oppression, and treason, Allah advises the believers:

⬧ If you suffer a setback, verily a setback has been there for the other party too. We make such days of adversity go around amongst the humans so that Allah may set apart those who believe and choose His witnesses from amongst the Believers. Allah' makes a distinction between True Believers from those who reject Faith.

⬧ Fight the unbelievers who surround you. Let them find you firm, and know Allah is always with those who have *taqwa*, who are Allah-wary.

Make careful preparations and take precautions for the endeavor. Then go forth in groups or all together. Remember Allah's blessings on you. When a people planned to stretch their hands against you, Allah held back their hands to protect you from your enemies. Perform Jihad and strive your utmost in Allah's Cause, and approach Him so that you may prosper. "When you meet the infidels rank upon rank, in conflict never turn your backs to them. Respond to Allah and His Messenger when He calls you to that gives you life. And know that

Allah intervenes in the tussle between man and his heart, and it is to Allah that you shall return. Fear treachery or oppression that afflicts not only those who perpetrate it but affects guilty and innocent alike. Know that Allah is strict in punishment.

When you meet the enemy force, stand steadfast against them, and remember the name of Allah much, so that you may be successful. And obey Allah and His messenger, and do not dispute with one another lest you lose courage, and your strength departs and be patient. Allah is with those who patiently persevere.

Go forth, advance! Whether equipped well or lightly, perform jihad strive your utmost and struggle with your wealth and your persons in the cause of Allah. That is best for you, if you knew.

Remember the Grace of Allah, bestowed upon you, when there came down hordes to overpower you. We sent against them a hurricane and forces that that you did not see but Allah sees all that you do.

Behold! They came on you from above you and from below you, your eyes became dim, and the hearts gaped up to the throats, and you imagined various vain thoughts about Allah!

Be not weak and ask for peace, while you are having an upper hand: for Allah is with you and will never decrease the reward of your good deeds.

Allah loves those who fight in His cause in array of unison and solidarity.

8. *Fitnah*

In the twenty-first century, the weakness, poverty, disunity, and fragmentation of the *ummah* arise from its lack of appreciation of the immense store of understanding and knowledge that is in the Koran.

Muslims look at the word of Allah but do not see it. They listen to the word but do not hear it. Allah's *nur*, His light, is with them, but they do not let it enter their hearts. The mirror of their *nafs* is covered with the smoke of their greed and craving of worldly wealth. They cannot see Allah's *nur* through the smoky darkness in their heart. *Fitnah*, treachery, and oppression are by-products of darkened hearts, causing blindness to the *nur* of Allah. Without the *nur* of Allah, there cannot be *taqwa* of Allah; and in the absence of the consciousness of the reality of Allah, the darkened soul is open to the evil of Satan.

Fitnah: Muslim societies have been plagued by *fitnah* and oppression since the death of the blessed *nabi*. In Muslim countries, *fitnah* is the result of the combination of internal and external forces. Although the perpetrators of *fitnah* often proclaim Allah as their Savior, their actions always belie their faith in Him.

Internal *Fitnah*: Hundreds of years of rule of sultans and later of Western colonial masters produced three unique sources of internal *fitnah* that rules the roost in our day.

a. **The Fitnah of Priesthood.** There is no priesthood in Islam; the believer has a highly personal and exclusive relationship with Allah. Such relationship does not permit the intervention of another human being between Allah and His believer. When the blessed Muhammad was taken up by Allah, every believer inherited the Koran, Allah's covenant, and His *din*. Every believer became the successor, inheritor, and custodian of the prophet's legacy till the end of time.

The priests and clerics of Islam assumed the legacy of the pagan priesthood and began to speak on behalf of Allah. Through distortion and misrepresentation of the word of Allah and the pronouncements of His *nabi*, over the last fourteen hundred years, the priests and imams of Islam have created divisions and schisms in Islam to generate hundreds of self-righteous sects and subsects among Muslims. Each sect is the enemy of the other. Every group has the dagger in the back of the other. This gradually smoldering *fitnah* of the priesthood is slowly consuming the body of the *ummah*.

Islam is a relationship between Allah and His believers. The *din* of Allah is an all-encompassing and highly personal type of relationship in which Allah's *nur* resides in the believer's heart. The believer is conscious of Allah's closeness and mercy and obeys, trusts, and loves Allah. Allah in return loves those who love Him and perform beautiful deeds.

Allah has granted knowledge and wisdom of *furqan* and *taqwa* to the believers who have opened their hearts and minds to Him. Man has been granted the freedom of choice in doing what is wholesome and beautiful or what is corrupt and ugly. This knowledge reminds the human of the scales of Allah's justice; the two hands of Allah—His mercy and His wrath—are reflected in the human domain, where people have been appointed His vicegerents. Deeds of goodness and wholesomeness are associated with mercy, paradise, and what is beautiful. Evil and corruption is rewarded with wrath, hell, and what is ugly.

Everything in the universe is connected to Allah through its creation, birth, sustenance, existence, demise, and death. Every particle and atom spins at the command of Allah's majesty; it has done so for billions of years and will continue to do so at Allah's command. They continue to spin in the cells of the living when they are alive and when the cells are devoid of life at Allah's command. Nothing ever happens without Allah's will and knowledge. No human, howsoever proud or strong, is independent of Him. The newborn is thus physically connected to Allah through His mercy. The particles and atoms in his cells spin at Allah's mercy in life and in death. Through Allah's mercy, his cells grow and multiply with sustenance from Allah.

Every man and woman in this journey is born alone and innocent. The individual leads his short life in this world, and when he dies, he leaves this world alone. In death, his cells disintegrate, yet the particles and atoms continue to spin at Allah's command forever. His life was a miracle and a mirage. Now the human was here, and in an instant, he was gone and all alone. The only reality is Allah. Every substance and relationship the human accumulated is left behind—parents, friends, wealth, children, priests, kings, human laws, honors, comforts, and so on. They all accompanied the human to the edge of his life and then parted to wait for their own demise one day.

In this journey, the human is presented with Allah's covenant as his guide, *taqwa* of Allah as his shield against evil, and *furqan*, the criterion to distinguish between the right and evil, as Allah's compass to the straight path of righteousness. If the human accepts these, he becomes a believer and among the righteous. The way to righteousness is in Allah's guidance and in His covenant in the Koran. Righteousness lies in the inspiration from the Koran through its recitation at leisure, at dawn, during the day, and under the glow of the lamp at night. Every little bit of devotion makes the *nur* of Allah glow in the heart till the believer is connected to Him and begins to follow His path. In this path, the believer does what is righteous and what is beautiful. Beautiful actions please Allah.

This communion between the believer and Allah is exclusive. Submission establishes the link between the believer and Allah. The believer asks, and Allah gives. The believer loves Allah, and Allah loves him in return. The believer asks for the straight path, and Allah shows him the way. The believer praises Allah, and Allah showers His mercy and grace on him. The believer remembers Allah, and Allah responds to those who praise Him, thank Him, and ask Him.

The believer on his chosen journey on the path of Allah is well equipped. He has Allah's protection, guidance, and direction. Does the believer need dogmas and laws based on human systems? Aren't Allah's word and the covenant sufficient as guidance? Allah is the absolute truth (*haqq*). All worldly, human, and priestly systems are not based on *haqq*. Allah is the only *Haqq*. What is not *haqq* is *batil*, the untruth. Those who let go of Allah's hand and clutch at the human priestly dogma and creed have fallen astray in Satan's footsteps.

The most important theological point made by the Koran is that there is one God, Allah, universal and beyond comparison, who creates and sustains both the material world and the world of human experience. Allah is *Haqq*, the absolute truth. All other forms of so-called truth are either false in their initial premises or contingently true only in limited situations. The recognition of this fact is of paramount importance to all believers. That Allah is *Haqq* is undeniable. *Haqq* does not fall into the domain of human fancy nor human ideas, but it stands for beliefs that manifest in concrete form. These beliefs must be in harmony with changing needs of time and with Allah's laws of the universe. No belief relating to this world can be called *haqq* unless its truth is established by positive demonstration of Allah's reality. This truth is permanent and unchanging.

There is no priesthood in Islam. *Haqq* does not need priests. Yet there are people among the believers who talk, dress, and preach like priests. They are indeed priests. They preach dogma and creed to the believers in the name of Allah and His blessed prophet. Yet what they preach distances the believers from Allah, the Koran, and the blessed prophet. The priests spread hatred among the believers and discord in the *ummah*. They concern themselves with obscure *Hadith* and man-made Sharia and *fiqh* that do not constitute the *din* of Allah. Their teachings and fatwas often contradict the Koran and the spirit of the blessed prophet's teaching.

If miraculously one day all the mullahs, self-proclaimed ulema, ayatollahs, imams, and Wahhabi preachers were to disappear from the face of this earth, from that day on, there will be no Shia, no Sunni, nor any other sect in the world. Every Muslim will be a believer of Allah. These preachers sustain one another through their own inbred dogma and creed. In turn, the mullahs and priests sustain their sects through their man-made belief systems. It is a cycle in which the priests continue to perpetuate their creeds generation after generation with "quote and reference" to their earlier imams and priests, repeating distortions, misquotations, and misrepresentations. The believers cannot hear the gentle message of Allah over all the noise and commotion created by the mullahs and religious scholars in the world of Islam. In the same token, if there were no rabbis, Christian priests, ministers, clerics, preachers, pastors, bishops, popes, pundits, and mullahs, there will be no Judaism, Christianity, Hinduism, nor sectarian Islam. All those who believe in one God will then be the servants of the same Allah, the religion of Abraham, Moses, Jesus, and Muhammad.

Yet priests have been with us since the times when man attained civilization. The priesthood of the Sumerian civilization left a powerful legacy on the generations that followed. Within a short time, the priestly culture spread to all human civilizations—to the Indus valley, Babylon, Egypt, Greece, and Rome. Priesthood independently sprung up in the Americas.

Humans crave a belief in the supernatural. They seek comfort and security in the idea of supernatural protection from gods. Priesthood is ever present and ready to exploit this need. Sumerians and all other civilizations were served by many gods—gods of war, fertility goddesses, sun god, moon god, gods of rain, gods of death, and so on. Priests were at hand to provide the protection at a cost, an offering to gods. The cult of gods did not operate in isolation. Though communities had their own particular guardian gods, they did share other gods with other towns and villages. Devotees traveled to distant places to pay homage to their gods. There was considerable exchange and sharing of patronage, protection, and blessing of gods among varying communities. Priesthood became the original corporations and propaganda machine for their gods.

Such publicity also took advantage of the weaknesses and vulnerabilities of the people. The greater the insecurity among the population, the more the devotees of particular gods were, the greater the wealth and influence of the priests. There were festivals of all sorts involving seasons—planting of seed, harvest, fertility, human sacrifice, fire, light, and many others. The priests began to control commerce, levy tithe, lend money on interest, organize professional armies, and provide temple prostitutes, alcohol, and protection against calamities. What mattered in the end was power and wealth. Priesthood became a network of guilds connected through secret societies that began to control the affairs of the world for all times to come.

Thirty-eight hundred years ago, the blessed *nabi* Ibrahim saw through the deceit and falsehood of the cult of false gods of Mesopotamia. He began to speak out. Being a danger to the cult of the priests, he was threatened to be silent or else. Thirty-two hundred years ago, when the blessed *nabi* Moses spoke against the same false gods, the priesthood persistently undermined and frustrated his efforts by worshipping the golden calf. Two thousand years ago, Jesus found the cult of the rabbis thoroughly objectionable. When he persisted in speaking against godlessness and corruption of the temple, the priests, and the moneylenders, he was nailed to the cross. Fourteen hundred years ago, when Muhammad rebelled against the gods and priesthood of the Quraish, he was threatened with death and banished from his home. It was the same organism of priesthood developed by the Sumerians whose descendants fought tooth and nail to protect their conspiratorial privileges, threatened by Ibrahim, Moses, Jesus, and Muhammad.

Priesthood created a cult of gods, spoke for their gods, and then assumed the power and wealth of the same gods. The corporation of gods run by priests in the days of *Nabi* Ibrahim is the longest-living organism, with its neurons and synapses running through the worshippers of the golden calf and then the Pharisees down to our times—the descendants of the priesthood of the Quraish, the enemies of the blessed *nabi* Muhammad. They appointed and directed kings. The ruling classes and the priest class successfully formed the system that controlled every Muslim's religion and exploited all Islamic societies. Priesthood offered protection, vice, alcohol, gambling, and women to attract adherents to their gods. Priests directed trade and commerce and were the beneficiaries of usury. Priests foretold fortune and future, and for this supernatural prophecy, they gained the influence and gratitude of their followers.

The organism of priesthood has kept up with the times. It never let its tricks of the trade get stale. The religions required periodic stimulation from wars, miracles, festivals, human sacrifice, and coronations. Whenever the true prophets won over adherents from the priesthood of gods, the counteroffensive was never far behind.

Abraham reformed the Sumerian traditions in the name of the one true merciful God. He left behind many followers with oral and perhaps written traditions, which were passed on to the coming generations. The priesthood distorted his teachings. After eight lifetimes of seventy years, put end to end, *Nabi* Moses taught his people the worship of one merciful God. Moses reformed the pagan Egyptian traditions of his people. He spoke with God on Mount Sinai through the smoke and haze of the burning bush and climbed down to the desert carrying the Ten Commandments of God inscribed on two stone slabs. After a lifetime of struggle with his people and their traditional priesthood, he left an oral and written tradition. His people continued to revert to the pagan calf worship and pervert Allah's commandments.

When disputes arose questioning the divinity of Jesus Christ, it was a difference of opinion among the priests of the fourth century. The priests assumed the prerogative of God and formulated a doctrine that defined the relationship between humanity and God. This relationship was to become so convoluted that no two Christians have the same understanding of their relationship to their Maker. The trinity of God has an incongruent understanding for each person and each sect. For the human of common understanding, Jesus is God. Jesus, in fact, became God on May 20, 325. On that day, Jesus became the Creator, the Word, the Judge, the Redeemer, and the only Way. In return, the priest class retained and augmented the special hierarchical status as it was among the Sumerians, Babylonians, Egyptians, Israelites, and Byzantines as the spokespeople of their God and gods. They retained the power to guide, legislate, teach, judge, excommunicate, and execute. The priests wore crowns, regalia, and jewels; they carried ornamental staffs to signify divine connection. Their processions into the places of worship in full regalia with pomp and circumstance resembled more a spectacle and entertainment for the common folk than a true act of worship of the Creator. The priests spoke in strange tongues and words incomprehensible to men and women.

Three hundred years after the blessed *nabi* Muhammad died, movements similar to ones that occurred after the times of the blessed prophets Ibrahim, Musa, and Jesus came to pass in Islam. Three months before the blessed *nabi* died, he performed the hajj. After midday prayers on the ninth day of *Zul-hajj* (March 632 CE) at Arafat, the blessed *nabi* delivered the historic hajj khutbah that had come to be known as the farewell address. When the blessed *nabi* delivered the hajj khutbah, he knew that he had completed his earthly mission and that his days in the world were numbered. The blessed Muhammad was aware that he was dying, yet he did not appoint a successor. He was a *nabi* and a *rasul*.

Only Allah has the prerogative of appointing and sending His messengers to this world. When Blessed Muhammad died, he left in this world his mortal remains, the Koran, Allah's covenant, and the *din*. When Blessed Muhammad was taken up by Allah, every believer inherited the Koran, Allah's covenant, and His *din*. Every believer became the successor, inheritor, and custodian of the prophet's legacy till the end of time. It was the negligence and the inability of the believer to assume his authority as the custodian of the prophet's legacy and Allah's covenant that degraded the *ummah* for over fourteen centuries.

After the *nabi* passed away, the succession to the blessed *nabi* Muhammad's *presumed* temporal authority became a problem from the very beginning. The period of the first four caliphs is regarded by the Muslims as the ideal period of Islamic history, when Islam was practiced perfectly. This is far from obvious when one looks at the contemporary records. For one thing, three of the four caliphs were assassinated.

What is the source of the continuing strife among the Muslims? Pagan priesthood?

Mecca in the pre-Islamic times was a pagan sanctuary with a cube-shaped shrine as the center of heathen worship. Kaaba housed over 360 gods, with the presiding god called Hubal. According to legend, in the fourth century of the Common Era, Amr ibn Luhayy, a descendant of Qahtan, a sheikh of Hejaz, placed an idol called Hubal inside the Kaaba after the Quraish group of tribes supplanted the Khuza'ah as the protectors of the holy ancient place. Luhayy had traveled to Hit in Mesopotamia and brought back with him the cult of the goddesses al-Uzza and Manat and combined it with the cult of Hubal, the god of the Khuza'ah. Hubal is considered to be of Aramaic origin, and its name is a variation of Baal, the Sumerian god (hu' Baal). Hubal was one of the deities of the Quraish before Islam. Some of the deities of Kaaba had a universal following in the fourth century CE when Christianity had not yet gained a popular following in the Middle East. Al-Uzza was Venus of the Greeks, Aphrodite of the Romans, and Isis of the Egyptians. *Al-Lat* was the Athena of the Greeks and *Manat* of the Arabs and represented the goddess of fate for the Persians and the Romans. Hubal was the Semitic Baal, Adonis of the Syrian and Greek Pantheon, and Tammuz, the consort of Ishtar, of the Babylonians. And a six-day "funeral" for this god was observed at the very door of the temple in Jerusalem, to the horror of the reformer Ezekiel. Temples for the worship of Baal, Adonis, Tammuz, Venus, Athena, Uzza, Aphrodite, and Isis were commonplace in the Byzantine and Roman Empires. These gods formed the pantheon of the known world before the advent of Islam.

Arab tribes from all over Arabia assembled once a year for mass worship of their gods. The occasion was also used by the visiting tribes for trade of goods and as a social gathering. The traders and their caravans plied between Arabia and destinations in the Byzantine and Persian Empires as well as Yemen. Over thousands of years, Arab traders had acquired the paramount position of intermediaries in the exchange of goods between the Indian and Mediterranean traders. The trade, maritime, and the pilgrim connection provided Meccans and the Arab tribes freedom, prosperity, affluence, and luxury that were not within the reach of people of other settled communities of the Middle East. The Meccans loved their luxury, wine, and revelry that wealth brought with it. To satisfy their passionate search for pleasure, they held their celebrations and drinking parties to find satisfaction in their slave girls in the center of the city right in front of the Kaaba. There in the proximity of more than 360 images of gods belonging to over 300 Arabian tribes, the sacred elders, and the priests of the Quraish and their aristocracy held their salons and shared stories, wine, and pleasures of the flesh.

Pagan worship at the Kaaba gave rise to a number of offices assumed by the king or the head priest of Mecca. These offices were *hijabah, siqayah, rifadah, nadwah, liwa,* and *qiyadah.*

- *Hijabah:* bequeathal of maintenance of the house and guardianship over its keys.
- *Siqayah:* provision of fresh water and wine to the pilgrims.
- *Rifadah:* provision of food to the pilgrims.
- *Nadwah:* Chairmanship of all religious meetings and their arrangements.
- *Liwa:* One who carried the flag.
- *Qiyadah:* Commander and head of the army defending Mecca and its pilgrims.

These offices claimed a tithe and levy on each pilgrim, trader, and inhabitant of Mecca, which made the Quraish priesthood extraordinarily rich. Qusayy ibn Kilab, a man who had been brought up in Syria in around 480 CE, dispossessed the reigning tribe of Mecca, the Khuza'ah, with the help of the Quraish and assumed all the offices associated with the Kaaba. Thereafter, his clan became the richest and the most influential family in Arabia.

Where there is wealth, there is greed and craving. The descendants of Qusayy fell on one another to gain control over the guardianship, priesthood, and wealth earned by the gods of Kaaba. To avoid civil war and disintegration of the Quraish tribe, a peace treaty was worked out, and the offices of Kaaba were divided between the two contesting clans. The descendants of Abd Manaf (Hashim) were granted the *siqayah* and *rifadah*, and the descendants of Abd al-Dar (Abd Shams) kept the *hijabah*, the *liwa*, and the *nadwah*. This peace lasted till the advent of Islam. Hashim's descendants continued to provision water, wine, and food for the pilgrims. Abd Shams's descendants continued to administer the upkeep of the Kaaba and its defenses.

Most historians and Muslims do not recognize the pagan priesthood of the Quraish with Islam's later civil wars and its wars for acquisition. After the blessed *nabi* died, there was an immediate though subdued struggle to revive the priestly power that had been destroyed by the fall of Mecca and the destruction of its gods. Though the powers that be could not revive the gods of the Kaaba, they could, however, take over Islam and bide their time till an opportune moment. With the rise of Islam and the conquest of Syria and Egypt, the choicest jobs of the new empire were given to the Quraish and to other Meccans. Whereas the descendants of Hashim—the providers of water, food, and wine to the pilgrims—stayed back in Mecca and Medina, the descendants of Abid Shams, the standard bearers of the army, were sent to the conquered territories. Among them was

Mu'awiyah, the son of Abu Sufyan, the sworn enemy of Islam and the prophet. Both the son and the father were pagans till the last moment, till they could be pagans no more.

When Uthman ibn Affan was elected the third caliph, he filled the bureaucracy of the new empire with his kin, who were the descendants of Abid Shams. The corruption in the governance of Syria and the accumulation of wealth in the hands of Mu'awiyah and his kin incensed some soldiers to kill the caliph Uthman. The grabbing of power and wealth by one branch of the priestly family of the Quraish led to the murder of the caliph and a civil war between the next caliph, Ali ibn Abi Talib, and his stepmother-in-law, Lady Aishah, the blessed *nabi*'s widow. Ali ibn Abi Talib, *nabi* Muhammad's cousin and son-in-law (Hashmi), was elected caliph; but Mu'awiyah, son of Abu Sufyan of the clan of Abd Shams (Shamsi) who happened to be the governor of Syria at the time, refused to recognize him as the caliph. Five years of civil war resulted between Mu'awiyah, based in Damascus, and Ali ibn Abi Talib of Beni Hashim, based in Kufah.

This was a civil war among the descendants of Qusayy, who had earlier avoided a civil war and disintegration of the tribe of Quraish by dividing the spoils of their priestly inheritance. The gods of Mecca, who had provided power and wealth to the descendants of Qusayy, had been destroyed. This time, the war was fought for the control of wealth and power that the Islamic empire had garnered. Fighting among Muslims, bloodshed, and killing of Muslims are strictly forbidden. This was a civil war among the Quraish and also among the prophet's immediate family. They had been used to bloodshed in their priestly days. Historians tell us about the battles, but we do not know of the conspiracies and family intrigues among the Quraish that undermined the new Islam's order. What actually followed was totally against the teachings of Allah, the Koran, and the teachings of the blessed *nabi*. However, what did occur was a norm among the Quraish—a fight for the control and perpetuation of power of the priesthood.

In 661, Ali was assassinated, and Mu'awiyah assumed the caliphate by force of arms and established the Umayyad dynasty that ruled the Muslim world for ninety years, from 661 to 750. This was a victory of the dynasty of Abu Shams over the dynasty of Hashim. This war and the struggle had nothing to do with the blessed *rasul* of Allah, the Koran, nor the *din* of Islam. In 750 CE, there was another civil war among the Quraish; the descendants of Abbas, the *Nabi's* uncle, of the Hashim clan rose in revolt and overthrew the Umayyad— the descendants of Abu Sufyan of the Abu Shams clan—with much bloodshed and killing of Muslims by Muslims. The Hashemite slaughtered every Umayyad they could find. Thereafter, the Abbasid dynasty ruled the Muslim empire until 861. Abandoning Damascus, the Umayyad capital, the Abbasids built Baghdad as their capital.

After the succession to the presumed *temporal* authority of the blessed *nabi* had been usurped by different priestly branches of the Quraish, a descendent of Abbas began to coerce clerics and judges to present him the authority to change the Koran. When Al-Ma'mun came to the throne, difficulties to his rule were increasing. To deal with these, Al-Ma'mun set up the so-called inquisition (*mihnah*). The judges and people in authority had to state publicly that they believed that the Koran was created and rejected the view that it was an uncreated word of Allah. This was not a piece of theological hairsplitting but an important sociopolitical and legal question.

Soon after *Nabi* Muhammad's death, some people had the belief that the caliph was or should be a divinely inspired person whose decisions should be binding on Muslims. In other words, they wanted the caliph to carry a priestly authority both in temporal and spiritual matters, and this was also the viewpoint of the caliph Al-Ma'mun. If the Koran, though it was Allah's word, was created, then a leader inspired by Allah could presumably change it.

The opposite point of view was that of scholar-jurists, who had become an important class in Islamic lands. This, in effect, was a battle for the control of Islam between the descendants of the priesthood of the Quraish, Qusay's descendants, and the newly formed priest class from among the people. Quite a large population of the empire could not speak or read Arabic and required the services of ulema to understand the complex issues in the Koran. The scholars insisted that the Koran was the uncreated word of Allah and therefore unchangeable and that they alone were its authorized interpreters, and only they could pronounce how it was to be applied to contemporary situations. That implied that it was they and not the caliph who had the final word. In fact, the descendants of the priesthood of Hashim and Shams or the newfangled ulema had neither the wisdom nor the authority to change or interpret the Koran. Allah addresses the Koran to the *nabi* and to those who believe. After the *nabi* died, every believer inherited the Koran. When Allah speaks to those who believe, will He not inspire those whom He addresses with the understanding of His message?

The policy of inquisition was finally discontinued in around 850 CE because the people refused to accept the caliph's demands. It was a power struggle for the right to use the scriptures for the control of the religion as it had occurred among the pagans, the Israelites, the Jews, and the Christians.

Lady Fatimah and Ali ibn Abi Talib's descendants are held in high esteem by Muslims because they descended from the blessed prophet. Ali ibn Abi Talib, his sons Hassan and Hussein, and their descendants also deserve veneration and honor by every believer because of their beautiful character and honorable conduct. Over the last fourteen hundred years, the lines of descent and pedigree have been dimmed by time, diluted with outside genes, polygamy, concubinage, and false claims of prophetic blood. The blessed nabi said in his farewell address, "None is higher than the other unless he is higher in virtue."

In matters of *din*, every believer received the prophet's heritage, the Koran, and the *din*. Every believer receives Allah in his heart according to his virtue. The battles for the succession of the blessed *nabi* were the legacy of the pagan and priestly Quraish for the control of the center of the new faith and the Kaaba. These past struggles of the Quraish are irrelevant in today's world. Total Koran is the total *din*. Men and priests do not intervene in the believer's relationship with Allah. The division of Islam into the Sunni and Shia sects was the result of infighting among the descendants of Qusayy for the control of Islam. This battle has continued to this day, with the priest class battling to control the pulpit and the throne of the Islamic state. Over the centuries, priests have raised the flag of *fitnah* with a claim to be God, a prophet, the Mahdi, an imam of the *din*, and a spokesperson of Allah. Their claims were for supremacy over the believers. True Muslims are believers of Allah. Believers of Allah and His *din* are not Shia, Sunni, nor any other sect, which are inventions and innovations of priests of the pagans, Sumerians, Israelites, and Christians.

b. **The *Fitnah* of the State and Mercenary Armies of Islam.** The blessed *nabi* said, "All believers shall rise as one man against anyone who seeks to commit injustice, aggression, crime, or spread mutual enmity amongst the Muslims. All believers are bonded one to another to the exclusion of other men. The believers shall leave none of their members in destitution without giving him in kindness that he needs by the way of his liberty."

However, this fight for unity, equality, and justice did not occur in the lands of Islam; the army of God and of Islam did not arise to fight in the cause of Allah to defend against *fitnah*, tyranny, and oppression and to seek retribution against injustice. The absolute loyalty of the army of Islam is to God, the Koran, and the *ummah*. The army of Islam defends the believers, their faith, their land, their wealth, and their honor and fights only against *fitnah* for truth and justice. In case of injury to the believers, their faith, their land, their wealth, and their honor, the believers are obliged to exact retribution. No believer shall side with an unbeliever against a believer. Whosoever is convicted of killing a believer without a righteous cause shall be liable to the relatives of the killed. The killers shall be subject to retaliation by each believer until the relatives of the victim are satisfied with the retribution.

Had the Muslim communities stood united as one to avenge the blood of every fallen Muslim and rejected a separate peace with the pagans without all the Muslims participating in it, there would have been no *fitnah* and massacres in Algeria, Palestine, India, Afghanistan, Iraq, Bosnia, Chechnya, Kosovo, and Darfur. This unity demands revenge, retribution, and reprisal for every act of murder and injury in Dayr Yasin, Sabra, Shatila, Srebrenica, Janin, Sarajevo, Fallujah, Kosovo, Chechnya, Gujarat, Kashmir, Iraq, Guantanamo Bay, and Abu Ghraib. Had the Muslims stood up for one another and fought those who perpetrated the *fitnah*, they would not have been groveling in the dustheap of humanity today.

Contrary to the stipulations of the covenant of Allah, the present six-million-man mercenary armies of Muslim states serve to bolster illegal regimes of *Munafiqeen*, the traitors to the cause of Islam. Instead of relieving the believers from *fitnah* and oppression, they cause them.

They are the source of dichotomy and division in Islam; they are the defenders of the foreign hegemony over Islam. The armies of the sultans of previous centuries and the rulers of modern times are the perpetrators of *fitnah*, and they are the enemies of Islam. They are the defenders of the borders created by the Western colonial powers that divide Islam today. They are the *fitnah*.

The covenants of Muhammad and of Allah have established clear conditions when the believers will rise in arms and go to battle. The following conditions are summarized in the covenant of Muhammad, written in the first year after hijra:

- **Defense of the unity of all believers**: All believers shall rise as one against anyone who seeks to commit injustice, aggression, or crime or spread mutual enmity among the Muslims. All believers are bonded to one another to the exclusion of other men. The believers shall leave none of their members in destitution without giving him in kindness and liberty what he needs.

- **Retribution against injustice**: All believers shall avenge the blood of one another when anyone falls fighting in the cause of God. Whoever is convicted of killing a believer deliberatively but without righteous cause shall be liable to the relatives of the killed. Until the latter are satisfied, the killer shall be subject to retaliation by each believer.

- **This Pax Islamica is one and indivisible**: No believer shall enter a separate peace without all other believers whenever there is fighting in the cause of God except on the basis of equality and justice to all others.

The loyalty of the army of Islam is not to any individual, state, government, or party. It is to the precepts of the covenant of Allah and the Koran. This army is an organism ordained by Allah with the stipulations for its conduct laid down by His covenant summarized below:

> Allah has forbidden taking of life. "Take not life, which Allah has made sacred, except by the way of justice or law." *Fitnah*, treason and oppression are so vile and repugnant that Allah commands the Believers to fight those who assail them and inflict oppression. And fight them until there is no more *fitnah*, tumult or oppression, and there prevails justice and faith in Allah.

> Go forth, advance! Whether equipped well or lightly, perform jihad strive your utmost and struggle with your wealth and your persons in the cause of Allah. Allah loves those who fight in His cause in array of unison and solidarity. *Fitnah*, treachery, and oppression afflict not only that who perpetrate it but affects everyone guilty and innocent alike. Allah's command to fight *fitnah* is conditional, that if the oppressors cease, let there be no further hostility except to those who practice oppression. Do not transgress limits. Allah does not love transgressors. (Composite)

Contrary to the stipulations of the covenant of Allah, the present six-million-man mercenary Muslim armies serve to bolster illegal regimes of traitors to the cause of Islam. Instead of relieving the believers from *fitnah* and oppression, they cause them. They are the source of dichotomy and division in Islam; they are the defenders of the borders dividing the Islamic state. During the twentieth century, they have not successfully defended any Muslim people or a state. The Muslim armies and intelligence services in the twentieth century have detained, tortured, and killed more believers than their professed enemies did. State mercenary armies are a state within the Muslim state with loyalties to dubious and murky causes harmful to Islam.

What is the reason for the existence of Muslim mercenary armies? They bolster the corrupt and dishonest rulers and their governments against the wishes of their people. The Muslim rulers keep the Muslim world divided in the interests of the perpetrators of the *external fitnah*, the Western powers. In return for their services to their interests, the United States and other Western powers pay seven billion dollars annually to the mercenary armies of Egypt, Pakistan, Jordan, Oman, Morocco, Afghanistan, and Uzbekistan. Their officer class receives additional benefits under the table to look after the Western interests in their countries and in the Middle East. The Western civilization is clearly against the unity of Islam. The state mercenary armies of the Muslim countries are a curse to Islam and the source of the *internal fitnah*. Does the sight of companies of ill-clad, demoralized, poorly trained, and poorly equipped soldiers at the checkpoints in the streets of Syria, Jordan, Egypt, and Pakistan present a picture of an army protecting Islam from its enemy? The picture is that of *fitnah* and oppression of Muslims by the regimes of these countries. They prevent free movement of the citizens in their legitimate quest for freedom and work. The mercenary armies of Islam are the armies of occupation of the land of Islam.

The largest army on the earth:

Imagine a country with the largest land base, with coasts rimmed by thousands of miles of blue water oceans, and with a vast number of rivers flowing from hundreds of snowcapped mountains through its deserts, grasslands, fertile valleys, and plains into rich deltas, lakes, and oceans bursting with marine life and other resources—a land blessed by Allah with resources never equaled in history, peopled with devout and hardworking populations with the knowledge of how to utilize such resources in the service of Allah and His creatures. Again, see in your mind's eye an army, the largest in history of mankind, keeping this land, its borders and resources, its oceans and skies, and its people and wealth secure from marauders who have traditionally raided other lands for their resources.

These defense forces comprise an army of six million men in about 300 infantry and mechanized divisions equipped with 30,000 tanks and armored vehicles, an air force of 3,580 aircraft of varying models, and a naval force equipped with 230 coastal and oceangoing ships equipped with armaments bought from the West and Russia. There are also 60 submarines in the armada. These armed forces are also equipped with short- and medium-range missiles tipped with about 100 nuclear bombs. The country has a budding arms-manufacturing industry producing low- and medium-technology weapons. The annual budget of the combined forces is one hundred billion dollars, of which thirty billion dollars annually go to Western countries to purchase their discarded, obsolete weaponry. The West then uses these funds to refurbish its own arsenal with the latest high-tech weapons.

You might have guessed that we are talking about the combined might of the Islamic world at the beginning of the twenty-first century. This army has never won any battle of significance since the war for the Gallipoli Peninsula about a century ago. These armed forces have not defended in any significant manner the Islamic world since the disintegration of the Ottoman Empire. The wars of independence of Islamic lands from the colonial rule in India, Iran, Iraq, Syria, Egypt, Morocco, and Algeria were fought by the masses with civil disobedience and jihadi guerrilla warfare. The largest army in the world, the state-organized mercenary army of Islam, has failed to safeguard people from *fitnah* and oppression in Palestine, Iraq, Lebanon, Kashmir, Sinkiang, Iraq, Kosovo, Bosnia, Mindanao, Chechnya, and the other Muslim peoples of Russia.

The Muslim armies and security services are the source of *fitnah* oppression and treachery to the *momineen*, resisting the tyranny of the circle of evil of the *Munafiqeen* and the *Mutaffifeen*. What went wrong? The Muslim army of the twentieth and twenty-first centuries has its guns pointed toward its own people, whereas the external borders of Islam are guarded and patrolled by the naval fleets of America and United Europe. The Muslim state armies should be fighting the *fitnah*, treachery, and oppression by enemies of Allah and Islam—the *kafirun*, *mushrikun*, *Munafiqeen*, and *zalimun*, who have usurped and plundered resources of the believers for the last two hundred years. Instead, the Muslim armies and security services are themselves the source of fitnah, oppression, and treachery to the *muttaqeen*. Clear examples are the armed and security forces of Reza Shah Pahlavi of Iran, the mullahs of Iran, Saddam Hussein of Iraq, the Taliban of Afghanistan, the military dictators of Pakistan, the Saudi family of Arabia, Suharto of Indonesia, the Assad's of Syria, Anwar Sadat, and Hosni Mubarak and al-Sisi of Egypt, Gadhafi of Libya, the military tyrants of Algeria, and the corrupt royalty of Morocco. This is a clear testimony that the believers of the covenant of Allah and those who control the mercenary armies of Islam have not surrendered to the will of Allah and do not strive in His path. In fact, the armies of the Muslim states are the perpetrators of tyranny and *fitnah*.

c. **The *Fitnah* of the Rulers of Islam.** Islam is a religion of voluntary submission of a human to the will of Allah after a considered conviction that Allah is the only reality and that everything else springs out of that reality. Allah has given every human the freedom of choice whether to submit to His will. There is no compulsion in the matters of the *din*. And yet there are humans who, by force of arms, compel others to submit to their will. They demand obedience through imprisonment, torture, and murder. Every Muslim state in this day is a police state. Every Muslim ruler abuses his authority to plunder and debase the lands of Islam.

The Muslim states are governed by self-appointed kings, dictators, and politicians who are divorced from their *din* and their people, the believers. They belong to and serve the interests of the circle of evil. There is a clear reason for the glaring weakness of the state-run armies of the Muslim nation-states. They are governed by kings, dictators, and politicians whose only interest is the continuation of their power over their people.

d. **The External *Fitnah* and the Circle of Evil.** The circle of evil two hundred years ago began its control of the world's wealth through conspiracy, subterfuge, and secrecy by undermining the stability of countries through war, strife, and discord and by weakening governments through creation of confusion in financial markets. The Western armies and intelligence services are the foot soldiers of the circle of evil, and the rulers of both the East and the West are their pawns and puppets to be manipulated at will for the purpose of gaining control of the world's power and wealth. The circle of evil is the *external fitnah* whose intent is to destroy Islam. Its intent has always been to corrupt, divide, and control the wealth of the Islamic land through the manipulation of its rulers who were initially placed in positions of power by the circle with the help of the Western armies, intelligence, and diplomacy. The weakness of the mercenary armies of the modern Islamic states clearly arises from the nonfulfillment of Allah's injunctions in the covenant. Faith in Allah's promise and His power, unity of the *ummah*, justice, and struggle to end *fitnah* and tyranny are essential actions ordained in the covenant. When an individual believer reneges in the fulfillment of his covenant with Allah, he only does it to the detriment to his own soul. However, such an action on the part of the community and its appointed leaders leads to the undermining, enslavement, and impoverishment of the whole Islamic community for many generations.

The foundation of the regimes of the imperial families of the Arabian Peninsula, Jordan, Brunei, and Morocco and the imperial governments of Hosni Mubarak of Egypt and the generals of Pakistan are supported by the *external fitnah*—the British, the US, and NATO armed forces, intelligence, and diplomatic services in opposition to the aspirations of their own people. In return, these regimes provide services to the circle of evil to subvert, undermine, and weaken the neighboring Islamic and Arab countries of Iran, Afghanistan, Iraq, Syria, Libya, Algeria, Sudan, and Mauritania.

9. A just and moral society

The *ummah* is saddled with the curse and the internal *fitnah* of the priesthood, mercenary armies, and corrupt rulers and the *external fitnah* of the circle of evil. Yet the answer to the problem is simple. Let every believer take control of his home and his *din*. And let every community of the *ummah* take charge of its affairs and return to the governance on the basis of tawhid, truth, justice, and equality for all.

The precepts of the covenant of Allah ensure human dignity, equality, justice, consultative government, a state where there is realization of lawful benefits to the people, prevention of harm, removal of hardship, and education of individuals by inculcating in them self-discipline, patience, restraint, and respect for the rights of other humans. It is a system under which there is restitution of all wrongs and imbalances in society.

The Islamic society, as envisioned in the Koran and the Sunna, is a just and moral society—a society in which every individual—man and woman, from the highest to the lowest, from the first to the last—has equal, unimpeded, and unquestionable right and freedom to practice his faith in accordance with his beliefs as, in Islam, there is no compulsion in matters of religion; right to life, which includes mental and physical and emotional well-being; right to safeguard one's property; right to intellectual endeavors, acquisition of knowledge, and education; right to make a living; and right to free speech and action to enjoin good and forbid evil. In enjoying his freedoms, the individual ensures that his activities do not impinge on the similar rights of others. All of the above cannot occur till the *four curses of humanity* are eradicated from the governance of Islamic lands and the *din:* the cult of wealth and acquisition, the priest class, the mercenary military class, and the self-appointed rulers of Islam.

10. Knowledge and nur of Allah

The jihad to end the *fitnah* lies in seeking the knowledge of Allah. Knowledge is given to humans through their openness to Allah. Humans accept the concept of God as the Creator of everything that is. He wills, and it is. He is beyond human comprehension, and His divine systems do not conform to the human concepts, creed, and dogma. Allah, God the Creator, created the galaxies, worlds, stars, sun, moon, little atoms, protons, neutrons, and tiny particles that show the complexity of His genius.

Allah the Divine is open to the most miniscule of beings. From the vastest of the expanse to the minutest of the particle, there is a connection with Allah the Cherisher and the Nourisher of the universe. Within this communion of the divine with the creation passes the Spirit of Allah into His creatures. The human lays his heart and mind open to Allah in submission to receive His Spirit and guidance. In the space and emptiness of the universe, there flow currents and whispers of wind and energy. These winds of silence, light, and sound carry the divine whisper of Allah, and in this sound is Allah's knowledge. This knowledge descends into the believer's receptive heart in peace, silence, and tranquility. When the angels and the Spirit descend with Allah's guidance, the eyes perceive the most beautiful divine light, the ears hear the softest tinkle of the bell, the nose smells the fragrance of a thousand gardens, and the skin feels the most tranquil of the gentle breeze. When this happens, the soul has seen nirvana. This is the knowledge of Allah. And this is the knowledge of certainty. And the soul unites with Allah.

Allah has bestowed the human with a mind and free will. The mind has the ability to perceive ideas and knowledge from the divine and from the signs of Allah. The whisper of the divine, the rustle of the wind, the light of God (*nur*), the fragrance of God's creation, and the sensation of the divine touch all inspire the human mind with an endless stream of ideas and knowledge. Man has been granted knowledge and the ability to process his thoughts with free will.

The verse of the light encompasses the totality of the knowledge and guidance that Allah sent to the human through His prophets. The pagan in the human confused God's message and instead began to worship the messenger. With the end of the era of prophecy, man has the freedom to open his heart to the light of Allah and to learn to recognize the presence of Allah within himself, in his own heart.

> Allah is the Light of the heavens and the earth. The parable of His Light is as if there were a Niche and within it a Lamp: the Lamp enclosed in Glass; the glass as it was a brilliant star: lit from a blessed Tree, an Olive, neither of the East nor of the West, whose Oil is well-nigh luminous, though fire scarce touched it: Light upon Light! Allah guides whom He will to His Light: Allah sets forth Parables for men, and Allah is the font of all Knowledge, and knows all things. Lit is such a light in houses, which Allah hath permitted to be raised to honor and celebrate His name. In them He is glorified in the mornings and in the evenings, over and over again. (An-Nur 24:35–36, Koran)

The parable of divine light is the fundamental belief in one universal God for the whole humankind. Allah is the light of the heavens and the earth that bestows life, grace, and mercy on His creatures. Allah loves His creation, and His *nur* is ever luminous in the hearts of those who love Him, place their trust in Him, and open their heart and soul in submission to Him. In the hearts and minds laid open to Allah in submission is a niche in which glows the light, Spirit, and knowledge of Allah. Such is the glow and the luminescence of the divine light, Spirit, and wisdom; it shines with the brilliance of a star—a star that is lit from divine wisdom, the tree of knowledge, and the knowledge of Allah's signs. For those who believe, Allah is within, and the believer is aglow with Allah's brilliance—light upon light, light seen from the heavens and the earth. The dwellings in which Allah is glorified in the morning and in the evening over and over again are aglow with Allah's light and mercy.

Allah has granted knowledge and wisdom of *furqan* and *taqwa* to the believers who have opened their hearts and minds to Him. Man has been granted the freedom of choice in doing what is wholesome and beautiful or what is corrupt and ugly. It is only man among the creation who has been given the knowledge to distinguish right activity, right thought, and right intention from their opposites. This knowledge reminds the human of the scales of Allah's justice; the two hands of Allah—His mercy and His wrath—are reflected in the human domain, where people have been appointed Allah's vicegerents. Deeds of goodness and wholesomeness are associated with mercy, paradise, and what is beautiful. Evil and corruption is rewarded with wrath, hell, and what is ugly.

Islam is submission to Allah, *iman* is faith in Allah, and *ihsan* is performance of beautiful deeds. A believer with Allah in his heart does not require a hierarchical priesthood to seek Him. Jihad is to open one's heart to Allah and to obey His covenant. Jihad is attaining the knowledge of Allah, obeying the commandments of His covenant.

When the believers, those with *taqwa* of Allah, receive knowledge from Him, they also receive the knowledge to fight the *fitnah* among and around them. Allah shows the way. Allah's way is not terrorism, indiscriminate killing of innocent civilians, aerial bombing by mercenary armies, nor bombing of shrines and homes by passionate jihadis. Allah abhors killing and murder.

Fitnah is to be eliminated through the unity of the *muttaqeen* with unity of intention, purpose, and action. The sole purpose of the elimination of *fitnah* is to establish a just and a moral society. The Islamic society as envisioned in the Koran and the Sunna is a society in which every individual,—man and woman, from the highest to the lowest, from the first to the last—has equal, unimpeded, and unquestionable right to freedom; right to practice his faith in accordance with his beliefs as, in Islam, there is no compulsion in matters of religion; right to life, which includes mental, physical, and emotional well-being; right to safeguard one's property; right to intellectual endeavors, acquisition of knowledge, and education; right to make a living; and right to free speech and action to enjoin good and forbid evil. In enjoying his freedoms, the individual ensures that his activities do not impinge on the similar rights of others. This unity of purpose and action of the *muttaqeen* requires self-cleansing, faith, and organization. It begins with the knowledge that *fitnah* is rooted in the body politics of Islam; is set in the covetousness and cravings of the Muslims; is embedded in the social fabric of Islam; is implanted in the way Muslims treat their mothers, sisters, wives, and daughters; and has roots in the way Muslims treat other Muslims. And above all, the priesthood of Islam, the mercenary armies of Muslim states, and the rulers of Muslim states are the greatest purveyor of *fitnah*. Most Muslims lead a life of self-deception, delusion, and hypocrisy. Till the Muslims fight the *fitnah* within their own selves, in their society, and in their countries; obey the covenant of Allah; and lead their lives in *taqwa* of Him, only then will they achieve supremacy and control over their lives.

Allah declares:

> Here is a declaration to the human, a guidance and advice to those who live in awareness, (*Taqwa*, of Allah)!

> So, lose not hope nor shall you despair, for you shall achieve supremacy if you are true in Faith.

> If you have suffered a setback, verily a setback has been there for the other party too. We make such days of adversity go around amongst the humans so that Allah may distinguish

those who believe and choose His witnesses from amongst them. And Allah loves not the evil doers.

Allah's objective is to distinguish the True Believers from those who reject Faith. (Ali 'Imran 3:138–41, Koran)

The loyalty of the believer is not to any individual, a state, a government, or a party. It is to the precepts of the covenants of Allah and of the Koran. Similarly, the loyalty of those who administer the affairs of the believers and that of the army of Islam is to Allah and His covenant. The conduct of the believer, the state, and its army as an organism is ordained by Allah with stipulations laid down in His covenant as summarized below:

Allah has forbidden taking of life. "Take not life, which Allah has made sacred, except by the way of justice and law." *Fitnah*, treason, and oppression are so vile and repugnant that Allah commands the Believers to fight those who assail them and inflict oppression.

"And fight them until there is no more *fitnah*, tumult or oppression, and there prevails justice and faith in Allah. Go forth, advance! Whether equipped well or lightly, perform jihad strive your utmost and struggle with your wealth and your persons in the cause of Allah. Allah loves those who fight in His cause in array of unison and solidarity. *Fitnah*, treachery and oppression afflict not only those who perpetrate it but affect everyone guilty and innocent alike. Allah's command to fight *fitnah* is conditional, that if the oppressors cease, let there be no further hostility except to those who practice *fitnah*, oppression. Do not transgress limits. Allah does not love transgressors."

Various Ayas Composite.

The jihad of the twenty-first century is to receive knowledge from Allah, to be close to Him, and to lead a life in *taqwa* of Allah. The jihad is fighting for the unity of the *ummah* under one universal Allah through obeying His covenant. Fighting in the cause of Allah is through the destruction of *fitnah*. Destruction of *fitnah* begins within one's own self and then inviting people to do good, enjoining what is right, and forbidding what is wrong:

> Let there arise out of you a band of people inviting to all that is good, enjoining what is right, and forbidding what is wrong: they are the ones to attain happiness. (Ali 'Imran 3:103–5, Koran)

The Koranic principle of enjoining what is good and forbidding what is evil is supportive of the moral autonomy of the individual. This principle authorizes the individual to act according to his or her best judgment in situations in which his or her intervention will advance a good purpose. The following saying of the blessed *nabi* supports individual action by a believer:

> If any one of you sees an evil, let him change it by his hand, and if he is unable to do that, let him change by his words, and if he is still unable to do that let him denounce it in his heart, but this is the weakest form of belief.

This principle assigns to the individual an active role in the community in which he or she lives. *The Koran annunciated the principle of free speech fourteen hundred years ago.* Believing men and women are reminded that they are the best of people to be witnesses over other nations. Such a responsibility carries with it a moral burden of an exemplary conduct of one who submits to the divine truth and whose relationship with Allah is governed is by *taqwa*, the consciousness of humankind's responsibility toward its Creator. With that knowledge and faith, the believer is well equipped to approach others to enjoin what is right and forbid what is wrong. This moral autonomy of the individual, when bound together with the will of the community, formulates the doctrine of infallibility of the collective will of the *ummah*, which is the doctrinal basis of consensus.

11. The Believer All Together Inherited the Koran, the Din, and the Dar es Salaam

When the blessed prophet died, he left behind the Koran, the *din*, and the Dar es Salaam. The blessed prophet wisely did not nominate a successor to his spiritual and worldly legacy. The believers all together inherited the Koran, the *din*, and the Dar es Salaam till the end of time. Allah addresses all the believers, both men and women, in His covenant, guiding them to the conduct of this spiritual and worldly legacy of the blessed *nabi*.

Every believer has autonomy over their conduct in their spiritual and earthly affairs. Humans have enough freedom to make their own choices; if they make the choice to do beautiful and wholesome deeds (*saalihaat*) motivated by faith (*iman*) and God-wariness (*taqwa*), they please Allah and bring harmony and wholesomeness to the whole world, resulting in peace, justice, mercy, compassion, honor, equity, well-being, freedom, and many other gifts through Allah's grace. Others chose to do evil and work with corruption (*mufsidun*), destroying the right relationship among the creation, causing hunger, disease, oppression, pollution, and other afflictions. In the universal order, corruption (*fitnah*) is the prerogative of humans, and vicegerency gives them the freedom to work against the Creator and His creation.

Allah measures out the good and the evil, the wholesome and the corrupt. Allah commands humans to be righteous. In the commandments of the covenant, Allah addresses individual believers, who in unity form a community, the *ummah*. Nevertheless, the emphasis of the guidance is to the individual believer for his own conduct. The concept of the covenant also symbolizes the relationship between individual humans among Allah's creatures and the rest of His creation. They all share one God, one set of guidance and commandments, the same submission and obedience to Him, and the same set of expectations in accordance with His promises. They all can, therefore, trust one another since they all have similar obligations and expectations. In view of the Koran, humans, communities, nations, and civilizations will continue in harmony and peace so long as they continue to fulfill Allah's covenant.

12. Every Believer Has the Authority to Appoint Temporarily for a Fixed Period a Suitable Person to Administer the Affairs of His Country and His *Din*

On the death of the blessed prophet, every one of those who believed in Allah inherited the Koran, the covenant of Allah, and the Islamic state on the earth, the Dar es Salaam. Every individual believer, therefore, has the authority to appoint temporarily, for a fixed period, a suitable a person to administer the affairs of his country and his *din*. With his authority to give the custodianship of the affairs of the *ummah*, he also has the power to revoke this authority if the appointed person fails to do his mandate to the satisfaction of the majority of believers. The community as a whole, after consultation and in consensus, grants people among themselves with authority to manage its affairs (*ulil amri minkum*). Those charged with authority act in their capacity as the representative (*wakil*) of the people and are bound by the Koranic mandate to consult the community in public affairs, and general consensus is the binding source of the law. The community, by consultation and in consensus, has the authority to depose any person charged with authority, including the head of state in the event of gross violation of the law and disobedience of the covenant of the Koran.

Islam pursues its social objectives by reforming the individual. The ritual ablution before prayer, the five daily prayers, fasting during the month of Ramadan, and the obligatory giving of charity all encourage punctuality, self-discipline, and concern for the well-being of others. The individual is seen not just a member of the community and subservient to the its will but also morally as an autonomous agent who plays a distinctive role in shaping the community's sense of direction and purpose. The Koran has attached to the individual the duty of obedience to the government and the right to simultaneously question the rulers about government affairs. The individual obeys the ruler on the condition that the ruler obeys the law according to the Koran. This is reflected in the declaration of the blessed prophet that "there is no obedience in transgression; obedience is only in the righteousness." A citizen is entitled to disobey an oppressive command that is contrary to the Islamic law according to the covenant of Allah.

CHAPTER FOUR

WHAT IS WRONG WITH
THE HOUSE OF ISLAM?

When the people around the world see the wretched condition of
Muslims today, they pose the question "what is wrong with Islam?"
And the Muslims themselves wonder why—after all the submission,
prayers, and humility—they continue to be mired in the dustheap
of humanity. Muslims continue to be poor, ignorant, and disunited.
They cannot extricate themselves from the *fitnah* and oppression in
Palestine, Kashmir, Chechnya, Afghanistan, and Iraq.

So what went wrong with Islam? Islam is still strong, growing
stronger, and vibrant. There are more believers in the word than ever
in history. Yet there are many things that have gone wrong within
Islam. Muslims are blinded by blinkers of self-deception and delusion,
and they cannot see the *fitnah* among their own selves. Believers, in
isolation and in unity, need to look within themselves and in their
community and take stock objectively of their place with Allah and
in this world. In this unity of purpose and action, believers require
self-cleansing to enable them to observe themselves clearly, free of
delusion and self-deception. Such unity of purpose and action requires
a clean *nafs* with *taqwa* of Allah and knowledge of Him.

Knowledge

The twenty-first century is the one of learning, understanding, and communication. Such knowledge requires understanding of Allah's word, the revelations. Such understanding requires Allah's *nur* within the believer's heart. When the blessed *nabi* died, the era of prophecy ended with him. There were to be no more prophets or mass revelations by Allah. When the blessed *nabi* died, he bequeathed each believer the Koran and the knowledge of Allah. With submission to Allah's will, each believer has Allah in the niche of his heart. Allah speaks to the believer through each *ayah* and word of the Koran. The *nabi* was a beacon of Allah's *nur* on each believer's path to Allah.

The believer speaks to Allah through the Koran, salat, and *du'a*, and Allah responds in the believer's heart. This gives the believer peace and tranquility. Submission gives *iman*, which promotes beautiful deeds. Beautiful deeds bring the believer closer to Allah. In closeness to Allah, the believer is aware of His presence, and he continues to perform wholesome deeds in *taqwa* of Allah, which shines the *nur* of Allah on the believer's *nafs*. This blows away the smoke of desire and craving from the *nafs*. And it shines like a mirror with Allah's *nur*.

Fitnah is rooted in cravings and greed of man. Desire and craving for the shiny goods of this world muddies the *nafs*, and man cannot see Allah's presence within him. Man slips and strays from the path of Allah and is then lost. And the Koran speaks of such people thus:

> These are they who have bartered guidance for error: but their traffic is profitless, and they have lost true direction.
>
> Their similitude is that of a man who kindled a fire; when it lighted all around him, Allah took away their light and left

them in utter darkness. So, they could not see. Deaf, dumb, and blind, they will not return to the path. (Koran 2:15–18)

Those with *taqwa* of Allah, the *muttaqeen*, are conscious that *fitnah* is rooted in the cravings of man. Cleansing of the *muttaqeen* begins with the knowledge that *fitnah* is set in the covetousness and cravings of Muslims; is rooted in the body politics of Islam; is embedded in the social fabric of Islam; is implanted in the way Muslims treat their mothers, sisters, wives, and daughters; and has roots in the way Muslims treat other Muslims. And above all, the priesthood of Islam and the mercenary armies and rulers of Muslim states are the greatest purveyor of *fitnah*. Muslim rulers and their mercenary armies are the instruments of occupation and *fitnah* over the *ummah*. Muslims and their rulers plunder their kin and the community without shame or embarrassment. Some "Muslims" lead a life of self-deception, delusion, and hypocrisy. These drive a wedge among the *ummah*.

Evil and *fitnah* have companions—those who conspire and scheme, the ones who execute, those who condone, and everyone who sees evil and does nothing to avert it. When believers refuse to follow the evildoers and unjust rulers, the latter cannot rule over the *ummah*. Every believer has the power and authority to speak out against and cast out *fitnah*, deceit, injustice, treason, and evil among his community. This moral autonomy of the individual, when bound together with the will of the community, formulates the doctrine of infallibility of the collective will of the *ummah*, which is the doctrinal basis of consensus. This consensus is for the good as opposed to evil. When the Islamic rulers and the state fall into degradation and depravity because of the actions of those in authority, the burden of preventing such perpetration of *fitnah* and evil rests with every individual believer and in the community. When *fitnah* and evil occur in the Islamic society, those who bear the ultimate responsibility are the believers for not acting against it and letting it occur.

Till the Muslims fight the *fitnah* within their own selves, in their society, and in their countries and obey the covenant of Allah and lead their lives in *taqwa* of Him, only then will they achieve supremacy and control over their lives. Allah declares:

> Here is a declaration to the human, a guidance and advice to those who live in awareness, *Taqwa*, of Allah!
>
> So, lose not hope nor shall you despair, for you shall achieve supremacy if you are true Believers.
>
> If you have suffered a setback, verily a setback has been there for the other party too. We make such days of adversity go around amongst the humans so that Allah may distinguish those who believe and choose His witnesses from amongst them. And Allah loves not the evil doers.
>
> Allah's objective is to distinguish the True Believers from those who reject Faith. (Ali 'Imran 3:138-41, Koran)

This is a test from Allah to distinguish the true believers from the *kafireen*.

The House of Islam

The house of Islam has four walls. The front wall represents the law that every believer pledges to submit to and to have faith in and obey. So the front wall and the facade of the house of justice and righteousness are the great guide, the book of truth, and the Koran.

1. The Front Wall: The Law

The law is the Koran and the guidance of the blessed prophet in matters of the *din*. In the fifteenth century hijra, one and a half billion believers wished to conduct their daily lives in accordance with the decrees of the Koran and the teachings of the blessed prophet. The Koran is the ever-living word of Allah, the truth for all times. The prophet said, "The Qur'an consists of five heads, things **lawful**, things **unlawful**, clear and positive **precepts, mysteries** and **examples**. Then consider that is **lawful** which is there declared to be so, and that which is forbidden as **unlawful**; obey the **precepts**, believe in the **mysteries** and take warning from the **examples**."

The Koran, in clear terms, addresses the believers about what is permissible and what is forbidden. And the Koran is plain and clear on guidelines, principles, and the law (precepts). And on these matters, the blessed prophet said, "My sayings do not abrogate the Word of Allah, but the Word of Allah can abrogate my sayings."

The prophet also said, "Convey to other persons none of my words, except that you know of a surety."

> The Blessed Prophet said: "I am no more than a man; when I order you anything respecting religion, receive it, and when I tell you anything about the affairs of the world, and then I am nothing but a man."

Allah proclaims:

> To you we revealed the Book of Truth, confirming the Scripture that came before it, and guarding it in safety: so, judge between them by what Allah hath revealed, and follow not their vain desires, diverging from the Truth that has come to you. *To each among you We have prescribed a Law and an Open Way.* If Allah had so willed, He would have made

you a single People, but (His plan is) to test you in what He has given you, so strive as in a race in all virtues. The goal of you all is to Allah; it is He that will show you the truth of the matters in which you dispute. (Al-Ma'idah 5:48, Koran)

Those who reject the Truth, among the People of the Book and among the kafiru, were not going to depart from their ways until there should come to them clear Evidence, a Messenger from Allah, rehearsing scriptures kept pure and holy: Wherein are laws right and straight. (Al-Baiyina 98:1-3, Koran)

In the above two *ayahs*, Allah proclaims that He sent the book of truth with purified pages. *In this book are laws, right and straight, from Allah.* The prophet says that the Koran contains clear and positive precepts, guidelines and laws, and what is lawful and what is unlawful.

Allah has made the laws, permissions, and prohibitions lucid and clear in the covenant. The believers do not require a hierarchy of clergy, priests, and self-proclaimed ulema. Why do believers need imams and the *masha'ikh* of the *madhahib* to direct their lives when Allah is the Teacher and the Guide? And Allah is accessible to the believer at all times.

So the front wall and the facade of the house of justice and righteousness are the greatest guide, the book of truth, and the Koran. The Koran defines the *lawful* and *unlawful* things and presents clear and positive *principles, mysteries,* and *examples.* The *nabi* said, "Then consider that is lawful, and declared to be so, and that which is forbidden as unlawful; obey the precepts, believe in the mysteries and take warning from the examples." The precepts of the covenant of Allah ensure human dignity, equality, justice, consultative government, a state where there is realization of lawful benefits to people, prevention of harm, removal of hardship, and education of individuals by inculcating in them self-discipline, patience, restraint, and respect for the rights of other humans. It is a system under which there is restitution of all wrongs and imbalances in society.

The Islamic society as envisioned in the Koran and the Sunna is a moral and a just society in which every individual—man and woman, from the highest to the lowest, from the first to the last— has equal, unimpeded, and unquestionable right to freedom; right to practice his faith in accordance with his beliefs as, in Islam, there is no compulsion in matters of religion; right to life, which includes a mental, physical, and emotional well-being; right to safeguard one's property; right to intellectual endeavors, acquisition of knowledge, and education; right to make a living; and right to free speech and action to enjoin good and forbid evil. In enjoying his freedoms, the individual ensures that his activities do not impinge on the similar rights of others.

2. The Rear Wall: The Ruler

The back wall of the house of justice for the last fourteen hundred years had been usurped by traitors to Islam and Allah. The rulers of Islam took possession of people's vicegerency by conquest or force of arms. Islam is a religion of voluntary submission of a human to the will of Allah after a considered conviction that Allah is the only reality and that everything else springs out of that reality. Allah has given every human the freedom of choice whether to submit to His will. There is no compulsion in matters of the *din*. And yet there are humans who, by force of arms, compel others to submit to their will. They demand obedience through imprisonment, torture, and murder. Every Muslim state in this day is a police state. Every Muslim ruler abuses his authority to plunder and debase the lands of Islam.

The covenant's criterion of consultative and participative government was lost within seventy years after the blessed *nabi* died. It has not been restored yet. No person has the right to impose himself and his family and clan as the ruler above the believers. The believers are free humans answerable to Allah only and governed by His covenant. The believers, both men and women, are not subject to other humans.

Allah has granted each believer the right to freedom to practice his faith in accordance to his beliefs as, in Islam, there is no compulsion in matters of religion; right to life, which includes mental, physical, and emotional well-being; right to safeguard one's property; right to intellectual endeavors, acquisition of knowledge, and education; right to make a living; and right to free speech and action to enjoin good and forbid evil. In enjoying his freedoms, the individual ensures that his activities do not impinge on the similar rights of others.

The believers, however, from time to time, choose people among themselves to administer their affairs and that of their community. The administrator of affairs, the *amri minkum,* and his bureaucracy should deal with every individual and his or her problems with empathy, sympathy, and compassion. The word *compassion* is commonly translated to mean "sympathy," which is not quite correct. One with compassion does have empathy or sympathy with a subject, but when an injustice is committed, his inner self will compel him to correct the injustice with an action as opposed to just feeling passive sympathy. There should be a restitution of all wrongs and imbalances in society.

> O you who believe! Obey Allah, and obey the messenger, and those charged with authority among you. If you differ in anything among yourselves, refer to Allah and His Messenger.

If you do believe in Allah and the last day: that is the best,
and most suitable for final determination. (Koran 4:59)

The community, the *ummah*, as a whole, after consultation and consensus, grants people among themselves with authority to manage its affairs (*ulil amri minkum*). Those charged with authority act in their capacity as the representative (*wakil*) of the people and are bound by the Koranic mandate to consult the community in public affairs, and general consensus is a binding source of the law. The community, by consultation and in consensus, has the authority to depose any person charged with authority, including the head of the state, in the event of gross violation of the law and disobedience of the covenant of the Koran.

Islam pursues its social objectives by reforming the individual. The ritual ablution before prayer, the five daily prayers, fasting during the month of Ramadan, and the obligatory giving of charity all encourage punctuality, self-discipline, and concern for the well-being of others. The individual is seen not just a member of the community and subservient to the community's will but also as a morally autonomous agent who plays a distinctive role in shaping the community's sense of direction and purpose. The Koran has attached to the individual's duty of obedience to the government a right of to simultaneously dispute with the rulers over government affairs. The individual obeys the ruler on the condition that the ruler obeys the Islamic law according to the Koran and the Sunna. This is reflected in the declaration of the Hadith that "there is no obedience in transgression; obedience is only in the righteousness." The citizen is entitled to disobey an oppressive command that is contrary to the Islamic law according to the covenant of the Koran.

Even though these laws are part of the commandments of the Koran, the ulema-jurist-priests who became the administrators of Sharia chose to ignore them. Thus, the true Sharia in practice had and has no authority over the governing structure of Muslim countries. This practice has become ingrained in the Islamic society, which became a society governed by state elites who patronized priests and religious leaders, who in turn legitimized the un-Koranic regimes. The collaboration of elites of state and religion and the cooperative relationship between these two institutions has, for many centuries, become the Muslim solution to the problem of state and religion. It totally bypassed the common person, the vicegerent of God. This arrangement continues to be perpetuated into today's Islamic society. The ruler-mullah alliance continues to be above the Sharia law and the customary law. The Sharia does not have authority over governance. These two establishments are not accountable to the Islamic populace. The Sharia law is subject to manipulation and falsification and has therefore sadly failed.

The ulema in Saudi Arabia, Iran, Sudan, and Egypt continue to issue fatwa at the behest of the corrupt ruling class. In fact, the ruling class in Islam is the source of *fitnah*. The Sharia and *fiqh* have failed, and it collapsed in AH 665 when the gates to *ijtihad* were slammed shut, and it has not since revived. In Islam, there are no professional ruling classes, sultans, politicians, priests, nor mercenary generals. The believer is independent and free, answerable only to Allah. The believer, in consultation with other believers, employs administrators, civil servants, and soldiers to run his or her affairs. Such state functionaries are the employees of the believers and not the masters. The Muslim states acquired un-Islamic regal, political, economic, and ecumenical systems from the Romans, Persians, Hindus, Central Asian nomadic tribes, and imperial European colonists. Once the

Mu'awiyah and Abbasi caliphs began to wear the Roman and the Persian crowns, the populace could never impose the Sharia law on them. Since then, the same pre-Islamic injustice and oppression of the Roman, Persian, Mongol, Hindu, and European civilizations has continued to percolate in the un-Koranic ruling classes of Islam. It is the governance of the Islamic state that has gone wrong.

3. The Right Wall: The Faqihs and the Priests

When the blessed prophet passed away, there was no clergy and priest class in Islam. During the following two hundred years, there arose hundreds of *madhahib*, each with an imam. The Sharia of the early *madhahib* failed as a tool of jurisprudence and justice. However, the work of the earlier imams documented sources from the Koran and the teachings of the blessed prophet as the source of Sharia. Injunctions of the Koran and Sunna provide the core of Sharia and are collectively called the *nusus*. Sharia comprises the guidance that Allah revealed to the His blessed messenger, relating moral values and practical legal rules. Islam morality (*ilm al akhlaq*) educates the individual in moral virtue, exercise of self-discipline, and restraint in the fulfillment of natural desires. The Sharia provides clear rulings on the fundamentals of Islam, its basic moral values, and practical duties such as prayers, fasting, zakat, hajj, and other devotional matters. It also pronounces on what is lawful (halal) and unlawful (haram). All this, in effect, is documentation of what the prophet had expounded in his lifetime. The Koran provided the law. Allah's covenant clearly states what is lawful and what is forbidden. It was not the law that failed. What failed was the legal system, the jurisprudence, and the *fiqh* that man created.

The blessed *nabi* said,

> Do you know what saps the foundation of Islam, and ruins it?
> The errors of the learned destroy it, and the disputations of
> the hypocrite and the orders of the kings who have lost the
> road.

What the *nabi* said actually began to occur soon after his death. Islam has been beset by the triple menace of the errors of jurist-scholars, the malice of hypocrites, and the tyranny of rulers. The followers of earlier imams became a hierarchy of priestly bureaucracy. Muslim society became, in practice, a society governed by self-appointed rulers who patronized religious hierarchy, the ulema that in turn legitimized un-Koranic rulers. In between were the opportunists, hypocrites, and Muslims in name only, who cause *fitnah* and dissension and benefit from disputes among Muslims.

The ruling elite supported the clerics, clergy, and jurists; and in return, the scholars of Islam sanctioned the un-Islamic practices of the elite. The mullahs had endowments, allowances, and positions of power above their fellow men; and in return, they overlooked the oppression and tyranny of the elite over the people. The Sharia based on the Koran endowed the *ummah*, in theory, with human dignity, equality, justice, consultative government, a state where there is realization of lawful benefits to peoples, prevention of harm to people (*darar*), removal of hardship (*haraj*), and education of individuals by inculcating in them self-discipline, patience, restraint, and respect for the rights of others. Sharia was supposed to bring about restitution of all wrongs and imbalances in society. Under the reign of the caliphs and the clerics, none of the above happened.

Even today in the states with the mullah-politician alliance where Sharia is supposedly practiced, there is injustice and open corruption under the Taliban, ayatollahs, Wahhabi, and Pakistani mullah-politician-generals. These are the most oppressive regimes in the world. The political mullahs, like other politicians, are interested in power; the only difference between them and the ordinary politicians is that the clerics choose the religious sentiment as their weapon. When in power, the ayatollahs, mullahs, and Wahhabi all unashamedly and openly practice torture and torment on their citizens and their political opponents alike. Whereas Allah and the blessed prophet advocate knowledge and education, the mullahs oppose acquisition of knowledge and education, especially the knowledge of literature, arts, and sciences by both men and women.

The Koran endowed women with equality and freedom, human dignity, justice, rights to free speech, a share in consultative government, a state where there is realization of lawful benefits to women, prevention of harm to women, removal of hardship, and education of individuals by inculcating in them self-discipline, patience, restraint, and respect for rights of others—a system where there is restitution of all wrongs and imbalances in society. The mullahs, for thirteen hundred years, have opposed these freedoms granted to women by Allah. Allah sent down his *din* to both men and women. He asked humans to believe in Him and worship Him with daily salat. The ulema and the mullahs make women unwelcome in Allah's house, the mosque. They falsify Hadith and misrepresent the Koran to keep women out of mainstream Islam. Allah asked men to lower their gaze and avoid *Fahasha*; instead, men and mullahs chose to shut the women behind closed doors and windows rather than subdue their own lust. They insist on shrouding women head to toe by misrepresenting the Koran and the Hadith.

Mullahs and the *madhahib* had no jurisdiction over God-fearing and upright women's right of worship nor in the manner of their apparel. Worship of Allah and a believing woman's apparel are matters of concern between Allah and the believer. Islam is a religion of self-surrender; it is the conscious and rational submission of dependent and limited human will to the absolute and omnipotent will of Allah. The type of surrender Islam requires is a deliberate, conscious, and rational act made by a person who knows with both intellectual certainty and spiritual vision that Allah, who is subject of Koranic discourse, is the reality. The knower of God is a Muslim (fem. *Muslimah*), "one who submits" to the divine truth and whose relationship with God is governed by *taqwa*, the consciousness of humankind's responsibility toward its Creator. After submission, the believer develops a personal relationship with Allah.

Allah addresses women and men in His covenant about their conduct and in matters of worship and dress. The mullah and the ulema have no part in this relationship. They have their own obligations to Allah for the benefit of their own souls. The believer has the right to approach any knowledgeable person to seek advice and spiritual discourse. There is no hierarchical priesthood in Islam. Therefore, there is no guardian or keeper of the Sharia, nor is there any religious constabulary. Allah is the seer and knower of all things. He does not need spies and enforcers to run His *din*.

The blessed prophet said Allah is the best of judges and that the command (*hukm*) rests with Him, and the prophet himself was the subject of Allah's command and was powerless to hurry, delay, or alter Allah's *hukm*.

> Say: "For me, I work on a clear Sign from my Lord, but you reject Him. What you would see hastened, is not in my power. The Command, Hukm, rests with none but Allah: He declares the Truth, and He is the best of judges." (Al-An'am 6:57, Koran)

> They take their priests and their rabbis their lords in derogation of Allah, and (they take as their Lord) Christ, the

son of Mary; yet they were commanded to worship but One God: *La Ilaha illa Huwa*, none has right to de worshipped but He. Praise and glory to Him: (far is He) from having the partners they associate (with Him). (At-Tawbah 9:31, Koran)

This *ayah* in At-Tawbah is reflective of the existence of a situation in the Muslim world today, which is similar to the one alluded to the Koran. The Muslims began to take their imams, priests, and scholars as their lords. Although the priests do not pretend to be divine, they pretend to possess an aura of holiness, and they decree *ahkam*, which is the prerogative of Allah. Their commandments to their followers occasionally are in contradiction to the message of the Koran. Also, they interpret Sharia by overriding the verses of the Koran with falsified sayings of the blessed prophet. They also place greater weight to Hadith collections of the third century than to Allah's word. The result is that, over the centuries, in practice, the *din* of Allah has become Mohammedanism rather than submission to the will of Allah. In fact, in the khutbah, the worshippers hear more about the blessed *nabi*, Ali, Hasan, Hussein, Abu Bakr, Umar, and Usman than the name of Allah and the contents of the Koran. The blessed *nabi* brought the message of one Creator, Allah, the God whom *Ibrahim* submitted to and placed all his trust in. In the scheme of things of the *din*, Allah is the Real, supreme, and worthy of worship. Humans, whatever their lineage, are mortal and insignificant. The mullahs and priests have distorted Islam into something that it is not. That is what went wrong with Islam.

4. The Left Wall: The Community of Islam, the Ummah

The *ummah* forms the fourth wall of the house of justice and righteousness. The *ummah* is united as one people and one nation, whose hearts Allah joined in love so that they are brethren to one another. It enjoins good and forbids evil. It is committed to truth, administers justice on the basis of truth, has been commanded by Allah to act justly to others and to one another, and in its advocacy of truth is a witness over itself and over mankind. The *ummah* observes due balance and moderation in all its actions, avoids extremism, and does not to transgress due bounds in anything. Men and women are straight and honest in all their dealings. Every believer maintains himself in a permanent state of surrender to Allah. The *ummah* is united in a single brotherhood not to be divided into sects, schisms, principalities, states, or kingdoms. Allah has promised *Azabu azeem*, a dreadful penalty, to those causing divisions among the *ummah*. This community looks after its own members in peace, tribulation, and adversity and in times of stress.

Although the *ummah* is sovereign and Allah's vicegerent on the earth, in spite of its autonomy and sovereignty, it has been subject to *fitnah*, tyranny, and oppression by its own members and outsiders. For thirteen hundred years, the ruling class and priesthood began to control the direction of Islam. Every wrong and distortion stem from such control.

In a just and moral society, a community is made up of community upon community at its base as in a pyramid that gradually tapers to an apex where the ultimate guardian of justice is represented by Allah's covenant, the Koran. Governance is based on transparent, honest, truthful statecraft where justice that is practiced by the *ummah*'s *wakil* at the top is seen by the whole *ummah* at the base. In the same context, the community at the base ensures that there is honesty in its governance, that the community bureaucracy is free from moral and economic corruption, and that each community also acts as the custodian of the covenant of Allah and ensures that its precepts are acted on in the interests of the community. The precepts of Allah's covenant ensure human dignity, equality, justice, consultative government, a state where there is realization of lawful benefits to peoples, prevention of harm to people, removal of hardship, and education of individuals by inculcating in them self-discipline, patience, restraint, and respect for the rights of others. It is a system where there is restitution of all wrongs and imbalances in society.

What failed was the legal system, the administration of justice, the jurisprudence, the *fiqh* that man created. There was nothing wrong with the law of the covenant of Allah. What went wrong was the destruction of a perfect legal system by human ego and noncompliance and disobedience of the law by those who practiced the governance of the Islamic state.

The contemporary state of Islam: The front wall representing the law, the Koran, and the right wall representing the *ummah* are still standing. Two walls of the house of justice and righteousness withstood the test of time and stood on their foundations. The walls lost the paint and plaster and looked somewhat dilapidated. The front facade representing the law and justice is still standing. This is the law of the Koran and the covenant. The right wall representing the *ummah* of the believers is also intact as the believers and most of the members of the *ummah* have continued to observe their covenant with Allah.

What has gone wrong? The back wall representing the rulers continues to crumble to dust. It is continually being rebuilt with ever-changing facade and fascia of granite and marble. Its foundations are on the sand of deceit and falsehood, threatening the continuation of the cycle of collapse and refurbishing.

The fourth wall representing scholar-jurists, faqih, mujtahid, and mullahs is in utter ruin, confusion, and disarray. There are books, manuscripts, and parchments—some whole, others moth eaten—strewn everywhere, a scene of utter confusion. Strewn around are also loudspeakers and sound systems that the mullahs use to shout at one another and at the people. The mullahs aggrandize themselves with grand names, regalia, and titles. All of them regard themselves as ulema, the holders of ultimate knowledge. But they refuse to broaden their horizons with the acquisition of broader knowledge of Allah's creation and signs, required to live today's life of human survival and spirituality. They have failed to learn from the signs of Allah.

The blessed prophet had said,

> Do you know what saps the foundation of Islam, and ruins it? The errors of the learned destroy it, and the disputations of the hypocrite and the orders of the kings who have lost the road.

What the prophet said actually began to occur. The followers of earlier imams, and the later scholars became a hierarchy of priestly bureaucracy. Muslim society became, in practice, a society governed by state elites who patronized the religious figures and the ulema that, in turn, legitimized the un-Koranic rulers. This collaboration of rulers and priestly hierarchy and the cooperative relationship between these two institutions has, for many centuries, degraded the justice system and the law prescribed by the Koran. It prevented the orderly development of representative and consultative government representing the common man. Education, public services, elimination of poverty, equality of man and woman, human dignity, and common suffering were not pursued by the rulers or by the clerics.

The rulers and the priests pursued power and wealth from the believers. The mullahs had endowments, allowances, and positions of power above their fellow men; and in return, they overlooked the *fitnah*, oppression, and tyranny of the elite over the people. The Sharia based on the Koran endowed the *ummah* with human dignity, equality, justice, and consultative government. It envisaged a state in which there is realization of lawful benefits to peoples, prevention of harm to people, removal of hardship, and education of individuals by inculcating in them self-discipline, patience, restraint, and respect for rights of others. Under the mullah-elite hegemony, this did not take place. Whereas Allah and the blessed prophet advocated knowledge and education, the mullahs opposed acquisition of knowledge and education, especially the knowledge of numbers and sciences by both men and women. The Koran endowed women with equality, freedom, human dignity, justice, rights to free speech, a share in consultative government, lawful benefits, education, prevention of harm to women, removal of hardship, and restitution of all wrongs and imbalances in society. The mullahs, for thirteen hundred years, opposed these freedoms granted to women by Allah.

The Renewal of Islam in the Twenty-First Century

In a just society, in the Dar es Salaam, the Sharia, and the institution of justice has to be made accountable to the law of the Koran and to the contemporary Muslim world. The house of justice and righteousness will stand with three walls, that of a pyramid, with Allah's mercy and beneficence at the top.

The front wall will represent the law, the Sharia based on the decrees of the Koran and the prophet's pronouncements on *din*. The Koran is the ever-living word of Allah, the truth for all times. The prophet said, "The Qur'an consists of five heads, things **lawful,** things **unlawful,** clear and positive **precepts, mysteries** and **examples.** Then consider that is **lawful** which is there declared to be so, and that which is forbidden as **unlawful**; obey the **precepts**, believe in the **mysteries** and take warning from the **examples**." The Koran, in clear terms, addresses the believers about what is permissible and what is forbidden. And the Koran is plain and clear on guidelines, principles, and the law (precepts).

And on these matters, the blessed prophet said, "*My sayings do not abrogate the Word of Allah, but the Word of Allah can abrogate my sayings.*"

The prophet also said, "*Convey to other persons none of my words, except that you know of a surety.*"

The blessed prophet also said:

> I am no more than a man; when I order you anything respecting religion, receive it, and when I tell you anything about the affairs of the world, and then I am nothing but a man.

The term *islam* signifies the idea of surrender or submission to the will of Allah. Islam is a religion of self-surrender; it is the conscious and rational submission of dependent and limited human will to the absolute and omnipotent will of Allah. The surrender that Islam requires is a deliberate, conscious, and rational act made by a person who knows with both intellectual certainty and spiritual vision that Allah, who is the subject of Koranic discourse, is the only reality. The knower of God, upon his surrender to Allah's will, accepts His covenant and consciously agrees to follow its commandments. The believer chooses Allah's path according to his own free will and choice. The knower of God is a Muslim, "one who submits" to the divine truth and whose relationship with God is governed by *taqwa*, the consciousness of humankind's responsibility toward its Creator. The act of submission and acceptance of Allah's covenant establishes a relationship between Allah and the believer, in which Allah is ever present in the conscious, heart, and mind of the believer. The concept of *taqwa* implies that the believer has the added responsibility of acting in a way that is in accordance with three types of knowledge: *ilm al-yaqin, ain al-yaqin,* and *haqq al yaqin* (knowledge of certainty, eye of certainty, and truth of certainty).

Islam is a religion of voluntary submission of a human to the will of Allah after a considered conviction that He is the only reality and that everything else springs out of that reality. Allah has given every human the freedom of choice whether or not to submit to His will. There is no compulsion in the matters of the *din. Yet there are humans who, by force of arms, compel other humans to submit to their will.* They demand obedience through imprisonment, torture, and murder. Every Muslim state in this day is a police state. Every Muslim ruler abuses his authority to plunder and debase the lands of Islam.

So in a just and a moral society, the law is paramount. The law is the Koran. Under this law, Allah has given every human the freedom of choice whether to submit to His will. Those whom Allah has granted the freedom of choice of belief in Him have the same divine right to choose their *wakil* to administer their affairs. With the right to choose their *wakil* comes also the right to dismiss such a person who does not perform to their expectations. These decisions have to be made in unity, consultation, and consensus. In the end, the decision of the majority will prevail, to be accepted by all.

The second wall of the house of justice and righteousness will represent the believers. The believers are free humans answerable to Allah only and governed by His covenant. The believers, both men and women, are not subject to other humans. Allah has granted each believer the right to freedom; right to practice his faith in accordance with his beliefs as, in Islam, there is no compulsion in matters of religion; right to life, which includes mental, physical, and emotional well-being; right to safeguard one's property; right to intellectual endeavors, acquisition of knowledge, and education; right to make a living; and right to free speech and action to enjoin good and forbid evil. In enjoying his freedoms, the individual ensures that his activities do not impinge on the similar rights of others.

The major issue with Islam today is illiteracy and lack of knowledge of the *din*. People lack understanding of the Koran and Allah's message. Islam is still strong, growing stronger, and vibrant. There are more believers in the word than ever in history. Yet there are many things that have gone wrong within Islam. Muslims are blinded by blinkers of self-deception and delusion, and they cannot see the *fitnah* among their own selves. Believers, in isolation and in unity, need to look within themselves, in their community, and in the *ummah* and take a stock objectively of their place with Allah and in this world. In this unity of purpose and action, believers require self-cleansing to enable them to observe themselves clearly, free of delusion and self-deception. Such unity of purpose and action requires a clean *nafs* with *taqwa* of Allah and knowledge of Him.

They need to understand each word of Allah's message and each covenant they have made with Him and to obey it diligently. They need to read and learn the Koran in their own language. Devotional reciting of the Koran should be in Arabic but, for a clear understanding, Allah's word should be read in their own language. Similarly, in personal salat and *du'a*, they may beseech Allah in their vernacular and say communal prayers in Arabic. Over a short time, each person will have mastery of Allah's word and understand their *din*, rights, and obligations. The Koran is the *din*, covenant, Sharia, and law.

When the people know their Koran, they will know their din. They will not be misguided by the ulema. The battles for the succession of the blessed *nabi* were the legacy of the pagan and priestly Quraish for the control of the center of the new faith and the Kaaba. These past struggles of the Quraish are irrelevant in today's world. Total Koran is the total *din*. Men and priests do not intervene in the believer's relationship with Allah.

The division of Islam into the Sunni and Shia sects was the result of infighting among the descendants of Qusayy for the control of Islam. This battle has continued to this day, with the priest class battling to control the pulpit and the throne of the Islamic state. Over the centuries, priests have raised the flag of *fitnah* with a claim to be God, a prophet, the Mahdi, imam of the *din*, and spokespeople of Allah. Their claims were for supremacy over the believers. True Muslims are believers of Allah. Believers of Allah and His *din* are not Shia, Sunni, nor any other sect, which are inventions and innovations of priests, like the priests of the pagans, Sumerians, Israelites, and Christians.

The third wall will represent the administrators of the affairs of the *ummah* appointed by the community. The *ummah* will from among themselves choose believing men and women of wisdom and learning from all walks of life to put together laws based on the decrees and the spirit of the Koran and what the prophet taught as uniform laws for the whole *ummah* to suit the circumstances of contemporary times. Since the days of the blessed *nabi*, the world has changed. Since then, there has been an industrial revolution. The darkness of the night has shrunk by six hours. A traveler can go around the world in a few hours. Information travels fast, and the knowledge of the sciences and arts is rapidly disseminated. Consequently, practical literacy has expanded; and with this, a layperson—the common believer—has accumulated more knowledge of his *din* than the old-time imam, mullah, and scholar.

The precepts of the Koran are there for all times. The Koran is the living word of Allah. The Hadith collections of the third century have become fixed in the third-century mores and knowledge. The everlasting wisdom and knowledge of the Koran has, by far, surpassed the tradition and stories of the old-time Hadith related through the minds of people one thousand years ago. They do not always accurately represent what the blessed *nabi* taught in his time.

Sharia is the law of the Koran, occasionally to be supplemented by the practice and teachings of the blessed prophet. Whereas the law of the Koran is *wahiy* revelation and is mandatory, the Sunna is not a revelation, and only its parts dealing with matters of *din* constitute the mandatory part of law. *Mutawatir* Hadith are word-for-word transmission of what the *nabi* said. There are no more than ten such Hadith. Another kind of Hadith is known as *conceptual mutawatir,* whereas the concept is taken from the prophet, but the words are that of the narrator. These kinds of *mutawatir* are frequent. They are sayings and the acts of the blessed prophet that explain the essentials of faith, the rituals of worship, the rules that regulate the punishments, and the description of the lawful and the unlawful. The blessed prophet said, *"I am no more than a man; when I order you anything respecting religion, receive it, and when I tell you anything about the affairs of the world, and then I am nothing but a man."* Therefore, the prophet's worldly deeds and sayings do not constitute the *din* or the law.

Fiqh and *ijtihad* are human and often have been mutually contradictory, and they form the law, which is transient and contingent on local circumstances and level of human development and always to be ordained on the basis of principles of the covenant of the Koran. These laws are human and therefore are subject to change by man according to his changing needs, nevertheless in accordance with the covenant of Allah.

What Is Wrong with Contemporary Islam?

1. The Betrayal of the Covenant: Ruling Elite and the Justice System

The prophet said, "The Qur'an, consists of five heads, things lawful, things unlawful, clear and positive precepts, mysteries and examples. Then consider that is lawful, which is there declared to be so, and that which is forbidden as unlawful; obey the precepts, believe in the mysteries and take warning from the examples." The only purpose of the Sharia is to ensure that the laws are just and that justice is done. Justice (*'adl*) is a divine attribute defined as "putting every object in the right place." Wrongdoing is a human attribute defined as "putting things in the wrong place, negative acts employed by human beings." Sharia should ensure human dignity, equality, justice, consultative government, a state where there is realization of lawful benefits to people, prevention of harm, removal of hardship, and education of individuals by inculcating in them self-discipline, patience, restraint, and respect for rights of others. Sharia is a system under which there is restitution of all wrongs and imbalances in society. When the law and the justice system does not fulfill these requirements, it cannot be deemed to be according to Allah's laws and does not fulfill the requirements of Sharia.

When the rulers of Islam; the caliphs, sultans, kings, and emirs; the colonial rulers and their Muslim successors; and the politicians and dictators imposed themselves over the Muslim societies, they threw aside the authority of the Koran and the Sharia. They enlisted as their supporters and helpers people who perpetrated *fitnah* and oppression over the believers. The tribal rulers brought their eunuch and slave armies, and the colonial capitalists brought their banks, merchants, and civil servants. Out of this chaos evolved the indigent babu, sahib, and effendi class of pashas, beys, deputy commissioners, tax collectors, and moneylenders and the new brown capitalist class emulating their earlier white masters. This new class fraternized with the drawing room politicians and the *darbari* mullahs to form the new ruling elite of Islam in the late twentieth century. The captains and colonels in their colonial-era khaki uniforms charged into the foray to grab power in the land of Islam. This scum—a blend of colonial servants, politicians, merchants, mullahs, and the subservient colonial colonel class—became the rulers of Islam for the next sixty years. For them, the knowledge of Allah and the Koran was too unbecoming for their lifestyles.

Secularism became the name of the game, and Western institutions formed the rules for the play. Capitalistic colonialism continued to rule Islam through these proxy rulers of Islam. Without the love of Allah and of their people, they fell victim to the desires and cravings of their newfound power and wealth. They have continued to suck the lifeblood out of their land and their nation. The post-twentieth-century governance is the extension of the un-Islamic ruling arrangement of the nomadic Mongol and Turkish tribal formations that gave birth to the Ottoman, Safavid, and Mogul Empires. The new ruling class is imbued with the culture of *fitnah*, parasitism, and corruption that their class had inflicted on the *ummah* in the previous centuries. The conquerors had their reward of gold and real estate of the conquered people. The power to pillage and snatch passed down step by step from the highest in the hierarchy to the meanest, sucking their victims of everything but the barest means of survival. This class carried their wealth of gold and precious stones in their proverbial turban and saddlebag, building no infrastructure nor institutions for the benefit of their people.

The subject population belonged to a lesser order of existence. All commoners were considered to be the flocks to be shorn in the interests of the elite. The small community and village organizations were left under the control of the tax collector, the landlord, or the clerical and priestly leaders. These leaders were part of a feudal, religious, and military hierarchy of state functionaries reporting to the sultan and the imperial authorities. These leaders assisted the state in collecting taxes and enforcing social discipline. The sultans operated on the principle that the subjects should serve the interests of the state. The economy was organized to ensure the maximum flow of tax revenues, goods in kind, and all the services required by the sultans, emirs, and elites. The populace was systematically taxed by maintaining a systematic record of the population, households, properties, and livestock.

The sultan owned all the lands of the Muslim empires; some lands, estates, and the *tapulu* were on perpetual lease to the peasants, and *mukatalu* lands were leased to a tax collector in return for a fixed payment for a lease. The economic policy on taxation and trade was aimed at accumulation of as much bullion as possible in the sultan's treasury. The Muslim rulers did not see trade policy or scientific and technological development as means of creating wealth. Rather, they sought wealth from conquered and annexed territories. The rulers and their religious, feudal, and military helpers were above the law—the law of the Sharia and the laws of the land. The laws of the Koran and Sharia were meant to control the flock but not the shepherd.

In the postcolonial era, power was handed down to the opportunist emirs and sheikhs in the Arab world and to politicians and bureaucrats in countries such as Pakistan and Egypt. The intelligence services of Britain and the USA discovered that it was simpler to bribe, sweet-talk, and manipulate the simple Bedouin and the colonel class than the nationalist and wily politicians. It was by no sheer coincidence that all Islamic states gradually came to be run by sheikhs and military dictators acceptable to the West. The West required influence in the lands of the Muslims, and there were droves of willing Muslims bidding to be hired. During the previous two hundred years, the Muslim society underwent a slow but perceptible change. In the late twentieth century, the believers found an alien culture in their midst. This alien society comprised constables, lance corporals, captains, session judges, deputy commissioners, inspectors, barristers, brigadiers, and an assortment of people with colonial names who had, in an earlier period, greased the smooth running of the colonial empire by intimidating the natives. After the wars of liberation, Muslims found that the same people had reinvented and organized themselves into senior civil servants, police commissioners, army generals, ministers of the government, governors, and presidents.

The culture and society of the *ummah* bifurcated into two divergent groups. The tiny minority comprising the alien class of policemen, civil servants, judiciary, and soldiers trained in the colonial approach of governance became emboldened sufficiently to believe that they were the new ruling class of Islam and had the divine right to intimidate, direct, punish, and control the remaining majority. They put their beliefs into practice and began to seize and extort the wealth and property of the citizens at checkpoints, courthouses, roadsides, airports, shopping areas, and all other public and private places. Their position provided them an assured authority to arrest, interrogate, imprison, and torture any citizen who infringed on their pleasure. The members of this privileged class had been initiated and indoctrinated to believe in their superiority over the common folks like the previous, white-skinned colonials had been.

Citizens are expected to bribe for the services of the lowly peon all the way up to the ranks of the mighty prime ministers, the presidents, and their bureaucracy. Their offices have little traps set up as in the game of Monopoly where the humble citizens are required to make offerings before they can have any official work done. Bribery and theft of public and private wealth goes on in open view. During the late twentieth century, politicians and officials of Muslim countries like Egypt and Pakistan had the honor of being the most corrupt in the world. When traveling in Pakistan and Egypt, one has to wonder whatsoever happened to those with *taqwa* of Allah.

The one and a half billion believers are in the clutches of this alien class of people who look like and pretends to be *Muslim*, yet their actions impose *fitnah* on the believers. Through their actions, *fitnah* has become rooted in the body politics of Islam; is embedded in the social fabric of Islam; is implanted in the way Muslims treat their mothers, sisters, wives, and daughters; and has roots in the way Muslims treat other Muslims. And above all, the priesthood of Islam, the mercenary armies of Muslim states, and the rulers of Muslim states are the greatest purveyor of *fitnah*. Muslim rulers and their mercenary armies are the instruments of occupation and *fitnah* over the *ummah*. Such "Muslims" and their rulers plunder their kin and the community without shame or embarrassment.

Some Muslims lead a life of self-deception, delusion, and hypocrisy that drive a wedge among the *ummah*. Cleansing of the *muttaqeen* begins with the knowledge that Islam abhors *fitnah*, oppression, and tyranny. Those who call themselves *Muslim* and inflict *fitnah* on Muslims in the name of Islam cannot be the people of belief in Allah. That *fitnah* is set in the covetousness and cravings of those who disobey Allah's commandments, and inflicting *fitnah* on the believers of Allah belie their belief in Allah. Thus, such people cannot themselves be a part of the *ummah*. Believers, beware!

Stand firmly for Allah as a witness of fair dealing. Let not the malice of people lead you to iniquity. Be just, that is next to worship. Be with taqwa of Allah, fear Allah.

⬦ O you who believe! Fear Allah and speak always the truth that He may direct you to righteous deeds and forgive you your sins: he that obeys Allah and His Messenger have already attained the highest achievement. (Al-Ahzab 33:69–73, Koran)

⬦ Stand firm for justice as witness to Allah be it against yourself, your parents, or your family, whether it is against rich or poor, both are nearer to Allah than they are to you. Follow not your caprice lest you distort your testimony. If you prevaricate and evade justice Allah is well aware what you do. (An-Nisa 4:135, Koran)

⬦ O you who believe! Stand firmly for Allah as a witness of fair dealing. Let not the malice of people lead you to iniquity. Be just, that is next to worship. Be with taqwa of Allah, fear Allah. Allah is well aware with what you do. (Al-Ma'idah 5:8, Koran)

⬦ Betray not the trust of Allah and His Messenger. Nor knowingly misappropriate things entrusted to you. (Al-Anfal 8:27, Koran)

Be honest in handling property, goods, credit, confidences, and secrets of your fellow men and display integrity and honesty in using your skills and talents.

⬦ If you have taqwa of Allah, and fear Allah, He will grant you a Criterion to judge between right and wrong and remove from you all misfortunes and evil and forgive your sins. Allah is the bestower of grace in abundance. (Al-Anfal 8:29, Koran)

◇ Be in taqwa of Allah, fear Allah, and be with those who are true in word and deed. (At-Tawbah 9:119, Koran)

◇ Deal not unjustly, and ye shall not be dealt with unjustly. (A-Baqarah 2:277–80, Koran)

◇ Whenever you give your word speak honestly even if a near relative is concerned.

◇ And come not near the orphan's property, except to improve it, until he attains the age of full strength.

◇ And give full measure and full weight with justice. No burden we place on any soul but that which it can bear. (Al An 'am 6:151–52, Koran)

Justice (*'adl*) is a divine attribute defined as "putting in the right place." The opposite of *'adl* is *zulm*, which in Koranic terms means "wrongdoing." Wrongdoing is a human attribute defined as "putting things in the wrong place." *Zulm* is one of the common terms used in the Koran to refer to the negative acts employed by human beings. Wrongdoing is the opposite of justice, and justice is to put everything in its right place and every act of the humans to be performed as prescribed by Allah. Hence, wrongdoing is to put things where they do not belong. Hence *zulm* is injustice, for example, associating others with Allah; others do not belong in the place for the divine. It is to place false words in place of the truth; it is to put someone else's property in place of your own. The other examples are taking a life against the divine commandments, replacing people's liberty with oppression, waging war instead of peace, and usurping people's right to govern them.

The Koran repeatedly stigmatizes humans of wrongdoing. When it points out who is harmed by injustice or wrongdoing, it always mentions the word *nafs* or self. People cannot harm Allah. By being unjust, doing wrong, or putting things in the wrong place, people harm themselves. They distort their own natures, and they lead themselves astray. Whom can one wrong? It is impossible to wrong or do injustice against Allah since all things are His creatures and do His work. Hence, wrongdoing and injustice is an activity against people and Allah's creation.

Allah had prescribed His covenant to humans for the good of human beings. People, tribes, and nations are being helped since Allah leads them into accord, harmony, and justice, which in turn create peace in the world. Allah has laid out all the basic principles for justice in His covenant for humans to live in harmony. Those who refuse to follow His commandments are therefore ungrateful and hence *kafirs*. Thus, they are wrongdoers (*zalimun*) and only harm themselves. Of the 250 verses where the Koran mentions *zulm* or *zalimun*, it mentions the object of wrongdoing in only 25 verses. In one verse, the object of wrongdoing are *people:*

> The blame is only against those who oppress men with wrongdoing and insolently transgress beyond bounds through the land, defying right and justice: for such there will be a Penalty grievous.
> (Ash-Shura 42:42, Koran)

In a second verse, the object of wrong and injustice are the signs of Allah:

> The weighing that day will be true. He whose scales are heavy, are the prosperous. Those whose scale are light; they have lost themselves for wronging Our Signs. (Al-A'raf 7:8–9, Koran)

Allah reveals His signs in nature and in scriptures so that the people may be guided. By disobeying these signs, they are wronging only themselves. In the remaining 23 verses in which the object of wrongdoing is mentioned, the wrongdoers are said to be only wronging themselves.

> Verily Allah will not deal unjustly with humans in anything: it is the human who wrongs his own soul. (Yunus 10:44, Koran)

> And We wronged them not, but they wronged themselves. (Hud 11:101, Koran)

> If anyone does evil or wrongs his own soul but afterwards seeks Allah's forgiveness, he will find Allah Oft-Forgiving, Most Merciful. (An-Nisa 4:110, Koran)

The Koran admonishes:

> Deal not unjustly and you shall not be dealt with unjustly. (Al-Baqarah 2:278)

Allah has granted each believer, man and woman, the right to freedom; right to practice his faith in accordance to his beliefs as, in Islam, there is no compulsion in matters of religion; right to life, which includes mental, physical, and emotional well-being; right to safeguard one's property; right to intellectual endeavors, acquisition of knowledge, and education; right to make a living; and right to free speech and action to enjoin good and forbid evil. In enjoying his freedoms, the individual ensures that his activities do not impinge on the similar rights of others.

> The blame is only against those who oppress humans, (insan: (men and women) with wrongdoing and insolently transgress beyond bounds through the land, defying right and justice: for such there will be a Penalty grievous (Ash-Shura 42:42)

2. The Betrayal of the Covenant: Theft, Deception, Fraud, Dishonesty, and Injustice

> Betray not the trust of Allah and His Messenger. Nor knowingly misappropriate wealth entrusted to you, whether on behalf of an orphan or another party. Be honest in handling property, goods, credit, confidences, secrets of your fellow men and display integrity and honesty in using your skills and talent. Whenever you give your word speak truthfully and justly even if a near relative is concerned.

The *amri minkum*, those entrusted with the administration of the affairs of the believers should not betray the trust of Allah, the messenger, and the believers and knowingly misappropriate the wealth of the Muslims. The populations of the Islamic lands are akin to the orphans whose land and heritage has been forcibly sequestered by conquest, to be redeemed and accounted for from those who seized it for every grain of sand and every grain of stolen gold. The dictators, the royals, and their circle of sycophants and cheerleaders in all Muslim nation-states have siphoned off the cream of their national wealth. Suharto, Asif Ali Zardari, Benazir Bhutto, Nawaz Sharif and his family, Reza Shah of Iran, the Saudi royal family, the sheikhs of the Gulf states and Oman, Saddam Hussein, Anwar Sadat, Hosni Mubarak, their families, and the inner circle of their regimes plundered their nation's treasuries of trillions of dollars over the years of their prolonged reign.

However, the greatest pillage and plunder in history took place systematically when the descendants of ten barefoot, camel-herding Bedouins took control of the Arabian Peninsula with the help of British money and arms. In the latter half of the twentieth century, over a short period of fifty years, they took a heist of tens of trillion dollars. In the Arabian Peninsula, in the kingdoms of Oman, Kuwait, the United Arab Emirates, Qatar, Bahrain, and Saudi Arabia, there are now six kinglings and over two hundred billionaires and thousands of millionaires among this narrow circle of ten clans. Over this short period, the tent dwellers who had never been inside the confines of a dwelling now own hundreds of palaces in Arabia, Europe, and America. Yet the plunder goes on and on.

Each lowly member of these clans receives an allowance of millions of dollars per year. The total amount of petty cash taken out by the thirty thousand "princes" in allowances, salaries, commissions, and expenses is to the tune of thirty to fifty billion dollars annually, which is more than the total annual combined budget of nation-states of Pakistan, Afghanistan, Iran, Syria and Jordan, with a population of 250 million people. The number of princes increases daily, requiring a special office of the state to keep track of their allowances. The cost of security of the royal families (90,000 troops) and of maintenance of personal jets, helicopters, yachts, and private royal air terminals in Jeddah and Riyadh is an additional several billion dollars. Such decadence occurs when most of the Arabs and Muslims live in conditions of utter poverty and deprivation.

Mohammed bin Salman, the Saudi crown prince, has recently acquired a pleasure yacht in the Red Sea for half a billion dollars and a portrait of Jesus Christ by Leonardo da Vinci for another half a billion to decorate his boat. There is a hazy distinction between people's wealth and personal spending for pleasure.

3. The Betrayal of the Covenant: Secret Pacts with the Kafireen, Circle of Evil, the Coalition of the Yahudi, Salibi, and the Munafiqeen

Sharif Hussein and his sons Faisal and Abdullah continued to be clients and servants of the British. For a few thousand pounds and personal glory, they and their descendants sold the honor of Islam for the next one hundred years. Ibn Sa'ud's sons inherited their father's debauchery and treason to Islam for their personal gain. Treason runs deep in the veins of the descendants of Sharif Hussein and 'Abd al-'Aziz.

The traitors are *Munafiqeen* who have taken their *awliya* from among the *kafireen*. According to the Koran those who take their *awliya* from among the *kafireen* are of the *kafireen* (Al-Ma'idah 5:51). This circle of evil—the coalition of the *Yahudi*, *Salibi*, and the *Munafiqeen*—triumphed over Islam for over one hundred years. The Jewish money in London, New York, Berlin, and Paris and the Christian powers of Europe and America collaborated with the *Munafiqeen*—Enver Pasha, Cemal Pasha, Talat Pasha, Sharif Hussein and sons, and 'Abd al-'Aziz and sons—to defeat the *ummah*. Together, they fragmented the Muslim lands into scores of impoverished mini-client-states of the West for the political and economic exploitation by the *Yahudi*, *Salibi*, and *Munafiq* coalition. The collaboration, the fragmentation, and the exploitation are still ongoing.

Time and again, we find shame and ignominy brought to Islam by professional rulers of Islam who sat on the throne with the help of mercenary armies and ruled the believers against the dictates of the law, the Koran, and the covenant of Allah. Knowledge of Islam's flawed history is essential to prevent the rule of traitors in the future. To know the past is to forecast the future. When the believers celebrate their heroes, they must also commemorate their traitors so that the history of Islam's ignominies does not repeat itself. Freshening of such painful memories is an essential part of an *ummah*'s maturity into righteousness and greatness.

Islam regards secret pacts with enemies and hostile actions against one's own people as treason. During the period when the *nabi* was in Medina, there were people who professed Islam and at the same time conspired with the enemy, the *kafirun*, against fellow Muslims. The Koran has the following description of the fate of the *Munafiqeen*.

> Of the people there are some who say: "We believe in Allah and the Last Day;" but they do not really believe.
>
> Fain would they deceive Allah and those who believe, but they only deceive themselves, and realize it not!
>
> In their hearts is a disease; and Allah has increased their disease: and grievous is the penalty they incur, because they are false to themselves.
>
> When it is said to them: "Make not mischief on the earth," they say: "Why, we only want to make peace!"
>
> Of a surety, they are the ones who make mischief, but they realize (it) not. (Al Baqarah 2:8–12, Koran).
>
> Allah will throw back their mockery on them, and give them rope in their trespasses; so, they will wander like blind ones to and fro.
>
> These are they who have bartered guidance for error: but their traffic is profitless, and they have lost true direction.
>
> Their similitude is that of a man who kindled a fire; when it lighted all around him, Allah took away their light and left

> them in utter darkness. So, they could not see. Deaf, dumb, and blind, they will not return to the path. (Koran 2:15–18)

Islam's history is laden with stories of covetous adventurers who, for little personal gain or a purseful of gold, stabbed the *ummah* in the back.

a. 1095 CE: The One-Thousand-Year War

November 25, 1095 is a milestone in the history of Europe and Christendom. On this day at the Council of Clermont, Pope Urban II—addressing a vast crowd of priests and knights and poor folk—declared a holy war against Islam. For Europe, this was a defining moment, and this event has ongoing repercussions until today in the Middle East. This holy war, begun in the twilight of the eleventh century, is still ongoing under various guises and forms into the beginning of the twenty-first century. NATO troops in Afghanistan, Kosovo, Bosnia, and Iraq (the coalition) are the legacy of the Council of Clermont, now called the Council of Europe, and the NATO.

The pope declared the race of Seljuk Turks who had recently converted to Islam to be barbarians. They had swept into Anatolia and seized lands from the Christian empire of Byzantium. The pope declared that the Turks were an accursed race, utterly alienated from God who had not entrusted their spirit to God[32]. Killing these godless monsters was a holy act; it was a Christian duty to "exterminate this vile race from our lands"[33]. Once they had purged the Asia Minor of this Muslim filth, the knights would engage in a still holier task. They would then march to the holy city of Jerusalem and liberate it from

---

[32] Robert the Monk, *Historia Iherosolimitana*. Quoted by August C. Krey, *The First Crusade: The Accounts of Eyewitnesses* (Princeton and London, 1921).

[33] Fulcher of Chartres, *History of the Expedition to Jerusalem, 1095–1127*, trans. Rita Ryan (Knoxville, 1969), 66.

the infidel. It was shameful that the tomb of Christ should be in the hands of Islam.

Since that time, there has been a constant onslaught against Islam by the West. When the Euro-Christian states were not fighting against one another, they grouped together in a pack to attack the Muslim states. On the surface for the public consumption, they fought for their religion to destroy the infidel, but the true motive underlying the thousand-year war was always economic exploitation of the East by the top echelons of Euro-Christianity. The thousand-year incursions of exploitation have changed its stance every so often that the historians have lost the truth between the Crusades; Venetian trade; voyages of discovery; slave trade; colonialism; racism; economic subversion of the natives; piracy in the open seas; maritime ambushes and robbery of coastal cities; plunder of mineral, agriculture, and human resources; opium trade; capitalism; socialism; communism; world wars, both hot and cold; globalization of world trade in the hands of a few nations; and finally the control of oil.

When Damascus fell to the British troops in September 1918, Gen. Edmund Henry Allenby made it a point to visit the tomb of the great warrior Salah al-Din Yusuf ibn Ayyub, the liberator of Jerusalem. Upon approaching the grave of the sultan, he kicked it with his riding boot and uttered, "Finally, the Crusades have been avenged." Allenby, the Christian conqueror of Damascus, had remembered Pope Urban's one-thousand-year-old call to arms against Islam.

b. 1492 CE: The Fall of Spain

When the *Muwahhid* dynasty ended, more than half the northern part of Spain and all the western provinces were in Christian hands. Muslim Spain had come under anarchy once again. Muslim territories were broken into small fragments, each at war with the other. Every

Muslim chief invited Christian troops against another and offered them some cities and forts in return for their military help. This depravity of Muslim rulers was very pleasing and encouraging to the Christians. By the middle of thirteenth century, many Muslims in Spain had become subject to Christians either by conquest or by treaty. Such Muslims were called Mudejares. They had preserved their religion and the laws but had begun to forget Arabic and to adopt Romance tongue.

The Nasrid sultans were embroiled in their dynastic quarrels that had been a perpetual curse of the Muslim sultans. The final ruin of the Muslim kingdoms was hastened by the irresponsible move by Sultan Abu al-Hasan ʿAli, who refused to pay customary tribute to Ferdinand and commenced hostilities by attacking Castilian territory. Ferdinand in 1482, in a surprise attack, took Al-Hammah, which stood at the foot of the Sierra de Alhama, and guarded the southwestern entrance of the Granadan domain. At this time, a son of Abu al-Hasan—Abu ʿAbd Allah Muhammad—instigated by his mother Fatima, raised the banner of rebellion against his own father. Fatima took revenge against her royal husband for his attachment and attentions toward a Christian concubine and her children. Supported by the garrison, Abu ʿAbd Allah in 1482 seized Alhambra and made himself master of Granada.

In the following year, Abu ʿAbd Allah—whose name became corrupted to Boabdil in Spanish—had the temerity to attack the Castilian town of Lucena, where he was beaten and taken captive. Abu al-Hasan ʿAli reinstated himself to the Granada throne, where he ruled till 1485, when he abdicated in favor of his brother Muhammad XII, nicknamed al-Zaghall. Ferdinand and Isabella saw a perfect tool in their prisoner Abu ʿAbd Allah in their plan for destruction of Islam and its presence in Spain. Supplied with Castilian men and money, Abu 'Abd Allah in 1486 occupied part of his uncle's capital and once more plunged Granada into a destructive civil war. In the meantime, the Castilian army was advancing. Town after town fell before it. Malaga was captured in the following year, and its Muslim inhabitants were sold in slavery. The noose was getting tighter around the doomed capital. Al-Zaghall made a few unsuccessful stands against the armies of Ferdinand and was defeated. Abu 'Abd Allah fought alongside the Christian armies of Ferdinand against his uncle.

No sooner had al-Zaghall been disgracefully disposed of by his nephew than Abu 'Abd Allah was ordered by Ferdinand to vacate the city and surrender Granada to Isabella and Ferdinand. Abu 'Abd Allah refused to comply. In the spring of 1491, Ferdinand with an army of ten thousand horses marched on Granada and occupied all the land around it. He destroyed crops and farms in a blockade to starve the population into submission. When the winter came, extreme cold and heavy snow barred all access to the outside world. Food became scarce, and the population starved. In December 1491, the hardships of the people had reached their extreme, and the garrison agreed to surrender. The following terms for the surrender were agreed. Abu 'Abd Allah and his officers and people would take an oath of obedience to the Castilian sovereigns. The Castilians entered Granada on January 2, 1492, and supplanted a cross on the crescent on the towers of the fortress.

The sultan Abu 'Abd Allah, with his queen, richly dressed, left his red fortress, never to return. As he rode away, he turned to take a last look at his capital, sighed, and burst into tears. His mother, till then his evil genius, turned to him with the words *"You do well to weep like a woman for what you could not defend like a man."* The rocky eminence where he took his sad farewell look is still known by the name *El ultimo suspiro del Moro* (the last sigh of the Moor).

Ferdinand and Isabella failed to abide by their terms of capitulation. A campaign of forced conversion of Muslims was inaugurated in 1499. All books in Arabic were burned in a bonfire of Arabic manuscripts in Granada. In 1501, a royal decree was issued that all Muslims in Castile and Leon should either convert to Catholicism or leave Spain. In 1526, Muslims of Aragon were confronted with the same choices. In 1556, Phillip II promulgated a law requiring the remaining Muslims to abandon at once their language, worship, and institutions and in 1609 their manner of life. The final order of expulsion of all Muslims from Spain was signed by Phillip III, resulting in forcible deportation en masse of all Muslims from Spanish soil. Some half a million Muslims landed on the shores of Africa or took ships to distant lands of Islam. Between the fall of Granada and the first decade of the seventeenth century, it is estimated that three million Muslims were banished or executed.

c. 1757–1761: The Battle of Plassey

In the history of Islam, there are defining moments when an individual's greed left a lasting impact on the freedom of the Muslim community, lasting over several hundred years. Abu 'Abd Allah's avariciousness in conjunction with Isabella and Ferdinand dealt the death blow to seven hundred years of *Islamic* civilization in Spain and the death and expulsion of three million Muslims from Spain.

Half a world away to the east in 1757, the French and the English had been jockeying for primacy of control of trade in the Indian peninsula. The Europeans had brought a powerful navy with guns that the Indians could not match. A small number of well-trained Europeans and European-trained Indian mercenary infantrymen armed with muskets could load and fire with synchronized rapidity that could produce enough firepower to halt a conventional Indian cavalry charge. Armed with this knowledge, the English set out to control revenue-bearing Indian real estate and land. Added to their weapons was the skill to divide, rule, and bribe Indian Muslim noblemen. The covetousness of these noble grandees lost India to Islam.

The English had made Calcutta a wealthy trading post and submitted considerable revenues to the nawab of Bengal. The English provided refuge to some rebels, and the nawab of Bengal Siraj al-Dawlah, a grandson of a previous Mogul governor, demanded their return. When he received no response, Siraj attacked Calcutta and drove the English out. Siraj suddenly found himself the master of Calcutta with an assortment of Englishmen, women, and children who failed to get away with the remaining English who had made a panic-stricken dash to the ships and sailed away. Unharmed, the group was lodged overnight in the detention cell of the fort built by the English for their prisoners. How many were detained is not certainly known, but next morning, only twenty-three staggered out. Dehydration and suffocation had tragically accounted for possibly fifty lives.[34]

The tragedy was apparently unintended. Nevertheless, Siraj was held responsible. Clive, the commander of the British garrison, was thirsting for revenge. Seven months later in 1757, he marched back to the Hugli River and retook Calcutta. He continued the hostilities and marched up the river to Murshidabad, Siraj's capital. In the meantime, Siraj's army took up defensive position at Plassey. Siraj had a well-trained army of fifty thousand; so was the disposition of his troops. Against him were three thousand British troops with slightly superior artillery. Had the battle been fought, the odds would clearly be in Siraj's favor.

---

[34] John Keay, *India: A History* (HarperCollins), 389–91.

Clive had little hope of victory and rested his hopes entirely on the treachery of the dignitaries of the Muslim army. He had already negotiated a secret pact with Mir Jaffar, Siraj's commander in chief and a relative. Mir Jaffar deserted with more than half of Siraj's army and joined Clive. Siraj had to run for his life. Clive personally placed Mir Jaffar on the throne of Bengal. British arms had put Ja'far on the throne, and now the British palms waited his greasing. For the British services, Mir Jaffar paid out over £1,250,000 (three billion dollars in today's money) from the Bengal treasury, of which over £400,000 was paid to Clive in the form of revenue-bearing estates. The demands of the British for more revenue continued to increase. When in 1760–61 Mir Jaffar refused to comply with the British demands, he was promptly replaced on the throne by the British with his son-in-law.

The circle of evil of the *Munafiqun*, hungry for power and wealth, collaborated with the evil of the West in their hunt for power and gold. Mir Jaffar opened the gates of Muslim India to the British for subjugation and plunder, which lasted another two hundred years. The British now discovered that revenue rights were much more profitable than the profits of trade. The revenue receipts from the Indian farmer would quickly eliminate the need to finance imports from India with export of bullion from Britain. In Bengal and later in the rest of India, relieving the ruling princes of revenue rights became a standard practice of the British. In the wake of Plassey, the British traders fanned out into Bengal, Bihar, and beyond to acquire monopoly rights over choice export commodities of saltpeter, indigo, cotton, and opium and over the lucrative internal trade in sea salt. Acquisition of Bengal enabled the British to siphon off the Indian revenue direct from the Indian peasant to the stately homes of Britain, the foundation of the English wealth and power. This wealth was the engine of the industrialization of England, Germany, and the USA, while India was systematically impoverished.

d. 1907–1925: Traitors Within: The Shame of Islam

In July 1908, army units of the Ottoman Army in Macedonia revolted against Sultan Abdul Hamid II and demanded a return to constitutional rule. Again, on April 24, 1909, troops loyal to the revolution marched from Macedonia and took the capital, Istanbul. The Young Turks were aided in their march onto Constantinople by the Central Powers, especially by the *Neue Freie Presse* of Vienna. And three days later, Sultan Abdul Hamid was deposed.

On the twenty-seventh of April 1909, the 240 members of the Ottoman senate agreed under pressure of the national Young Turks to remove Abdul Hamid from power. The appearance of four people in the sultan's office on that day—an Arab, a Turk, a Jew, and a Christian—who came to remove him from power was a premonition of the dismemberment of the Islamic world from treachery of the Arabs and the Turks in collusion with Jews and Christians. The caliphate effectively came to an end with the fall of Abdul Hamid.

Foreign powers took advantage of the political instability in Istanbul to seize portions of the Ottoman Empire. Austria annexed Bosnia and Herzegovina immediately after the 1908 Turkish revolution, and Bulgaria proclaimed its complete independence. Italy proclaimed war in 1911 and seized Libya. After a secret pact, Greece, Serbia, Montenegro, and Bulgaria invaded and defeated Ottoman forces in Macedonia and Thrace in October 1912.

After a series of disasters, in January 1912 in a coup d'état,[35] the most authoritarian elements of the Young Turks movement took control of the Ottoman government. Kamil Pasha was driven from

---

[35] John Ridley-Dash, *The Demise of Ottoman* (Girne American University, 1995).

power and Nazim Pasha was murdered by Enver Bey. The leadership of the Committee of Union and Progress emerged as a military dictatorship with power concentrated in the hands of the triumvirate of Mehmed Talat Pasha, Ahmed Cemal Pasha, and Enver Bey. Enver, as war minister, was acknowledged as the leader of the group in the government.

On January 13, 1913, Talat and Enver hastily collected about two hundred followers and marched to the Sublime Porte, where the ministers were meeting. Nazim Pasha, hearing the uproar, stepped into the hall, courageously faced the crowd with a cigarette in his mouth and hands thrust in his pockets, and said in good humor, "Come, boys, what is this noise about? Don't you know it is interfering with our deliberations?" The words had hardly left his mouth when he fell dead. A bullet had pierced his heart. The mob led by Enver and Talat then forced their way into the council chamber. They forced Kamil Pasha, the grand vizier, to resign his post by threatening him with the fate that had befallen Nazim.

Assassination became the method by which these conspirators usurped the supreme power. So, assassination continued to be the instrument by which they kept their hold on power. The Young Turks destroyed Abdul Hamid's regime to restore a democratic constitutional government; instead, they created a reign of terror. Men were arrested and deported by the score, and hangings of opponents became a common occurrence.

Early in January 1914, Enver—then only thirty-two—became war minister. Enver's elevation to the ministry of war was virtually a German victory. He immediately instituted a drastic reorganization of the armed forces. By March 1914, Germans—with the help of Talat, Enver, and Cemal—had tightened their hold on Turkey. Liman von Sanders was first made the head of the first army corps and then the inspector general of all the Turkish armed forces. Another German general, Bronsart von Schellendorf, was appointed the chief of staff, and scores of German officers held commands of first importance. And the Turkish politician Enver Pasha, an outspoken thirty-four-year-old champion of Germany, was minister of war. The Kaiser had almost completed his plans to annex the Turkish Army to his own.

Enver secretly signed a treaty of Turko-German alliance on August 2, 1914. Only five people in Turkey knew of this treaty, which brought on the final disintegration of the Ottoman Empire. The puppet grand vizier Said Halim, Talat, and Cemal were convinced by Enver of the wisdom of supporting the Germans in case the war broke out. Enver Pasha chose to ally Turkey with the Central Powers by citing Germany's earlier victories in the war. Thus, the Ottoman Empire joined the Central Powers to form a triple alliance without the knowledge of the cabinet, the parliament, the army generals, and the Ottoman populace. The empire was ruled by three collaborators and puppets of Germany, traitors to Islam, to the Muslims in Turkey, and to the whole of the *ummah*. They acted secretly as collaborators with a foreign government working toward the destruction and disintegration of the only free Islamic state.

Two German warships, the battleship *Goeben* and the cruiser *Breslau*, that were caught in a neutral Turkish port when the war broke out in Europe were handed to the Ottoman Navy. In October, they were put out to sea, flying the Ottoman flag with German officers and crew, and shelled Odessa and other Russian ports. Enver Pasha, as the Ottoman war minister, gave secret orders in a sealed envelope to Admiral Souchon, the commander of the Turko-German fleet, only to be opened when the fleet was deep in the Black Sea. The orders read:

War minister Enver Pasha to Admiral Souchon October 25, 1914.
The entire fleet should maneuver in the Black Sea. When you
find a favorable opportunity, attack the Russian fleet. Before
initiating the hostilities, open my secret orders given to you
personally this morning. To prevent transport of material to
Serbia, act as already agreed upon. Enver Pasha.

(Secret Order): *"The Turkish fleet should gain the mastery of*
the Black Sea by force. Seek out the Russian fleet and attack
her wherever you find her without declaration of war. Enver
Pasha"

Souchon now had a surprise for Enver. Rather than causing an incident at sea, the admiral attacked simultaneously the Russian ports of Sebastopol, Theodosia, Novorossiysk, and Odessa on the morning of October 29. This action in effect declared a war on Russia and its allies Britain and France. Once again, Enver acted secretly at the behest of Germany. He did not consult his coconspirators, Talat and Cemal, before ordering the attack on Russia or the declaration of war against the Western allies. He kept his cabinet colleagues, the parliament, and the people of the empire in the dark, who on the morning of October 29, 1914, were surprised to find themselves at war.

The conspiracies, utter stupidity, and lust for power of three men—Talat, Cemal, and Enver—led to the dismemberment of the Ottoman Empire. For another one hundred years, this land of Islam was to know no peace. It became the prey of the circle of evil of the Euro-Christian, Jew, and Arab conspirators.

e. 1914-Present: The Hashemites: From Common Traitors to Kings of Arabs

According to some sources, Sharif Hussein's son Abdullah had made contacts with the British consul general in Egypt, Lord Kitchener, as early as 1912, if not 1913.[36] Kitchener established a line of communication with Hussein's family through Hussein's representative, Muhammad al-Faruqi. Kitchener's letters to Hussein contained statements pledging British support in the event of an Arab uprising against the Turks and promising an independent Arabia after the war. In January 1915, Lord Kitchener was replaced by Sir Henry McMahon. In the ensuing correspondence, Hussein set forth a list of demands calling on the British government to support the independence of "Arab countries" within an area bounded on the north by the Mersin-Adana line and the thirty-seventh parallel, on the east by the Persian frontier and the Persian Gulf, on the south by the Indian Ocean (excepting Aden), and on the west by the Red and Mediterranean Seas. Hussein also requested the establishment of an Arab caliphate to supplant the Turkish sultan. In exchange for these concessions, Hussein offered economic preference to Great Britain and a defensive alliance.

In reply, McMahon dispatched on October 24 a letter that more precisely outlined the territorial parameters within which the British were prepared to recognize the Arab independence. These boundaries corresponded roughly with those asked by Hussein earlier with several important differences. In view of Britain's established position and interests, the vilayets of Basra and Baghdad were excluded. Also excluded were the areas of Syria, west of the district of Damascus, Homs, Hama, and Aleppo, as well as districts of Mersin

---

[36] Bruce Westrate, *The Arab Bureau: British Policy in the Middle East, 1916–1920* (Pennsylvania State University Press, 1992).

and Alexandretta. Hussein's response on November 5 accepted the exclusion of Mersin and Alexandretta but objected to the exception of what essentially were Lebanon and the coastal Latakia area. Hussein was willing to accept the British claim to the two Mesopotamian vilayets in exchange for monetary compensation, pending the region's eventual return to Arab rule. In his letter on December 14, McMahon held firm to his stance on the Syrian littoral, citing the prior French interests precluding the inclusion of the area to the Arab zone.

Hussein was never promised personal rule of the territory in question. An Arab caliphate was only obliquely referred to in the correspondence. Hussein did not make any attempt to clarify the position taken by the British before he led a revolt against his caliph, sultan, country, and coreligionists under the protection of an alien, infidel, colonial, expansionist power with the full knowledge that parts of the Islamic state—including Syria, Lebanon, Palestine, and Iraq—would pass from Islamic rule to an economic and colonial subjugation of a non-Muslim power. For the sake of his own hunger for power, he used his holy prophetic bloodline to break up the united Islamic state when what its people most needed was a moral and just leadership to steer the state into the path of Allah. He could have drawn on his authority, knowledge, and influence to correct what was wrong in the *ummah* rather than subvert it. He appealed to an infidel power for his own personal elevation to the position of caliph, the spiritual and temporal leadership of the whole Islamic nation.

At that time, there was another player in the treason game with the British. He was the young Bedouin tribal leader 'Abd al-'Aziz (Ibn Saud). He was a master of the *ghazzu*, raiding other tribes to steal their women, camels, sheep, and grain. He was backed by the religious zealots of the Wahhabi sect, who had little regard for life and sought death in the hope of martyrdom and ascent to heaven. Bedouin sheikhs frowned on *ghazzu* as an unwholesome and dishonorable activity. The heads of major Bedouin tribes who claimed hegemony over large tracts of land did not practice it. The way of robbery and plunder as practiced by 'Abd al-'Aziz was contrary to all Koranic teaching and Arab traditions of generosity to the vanquished. 'Abd al-'Aziz prided himself on never taking any prisoners; he murdered all the men of the raided tribe to prevent future retaliation.

Ibn Sa'ud's political emergence began in 1902, when he reclaimed Riyadh[37], the city where his family had been local sheikhs, appointed by local emirs. His first merciless act was to terrorize the population by spiking the heads of his enemies and displaying them at the gates of the city. His followers burned 1,200 people to death. While conducting a raid, he and his followers were very much in the habit of taking young maidens back as slaves and as gifts to friends. This as how Ibn Sa'ud lived at the turn of the century before he became a king when he was a mere head of a small tribe.

The third player was Lawrence. Thomas Edward Lawrence was the illegitimate child of an illegitimate child. His father was Thomas Chapman and his mother, Thomas Chapman's family governess, was the offspring out of wedlock of an English mother and a Norwegian father. In 1913 and 1914, Lawrence worked on a geographical survey of the Negev desert under the archaeological rubric of the Palestine Exploration Fund. Lawrence acquired a great deal of vital cartographic and geographic data for the British intelligence before the venture was terminated by the Turkish authorities in early 1914. When the war began, he found himself as an intelligence officer on the staff of Lord Horatio Herbert Kitchener with David Hogarth, his mentor, a key figure in the British administration in the Middle

---

[37] Said K. Aburish, *The Rise, Corruption, and Coming Fall of the House of Saud* (St. Martin's Griffin, New York).

East. Hogarth later became the head of the Arab Bureau, planning and executing the so-called Arab Revolt. Kitchener, the British consul general in Egypt was in secret contact with Abdullah, son of Sharif Hussein of Mecca, who at the time was a member of Parliament in Istanbul. Sharif Hussein ibn Ali was the Turkish-appointed governor as a caretaker of the Muslim holy shrines of Mecca. Kitchener's strategy was to establish a channel of communication with Hussein to take advantage of the situation in the event of war with Turkey as the Arab lands were critical to the British position in India and Egypt. Winston Churchill underlined the strategic importance of the Persian Gulf oil and the huge refinery at Abadan and made clear the intention of the British government to become the owners and the controllers of the Gulf oil required by the British navy. This vital priority led to the occupation of Basra in 1914 and later the invasion of Mesopotamia.

In June 1916, supported by Abdullah, Faisal, and his other sons, Hussein proclaimed the Arab Revolt against the sultan and the caliph of the Ottoman Empire. For Hussein and sons, it was an act of treason—treason against their religion, people, and sovereign to whom they had sworn allegiance and loyalty. Faisal, who was a serving officer in the Ottoman Army, deserted his post in Syria to join the revolt. It proved to be a dud. Hussein, it turned out, had no following at all. Muslims did not respond to his call, nor did the Arabs. Under his banner, or rather the one that a British official designed for him, those who rallied under him were closer to one thousand rather than one hundred thousand, and they were Bedouin tribesmen and not soldiers. And those who did join were bribed with British gold.

In the make-believe world of Lawrence, Faisal ibn Hussein became Prince Faisal, the field commander of the Arab armies of under one thousand men; and at Faisal's request, Lawrence was assigned to be the British liaison officer with him. With such untrained and undisciplined band of men in Faisal's army, a frontal attack on the Ottoman troops would be suicidal. Some Bedouin men had qualms against fighting face-to-face against fellow Muslims. Over half the Ottoman Army was ethnically Arab. Lawrence, therefore, believed that Faisal's Bedouins would be better employed in fighting a guerilla war than in trying to fight a conventional one. Their object was to take the city of Medina, which lay to the north and blocked Faisal's force from riding to Palestine, where the Middle East war was to be fought.

Faisal's men raided a single-track railway from the Ottoman Palestine, which was the only source of reinforcement and supply to Medina's defenders. A British officer, Herbert Garland, taught Faisal's Bedouins to dynamite the railroad. Garland, Lawrence, and other British officers went on to dynamite it repeatedly. The campaign failed. The Ottoman Muslim forces repaired the railway after each attack and kept it running. Medina never fell to Faisal or to the British. The Ottoman Muslim garrison held on till the end of the war, blocking the land road to Palestine. The Arab and Muslim defenders of Medina and Asir stood their ground to the last day of the war.

June 1916 was a historical moment when, for the first time in the history of Islam since the Battle of Badr in the first year of hijra, the combined forces of the *kafireen* and *Munafiqeen* attacked the city of the prophet of Islam, though unsuccessfully. This attack introduced the combined evil dominion of the *Mutaffifeen*, *kafireen*, and *Munafiqeen* to the heartlands of Islam for the next century to come.

Medina continued to stand in Faisal's way, and had Lawrence not thought of a way around it using the Red Sea route, Hussein's revolt would have stayed bottled up in the Hejaz desert. Now that Lawrence had secured a port in Palestine, General Allenby sent boats to bring Faisal and about a thousand Bedouin followers from Ragheb on the Red Sea to Aqaba. Faisal arrived in Aqaba as a conqueror, and so the world was told by the British media and by Prime Minister Lloyd George's secretariat. In Aqaba, Faisal was reinforced by about twenty-five hundred men, Auda abu Tayi's Bedouins, and some Arab deserters from the Ottoman Army. All together, they formed a camel cavalry corps that harassed the Turkish flank when Allenby's Egypt-based army invaded Palestine and marched into Syria.

Faisal's camel corps presented a pretense that Syria was liberated by the Arabs themselves. In fact, there were a million British troops fighting in the Middle East in 1918 and only thirty-five hundred Husseini troops, and on the face of it was a British war of conquest over the Arabs and not a war of liberation for the Arabs. The British on May 9, 1916, in a secret convention, had already promised Arab Syria to the French (Sykes-Picot Agreement) and on November 2, 1917, in the Balfour Declaration, gave away Arab Palestine to the Jews. The Lawrence-Hussein-sons puppet show was being cleverly orchestrated from London. Each one of the players understood their role and the reward for their part except Hussein and sons. The ambiguous language, willful face-to-face lies, secret agreements, double dealings, deception, flattery, and bribery as a skill and art had become the trademark of English diplomacy over the previous one hundred years. The Arabs and the Bedouins had their own share of guile and cunningness; they were, however, no match for the Anglos as the next one hundred years would reveal. And the Arab leaders never learned.

For his treachery, Sharif Hussein received his first reward in gold sovereigns in March 1916, a shipment in the amount of £53,000, three months before he announced his revolt. Commencing on August 8, 1916, the official allowance was set at £125,000 a month, a sum that was frequently exceeded on Hussein's demand. For example, in November 1916, £375,000 in gold sovereigns was dispatched to Hussein by the British for hajj expenses. The money was to have been used by Hussein to pay his armies and to bribe the sheikhs and the tribes into joining his revolt. The payments were broken down into five categories representing the four armies under the command of Hussein's sons and an allotment for the upkeep of the mosque at Kaaba and for hajj facilities as well as for the operation of Hussein's government in Mecca and Jeddah. Forty thousand pounds was allocated to Faisal, £30,000 to Abdullah, £20,000 each for Ali and Zeid, and £15,000 for expenses at Mecca and Jeddah.

The year 1916 must have been the lowest point in the history of Islam. It was surrounded by powerful enemies around the world and inside; it was being destroyed by self-serving traitors at the very heart of the faith, the Kaaba. For the first time in the history of Islam, the very upkeep of the Holy Mosque of Mecca and the Kaaba and the hajj expenses were being paid for by the *kafireen* at the behest of the *Munafiqeen* under the claim of their lineage from the holy prophet. While claiming their bloodline, they forgot the teachings of the Koran and the example of the prophet.

The British were unable to make all the payments from their London treasury, so in the spring of 1917, the British drew gold out of the rapidly diminishing Egyptian treasury. The source of gold in the Egyptian treasury was the sweat and blood of the Egyptian peasant. Hussein had insisted that he needed additional £75,000 monthly to meet his bloated payroll. The Egyptian peasants were in double jeopardy as they not only had to pay in taxes for Hussein's misadventure but also had to provide free labor of one hundred thousand men for the transport of troops, equipment, and supplies to the British Expeditionary Force of General Allenby from Egypt to Palestine. The British-controlled Egyptian treasury, by June 1917, had only £200,000 in reserve that was available for Hussein. To meet Hussein's demand for additional cash, there was a scramble for alternative source for money. Silver was scarce in India, and agriculture goods were too dear in Egypt. Hussein demanded that the total payment be made in gold; however, he was eventually forced to accept shipments of Indian paper rupees and goods in lieu of precious metals.

f. 1902–Present: The Saudis: From Desert Thugs to Kings of Arabs and Servants of the *Kafireen*

The Ottomans, with German finance and technology, planned a railway from Berlin through the Ottoman Empire to end in the Persian Gulf at Kuwait, which was the only deep-water harbor in the region. The railway threatened the growing British influence in the region, and the British quietly preempted the German move by signing an agreement with Sheikh Mubarak Al-Sabah of Kuwait. The gist of the agreement signed on January 23, 1899, stated that the sheikh would not receive the agent or representative of any other power without the sanction of the British government, nor would he cede, sell, lease, mortgage, or give for occupation any part of his territory to any other power without the British permission. There was in the treaty no mention of the establishment of a protectorate over Kuwait, although the British Crown assumed that to be the case. Britain then appointed a resident political officer in Kuwait a year after the signing of the treaty.

Ibn Sa'ud, a homeless and hungry tent-dwelling Bedouin youth living in Kuwait, was looking for adventure and a sponsor. At least on two occasions, he wrote to the Ottoman sultan, offering his services; however, he was turned down. The British were looking for influence and contacts in the interior of Arabia and had sent several intelligence agents in the form of explorers. The first British contact with 'Abd al-'Aziz probably occurred soon after the political agent had established himself in Kuwait in 1901. By 1904, 'Abd al-'Aziz was already in the pay of the British and, till 1911, continued to receive small amounts of money. The British scouts had recognized him as potentially useful and kept him in reserve in case hostilities broke out against the Turks.

'Abd al-'Aziz certainly had a mysterious source of support when he raided Riyadh with equipment and camels and with a number of men, which were thought to be beyond his means. After he captured Riyadh, relative peaceful equilibrium of the desert was disturbed by the young Bedouin tribal leader, Ibn Sa'ud. He was a master of the *ghazzu*, raiding other tribes to steal their camels, sheep and grain. He was backed by the religious zealots of the Wahhabi sect, who had little regard for life and sought death in the hope of martyrdom and ascent to heaven. Ibn Sa'ud used much of the money from the British to sponsor colonies of the Ikhwan brotherhood, fanatics of the Wahhabi sect, to which Ibn Sa'ud belonged. The Ikhwan formed the backbone of Ibn Sa'ud's conquering army, whose savagery wreaked havoc across Arabia.

Ibn Sa'ud had no formal education. His literary talent, if any, was extremely restricted; and therefore, his worldview was limited by his own experience of the life of a Bedouin and the tribal code, which had barely changed for fourteen hundred years. His resting place was a tent or under the starlit sky. Food and water were scarce; security and refuge was with the family, clan, and tribe. Intertribal disputes and feuds were frequent and were settled by the sword; raiding the neighboring tribes for their goods and animals was a sport. Killing another Muslim and looting his property in a *ghazzu* was perfectly acceptable and did not cause remorse, slavery was practiced and prevalent, and women were nonentities and not worthy of equality with men. 'Abd al-'Aziz once boasted that he had never had a meal with a woman and that he never looked at the face of the woman he made love. Yet he had been married to over a hundred women and had a similar number of concubines and sex slaves. Religion and spirituality was judged through the narrow tunnel vision of Wahhabi men of religion in a nomadic social setting where neither the Koran nor other religious texts were available to the common man. Any person not following the narrow edicts of the Wahhabi sect of Islam was automatically a heretic and therefore an infidel and punishable by public flogging, amputation, or beheading.

Armed with these moral values and ethics, 'Abd al-'Aziz set out to conquer Arabia with the financial and military assistance of the British. His first victims were the Ibn Rashid's of the Ottoman-controlled part of the Arabian Peninsula. The defeat of the Ibn Rashid's was, in effect, a British victory. Sir Percy Cox, a British resident in the Persian Gulf, wrote, 'With Ibn-Saud in Hasa (the Gulf Coast of Arabia) our position is very much strengthened." Percy Cox openly encouraged Ibn Sa'ud to attack the remaining territory of the Ibn Rashid's to divert them from reinforcing Turkish troops against the British. Ibn Sa'ud had constant British financial aid, arms, and advisers, initially William Shakespeare and Percy Cox and later Harry Saint John Philby.

After they helped him master eastern Arabia in 1917, the British found another use for Ibn Sa'ud. In 1924, Hussein declared himself caliph of Islam without the consent of the British. Abdullah being entrenched in Amman and Faisal in Baghdad and the elevation of Sharif Hussein to the leadership of whole Islam threatened Britain's growing interests in the Middle East. These interests included strategy to continue to divide and rule the Middle East through subservient local notables. Although Hussein's sons were pliable and obedient to these imperialistic plans, Hussein demanded that Britain live up to its promises to grant Arab's independence and a free hand in all the Arab countries. He objected to British plans to provide Jews with a national home in Palestine. Ibn Sa'ud started his thrust into Hejaz; although the British ostensibly cut off the arms supplies to both sides, most historians believe that the British continued to supply small but crucial amounts of money and arms to Ibn Sa'ud and his merciless Ikhwan. Some of the military equipment used by Ibn Sa'ud was expensive and could not have been obtained without outside help and could not have been used without instructors. At the time, statements by British officials did point to the British hand in Ibn Sa'ud's attack on Mecca. Arthur Hirtzel—a Jew, head of the British India Office at that time—expressed the need for Ibn Sa'ud to establish himself in Mecca.

In 1925, Hejaz fell to Ibn Sa'ud's Ikhwan army. The most advanced and settled part of Arabia with a long history of contact with the outside world, constitutional government, established institutions, and established justice system fell to an anarchist tribal army of religious fanatics. If the British secret planners had wanted to destroy and divide the heart of Islam, they could not have chosen a more competent and effective allies. Ibn Sa'ud's Ikhwan soldiers killed hundreds of males, including children; pillaged homes of the conquered populace for money, gold, and valuable objects; murdered non-Wahhabi religious leaders; and destroyed whole towns. Tolerance of others' beliefs was against Wahhabi and Ikhwan teachings and traditions. They committed massacres in At Ta'if, Bureida, and Al Huda. They tried to destroy the tomb of the prophet and remove the domes of the major mosques. They also desecrated the Sunni graveyards of Mecca. They carried out genocide against Shias of eastern Arabia.

The Ikhwan forces of Ibn Sa'ud indulged in mass killings of mostly innocent victims, including women and children. Ibn Sa'ud's cousin Abdallah bin Mussallem bin Jalawi beheaded 250 members of the Mutair tribe, and Ibn Sa'ud himself set an example for his followers by personally beheading 18 rebels in a public square of the town of Artawaya. The Shammar tribe suffered 410 deaths, the Bani Khalid 640, and the Najran a staggering 7,000. Ibn Sa'ud used massacres to subdue his enemies No less than a 400,000 people were killed and wounded in the Saudi campaign to subdue the Arabian Peninsula. The Ikhwan did not take prisoners and mostly killed the vanquished. Well over a million inhabitants of the territories conquered by Ibn Sa'ud fled to Kuwait, Egypt, Iraq, Jordan, and Syria. By the time Ibn Sa'ud and his family had subdued the country, they had carried out 40,000 public executions and 350,000 amputations, respectively 1 and 4 percent of the estimated population of 4 million.[38]

To summarize the brutality and the insensitivity of Ibn Sa'ud's regime, one has to understand the degree of devastation of the country, which he proudly named after himself in 1932. At the turn of the twentieth century, the population of the territory that became Saudi Arabia was an estimated 3.5 million. By the time, 'Abd al-'Aziz established his control over the kingdom, a million inhabitants had fled the country, 400,000 were killed or wounded, 40,000 were beheaded in public squares, and 350,000 had their limbs amputated for opposing the Saudi regime. Thus, to accommodate 'Abd al-'Aziz in his newfound kingdom, an estimated 30 percent of the population chose exile, 13 percent were killed in war or beheaded in public squares, and 10 percent had their limbs amputated. This left only 47 percent of the population of able-bodied men women and children in the kingdom. Assuming that of the 2.5 million people remaining

---

[38] Ibid., 24–27.

after the ones who fled the country, 1,250,000 were male and the same number were females, both adult and children, and again assuming that most of the people killed, executed, and dismembered were males, then we are forced to assume that by mid-1930s, the total population of males in Saudi Arabia was only 810,000, of whom 460,000 were able bodied and the remaining 350,000 amputees, mutilated by the state. The ratio of able-bodied men to women was almost 1:3. This would explain the destitution of Saudi Arabia before the discovery of oil when most of the able-bodied, educated, cultured, and enterprising men was eliminated, leaving uneducated Bedouins to run the country. This also explains why after each man took four wives, still, there were plenty of women left to marry. In a culture where women had equality with men, suddenly, women were the underdog, unable to resist the inequity. This would also explain the need for foreign workers to man most jobs in the kingdom and why the Saudis have not been able to raise a large enough army, having to depend on the Americans for the defense of their country.

In the hot wind and sand-blown desert, this genocide and iniquity went unnoticed by the world, while similar crimes later during the century in Nazi Germany caused public outcry. It was so because it was a Muslim carrying out genocide against Muslims in the name of Islam with the British-supplied arms for the greater glory of the British Empire. Lord Crewe, a British minister, had proclaimed, "What we want is not a united Arabia, but a disunited Arabia split into small principalities under our suzerainty." With ongoing turmoil within his own kingdom and skirmishes with Hejaz and later with Jordan, Iraq, and Yemen, Ibn Sa'ud afforded Britain the comfort of keeping the Arabs and Muslims divided. This protected its commercial and political interests by opposing a unified Muslim state.

g. 1915 to Present: Creation of Israel, a State for the Jews in the Land of Islam

Alfred Milner, son of a university lecturer, was born in Bonn, Germany, in 1854. After childhood in Germany, he came to England and completed his education at the Oxford University. George Joachim Goschen, who was the chancellor of the Exchequer, brought Milner into the British establishment as his private secretary. On Goschen's recommendation, Milner was appointed undersecretary of finance in Egypt in 1890 and was responsible for the taxation of the Egyptian population to pay off the Egyptian debt to the Jewish bankers.

Cecil Rhodes and Milner were members of a secret society that was patterned on the organization of Jesuits. It was also based on political, personal, and family relationship built over a long period. Financial backing came informally from the fortunes of Cecil Rhodes, the Rothschilds, and other Jewish bankers. There was, by the turn of the century, an acceptance of social mixing among the moneyed Jews and the British aristocracy. Among the first initiates to the Round Table were Rhodes, Lord Rothschild, Milner, Grey, Balfour, Lord Rosebery (Lord Rothschild's son-in-law), and Alfred Beit, a Jewish business genius who handled all of Rhodes's business affairs. Among others to join later was Winston Churchill, who as well as his father, Randolph, before him had been allowed to live a life of opulence, thanks to the benevolence of Lord Rothschild.

The Round Table was originally a major fief within the great nexus of power, influence, and privilege controlled by the Cecil family. The method used to control the center of power was penetrating the fields of politics, education, and journalism; recruitment of men of ability chiefly from All Souls College at Oxford; and linking these men to Cecil and the Round Table block by matrimonial alliances and then granting them positions of power and titles. Milner had recruited Leo Amery, a secret Jew, when he was still at Oxford. Amery was an eminent scholar and, at the time, was regarded as the chief imperial theorist. He served as the *London Times* chief war correspondent during the Boer War and into the period leading to the Great War. Milner actively supported his effort to be elected to Parliament in 1906.

David Lloyd George appointed Milner to his war cabinet in 1916 as secretary of war. Milner, a Jew in league with Cecil Rhodes and Lord Nathaniel (Natty) Rothschild, had intrigued to instigate the Boer War in 1902 to establish British control over the whole of southern Africa. The aim was to exploit extensive mineral wealth of that region. After becoming the secretary of war, Milner brought Leo Amery, another Jew albeit a secret one, as the secretary of the war cabinet. Milner had maintained his contacts with the Rothschilds; in 1912, he had helped Natty Rothschild unify the divided Jewish community of London, less than one spiritual head, Chief Rabbi Joseph Herman Hertz.[39]

British cabinet minister Herbert Samuel, a Jew, wrote a memorandum "The Future of Palestine" in 1915, when Palestine was still a Turkish possession. He argued that Palestine should become a British protectorate, "into which the scattered Jews in time swarm back from all quarters of the globe, in due course obtain home rule, and form a Jewish Commonwealth like that of Canada and Australia." Lord Walter Rothschild, Natty Rothschild's successor as the leader of the British Jews, bent the ears of the prime minister, Lloyd George, and his foreign secretary for a declaration about Palestine. Balfour suggested that "they submit a declaration for the cabinet to consider."

---

[39] Ferguson, *House of Rothschild*, 259.

The declaration was written by Milner and revised several times. The final version was drafted by Leo Amery, which read,

> His Majesty's Government view with favor the establishment in Palestine a national home for the Jewish people and will use their best endeavors to facilitate the achievement of this object, it being clearly understood that nothing shall be done which may prejudice the civil and religious rights of existing non-Jewish communities in Palestine, or the rights and political status enjoyed in any other country.

The British cabinet approved the declaration, which was addressed to Lord Walter Rothschild and signed by the foreign secretary Balfour. The Balfour Declaration, as this Jewish Magna Carta came to be known, gave birth illegitimately to the state of Israel. The document was written by Lord Alfred Milner, a Jew; it was revised and finalized by Leo Amery, another Jew, at the behest of Lord Walter Rothschild. And it was addressed to Lord Walter Rothschild, the leader of the Jews of London, for the purpose of the creation of a state for the Jews in the name of the British government on a land that did not belong to the Jews or to the British. In fact, this was an agreement among a group of conspirators belonging to a secret organization that had a long history of fraud and extortion to grab the world's wealth.

In this case, the plotters made full circle in their relationship. Lord George Joachim Goschen, a German Jew, patronized Alfred Milner, another German Jew, and brought him into the English establishment and introduced him to the Rothschilds. Milner, in turn, brought Leo Amery, a secret Jew, into the war cabinet, and they together wrote the Balfour Declaration for the Lord Rothschild. To complete the circle, George Goshen's daughter Phyllis Evelyn Goschen married

Francis Cecil Balfour, Foreign Secretary Balfour's son, on August 31, 1920. From among the same group of conspirators, Herbert Samuel was appointed the high commissioner to Palestine to establish Jewish immigration; Rufus Isaacs (as Lord Reading) was appointed viceroy of India with authority over the affairs over Iraq, Persian Gulf, Palestine, and Arabia.

From this time, Zionists became the allies of the British government, and every help and assistance was forthcoming from each government department. Space was provided for the Zionists in Mark Sykes's office with liaison to each government department. The British government provided financial, communication, and travel facilities to those working in the Zionist office. Mark Sykes, who had negotiated the Sykes-Picot agreement giving Syria to the French, was now working for the Zionists, offering them a part of the same territory. In the meantime, through secret communications, the British, USA, France, Italy, and Vatican had all come to a secret understanding of establishment of a Jewish nation in Palestine. The Balfour Declaration was the culmination of secret negotiations and maneuverings among these powers whose price would be paid to the international Jewry for financial and intelligence support in the war against the Germans and the Turks.

The Koran speaks of the deceivers thus:

> O you who believe! Take not for friends Unbelievers rather than Believers: do you wish to offer Allah an open proof against yourselves? (4:144)

Allah, in the covenant, also reminds the believers repeatedly not to take the *kafirun* (infidels), Jews, and Christians as their *awliya* (friends and protectors) in place of believers. They are friends and protectors unto one another. He who among believers turns to them is one of them. Allah does not guide those who are unjust and evildoers (*zalimun*). He from among the believers who turns to them is from among the *kafirun*, *Munafiqeen*, *mushrikun*, and *zalimun*.

h. 1921–1970: Treaty of Versailles: The Traitors of Islam

Faisal's camel corps presented a pretense that the Arabs themselves liberated Syria. In fact, there were a million British troops fighting in the Middle East in 1918 and only thirty-five hundred Husseini troops, and on the face of it was a British war of conquest over the Arabs and not a war of liberation for the Arabs. The British, on May 9, 1916, in a secret convention, had already promised Arab Syria to the French (Sykes-Picot Agreement) and on November 2, 1917, in the Balfour Declaration gave away Arab Palestine to the Jews. The Lawrence-Hussein-sons puppet show was being cleverly orchestrated from London. Each one of the players understood their role and the reward for their part except Hussein and sons. The ambiguous language, willful face-to-face lies, secret agreements, double dealings, deception, flattery, and bribery as a skill and art had become the hallmark of English diplomacy over the previous one hundred years. The Arabs and the Bedouins had their own share of guile and cunningness; they were, however, no match for the Anglos and the Franks as the next one hundred years were to reveal. And the Arab leaders never learned.

For his treachery, Sharif Hussein started to receive his reward in gold sovereigns from March 1916 onward, three months before he announced his revolt. The total shipments were in the amount of £1,928,000. The payments were broken down into five categories representing the four armies under the command of Hussein's sons and an allotment for the upkeep of the mosque at Kaaba and for hajj facilities as well as for the operation of Hussein's government in

Mecca and Jeddah. Forty thousand pounds per month was allocated to Faisal, £30,000 to Abdullah, £20,000 each for Ali and Zeid, and £15,000 for expenses at Mecca and Jeddah. The year 1916 must have been the lowest point in the history of Islam. At that time, it was surrounded by powerful enemies around the world; and inside, in its very heart, the Kaaba, it was being destroyed by traitors to Islam. For the first time in the history of Islam, the very upkeep of the Holy Mosque of Mecca, the Kaaba, and the hajj expenses were being paid for by the *kafireen* at the behest of the *Munafiqeen* under the claim of their lineage to the holy prophet. In this claim of their bloodline, they forgot the teachings of the Koran and the example of conduct set by the prophet.

The covenant of Allah states:

> When you hold secret counsel, do it not for iniquity and hostility, and disobedience to the teachings of the Messenger; but do it for righteousness and self-restraint; and fear Allah, to whom ye shall be brought back.

> The Satan inspires secret counsels, in order that he may cause grief to the Believers; but he cannot harm them in the least, except as Allah permits; and on Allah let the Believers put their trust.

No believer, individual, community, or ruler shall make a compact on behalf of the *ummah* or part of it in secret with the unbelievers. Islam regards secret pacts with enemies and hostile actions against one's own people as treason. During the blessed prophet's lifetime in Medina, some people professed Islam yet conspired with the *kafirun* against their fellow Muslims. The Koran has the following description of these *Munafiqeen.*

Fain, would they deceive Allah and those who believe, but they only deceive themselves, and realize it not! In their hearts is a disease; and Allah has increased their disease: and grievous is the penalty they incur, because they are false to themselves. When it is said to them: "Make not mischief on the earth," they say: "Why, we only want to make peace!" Of a surety, they are the ones who make mischief, but they do not realize. (Al-Baqarah 2:8–12, Koran)

Allah will throw back their mockery on them and give them rope in their trespasses; so they will wander like blind ones to and fro. They have bartered guidance for error: but their traffic is profitless, and they have lost true direction. Their similitude is that of a man who kindled a fire; when it lighted all around him, Allah took away their light and left them in utter darkness. So, they could not see. Deaf, dumb, and blind, they will not return to the path. (Koran 2:15–18)

In our age, there are people who think they can get the best both worlds by compromising their nation and Islam's interests with the enemy. Winston Churchill created Transjordan, an unsustainable country, as an instrument of British control over the Arabs. He appointed Emir Abdullah as an instrument of British policy to help moderate and dampen the Palestinian opposition to the Jewish settlement in Palestine. He appointed Sir Herbert Samuel as the high commissioner to guide Abdullah in this direction. At the Cairo conference, Lawrence summed up the British position by declaring, "It will be preferable to use Transjordan as a safety valve, by appointing a ruler who would bring pressure to bear, to check anti Zionism[40]." The West used Abdullah to undermine Arab efforts against Israel in 1948. Abdullah secretly met Zionist leaders from 1922 onward, merely a year after the creation of Transjordan. These

---

[40] Uriel Dann, *The Great Powers in the Middle East*, 94.

meetings continued during the Palestinian disturbances in 1932 and 1936. The amity between the two conspiring sides was so total that, in a meeting, Abdullah and the Jewish envoy discussed ways of eliminating the mufti of Jerusalem, the leader of Palestinians, and enemy of both sides[41]. He secretly conspired with Chaim Weizmann for the partition of Palestine in 1947.

Abdullah's grandson Hussein started his secret contacts with the Israeli leaders in 1957, and by 1963, meetings[42] with the leaders became a regular occurrence. In 1963, Hussein made secret visit to Tel Aviv. In the period preceding 1967, Hussein performed several treasonable acts, which were openly anti-Arab and anti-Islam. In response to the creation of PLO, which wanted to replace him as the Palestinian representative, Hussein's[43] intelligence service provided the names and location of the Palestinian fighters infiltrating and battling the Israelis. Hussein did not stop there. His intelligence service also provided Israeli's information about other Arab countries.[44]

From 1970 onward, there were several secret meetings between Hussein and the Israeli defense minister Moshe Dayan and with Israeli prime minister Golda Meir.[45] This extensive period of secret Jordanian-Israeli cooperation produced the most treasonable act of Hussein's life, informing Israel of the impending Egyptian Syrian attack of October 1973.[46]

The rulers of Islam, who work against their own faith and their own people, have a disease in their hearts. They make mischief on the earth against their own faith and nation in secret collusion with the

---

[41] Shlaim, *Partition*, 203.

[42] Raviv and Melman, *Every Spy*, 213.

[43] Black and Morris, *Secret War*, 238.

[44] Raviv and Melman, *Every Spy*, 214.

[45] Heikal, *Secret Channels*, 310.

[46] Black and Morris, *Secret War*, 265.

enemies in return for personal power and wealth. Allah promises a grievous penalty for them because they are false to themselves and do not realize it.

i. 1973–1979: Betrayal of the Covenant: Treason

Anwar Sadat and the Egyptian Army won partial victory over the Jewish state of Israel in 1973. The victory made Sadat a hero in the eyes of many Arabs, if not equal to then almost comparable to the great Arab hero Gamal Abdel Nasser. Puffed up by success and sycophancy from the likes of Henry Kissinger, Sadat forgot his own roots and began to take advice and comfort from Kissinger and the Israeli lobby in Washington. Against the advice of his closest advisers and the leaders of other Arab countries, he made a secret trip to Israel and addressed the Knesset, the Israeli parliament. Under the American tutelage and patronage, he abandoned his Arab allies, negotiated, and signed a peace treaty with many secret appendices with Israel at the expense of the Palestinians and Syrians. Therefore, all Palestine and the Golan Heights are under Israeli occupation. The Arabs are disunited and in disarray. Sadat sold out Egyptian sovereignty, the Islamic nation, and the holy Islamic places in Jerusalem for four billion dollars a year. Sadat took Jews and Christians as his *awliya* and willfully disobeyed the covenant that every Muslim, if he was a believer, has pledged to obey. He also disobeyed the provisions of the covenant of Yathrib and the prophets teaching:

> Just as the bond to Allah is indivisible, all the believers shall stand behind the commitment of the least of them. All believers are bonded one to another to the exclusion of other men. This Pax Islamica is one and indivisible. **No believer shall enter a separate peace without all other believers whenever there**

is fighting in the cause of God but will do so only on the basis of equality and justice to all others. In every expedition for the cause of God we undertake, all parties to the covenant shall fight shoulder to shoulder as one man. All believers shall avenge the blood of one another when any one falls fighting in the cause of God.

Once again, the *Yahudi-Salibi* ingenuity used a *Munafiq* to sow the seeds of discord in the Islamic world.

j. 1979–1991: Saddam, the Servant of the *Kafireen*, Traitor to Islam

Saddam Hussein replaced al-Bakr as president of Iraq in July 1979. The bloodbath that followed eliminated all potential opposition to him. Saddam was now the master of Iraq with no one around him daring to question his actions. Two actions that he initiated led the Islamic community to disastrous disunity and debt. He attacked his fellow Muslims, Iran in 1980 and Kuwait in 1990.

The Iran-Iraq War turned out to be a battle between two egomaniac personalities, each with a Messiah complex, with neither of them willing to call a truce and a halt to the hostilities. The result was emaciation and bleeding of both countries to near bankruptcy. The Iraqi troops launched a full-scale invasion of Iran on September 22, 1980. France supplied high-tech weapons to Iraq, and the Soviet Union was Iraq's largest weapon supplier. Israel provided arms to Iran, hoping to bleed both the nations by prolonging the war. At least ten nations sold arms to both warring nations to profit from the conflict.

The United States followed a more duplicitous policy toward the warring parties to prolong the war and cause maximum damage to both of them. The United States and Iraq restored diplomatic relations in November 1984. Washington extended a $400 million credit guarantee for the export of US goods to Iraq. The CIA established a direct Washington-to-Baghdad link to provide the Iraqis with faster intelligence from US satellites.[47] The satellite data provided to Iraqis was some factual and some misleading information. Casey, the CIA director, was urging Iraqi officials to carry out more attacks on Iran, especially on economic targets.[48]

The US policy toward Iran was two faced as it followed two tracks at the same time. On the one hand, the US government carried out a covert program to undermine the government of Iran[49]. Starting in 1982, the CIA provided $100,000 a month to a group in Paris called the Front for the Liberation of Iran, headed by Ali Amini, who had presided over the reversion of Iranian oil to foreign control after the CIA-backed coup in 1953. The United States also provided support to two Iranian paramilitary groups based in Turkey, one of them headed by Gen. Bahram Aryana, the Shah's army chief.[50] The United States also carried out clandestine radio broadcasts into Iran from Egypt, calling for Khomeini's overthrow and urging support for Bakhtiar. Simultaneously, the United States pursued the second track of clandestinely providing arms and intelligence information to Iran in 1985 and 1986. In 1984, Washington launched Operation Staunch in an effort to dry up Iran's sources of arms supplies by pressuring US allies to stop supplying arms to Iran. While Washington was pretending to be neutral in the war and trying to make everyone else

---

[47] Stephen Engelberg, "Iran and Iraq Got Doctored Data, US Officials Say," *New York Times*, Jan. 12, 1987, A1, A6.

[48] Bob Woodward, *Veil*, 480.

[49] The Tower Commission, *President's Special Review Board* (Bantam Books, New York), 294–95.

[50] Leslie H. Gelb, "US Said to Aid Iranian Exiles in Combat and Political Units," *New York Times*, March 7, 1982, A1, A12.

stop selling arms to Iran, the United States made secret arms transfers to Iran and encouraged Israel to do the same.[51] The United States provided intelligence to Iranians, which was a mixture of factual and bogus information. The USA did, however, provide full critical data to Iran before its critical victory in the Fao Peninsula in February 1986.

The Iran-Iraq War was not between good and evil. Islam forbids fighting among the Muslims and forbids murder and the taking of life unless it is in the cause of justice. Saddam Hussein launched a murderous war to regain a few square miles of territory that his country had relinquished freely in 1975 border negotiations. There were one and a half million Muslim casualties in this senseless fraternal war. The war ended in a cease-fire that essentially left prewar borders unchanged. The covenant of Allah not only forbids such an internecine war but also provides a mechanism for dispute resolution. Instead of condemning the aggressor, the Arab states sided with Saddam Hussein, providing him with funds for further bloodletting. Saddam Hussein used banned chemical weapons against fellow Muslims, the Iranians and Kurds. The eight-year-long war exhausted both countries. The primary responsibility for the prolonged bloodletting must rest with the governments of the two countries, the ruthless military regime of Saddam Hussein and the ruthless clerical regime of Ayatollah Khomeini in Iran. Whatever his religious convictions, Khomeini had no qualms about sending his followers, including young boys, to their deaths for his own greater glory. This callous disregard for human life was no less characteristic of Saddam Hussein.

---

[51] Leslie Gelb, "Iran Said to Get Large Scale Arms from Israel, Soviets and Europeans," *New York Times*, March 8, 1982, A1, A10; Anthony Cordesman, *The Iran-Iraq War*, 31.

Saudi Arabia gave $25.7 billion and Kuwait $10.0 billion to Iraq to fuel the war and the killing of Muslims by Muslims. Saddam also owed the Soviets, USA, and Europe $40 billion for the purchase of arms. The cost of war to the Iranians was even greater. The rest of the world community sold arms for eight and a half years and watched the bloodletting. The USA sold arms and information to both sides to prolong the war strategically and to profit and gain influence and bases in the Gulf countries. Ayatollah Khomeini, in particular, was a hypocrite in dealing with Israel in secret, especially when his public pronouncements were venomously anti-Israel.

Iran, Iraq, and all the Arab states of the Persian Gulf took Western countries, the Soviet Union, and Israel as their *awliya* in contradiction to the commandments of the covenant. The ayatollah and his clerics should have known and understood their obligations to Allah and to their people as spelled out in Allah's covenant. The uncontrolled Arab Iranian hostility left a deep, festering wound in the body of the nation of Islam. The West made gains by setting up permanent bases in Saudi Arabia, Oman, the United Arab Emirates, Bahrain, Qatar, and Kuwait. This is the land that Muhammad, the blessed messenger of Allah, freed from the infidels, only to be handed over to infidels by the *Munafiqeen*.

k. 1990–2006: Saddam Opens the Gateway of Islam to the *Kafireen*

On August 2, 1990, Saddam Hussein was into mischief again. He invaded and occupied Kuwait. The sheikh of Kuwait and his family fled to Saudi Arabia. A coalition of Arabs, NATO, and many other countries carried a massive bombardment of Baghdad and other parts of Iraq on January 17, 1991, destroying the military installations, industrial units, and civilian infrastructure of Iraq. On February 24,

1991, American-led forces launched a ground offensive into Iraq and defeated the Iraqi Army. A United Nations resolution placed Iraq under an embargo till Iraq gave up all its biological and chemical weapons and also all nuclear weapon-making material.

After the Kuwait war at the invitation of King Fahd, the USA has continued to maintain large operational army and air force bases and command and control facilities that enable them to monitor all air and sea traffic as well as all civilian and military communications in the Middle East. Bahrain, in the meantime, has become the headquarters of the naval fleet command. Qatar has the longest runways in the Middle East and host to the United Stated Central Command Center. The Middle East, at the beginning of the twenty-first century, is under the absolute military and economic grip of the USA and NATO. The circle of evil—the *Yahudi*, *Salibi*, and *Munafiqeen*—continues to dominate the lives of the Muslims.

I. 1992–Present: The American Empire: The Circle of Evil

After Saddam Hussein's Iraq was thoroughly trounced by the United States and its NATO and Arab allies in February 1991, the Western countries used their power in the United Nations Security Council to set up an embargo on Iraq. No food, medicines, or equipment for use in the reconstruction of the destroyed power and water purification plants was allowed into Iraq. Over the following twelve years, over half a million Iraqi children died and five million children suffered from malnutrition and disease. Iraq suffered from depravation and disease created by the United Nations, a world body established to bring about peace and reduce suffering in the world. Eventually, when the UN did start the oil-for-food program, the funds were skimmed by the United Nations to pay for war reparations, and the food aid meant for the victims of the embargo did not always get to them.

m. The New American Century

Iraq was thoroughly humiliated and defeated in February 1991. This was considered by the Americans to be a magnificent victory. In fact, the war was between a war-weary Iraq, with a population of eighteen million people, and a coalition of the world's most developed countries and the wealthy Arabs. The Arabs supplied over a hundred billion dollars and all the air, land, and naval bases to fight this war. After its humiliating defeat in Vietnam, the USA had avoided any frontal assault on any country till the war on Iraq. Actually, the Americans had been bold enough to attack two ministates, Granada and Panama, which had only parade ground armies and won hands down.

In early 1990s, emboldened with these victories and by the fall of Soviet Russia from internal decay, a group of Republican politicians founded the Project for the New American Century. They planned and conspired to take the White House and the two other branches of government as well. They began to lay on the drawing board their vision about how the United States should move in the world when the time came.

Donald Rumsfeld, Dick Cheney, James Woolsey, Paul Wolfowitz, Richard Perle, Bill Kristol, James Bolton, Zalmay M. Khalilzad, William Bennett, Dan Quayle, and Jeb Bush led the Project for the New American Century. They were representing ideas and ideologies of faceless, influential, wealthy individuals and corporations that helped them set up think tanks and provided them funds to buy up media outlets—newspapers, magazines, TV networks, radio talk shows, and cable channels. Through the inside manipulations of the governor of Florida, Jeb Bush, and through the friendship of Dick Cheney with his fishing pal, justice of the Supreme Court Antonin Scalia, George W. Bush was selected the president of the United States. The new president was a foreign policy novice and described by some as intellectually incurious who had struggled with alcoholism all his life.

In our age, we have people who think that they can get the best both the worlds by compromising their nations and Islam's interests with the enemy. Beyond what has been stated, more than their diplomatic, economic, and military strength is the power provided to United States, Britain, and Israel by the traitors of Islam. They constitute the other half of the circle of evil that is destroying Islam. They pretend to be Muslims. They pray, they fast, and they go for the hajj pilgrimage. Their fingers robotically sift through their prayer beads. Allah has bestowed on them so much wealth and power that their next one hundred generations will be able to live lavishly off their wealth. They love the luxury of their private Gulf Stream jets and granite places with silken rugs and gold plumbing fixtures. Dozens of attendant's rush to their raised brow. Are they happy? Moreover, are they in peace with Allah's grace upon them? No. Wealth and power is not enough; they want more of it.

The Circle of Evil among the Muslims: Nine countries collectively have acted as the Muslim part of the circle of evil. They are Egypt, Pakistan, Bahrain, Kuwait, Qatar, United Arab Emirates, Oman, Jordan, and Saudi Arabia. In the Afghanistan and Iraq invasions of 2004–2006, an estimated 260,000 Muslim men, women, and children were killed, and hundreds of thousands injured and millions made homeless by bombing. Two sovereign Islamic nations have been decimated, their state structure shattered, and economies annihilated. It would take at least thirty years to rebuild these nations and rehabilitate their citizens. The loss was not to the Taliban or to Saddam Hussein. The loss is to the unity of the *ummah*, the unity that has been ordained in the covenant with Allah. Who will assist in the destruction of Islam perpetrated by a secret cabal of *Yahudi-Salibi* conspirators in Washington? In the twenty-first century, treason is hard to hide.

Pakistan: Pakistan's illegitimate dictator Musharraf, who had stolen the government by force of arms, craved for legitimacy. Power corrupts, and absolute power corrupts absolutely. Any power and wealth acquired with *harramma* will continue to be maintained with *harramma*. Those who promote disunity of the *ummah* are promised severe retribution. Disobedience of the covenant of Allah is haram and is cursed. Haram will breed more haram and Allah's wrath. It reminds us of how the scales of Allah's justice, the two hands of Allah—His mercy and His wrath—are reflected in the human domain, where people have been appointed Allah's vicegerents. Deeds of goodness and wholesomeness are associated with mercy, paradise, and the beautiful. Evil and corruption is rewarded with wrath, hell, and the ugly.

The other "Muslims" who perpetrate evil association with the *kafireen* are princes and kings of Arabia, the land of Islam, Allah's blessed prophet, and the holy shrines of Mecca and Medina. Bahrain, Kuwait, Qatar, United Arab Emirates, Jordan, Oman, and Saudi Arabia united with the evil to destroy the lives of 50 million Muslims in Iraq and Afghanistan and the faith of 1.5 billion believers. Although *Bahrain* is a constitutional monarchy, it is run like a family enterprise by the Al Khalifah family. In 1992, the sheikh gave himself the title of king. The king, the crown prince, the commander in chief, the prime minister, the defense minister, housing minister, the interior minister, the oil and development minister, and the foreign ministers are related through blood and marriage, and they all are kith and kin of the Al Khalifah family, afraid to share governance with their 724,000 subjects. This family has carved most of Bahrain's agriculturally fertile land for their own private use. Members of the Al Khalifah family control over 80 percent of the agriculture land in Bahrain. They have allocated themselves virtually all the coastal land. Thirty-three percent of all oil revenue goes to the members of the Al Khalifah family; the instruments of the state are run on the rest. Two percent of the population owns 90 percent of the wealth of the islands. To safeguard the wealth and position of this family, the Al Khalifah clan has secret treaties with the United States to protect the family from their subjects and from their neighbors. They act as the springboard for the United Stated Army, Marines, and Navy in their two invasions of Iraq and Afghanistan and in the ongoing hostilities against Iran. The Al Khalifah family has permitted the American Fifth Fleet to be based in Bahrain. The Fifth Fleet, for over thirty years, has menaced the Persian Gulf and has worked against the freedom of Iran and Iraq.

Kuwait: Kuwait, an oil-rich patch of desert, was carved out of the Basra district of the Ottoman Empire through the connivance of the British to circumvent the German plan to build railways from Berlin through the Ottoman Empire to Kuwait in the Persian Gulf. Kuwait, being the only deep- water harbor on the western edge of the Persian Gulf, provided the British with a supply and refueling center for its navy. It has continued to be subservient to the *kafireen* to maintain the Sabah family's power and riches. The Sabah family, like other Arab monarchies, runs their country as a family incorporation, all ministries being run by the family. Most of the country's wealth reverts to the royal family.

n. 2003–present: Muslim Complicity in the Invasion of Iraq

Bahrain, Kuwait, Qatar, United Arab Emirates, Oman, Jordan, Pakistan, and Saudi Arabia willingly provided Britain and the United States facilities for overflight, air operations, basing, port facilities, and facilities to preposition equipment for the Iraq invasion. It should come as no surprise to Muslims around the world that the Saudi royal family directly participated in the American invasion of Iraq and the slaughter of approximately 260,000 Iraqis and in the destruction of Iraq's infrastructure.

Treason among Us: On Friday, November 15, 2002, the Saudi ambassador Prince Bandar bin Sultan came to the Oval Office to see Pres. George W. Bush. Dick Cheney and Condoleezza Rice were also there. Bandar had been a long-term fixture in Washington, having served during four American presidencies. He had a ready access to American presidents, particularly the first President Bush, and the Bush family regarded him as a member of the family, where the prince had acquired the name Bandar Bush. On the same token, the Saudis had reputedly invested $1.4 billion in the Bush family, and the American president could safely be named George Bush Ibn Sa'ud. In this relationship, the Saudis do the American bidding in the Middle East, and the Americans protect the royal family interests and investments. In spite of this deep relationship and $3 trillion Saudi investment and support to the American economy, the Saudis do not have the resolve and will to use their clout to solve the Palestinian problem.

Bandar handed the president a private letter from Prince Abdullah, the de facto ruler of Saudi Arabia, and provided an English translation of the text. The text, in summary, congratulated the president's victory achieved by the Republican Party under his leadership. It stated that Prince Bandar was authorized to convey and discuss his message to the president face-to-face. As instructed Bandar then said formally, "Since 1994, we have been in constant contact with you at the highest level regarding what needs to be done with Iraq and Iraqi regime. Now, Mr. President, we want hear from you directly on your serious intention regarding this subject so we can adjust and coordinate so we can make right policy decision."

In 1994, King Fahd had proposed to President Clinton a joint US-Saudi covert action to overthrow Saddam, and Crown Prince Abdullah in April 2002 had suggested to Pres. George Bush that they spend up to $1 billion in a joint operation with the CIA. "Every time we meet, we are surprised that the United States asks us to give our impression about what can be done regarding Saddam Hussein," Bandar said, suggesting that the repeated requests caused them to "begin to doubt how serious America is about the issue of regime change. Now tell us what you are going to do."

Bandar read, "If you have a serious intention, we will not hesitate so that our two military people can then implement and discuss in order to support the American military action or campaign. This will make Saudi Arabia a major ally for the United States."

President Bush thanked the ambassador and said that he always appreciated the crown prince's views; he was a good friend and a great ally. Bush added that when he made up his mind on the military option, he would contact the crown prince before his final decision.[52]

On January 11, 2003, Dick Cheney invited Prince Bandar bin Sultan, the Saudi ambassador, to his West Wing. Present on this occasion were Defense Secretary Don Rumsfeld and Joint Chief of Staff Chairman Gen. Richard Myers. The American defense officials appraised Bandar, a foreigner, of their battle plans against Iraq, even before Colin Powell, the US secretary of state, knew of them. General

---

[52] Bob Woodward, *Plan of Attack* (Simon & Shuster), 228–30.

Meyers unfurled a large map of the area and explained the first part of the battle plan. The plan involved a massive bombing campaign over several days. The United States would drop on Iraq four times the bombs that destroyed it during the forty-two days of the Gulf War. And during those days, Americans dropped more bombs on Iraq than were dropped by all the combatants during the Second World War. Bandar was informed that his fellow Arab and Muslim Iraqis were to be exploded, incinerated, and blown to bits with four times the explosives than had ever been used on this planet previously. Special forces, intelligence teams, and air strikes would be launched through the five-hundred-mile Saudi border with Iraq.

The next day, Bandar met George W. Bush. The Saudis wanted an assurance that, this time, Saddam would be totally finished, and the president reminded the ambassador of his briefings from "Dick, Rummy, and General Meyers," in which they had assured Bandar that, this time, Saddam indeed would be toast.[53] Bandar flew to Riyadh and provided a verbatim report of the battle plan to Crown Prince Abdullah. Abdullah advised Bandar to maintain strict secrecy till they could figure out their next move.

On Friday, March 14, 2003, Bandar was shown into the Oval Office; Cheney, Rice, and Card were there. Bandar was unshaven, he had put on weight, and the buttons on his jacket were straining. He was tired, nervous, and excited. He was sweating profusely. "What's wrong with you?" the president asked Bandar. "Don't you have a razor to shave with?"

"Mr. President," Bandar replied, "I promised myself I would not shave until this war starts."

"Well, then, you are going to shave very soon."

---

[53] Woodward, *Plan of Attack*, 263–68.

"I hope so," Bandar said. "By the time this war starts, I will be like bin Laden." He then indicated a long beard of a foot or two.

On Wednesday, March 19, 2003, at 7:30 p.m., Condoleezza Rice told Bandar, "The president has asked me to tell you that we are going to war. At about 9:00 p.m., all hell will break loose."

"Tell him he will be in our prayers and hearts," Bandar said. "God help us all."

Bandar then called Crown Prince Abdullah in a prearranged code in reference to an oasis, Roda outside Riyadh. "Tonight, the forecast is there will be heavy rain in the Roda," Bandar said from his car phone to Saudi Arabia.

Abdullah asked, "Do you know how soon the storm is going to hit?"

Bandar replied, "Sir, I don't know, but watch TV."

The American air campaign against Iraq was essentially managed from inside Saudi Arabia, where American military commanders operated an air command center and launched refueling tankers, F-16 fighter jets, and sophisticated intelligence-gathering flights, according to American officials.[54] Senior officials from both countries told the Associated Press that the royal family permitted widespread military operations to be staged from inside the kingdom during the invasion of Iraq.

Between 250 and 300 air force planes were staged from Saudi Arabia, including AWACS, C-130s, refueling tankers, and F-16 fighter jets, during the height of the war, the officials said. Air and military operations during the war were permitted at the Tabuk air base and the Arar regional airport near the Iraq border. "We operated the command center in Saudi Arabia. We operated aeroplanes out of Saudi

---

[54] "New Details on Saudi Help in Iraq War," Associated Press, April 25, 2004, http://wwwfoxnews.com/story/0,933,118084,00.html.

Arabia, as well as sensors and tankers," said Gen. T. Michael Moseley, a top air force general who was the architect of the campaign. During the war, US officials held a media briefing about the air war from Qatar although the air command center was in Saudi Arabia—a move designed to prevent inflaming the Saudi public.

When the war started, the Saudis allowed cruise missiles to be fired from navy ships across their airspace into Iraq. The Saudis provided tens of millions of dollars in discounted and free oil, gas, and fuel for American forces. During the war, a stream of oil delivery trucks, at times, stretched for miles outside the Prince Sultan air base, said a senior US military planner. The Saudis were influential in keeping down the world oil prices during the run-up to the Iraq War by pumping 1.5 million barrels a day. The Saudis kept Jordan supplied with cheap oil for its support in the Iraq War. Although King Abdullah of Jordan had met with the leaders of Turkey, Syria, and Egypt and made well-publicized statements against the war on Iraq, he had secretly committed to support the American war effort against Iraq. American troops and intelligence services operated from inside the Jordanian borders in their invasion of Iraq.

Saddam Hussein was a traitor to Islam and a tyrant and deserved humiliation. However, at the eve of the war, he contacted Egypt for asylum. The Egyptians, at the behest of the Americans, refused. Prince Bandar had been informed directly by Hosni Mubarak. Yet Iraqis were attacked, and the country decimated.[55]

The Saudis, Egyptians, and other Arab rulers were aware of the magnitude of the planned air attack on the Iraqi people. The invasion of Iraq ostensibly was to depose Saddam and his regime. Saddam tried to abdicate, leave Iraq, and sought asylum in Egypt. Yet the Arab rulers let the invasion go unchallenged and, in fact, assisted a *kafir*

---

[55] Woodward, *Plan of Attack*, 312.

power to occupy a sovereign Muslim country. They allowed 260,000 Iraqis to be blown to bits and hundreds of thousands of civilians to be maimed. Eighty percent of the population lost their jobs. The country was decimated. The infrastructure had been blown into stone age, and the desert had been poisoned with radioactive waste from spent ammunition for thousands of years to come.

Islam is a religion of peace, truth, justice, and harmony. Conflict and war is only permitted by the covenant of Allah in self-defense and to fight *fitnah*, treachery, oppression, and injustice.

The Circle of Evil: On Wednesday, March 19, 2003, at 9:00 p.m., the US armed forces attacked and invaded Iraq with a force of over 460,000 troops from all its armed services, supported by 46,000 UK troops, 2,000 from Australia, and a few hundred from Poland, Spain, Portugal, and Denmark. The "shock and awe" aerial bombardment unleashed 29,200 bombs and missiles on Iraq in the first five weeks of the war.

This war against Iraq, subsequent wars against Syria and Libya, and embargo and hostilities against Iran were initiated by a cabal of Jews in the American administration, the Pentagon, the CIA, and Bush's White House. The execution of the conflicts was aided by the *Munafiqeen* in the Arab kingdoms of Saudi Arabia, Emirates, Qatar, Egypt, Jordan, and Turkey, a NATO ally of the United States and Britain.

Together, they created the so-called Islamic State, the ISIS, a cruel and wild guerilla organization that created havoc in Syria and Iraq. There was nothing Islamic about it. Its actions were in each and every way opposed to the covenant of Allah. It was organized, funded, trained, and armed by the United States, Saudi Arabia, and Turkey to destabilize and destroy Syria and Iraq. Hundreds of Toyota Tundra trucks with thousands of armed guerrillas were let loose from Turkey into Syria and Iraq, where they captured eastern Syria up to Mosul in Iraq, allowing for the pretense of the second American invasion of Iraq, which is still ongoing. In fact, these two nations had already been pulverized by the US invasion. It was a matter of taking control and possession of the very heart of Islam by the circle of evil.

Subsequent planning had been even worse. Saudi Arabia had been taken over by a murderous crown prince, Mohammed bin Salman. He was known to murder and dismember his critics while still alive. He lured his critic journalist Adnan Khashoggi into the Saudi consulate in Istanbul and had him cut up and dismembered alive, screaming and still conscious. He collaborated with the Jewish crown prince Jared Kushner of the White House in Washington to sell and dismember the sovereignty of the Palestinian state for a paltry billion dollars.

The US invasion of Iraq was a crime of aggression under international law and was actively opposed by people and countries all over the world, including 30 million people who took to the streets in 60 countries on February 15, 2003, to express their horror that this could really be happening at the dawn of the twenty-first century. Seventeen years later, the consequences of the invasion had lived up to the fears of all who opposed it. Wars and hostilities raged across the region, and there were divisions over war and peace in the world.

Millions of Iraqis Killed and Wounded: Estimates on the number of people killed in the invasion and occupation of Iraq vary widely, but even the most conservative estimates based on fragmentary reporting of minimum confirmed deaths are in the hundreds of thousands. Serious scientific studies estimated that 655,000 Iraqis had died in the first three years of war and about a million by September 2007. The violence of the US escalation or "surge" continued into 2008, and sporadic conflict continued from 2009 until 2014.

Then in its new campaign against the Islamic State, the United States and its NATO allies bombarded major cities in Iraq and Syria with more than 118,000 bombs and the heaviest artillery bombardments since the Vietnam War. They reduced much of Mosul and other Iraqi cities to rubble, and a preliminary Iraqi Kurdish intelligence report found that more than 40,000 civilians were killed in Mosul alone. There are no comprehensive mortality studies for this latest deadly phase of the war. In addition to all the lives lost, even more people had been wounded. The Iraqi government's Central Statistical Organization said that 2 million Iraqis have been left disabled.

Millions More Iraqis Displaced: By 2007, the UN High Commissioner for Refugees (UNHCR) reported that nearly 2.0 million Iraqis had fled the violence and chaos of occupied Iraq, mostly to Jordan and Syria, while another 1.7 million were displaced within the country. The US war on the Islamic State relied even more on bombing and artillery bombardment, destroying even more homes and displacing an astounding 6 million Iraqis from 2014 to 2017. According to the UNHCR, 4.35 million people had returned to their homes as the war on Islamic State had wound down, but many faced "destroyed properties, damaged or non-existent infrastructure and the lack of livelihood opportunities and financial resources, which at times has led to secondary displacement." Iraq's internally displaced children represented "a generation traumatized by violence, deprived of education and opportunities," according to UN special rapporteur Cecilia Jimenez-Damary.

Even More Veterans Have Committed Suicide: More than 20 US veterans kill themselves every day––that is more deaths each year than the total US military deaths in Iraq. Those with the highest rates of suicide are young veterans with combat exposure, who commit suicide at rates "4-10 times higher than their civilian peers." Why? As Matthew Hoh of Veterans for Peace explains, many veterans "struggle to reintegrate into society," are ashamed to ask for help, are burdened by what they saw and did in the military, are trained in shooting and own guns, and carry mental and physical wounds that make their lives difficult.

Trillions of Dollars Wasted: On March 16, 2003, just days before the US invasion, VP Dick Cheney projected that the war would cost the United States about $100 billion, and that the US involvement would last for two years. Seventeen years on, the costs are still mounting. The Congressional Budget Office (CBO) estimated a cost of $2.4 trillion for the wars in Iraq and Afghanistan in 2007. Nobel Prize–winning economist Joseph Stiglitz and Harvard University's Linda Bilmes estimated the cost of the Iraq War at more than $3 trillion "based on conservative assumptions" in 2008. The UK government spent at least £9 billion in direct costs through 2010. What the United Sates did not spend money on, contrary to what many Americans believe, was rebuilding Iraq, the country our war destroyed.

Dysfunctional and Corrupt Iraqi Government: Most of the men (no women!) running Iraq today are still former exiles (collaborators and the Arab part of the circle of evil) who flew into Baghdad in 2003 on the heels of the US and British invasion forces. Iraq is finally once again exporting 3.8 million barrels of oil per day and earning $80 billion a year in oil exports, but little of this money trickles down to rebuild destroyed and damaged homes or provide jobs, health care, or education for Iraqis, only 36 percent of whom even have jobs. *All the Iraqi treasure, including gold, and all the oil money have been systematically stolen by the US government.*

Iraq's young people had taken to the streets to demand an end to the corrupt post-2003 Iraqi political regime and US and Iranian influence over Iraqi politics. More than 600 protesters were killed by government forces, but the protests forced PM Adel Abdul Mahdi to resign. Another former Western-based exile, Mohammed Tawfik Allawi, the cousin of former US-appointed interim prime minister Ayad Allawi, was chosen to replace him, but he resigned within weeks after the national assembly failed to approve his cabinet choices. The popular protest movement celebrated Allawi's resignation, and Abdul Mahdi agreed to remain as prime minister but only as a "caretaker" to carry out essential functions until new elections can be held. He had called for new elections in December. Until then, Iraq remains in political limbo, still occupied by about 5,000 US troops.

Illegal War on Iraq Has Undermined the Rule of International Law: When the United States invaded Iraq without the approval of the UN Security Council, the first victim was the United Nations Charter, the foundation of peace and international law since World War II, which prohibits the threat or use of force by any country against another. International law only permits military action as a necessary and proportionate defense against an attack or imminent threat. The illegal 2002 Bush doctrine of preemption was universally rejected because it went beyond this narrow principle and claimed an exceptional US right to use unilateral military force "to pre-empt emerging threats," undermining the authority of the UN Security Council to decide whether a specific threat requires a military response. Kofi Annan, the UN secretary-general at the time, said the invasion was illegal and would lead to a breakdown in international order, and that is exactly what has happened. When the United States trampled the UN Charter, others were bound to follow. Today we are watching Turkey and Israel follow in the United States' footsteps, attacking and invading Syria at will as if it was not even a sovereign country, using the people of Syria as pawns in their political games.

Iraq War Lies Corrupted US Democracy: The second victim of the invasion was American democracy. Congress voted for war based on a so-called summary of a National Intelligence Estimate (NIE) that was nothing of the kind. The *Washington Post* reported that only six out of one hundred senators and a few House members read the actual NIE. The twenty-five-page "summary" that other members of Congress based their votes on was a document produced months earlier "to make the public case for war" as one of its authors, the CIA's Paul Pillar, later confessed to PBS *Frontline. It was a lie.* It contained astounding claims that were nowhere to be found in the real NIE, such as that the CIA knew of 550 sites where Iraq was storing chemical and biological weapons. Secretary of State Colin Powell repeated many of these lies in his shameful performance at the UN Security Council in February 2003, while Bush and Cheney used these lies in major speeches, including Bush's 2003 State of the Union address. How is democracy––the rule of the people––even possible if the people elected to represent in Congress can be manipulated into voting for a catastrophic war by such a web of lies?

Impunity for Systematic War Crimes: The US government is criminal and is not accountable to its people nor to the world. Another victim of the invasion of Iraq was the presumption that US presidents and policy are subject to the rule of law. Seventeen years later, most Americans assume that the president can conduct war and assassinate foreign leaders and terrorism suspects as he pleases with no accountability whatsoever––like a dictator.

When President Obama said he wanted to look forward instead of backward and held no one from the Bush administration accountable for their crimes, it was as if they ceased to be crimes and became normalized as US policy. That includes crimes of aggression against other countries, the mass killing of civilians in US airstrikes and drone strikes, and the unrestricted surveillance of every American's phone calls, emails, browsing history, and opinions. But these are crimes and violations of the US Constitution and refusing to hold accountable those who committed these crimes has made it easier for them to be repeated.

Destruction of the Environment: During the first Gulf War, the United States fired 340 tons of warheads and explosives made with depleted uranium, which poisoned the soil and water and led to skyrocketing levels of cancer. In the following decades of "ecocide," Iraq has been plagued by the burning of dozens of oil wells; the pollution of water sources from the dumping of oil, sewage, and chemicals; millions of tons of rubble from destroyed cities and towns; and the burning of huge volumes of military waste in open-air "burn pits" during the war. The pollution caused by war is linked to the high levels of congenital birth defects, premature births, miscarriages, and cancer (including leukemia) in Iraq.

The pollution has also affected US soldiers. "More than 85,000 U.S. Iraq war veterans...have been diagnosed with respiratory and breathing problems, cancers, neurological diseases, depression and emphysema since returning from Iraq," as the Guardian reports. And parts of Iraq may never recover from the environmental devastation.

The Unites States' Sectarian "Divide and Rule" Policy in Iraq Spawned Havoc across the Region: In the secular twentieth-century Iraq, the Sunni minority was more powerful than the Shia majority; but for the most part, the different ethnic groups lived side by side in mixed neighborhoods and even intermarried. Friends with mixed Shia/Sunni parents tell us that before the US invasion, they didn't even know which parent was Shia and which was Sunni. After the invasion, the United States empowered a new Shiite ruling class led by former exiles allied with the United States and Iran, as well as the Kurds in their semiautonomous region in the north.

The upending of the balance of power and deliberate US "divide and rule" policies led to waves of horrific sectarian violence, including the ethnic cleansing of communities by interior ministry death squads under US command. The sectarian divisions the USA unleashed in Iraq led to the resurgence of al-Qaeda and the emergence of ISIS, which had wreaked havoc throughout the entire region.

Americas Plunder: Recall that one of the leading neocons who engineered the invasion of Iraq, Paul Wolfowitz, claimed the USA could finance its entire invasion of Iraq (he estimated the cost at about $70 billion) by plundering Iraq's oil. Today the cost of the occupation has reached over $3 trillion. Paul Wolfowitz is nowhere to be seen. Meanwhile, President Trump says the USA will grab Syria's oil fields.

So where did all the money go? A large amount for corrupt Iraqi politicians and more for the ten-plus US bases in Iraq, perhaps a modest payoff for neighboring Iran and Iraq's Shia clergy, or helping finance Iraq and Syria's ISIS. But that still leaves a huge amount of unaccounted cash from oil plundered by the USA. One day we may find out.

In recent weeks, Shia and Sunni Iraqis have been rioting to protest continuing US proxy rule via a Washington-installed puppet regime in Baghdad that, curiously, also has some Iranian support. As of this writing, 120 Iraqis have been shot dead and some 6,000 wounded. This has happened while scores of Palestinians are being killed by Israel in Gaza.

In the Cheney-Wolfowitz plan, Iraq was to serve as the principal US military base to control the entire Middle East, Iran, and Afghanistan. This did not happen because of fierce Iraqi resistance to US-British rule. But the USA has still kept some army, marine, and most importantly air bases in Iraq. Supposedly, "independent" Iraq is not allowed modern air or armored forces, and its airspace remains under US control. The US troops that were recently sent to Syria came from the Iraq garrison—a small version of Dick Cheney's imperial dream.

Ever since the 2003 invasion, Iraq has been ruled by a succession of US-appointed figureheads who have proved as corrupt as they are inept. During the war, the USA destroyed most of Iraq's water and sewage systems, causing some 500,000 children to die from waterborne diseases, wrecking much of its industry and commerce, leaving millions of men unemployed. Public services have broken down. Before the US invasion, Iraq led the Arab world in industry, farming, medicine, education, and women's rights. All that was destroyed by the "liberation."

o. 2001–Present: After Eighty-Seven Years, History Repeats Itself: More Traitors

Enver Pasha secretly signed a treaty of Turko-German Alliance on August 2, 1914. Only five people in Turkey knew of this treaty, which brought on the final disintegration of the Ottoman Empire. The puppet grand vizier Said Halim, Talat, and Cemal were convinced by Enver of the wisdom of supporting the Germans in case the war broke out. Enver Pasha chose to ally Turkey with the Central Powers by citing Germany's earlier victories in the war. Thus, the Ottoman Empire joined the Central Powers to form a triple alliance without the knowledge of the cabinet, the parliament, the army generals, and the Ottoman populace. The empire was ruled by three collaborators and puppets of Germany, traitors to Islam, to the Muslims in Turkey, and to the whole of the *ummah*. They acted secretly as collaborators, with a foreign government working toward the destruction and disintegration of the only free Islamic state.

Two German warships, the battleship *Goeben* and the cruiser *Breslau*, that were caught in a neutral Turkish port when the war broke out in Europe were handed to the Ottoman Navy. In October, they were put out to sea, flying the Ottoman flag with German officers and crew, and shelled Odessa and other Russian ports. Enver Pasha, as the Ottoman war minister, gave secret orders in a sealed envelope to Admiral Souchon, the commander of the Turko-German fleet, only to be opened when the fleet was deep in the Black Sea. The orders read:

> *War minister Enver Pasha to Admiral Souchon October 25, 1914. The entire fleet should maneuver in the Black Sea. When you find a favorable opportunity, attack the Russian fleet. Before initiating the hostilities, open my secret orders given to you personally this morning. To prevent transport of material to Serbia, act as already agreed upon. Enver Pasha.*

> *(Secret Order): "The Turkish fleet should gain the mastery of the Black Sea by force. Seek out the Russian fleet and attack her wherever you find her without declaration of war. Enver Pasha*

The admiral attacked simultaneously the Russian ports of Sebastopol, Theodosia, Novorossiysk, and Odessa on the morning of October 29. The first cannon shot from the Turkish fleet, in effect, declared a war on Russia and its allies Britain and France. Once again, Enver acted secretly at the behest of Germany. He did not consult his coconspirators, Talat and Cemal, before ordering the attack on Russia or the declaration of war against the Western allies. He kept his cabinet colleagues, the parliament, and the people of the empire in the dark, who on the morning of October 29, 1914, were surprised to find themselves at war.

The conspiracies, utter stupidity, and lust for power of three men—Talat, Cemal, and Enver—led to the dismemberment of the Ottoman Empire. For another one hundred years, this land of Islam was to know no peace. This land of Islam became the prey of the circle of evil of the Euro-Christian, Jew, and Arab conspirators.

p. The New American Century: The *Yahudi–Salibi-Munafiq* Conspiracy

At the end of the twentieth century, American planners formulated a new doctrine for the deployment of American might. It reads:

> The Unites States will rule the world. The United States will turn into the center of global empire. Washington will decide the fates of governments, divide up riches of foreign economies, and impose democracy in the American sense of the world. With overwhelming military superiority, the United States will prevent new rivals from rising to challenge it on the world stage. The United States will have dominion over friends and foes alike. The United States will be the bully on the block. If required, its armed forces will use overwhelming preemptive military force. It will prevent and discourage the development of nuclear programs in other countries.

In the American view, Iran, Iraq, and North Korea are the *axis of evil*, and the destruction of their military and economic prowess is a priority. Wars and military adventures benefit from coalitions, but the United States must determine and control all missions and lead the fights. The United States will not only be the most powerful but must be powerful to deter the emergence of rival powers.

After the wane of the Soviet Union, there was no threat to the security of the United States and its people; therefore, the American people demanded reduction in the defense expenditure. The defense industry and the financial institutions demanded continuing spending on armaments and defense industry to keep the economy running. America needed a threat to replace the Soviet Union. Inexplicably, this threat suddenly appeared from the caves in the Hindu Kush Mountains of Afghanistan. From a cave lit with a kerosene lantern in Tora Bora, on September 11, 2001, a man called Osama bin Laden directed and launched four massive airliners full of innocent passengers, which crash-landed into the Twin Towers of the World Trade Center and the Pentagon. The US Air Force shot down the fourth plane on the way to the White House. Three thousand people died. This catastrophe shook America and the world.

The Pentagon boosted its budget in increments from $260 billion to $480 billion over a period of twenty months. To the surprise of most people who were not aware, almost all the planners of the new American century were Jews. The conspirators Abram Shulsky, Robert Martinage, Paul Wolfowitz, Lewis Libby, James Lasswell, Mark Lagon, Phil Meilinger, Robert Kilebrew, William Kristol, Steve Rosen, Robert Kagan, Dov Zakheim, Fred Kagan, Donald Kagan, Devon Gaffney Cross, Stephen Cambone, Elliot Cohen, Alvin Bernstein, and Richard Perle are all Jews, and most of these men have spent some part of their life in Israel. They hold Israeli citizenship and are active in promoting pro-Israeli and anti-Arab and anti-Muslim causes. A few are right-wing Christian Zionists. All are committed to Israel and the Likud Party of the former Israeli prime minister Sharon.

This Jewish-Israeli transplant in Washington and the Christian right movement want to decisively shift the balance of power in the Middle East in favor of Israel so that it could effectively impose peace terms on Palestinians and Syrians, divide and fragment Arab and Muslim countries, and impose American/Israeli hegemony and economic and military control over the Middle East. They want to demonstrate to the world that America does have the will and power to disarm any rogue state that attempts to acquire weapons of mass destruction. They also want to demonstrate to any future rival powers that America could invade the Persian Gulf and deny any rival supplies of oil. In other words, comply with the American/Israeli wishes or else.

To achieve these objectives, the conspiring hawks planned to dominate the oil-rich arch of Islam extending from Syria on the Mediterranean to Afghanistan in the Hindu Kush Mountains. They planned to set up military bases in Iraq and link those to bases in Central Asia, Horn of Africa, Persian Gulf, and the Mediterranean.

The planning of invasion of Iraq and its execution were carried out secretly by a group of Jews working inside the Pentagon, namely, Paul Wolfowitz, Richard Perle, Douglas Feith, and Paul Nitze. In July 2001, at the Group of Eight summit held in Genoa, Italy, plans were discussed for the ouster of the Taliban from power. Wolfowitz, Perle, and Nitze were the people pushing for the American occupation of Afghanistan and Iraq. Bush's cabinet intended to take military action to take control of the Persian Gulf whether or not Saddam Hussein was in power. The blueprint written in September 2000 was supported by an earlier document written by Wolfowitz and Libby recommending maintaining American bases in Saudi Arabia and Kuwait to keep American control over the Arab oil. Another member of this team was the propagandist William Kristol, a Council on Foreign Relations (CFR) member.

Donald Rumsfeld (secretary of defense) and Paul Wolfowitz (deputy secretary of defense) set up a secret bureau within in the Pentagon. The Office of Special Plans (OSP) in the Pentagon dealt with the Middle East. Douglas Feith headed the Near East South Asia Center (NESA). Retired intelligence officers from the State Department, the Defense Intelligence Agency, and the Central Intelligence Agency had long charged that this office exaggerated and doctored the intelligence from Iraq and the Middle East before passing it along to the White House. Key personnel who worked in the OSP and NESA under the control of Douglas Feith were part of a broader network of Jews and Zionists who worked with similar Bush political appointees scattered around the American national security network. Their assignment was to move the country to war, according to the retired lieutenant colonel Karen Kwiatkowski. Kwiatkowski was assigned to NESA from May 2002 through February 2003.[56] Other political appointees who worked with them were William Loti, Abram Shulsky, Michael Rubin, David Schenker, Michael Makovsky, and Chris Lehman.

Along with Feith, all the political appointees have a common close identification with Ariel Sharon and the Likud Party in Israel. This group works closely with Richard Perle, John Bolton, Michael Wurmser, and Elizabeth Cheney. There are published reports that this group works with a similar group in the Israeli prime minister

---

[56] Jim Lobe, "Pentagon Now Home to Neoconservative Network," *Dawn*, Aug. 9, 2003.

Ariel Sharon's office in Jerusalem. The OSP and the NESA personnel are already discussing and planning "going after Iran and Syria" after the war in Afghanistan and Iraq. Political plans of the Likud Party and the Council for Foreign Relations work on behalf of the Jewish finance and defense industry to facilitate borrowing by the governments. It is amazing how in banking and wars Jewish names keep coming up.

In the arch of Islam, Iran is the keystone; and Syria, Iraq, Afghanistan, and Pakistan constituted the western and eastern halves of the arch. If Iran fell, the whole Muslim world would come tumbling down into the American lap. The planners decided to work on the weakest link of the chain. Afghanistan and Iraq had been devastated by twenty-five years of war, and Iraq had further been bled through the United Nations sanctions. Once Iraq and Afghanistan had been decimated and removed from the arch, then Iran and Syria would come tumbling down too.

After the fall of the Soviet Empire, the world was settling down to a slumber of peace, and the people of the world looked forward to a disarmed world. The planners of the new American century wanted an event so overwhelming and catastrophic that would propel the American people's psyche into a prolonged period of perpetual warfare. The assistance for such an event came from a very unsuspecting source.

q. Pakistan: The *Munafiq* Connection

Gen. Pervez Musharraf, in a bloodless coup d'état on October 12, 1999, ousted the elected Pakistani government, arrested the prime minister Nawaz Sharif, and installed his own military regime. Accusing the previous government of corruption and ruining the economy, Musharraf promised to bring economic progress and political stability, eradicate poverty, build investor confidence, and restore democracy as quickly as possible. Two years later, none of these promises had been fulfilled. The economy was on a knife-edge, and there was growing, popular discontent with falling living standards and lack of basic democratic rights. The regime was under fire not only from the political opposition but also from its supporters in the ruling military elite. The schisms in the military reflected the pressure that the regime was under both domestically and internationally.

While the USA and other major powers tacitly accepted the coup, they had become increasingly critical of Musharraf's failure to carry out the economic measures demanded by the International Monetary Fund and his failure to crack down on Islamic fundamentalism. The USA had effectively blocked IMF loans and had not lifted economic sanctions imposed on Pakistan after its 1998 nuclear tests. The USA also demanded that Musharraf put pressure on the Taliban regime in Afghanistan to hand over Osama bin Laden, whom the USA blamed for the terrorist bombing of US embassies in Kenya and Tanzania.

Musharraf's junta confronted serious debt problems as a result of the IMF's repeated delays in disbursing $1.56 billion in loans. Without the IMF's backing, Pakistan had been unable to reschedule its $38 billion in foreign loans and was at the risk of defaulting on repayments of $5 billion of its loans that were due by the end of the year. According to official records, Pakistan's foreign exchange reserves were down to a bare one-third of a billion dollars.

To impose its policies, the military regime resorted to an outright repression, making a mockery of its claims of returning Pakistan to democracy by 2002. All the evidence pointed to a regime with a rapidly dwindling base of support. Its only answer to protests and opposition was more repression and seeking respite from foreign sources.

There was evidence that Musharraf's junta was secretly cooperating and cozying up with the US military and intelligence services and covertly helping the USA in its operations in Afghanistan. With CIA backing and with the injection of massive amounts of US military aid, Pakistan's Inter-Services Intelligence (ISI) had, in the 1980s and 1990s, developed into a major intelligence network wielding enormous power over all aspects of Pakistani civilian and military life. The ISI had a staff of military and intelligence officers, bureaucrats, undercover agents, and informers estimated at 150,000.[57] With this active collaboration with the CIA, the ISI continued to perform covert intelligence operations in the interests of the United States in Afghanistan and Central Asia. The ISI had directly supported and financed a number of terrorist organizations, including al-Qaeda. This cooperation with the al-Qaeda began as an extension of American interest in the region, and it could not have continued without the consent and the knowledge of the CIA.

The Sequence of Events: April 4, 2000. ISI director Gen. Mahmood Ahmed visited Washington. He met officials at the CIA and the White House. In a message meant for both Pakistan and the Taliban, US officials told him that al-Qaeda had killed Americans and "people who support those people will be treated as our enemies." However, no actual action, military or otherwise, was taken against either the Taliban or Pakistan.

---

[57] Ahmed Rashid, "The Taliban: Exporting Extremism," *Foreign Affairs*, November–December 1999. See also Michel Chossudovsky, "Who Is Osama bin Laden?" *Global Outlook* no. 1 (2002).

May 2001. CIA director Tenet made a quiet visit to Pakistan to meet with Pres. Pervez Musharraf in May 2001. While in Islamabad, Tenet had an "an unusually long meeting" with General Musharraf. He also met with his Pakistani counterpart, ISI director Lt. Gen. Mahmood Ahmed.

July 2001. The BBC's George Arney reported on September 18 that American officials had told former Pakistani foreign secretary Niaz Naik in mid-July of plans for military action against the Taliban regime: "Mr. Naik said US officials told him of the plan at a UN-sponsored international contact group on Afghanistan which took place in Berlin. Mr. Naik told the BBC that at the meeting the US representatives told him that unless Bin Laden was handed over swiftly America would take military action to kill or capture both Bin Laden and the Taliban leader, Mullah Omar." The wider objective, according to Mr. Naik, would be to topple the Taliban regime and install a transitional government of moderate Afghans in its place, possibly under the leadership of the former Afghan king Zahir Shah. "Mr. Naik was told that Washington would launch its operation from bases in Tajikistan, where American advisers were already in place. He was told that Uzbekistan would also participate in the operation and that 17,000 Russian troops were on standby. Mr. Naik was told that if the military action went ahead, it would take place before the snows started falling in Afghanistan, by the middle of October at the latest."

July 2001. The FBI confirmed in late September 2001, in an interview with ABC News, that the 9/11 ringleader, Mohammed Atta, had been financed from unnamed sources in Pakistan in July 2001:

> As to September 11th, federal authorities have told ABC News they have now tracked more than $100,000 from banks in Pakistan, to two banks

in Florida, to accounts held by suspected hijack ringleader, Mohammed Atta. As well . . . "Time Magazine" is reporting that some of that money came in the days just before the attack and can be traced directly to people connected to Osama bin Laden. It's all part of what a successful FBI effort has been so far to close in on the hijacker's high commander, the money men, the planners and the mastermind.[58]

The FBI had information on the money trail. They knew exactly who was financing the terrorists. Less than two weeks later, the findings of the FBI were confirmed by Agence France-Presse and the *Times of India*, quoting an official Indian intelligence report. According to these two reports, the money used to finance the 9/11 attacks had allegedly been "wired to WTC hijacker Mohammed Atta from Pakistan, by Ahmad Umar Sheikh, at the instance of ISI Chief General Mahmood Ahmad."[59]

July 2001. At the Group of Eight summit held in Genoa, Italy, plans were discussed for the ouster of the Taliban from power. Wolfowitz, Perle, and Nitze were the people pushing for the American occupation of Afghanistan and Iraq. Bush's cabinet intended to take military action to take control of the Persian Gulf whether or not Saddam Hussein was in power. The blueprint written in September 2000 was supported by an earlier document written by Wolfowitz and Libby recommending maintaining American bases in Saudi Arabia and Kuwait to keep American control over the Arab oil.

---

[58] Statement of Brian Ross reporting on information conveyed to him by the FBI, ABC News, September 30, 2001.

[59] *Times of India*, Delhi, October 9, 2001.

Late August 2001. Barely a couple of weeks before September 11, Rep. Porter Goss, together with Sen. Bob Graham and Sen. Jon Kyl, were on a top-level intelligence mission in Islamabad. They held meetings with Pres. Pervez Musharraf and with Pakistan's military and intelligence brass, including the head of Pakistan's Inter-Services Intelligence, Gen. Mahmood Ahmed. Porter Goss, a Florida Republican and former CIA operative, was chairman of the House Intelligence Committee. He also chaired, together with Sen. Bob Graham, the Joint Senate House Committee on the September 11 attacks.

Amply documented, Porter Goss had an established personal relationship to the head of ISI, Gen. Mahmood Ahmed, who according to the *Washington Post* "ran a spy agency notoriously close to Osama bin Laden and the Taliban" (May 18, 2002).

According to the Council on Foreign Relations, the ISI had over the years supported a number of Islamic terrorist organizations while maintaining close links to the CIA:

> Through its Inter-Services Intelligence agency (ISI) Pakistan has provided the Taliban with military advisers and logistical support during key battles, has bankrolled the Taliban, has facilitated trans-shipment of arms, ammunition, and fuel through its territory, and has openly encouraged the recruitment of Pakistanis to fight for the Taliban.

> Pakistan's army and intelligence services, principally the Inter-Services Intelligence Directorate (ISI), contribute to making the Taliban a highly effective military force.

In other words, up to and including September 11, 2001, extending to December 2001, the ISI had been supporting the Taliban network.

And that was precisely the period during which Porter Goss and Bob Graham established a close working relationship with the ISI chief, Gen. Mahmood Ahmed. The latter had, in fact, "briefed" the two Florida lawmakers at ISI headquarters in Rawalpindi, Pakistan:

> Senator Bob Graham's first foreign trip as chairman of the Senate Intelligence Committee, in a late-August 2001, with House intelligence Chairman Goss and Republican Senator Jon Kyl of Arizona, focused almost entirely on terrorism. It ended in Pakistan, where (ISI Chief) General Mahmood Ahmed's intelligence agents briefed them on the growing threat of al Qaida while they peered across the Khyber Pass at an obscure section of Afghanistan, called Tora Bora. The Americans also visited General Ahmed's compound and urged him to do more to help capture Osama bin Laden. The general had not said much, but the group had agreed to discuss the issue more when he visited Washington on September 4, 2001.

September 4, 2001. Gen. Mahmood Ahmed arrived in the USA on an official visit.

September 4–9, 2001. He met his US counterparts, including CIA head George Tenet, according to official sources. He also held long parleys with unspecified officials at the White House and the Pentagon. But the most important meeting was with Marc Grossman, US undersecretary of state for political affairs.

September 9, 2001. The leader of the Northern Alliance, Gen. Ahmad Shah Masoud was assassinated on the ninth of September 2001. The ISI, headed by General Ahmed, was allegedly involved in ordering the assassination of General Masoud. Ahmad Shah Masoud was the last hurdle in the Northern Alliance's cooperation with the USA in the coming invasion of Afghanistan. The kamikaze assassination took place two days before the attacks on the Twin Towers and the Pentagon during Gen. Mahmood Ahmed's official visit to Washington (September 4–13, 2004). The official communiqué of the Northern Alliance pointed to the involvement of the ISI.

September 10, 2005. According to Pakistani journalist Amir Mateen in a revealing article published one day before the 9/11 attack[60]:

> ISI Chief Lt-Gen. Mahmood's week-long presence in Washington has triggered speculation about the agenda of his mysterious meetings at the Pentagon and National Security Council. Officially, he is on a routine visit in return to CIA Director George Tenet's earlier visit to Islamabad. Official sources confirm that he met Tenet this week. He also held long parleys with unspecified officials at the White House and the Pentagon. But the most important meeting was with Marc Grossman, U.S. Under Secretary of State for Political Affairs. One can safely guess that the discussions must have centered on Afghanistan, and Osama bin Laden. What added interest to his visit is

---

[60] Amir Mateen, "ISI Chief's Parleys Continue in Washington," *News*, September 10, 2001.

the history of such visits? Last time Ziauddin Butt, Mahmood's predecessor, was here, during Nawaz Sharif's government, the domestic politics turned topsy-turvy within days.

Morning of September 11, 2001. The three lawmakers Bob Graham, Porter Goss, and Jon Kyl and General Mahmood *all met in a top-secret conference room on the fourth floor of the US Capitol.* Also present at this meeting were Pakistan's ambassador to the USA Maleeha Lodhi and several members of the Senate and House intelligence committees. According to Graham's copious notes, they discussed "poppy cultivation" before they discussed terrorism. But then the Americans pressed Ahmed even harder to crack down on al-Qaeda. And then at "9:04 -- Tim gives note on 2 planes crash into World Trade Center, NYC" (*Washington Post*, May 4, 2003).

However, at no time since 9/11 had Rep. Porter Goss and his Senate counterpart, Bob Graham (chairman of the Senate Intelligence Committee), acknowledged the role of Pakistan's ISI in supporting al-Qaeda. In fact, quite the opposite. One year after the attacks, the former head of the ISI continued to be described as a bona fide intelligence counterpart supportive of the US "war on terrorism." In an interview in the *New York Times* on the first anniversary of 9/11, Sen. Bob Graham described his August 2001 encounter with General Ahmed:

> I had just come back a few days before September the 11th from a trip... [to] Pakistan and [a] meeting with President Musharraf and with the head of the Pakistani intelligence service.

While we were meeting with the head of the intelligence service, a general whose name was General Ahmed, he had indicated he would be in Washington in early September, we -- Porter Goss, myself -- had invited him to meet with us while he was there. It turned out that the meeting was a breakfast the day of September the 11ᵗʰ.

The head of the ISI arrived in the USA on the fourth. Graham stated in the interview that he got back a few days before 9/11, which suggested that the Goss-Graham mission could well have returned to Washington on board the same military plane as General Ahmed.

So we were talking about what was happening in Afghanistan, what the capabilities and intentions of the Taliban and Al Qaida were from the perspective of this Pakistani intelligence leader, when we got the notices that the World Trade Center towers had been attacked.

September 12–13, 2001. At 10:00 a.m. a day after the devastating terrorist attacks on New York's World Trade Center and Pentagon headquarters in Washington, Gen. Mahmood Ahmed, ISI chief, arrived at the State Department for an emergency meeting with the US deputy secretary of state, Richard Armitage. "General, we require your country's full support and cooperation," Armitage told Pakistan's spymaster and member of the triumvirate that ruled the country. "We want to know whether you are with us or not, in our fight against terror." The meeting was adjourned for the next day after the general had assured Armitage of Pakistan's full support.

"We will tell you tomorrow what you are required to do," Armitage said as they left the room.

Meanwhile at 1:30 p.m., Colin Powell spoke to President Musharraf on the phone. "The American people would not understand if Pakistan did not cooperate in this fight with the United States," Powell said candidly as one general to another. President Musharraf promised to cooperate fully with the United States.

It was 12:00 p.m. on September 13, 2001, when General Mahmood returned to the State Department for the second meeting. "This is not negotiable," said Armitage as he handed over a single sheet of paper with seven demands that the Bush administration wanted him to accept.

The general glanced through the paper for a few seconds and replied, "They are all acceptable to us."

The swift response took Armitage by surprise. "These are very powerful words, General. Do you not want to discuss with your President?" he asked.

"I know the president's mind," replied General Mahmood.

A visibly elated Armitage asked General Mahmood to meet with George Tenet, the CIA chief, at his headquarters at Langley. "He is waiting for you," said Armitage.

The American demands, to which General Mahmood acceded to in no time, required Pakistan to abandon its support for the Taliban regime and provide logistical support to the American forces. The list of demands included the following:

1. Stop al-Qaeda operations on the Pakistani border and intercept arms shipments through Pakistan and all logistical support for bin Laden.

2. Give blanket overflights and landing rights for US planes.

3. Provide access to Pakistan's naval bases, airbases, and borders.

4. Give immediate intelligence and immigration information.

5. Curb all domestic expression of support for terrorism against the United States and its friends and allies.

6. Cut off fuel supply to the Taliban and stop Pakistani volunteers going into Afghanistan to join the Taliban.

7. Break diplomatic relations with the Taliban and assist the USA to destroy bin Laden and his al-Qaeda network.

September 13, 2001. General Ahmed met Sen. Joseph Biden, chairman of the Senate Foreign Relations Committee.

The Decision to go to War: At meetings of the National Security Council and in the so-called war cabinet on September 11, 12, and 13, CIA director George Tenet played a central role in persuading Pres. George Bush to launch the "war on terrorism."

September 11, 2001, 3:30 p.m. A key meeting of the National Security Council (NSC) was convened, with members of the NSC communicating with the president from Washington by secure video.[61] In the course of this NSC videoconference, CIA director George Tenet fed unconfirmed information to the president. Tenet stated that "he was virtually certain that bin Laden and his network were behind the attacks.[62]"

---

[61] *Washington Post,* January 27, 2002.

[62] Ibid.

The president responded to these statements quite spontaneously, off the cuff, with little or no discussion, and with an apparent misunderstanding of their implications. In the course of this videoconference (which lasted for less than an hour), the NSC was given the mandate by the president to prepare for the "war on terrorism." Very much on the spur of the moment, the green light was given by videoconference from Nebraska. In the words of President Bush, "We will find these people. They will pay. And I don't want you to have any doubt about it."[63]

4:36 p.m. (one hour and six minutes later). Air Force One departed for Washington. Back in the White House, that same evening at nine, a second meeting of the full NSC took place, together with Secretary of State Colin Powell, who had returned to Washington from Peru. The NSC meeting (which lasted for half an hour) was followed by the first meeting of the so-called war cabinet. The latter was made up of a smaller group of top officials and key advisers.

9:30 p.m. At the war cabinet, "Discussion turned around whether bin Laden's Al Qaida and the Taliban were one and the same thing. Tenet said they were."[64]

11:00 p.m. By the end of that historic meeting of the war cabinet, the Bush administration had decided to embark on a military adventure that began the war on Afghanistan and Iraq. Astonishingly, within a course of forty-eight hours, the military junta of Pakistan took an about-turn to become a lynchpin in the US-led military operation in Afghanistan that ousted the Taliban regime. The speed of the quick about-turn surprised even the American authorities.

Events after September 11 during the week in Washington and Islamabad provided an interesting insight into the ad hoc and arbitrary

---

[63] Ibid.

[64] Ibid.

decision-making process of military dictatorships on crucial national security and foreign policy issues. Like the policy to support the Taliban regime, the decision to surrender the country's sovereignty was also taken just by two generals. There were no consultations at any level when President Musharraf abandoned support for the oppressive and reactionary regime in Afghanistan, gave the American forces complete access to Pakistani territory, and assisted in the invasion of an ally and an independent Muslim state. A similar sequence of events had occurred in the history of Islam eighty-seven years earlier when Enver Pasa secretly signed a treaty of Turko-German alliance on August 2, 1914.

On the evening of September 12, General Musharraf received a phone call from General Mahmood in Washington, who briefed him about his meeting with Armitage. Later, US ambassador Wendy Chamberlain met with him and conveyed a formal message from the American leaders for cooperation. The president assured her of Pakistan's full support.

As it occurred in Turkey eighty-seven years earlier, in Pakistan, there was no consultation with political leaders on the paradigm shift in the strategic discourse of the nation. General Musharraf took his handpicked, unelected cabinet into confidence, almost three days after his ISI chief had already signed on the dotted line to the US demands. He told the ministers that the decision to cooperate with the United States was necessary to safeguard Pakistan's nuclear assets and its Kashmir policy.

General Musharraf did not find it hard to convince his cabinet, but it was not so simple when it came to his corps commanders and members of his military junta. At least seven senior officers, including Lieutenant General Mahmood, who had earlier in Washington signed on the dotted line, showed reservations on the decision to pull out support for the Taliban regime. The people of Pakistan and the owners of the land were astonished when they found themselves involved in a long war on behalf of the *kafireen* against their own countrymen in Waziristan and against other Muslims in Afghanistan.

Musharraf acted swiftly and fired the dithering general Mahmood and the other reluctant generals who disagreed with him. Through a series of purges at the top level, General Musharraf consolidated his position with the new commanders backing him fully on the new policy on Afghanistan. The shift in Pakistan's Afghan policy and the decision to support the United States brought minor economic and political benefits to General Musharraf's regime. From a pariah state, Pakistan became the center of focus of the international community. Never before had so many head of states traveled to Pakistan as they did in the few weeks after September 11. Pakistan was, once more, the USA's strategic partner.

According to senior American sources, the US-led coalition could not have achieved its swift success in Afghanistan without the ISI's intelligence support. The agency, which had been deeply involved with the Taliban from its inception, guided the American forces to the bombing and the massacre of the Taliban, its own creation. For this treachery, Musharraf's junta extracted paltry economic aid and concessions from the USA and other Western countries. Pakistan sold its honor for a $1 billion loan write-off, $600 million in budgetary support, and debt rescheduling. Pakistan was sold for $1.6 billion. Musharraf sold the heritage of each Pakistani man, woman, and child for US$10 each, equivalent to five hundred Pakistani rupees.

Munafiqeen in Pakistan assisted a *kafir* power to occupy two sovereign Muslim countries, Afghanistan, and Iraq. They allowed 260,000 Afghans and Iraqis to be blown to bits and hundreds of thousands of civilians to be maimed. Eighty percent of the population lost their jobs. The countries were decimated. Their infrastructure had been blown into stone age, and the desert and the mountains had been poisoned with radioactive waste from spent ammunition for thousands of years to come.

Yet this is not the end. And yet to come is the invasion of Iran, Libya, and Syria. Do the Saudis, Pakistanis, and the Egyptians feel that they will be spared of this fate?

r. Carefully Planned *Yahudi-Salibi-Munafiq* Intelligence Operation

The 9/11 attacks on New York and Washington were carefully planned intelligence operations. The 9/11 terrorists did not act on their own volition. The suicide hijackers were instruments of a carefully planned international intelligence operation. The evidence confirmed that al-Qaeda was the brainchild of the CIA and supported by Pakistan's military intelligence, the Inter-Services Intelligence. And the ISI, in turn, was an arm of the CIA in South Asia and owed its existence to the CIA.

The spontaneity of the discovery of the culprits and the instant declaration of war against the Taliban and al-Qaeda is a play written long time ago by the authors of the new American century in which the actors recited the long-memorized lines. The prologue was the act in which the Twin Towers exploded in a haze of smoke and dust, a real smoke screen of deception and lies foreshadowing what was yet to come.

The ISI and the CIA began planning the massacre of the Twin Towers in April 2000. Such a gigantic explosive event was meant to be shown live on every television screen around the world to arouse sympathy for America as the victim and repulsion against the perpetrators of the ghastly event. It was the opening scene of America's war against the world.

The evidence showed an intense collusion and collaboration between the president of Pakistan and his top intelligence staff and the senior American officials, the overseers of US intelligence services from the House and the Senate of the United States, and the director of the CIA. And Mahmood Ahmed traveled to the United States for the final fine-tuning of the planned operation between his men and the US side. There is little doubt that the 9/11 episode was a well-orchestrated, well-planned, and technically high-precision job undertaken by skilled people in collaboration with those within the aviation authority, the air force, the FBI, the immigration services, and a centralized secret group of planners with international intelligence connections with the CIA, ISI, and others. And finally, the perpetrators sat down all together to watch the results of their handiwork in a top secret room on the fourth floor of the US Capitol. Mahmood's presence in Washington was to ensure that the Pakistani intelligence chief delivered all that he had promised and did not crawl out of his part of the bargain.

In this conspiracy of the circle of evil, over three thousand innocent men and women lost their lives. And it was just the opening shot in a long war against humanity.

- ◇ If anyone slew a person – unless it is for murder or for spreading mischief in the land – it would be as if he slew the whole people; and if anyone saved a life, it would be as if he saved the life of the whole people. (Al-Ma'idah 5:32, Koran)
- ◇ Take not life, which Allah hath made sacred, except by the way of justice or law: This He commands you, that you may learn wisdom. (Al-An'am 151–53, Koran)

The covenant of Muhammad written in Medina is the first constitution of Dar es Salaam. The covenant is a brief summary of the covenant of the Koran underlining the fundamental obligations of the individual believers to their community in times of conflict.

⋄ The Muslims constitute one Ummah to the exclusion of all other men.

⋄ All believers shall rise as one man against anyone who seeks to commit injustice, aggression, crime, or spread mutual enmity amongst the Muslims even if such a person is their kin.

⋄ Just as the bond to Allah is indivisible, all the believers shall stand behind the commitment of the least of them. All believers are bonded one to another to the exclusion of other men.

⋄ The believers shall leave none of their members in destitution without giving him in kindness that he needs by the way of his liberty.

⋄ This Pax Islamica is one and indivisible. No believer shall enter a separate peace without all other believers whenever there is fighting in the cause of God but will do so only on the basis of equality and justice to all others.

⋄ In every expedition for the cause of God we undertake, all parties to the covenant shall fight shoulder to shoulder as one man.

⋄ All believers shall avenge the blood of one another when anyone falls fighting in the cause of God. No believer shall slay a believer in retaliation for an unbeliever, nor shall he assist an unbeliever against a believer. Whoever is convicted of killing a believer deliberatively but without righteous cause shall be liable to the relatives of the killed. Until the latter are satisfied, the killer shall be subject to retaliation by each believer.

During the last two hundred years, Muslims have lost in the battlefield in every conflict against the West; and in doing so, they have been subjected to humiliation and colonization lasting more than a century. Why did that happen? Muslim communities are beset with traitors and *Munafiqeen*. They look like Muslims, dress like Muslims, and pray like Muslims. They frequently go for *umrah* and hajj, yet for a price, they disobey every article of the covenants of Muhammad and of the Koran. For the price of a kingdom and a fiefdom, they betray their *din* and the *ummah*.

During the last three centuries, the Muslim states had had many external enemies whose motives were varied. All of them used disgruntled Muslim princes, noblemen, and tribes with the temptation of wealth and territory in fostering their aim. Once the conquering armies managed to gain a stranglehold on the Muslim territory, the traitors were discarded like rags once their usefulness was over. Yet in Muslim history, there had never been shortage of such traitors. In recent history, those who invited and aided the infidels in the occupation of the lands of Islam are the generals of the Pakistan Army, Northern Alliance of Afghanistan, Kurds of Iraq, the Shias of Iraq, the Saudi royal family, the Jordanian royals, and the sheikhs of Qatar, Kuwait, Bahrain, United Arab Emirates, and Oman. The result is the occupation of Afghanistan and Iraq, with the resulting loss of life of over 260,000 believers in Afghanistan and Iraq in the years 2002–2006. The loss of life of over 1 million Iraqis caused by the United Nations sanctions was also aided and abetted by the rulers of the Arabian Peninsula, Turkey, Jordan, and Iran. In fact, all the Islamic states combined are in no better position now to solve their problems of defense, disunity, infighting, poverty, illiteracy, and poor world image than they had in 1909, when Caliph Abdul Hamid was deposed by their ilk. When the Koran says the following, it might as well have been addressed to the present rulers of Islam:

> When the Hypocrites come to thee, they say, "We bear witness that thou art indeed the Messenger of Allah". Yes, Allah knows that you are indeed His Messenger, and Allah bears witness that the Hypocrites are indeed liars.

> They have made their oaths a screen (for their hypocrisy), thus they obstruct (men) from the Path of Allah: truly evil are their deeds.
>
> That is because they believed, then they disbelieved: so their hearts are sealed, therefore they understand not.
>
> When you look at them, their figures please you, and when they speak, and you listen to their words, they are as worthless as decayed piece of wood propped up. They panic at every shout is against them. They are the enemies, beware of them. Let the curse of Allah be on them! How they are perverted! (Al-Munafiqun 63:1–8)

How apt and fitting are Allah's words with regard to rulers of Islam. You see them sitting on their grandiose gold-covered chairs with thick velvet cushions, dressed in silken robes with gold embroidery, attending meetings of the Arab League and the Organization of Islamic Cooperation. We say, "Wow, these are our princes of Islam, all of them meeting to seek ways and means of our deliverance from tyranny and oppression." After their hard and difficult deliberations, they speak out gently in soft tones of their anguish and concern about the state of the *ummah*. Their words are as worthless as a rotten, hollow, and crumbling log unable to support the truth. Their hypocrisy and lies have dogged the *ummah* year after year for the last three hundred years. They are insecure and panic stricken in case the believers seek justice and retribution. The Koran says these hypocrites are the enemies and beware of them.

> When you look at them, their figures please you, and when they speak, and you listen to their words, they are as (worthless as decayed) piece of wood propped up. They panic that every shout is against them. They are the enemies,

beware of them. Let the curse of Allah be on them! How they are perverted!

We have seen in this chapter that there is a distinct circle of evil that does Satan's bidding. A circle of smart financiers, usually Jews, spins the web of the devil or sets the trap using the Christian armies to snare the Muslims. There are traitors among the Muslims, the *Munafiqeen*, who finally snap shut the trap door. Throughout the history of man, this story has been repeated over and over again. The trap can be set only with deception and guile.

On the eve of the Iraq War while the Jews in the Pentagon were planning and the Pentagon and the White House were carrying on the troop deployment, the whole world knew what was happening. The Arab kings, the third dimension of the evil, were doing the bidding of the *kafireen*; the only people being fooled were the Arab and Muslim people. Yet the people who drove the fuel tankers to the air bases, the Saudi and Jordanian armies, the diplomats, and the news reporters knew the game plan. If anyone was deceived by Bandar and Abdullah and their royal kin, they wanted to be deceived.

In this day and age of paper and pen and electronic communication, every believer has access to the guidance of Allah and their covenant with Him. In Islam, there are no professional kings or rulers, nor are there professional politicians. Today the whole world knows of the *fitnah*, corruption, dishonesty, *Fahasha*, treachery, and disobedience to the covenant of Allah by the Muslim ruling classes and politicians. The kings and rulers of Islam cannot rule unless the believers want to be ruled by them. The *Munafiqeen* and the *Fahasha* cannot be the guardians of *Beit el Allah* and the guardians of the rites of hajj unless the Muslims allow them. If "Muslims" follow the lead of the *Munafiqeen*, disobey the covenant, and do evil, they themselves become tainted by the same evil. Every believer is reminded by his covenant to invite others to all that is good and right and forbid what is wrong.

> Let there arise out of you a band of people inviting to all that is good, enjoining what is right, and forbidding what is wrong: they are the ones to attain happiness. (Ali 'Imran 3:103–5, Koran)

The Koranic principle of enjoining good and forbidding what is evil is supportive of the moral autonomy of the individual. This principle authorizes the individual to act according to his or her best judgment in situations in which his or her intervention will advance a good purpose. The following saying of the blessed prophet supports individual action by a believer:

> If any one of you sees an evil, let him change it by his hand, and if he is unable to do that, let him change by his words, and if he is still unable to do that let him denounce it in his heart, but this is the weakest form of belief.

This principle assigns to the individual an active role in the community in which he or she lives. *The Koran annunciated the principle of free speech fourteen hundred years ago.* Believing men and women are reminded that they are the best of people, witnesses over other nations. Such a responsibility carries with it a moral burden of an exemplary conduct of one who submits to the divine truth and whose relationship with Allah is governed is by *taqwa*, the consciousness of humankind's responsibility toward its Creator. With that knowledge and faith, the believer is well equipped to approach others to enjoin what is right and forbid that is wrong. This moral autonomy of the individual, when bound together with the will of the community, formulates the doctrine of infallibility of the collective will of the *ummah*, which is the doctrinal basis of consensus.

When the blessed prophet died, he left behind the Koran, the *din*, and the Dar es Salaam. The blessed prophet wisely did not nominate a successor to his spiritual and worldly legacy. The believers all together inherited the Koran, the *din*, and the Dar es Salaam till the end of time. Allah addresses individual believers, both men and women, in His covenant, guiding them to the conduct of this spiritual and worldly legacy of the prophet. Every believer has the autonomy of their conduct of their spiritual and the earthly affairs. Humans have enough freedom to make their own choices: if they make the choice to do beautiful and wholesome deeds (*saalihaat*) motivated by faith (*iman*) and God-wariness (*taqwa*), they please Allah and bring harmony and wholesomeness to the world, resulting in peace, justice, mercy, compassion, honor, equity, well-being, freedom, and many other gifts through Allah's grace. Others choose to do evil and work corruption (*mufsidun*), destroying the right relationship among the creation, causing *fitnah*, hunger, disease, oppression, pollution, and other afflictions. In the universal order, corruption is the prerogative of the humans, and vicegerency gives the humans the freedom to work against the Creator and His creation. Allah measures out the good and the evil, the wholesome and the corrupt. Allah commands the humans to be righteous.

In the commandments of the covenant, Allah addresses individual men and women who in unity form a community, the *ummah*. Nevertheless, the emphasis of the guidance is to the individual believer for his and her own conduct. The concept of a covenant also symbolizes the relationship between humans, among Allah's creatures, and the rest of His creation. They all share one God, one set of guidance and commandments, the same submission and obedience to Him, and the same set of expectations in accordance with His promises. They all can therefore trust one another since they all have similar obligations and expectations. In view of the Koran, humans, communities, nations, and civilizations will continue to live in harmony and peace so long as they continue to fulfill Allah's covenant.

4. Betrayal of the Covenant: Inequity with Women

Allah has granted each believer, man and woman, equality—a right to freedom; a right to practice his faith in accordance with his beliefs as, in Islam, there is no compulsion in matters of religion; a right to life, which includes mental, physical, and emotional well-being; a right to safeguard one's property; a right to intellectual endeavors, acquisition of knowledge, and education; a right to make a living; and a right to free speech and action to enjoin good and forbid evil. In enjoying his freedoms, the individual ensures that his activities do not impinge on the similar rights of others.

Equality of Men and Women:

> You are forbidden to take women against their will.
> Nor should you treat them with harshness, on the
> contrary treat them on a footing of equality kindness
> and honor.

Fifty percent of the population of the believers, the women, have been excluded from the mainline Islam by the priests, mullahs, jurist-scholars, and Hadith scholars against the commandments of the Koran. Women were regarded as inferior beings in most pre-Islamic cultures, including the Arabs, Persians, Greeks, and Romans and also among the Hindus. Their status was not any higher among the Turkish and the Mongol tribes of Central Asia. In Judaism, women were forbidden from the inner sanctuary of the temple; and in the early Pauline Christianity, their position was relegated to the entrance or outside the church at prayer time.

Islam brought dignity and grace to the status of women—the mothers, wives, and the daughters. Women had their rights established and their social status elevated as equal to that of the men. They attended prayer services at the Prophet's Mosque; they held regular and frequent discourse with the prophet of Allah on religious, women's, and family issues. They participated in the battles alongside their men. Women worked outside their homes. The first person to convert to Islam, Khadijah, was a successful international trader and owned an import and export business, dealing in goods from India, Persia, Africa, Yemen, and the Byzantine Empire. She employed several men to assist her in her business. Other women memorized the Koran and taught other Muslims. Aishah gave regular talks and discourses on religious matters. Other women led the ritual prayers and *dhikr-e-Allah* gatherings.

The ulema and other followers of the Hadith collections of the third century over the last one thousand years have betrayed Allah and His messenger by excluding women from congregation prayers, businesses, public and social affairs, and most importantly education. The Muslim communities have betrayed Allah and His messenger concerning their obligations to their women—their mothers, wives, sisters, and daughters. Allah's covenant provides equality to every individual within the community, both men and women. Allah has elevated the rank and dignity of the children of Adam, both men and women, with special favors above that of most of His creation, including the angels. The dignity and favors promised by Allah include six special values: faith, life, intellect (education), property, lineage, and freedom of speech and action.

The Koran addresses men and women who submit to Allah, who believe, who are devout, who speak the truth, who are righteous, who are humble, who are charitable, who fast and deny themselves, who guard their chastity, and who remember Allah much and promises them a great reward and forgiveness for their transgressions. In this address, Allah treats individual men and women equitably with a promise of similar reward for their good acts. In Allah's eyes, all men and all women who do good deeds carry an equal favor with Him.

Allah admonishes both the believing men and women to lower their gaze and guard their chastity. Allah also admonishes women to dress modestly and to not display their adornments outside their immediate family environment. Allah commands believers, men and women, to turn *all together* toward Allah so that they may prosper. This can happen only when the believers, men and women, turn to Allah collectively as a community in a mosque as was customary during the lifetime of the *nabi* of Allah.

According to the Koran, men and women are autonomous and answerable to Allah for their own deeds and actions, and only they as individuals are rewarded or punished for their deeds. In a community, men as a group or the state has no sanction from the Koran to enforce any restrictions on the freedom of righteous and believing women. To every man and to every woman, Allah has bestowed rights to freedom, faith, life, intellect, property, and education. The authority of a ruler who denies these basic freedoms to men or to women is openly disputable. The individual obeys the ruler on the condition that the ruler obeys the Koran and Allah's covenant.

The Koran addresses men and women equally, subjecting them together to similar obligations of submission to Allah, regular prayer, giving in charity, modesty in dress and behavior, righteousness, humility, chastity, worship, truthfulness, remembrance of Allah, and being kind and just. Allah blessed mankind (*insan*) with dignity, justice, and equality and promised them with the same rewards as well as obligations. *Be steadfast in prayer and practice regular charity* is an ongoing and repetitive theme in the Koran. Allah calls those who believe, both men and women, to hasten to the congregation prayer on Friday, the day of assembly.

> O you who believe! (Men and women) When the call is proclaimed to prayer on Friday, the Day of Assembly hasten earnestly to the Remembrance of Allah and leave off business and traffic that is best for you if ye but knew!
>
> And when the Prayer is finished, then may ye disperse through the land, and seek of the Bounty of Allah: and celebrate the Praises of Allah often: that ye may prosper. (Al-Mumtahanah 62:9–10, Koran)

Women attended obligatory prayers, *jum'ah* prayers, and Eid prayers in the Prophet's Mosque. Whenever the apostle of Allah finished his prayers with *Taslim*, the women would get up first, and he would stay in his place for a while before getting up. The purpose of his stay was that the women might leave before the men who had finished their prayer.

Soon after the prophet died, there occurred an enormous expansion of the Islamic domain. Women, for a while, enjoyed their newly won freedom and dignity given by Islam and proclaimed by Blessed *Nabi* Muhammad. Soon afterward, the Arabs reached an unprecedented level of prosperity and began to accumulate large harems, wives, concubines, female slaves, and servants. These women were increasingly confined to their quarters and not allowed to go out unchaperoned. Subsequently, the architecture of the Middle East dwellings changed to suit the new circumstances. The courtyard of the house had high walls, and the only entrance was where the master of the house sat. The master of the harem was so jealous of the chastity of his women that he employed eunuchs as servants and guards in his house. The institution of eunuchs was a peculiar Middle Eastern practice related to the institution of the harems of the elite.

The trampling of women's rights was and is a betrayal of the blessed *nabi* Muhammad's emancipations of women's rights. As more Arabs, Romans, Persians, Hindus, Turks, and Mongols embraced Islam, they brought with them their peculiar bias against women and female infants. The Islamic emancipation of women was ignored; women were confined within their houses, covered head to foot in cloth, denied spiritual growth, and denied access to education and to places of worship. Shamefully, the scholars and the ulema encouraged this state of affairs. Women were gradually discouraged from praying in the mosque and were excluded from congregational worship. Women were deprived of education and knowledge of Islam; consequently, their children grew up in ignorance. The first school is in the cradle, and this is the school Muslim children were denied. Thus, over the centuries, the Muslims have betrayed the *rasul* of Allah and disobeyed His covenant.

Pre-Islamic Arab and other cultures regarded woman as their chattel and possession. Abduction and rape of opponents' women was a favored pastime of those victorious in battle to humiliate the vanquished. Thus, the birth of a female child was regarded as a matter of shame, which led to the practice of infanticide. This practice was forbidden earlier on during the prophet's mission. However, the primordial masculine instinct resurfaced in the new Muslim. His subconscious shame and embarrassment of the female in his household was sublimated into gentler and more socially acceptable alternative. As the Koran points out, he chose to retain the female child on sufferance and contempt rather than bury her in the dust.

What an evil choice they decide on!

The shame and cultural burden in some of the Muslim societies is so intense that, the female infant is buried in the coffin of Yashmaq (Burqa) in the confines of the brick walls of her house. She is not killed off physically, but nevertheless killed intellectually and spiritually, by withholding the intellectual and spiritual sustenance, which Allah has provided for her.

Indeed, lost are those who slay their children, foolishly and without knowledge, and have forbidden that which Allah has provided for them, and inventing lies against Allah. They have indeed gone astray and heeded no guidance. (Al-An'am 6:140, Koran)

When news is brought to one of them, of the birth of a female child, his face darkens, and he is filled with inward grief! With shame does he hide himself from his people, because of the bad news he has had! Shall he retain it on sufferance and contempt, or bury it in the dust? Ah! What an evil choice they decide on? (An-Nahl 16:58–59, Koran)

In a just and moral society, women should have all the freedoms bestowed by Allah's covenant. Women should themselves arise and demand their God-given birthright of freedom and equality. They should have an intellectual awakening to assert their rights.

Women in Communal Worship: Allah blesses mankind (*insan*), both men and women, with dignity, justice, and equality and promises them with the same rewards as well as obligations. *Be steadfast in prayer and practice regular charity* is an ongoing and repetitive theme in the

Koran. Allah calls those who believe, both men and women, to hasten to the congregation prayer on Friday, the day of assembly.

The whole world is the place of prostration, and every place where Allah is remembered is aglow in Allah's *nur*. Every place of prostration and Allah's remembrance has His presence and light. The believing men and women approach the Lord in His *taqwa* in awe and gratitude, supplicating in His presence, aware that He is there, and they see Him; however, if they do not see Him, they are aware that He sees them and is sentient of their prayer, gratitude, and supplication. Allah calls on all believers, men and women, to salat.

> Bow down, prostrate yourself and serve you're Lord, and do wholesome deeds that you may prosper. Establish regular Salaat, give regular charity, and hold fast to Allah. He is your Mawla, Protector, the best of Protectors and the best Helper. Those who do wholesome deeds, establish regular prayers and regular charity have rewards with their Lord. On them shall be no fear, nor shall they grieve. Seek help with patience, perseverance, and prayer. Allah is with those who patiently persevere.

When Allah calls all believers, men and women, to salat, to remember and praise Him, the believers purify themselves by washing their faces and their hands to the elbows, wipe their heads, and wash their feet to the ankles. If they are unclean, they purify themselves by bathing. They then approach their Lord, submit to Him, and renew their covenant with Him. Salat, *dhikr*, recitation, fasting, *taqwa* of Allah, and *furqan* are the beams of light that maintain the believer's connection with the divine light. *Islam* (submission, prostration) is the direct link between the believer and Allah. The believer asks, and Allah gives. The believer loves Allah, and Allah loves him in return. The believer asks for the straight path, and Allah shows him the way.

The believer prays to Allah, and Allah showers his mercy and grace on him. The believer remembers Allah, and Allah responds to those who praise Him, thank Him, and ask Him.

The believer, in every case, is the human, both man and woman. Allah addresses both man and woman equally. And Allah reassures them:

> On you there shall be no fear, nor shall you grieve. Seek help with patience, perseverance, and prayer. Allah is with those who patiently persevere.

Allah calls the believers to prayer; some believers are indeed afraid, and on some, there is indeed fear and grief. Places of prostration in the Islamic world are masculine preserves, men's clubs. Believing, upright women, if not totally forbidden, are indeed discouraged from praying in the mosques by men and those who control the mosques. Such actions amount to *fitnah*, oppression of women by these men. The mosques that do permit women to pray have separate entrance for the woman and a segregated and sometimes unclean, uncomfortable, unventilated prayer room for women and children. The khutbah and the prayers are inaudible. When Allah calls on the believers, he addresses both men and women together in unison.

Allah made tribes and nations from a single pair of male and female so that humans can communicate and come to know one another. Allah honors humans who have *taqwa* of Him and the ones who are righteous. The acts of good works and righteousness recognized in the Koran are:

> to show compassion, to be merciful and forgive others, to be just, protect the weak, defend the oppressed, to be generous and charitable, to be truthful, and to seek knowledge and

wisdom, to be kind, to be peaceful, to love others, and to perform beautiful deeds.

We created you from a single pair of a male and a female, and made you into nations and tribes, that ye may know each other. Verily the most honored of you in the sight of Allah is the one with taqwa of Allah, the most righteous of you. And Allah is All Knowing, All Aware. (Al-Hujurat 49:12–13)

The earliest Muslims gathered for prayers in a makeshift mosque partly open to the elements. The prophet of Islam led the prayers for everyone to see and hear. The men prayed behind the prophet, followed by rows of children and women occupying the back rows of the Prophet's Mosque, where they could be seen and heard by the rest of the congregation in the same small room. In between the prayers, men and women were able to mingle, and the blessed prophet was accessible to each person, if any man or a woman wanted a conversation or had questions.

Direct contact between the prophet, as the imam who led the prayers, and those who attended the prayers seems to have been an important element in the Friday khutbah. On Fridays, the blessed *nabi* preached the khutbah leaning on his staff. And the men, women, and children sat in front of him, their faces raised toward him; they listened as they watched him.

The idea is that the mosque is a privileged place, a collective space where the community debates important matters before making decisions. It is the fundamental concept of Islam, which provides the community autonomy and a voice through consultation and consensus. Everything passes through the mosque. The mosque, in the history of Islam, became the school for indoctrination of new converts. It became the nerve center of the community for ritual prayer, community organization, and socialization. In the mosque, worshippers came to know and bonded with one another. This is where the Ansar became the brethren of the Muhajirun.

The mosque became established as the place where dialogue between the leader and the people took place. Here, the teacher, the *nabi*, taught and preached; and the populace, both men and women, came to listen to him. The apparently simple decision to install a minbar in the mosque was treated by the prophet as a matter that concerned all Muslims. The prophet used to say the Friday prayers standing, leaning against a palm trunk. Not everyone could see the prophet clearly, and the believers urged the prophet to take his place on a platform at the time of prayer so that everybody could see him. Within a few months, the number of Muslims had grown considerably. "Why not build a pulpit like I have seen in Syria?" suggested a companion. The prophet asked those present for their advice on the question, and they agreed to the suggestion. A Medina carpenter cut a tree and built a pulpit with a seat and two steps up to the seat. Thus, the congregation—men in front, children in the middle, and women at the back—were able to see and hear the blessed *nabi* when he taught in the mosque.

The premise that women are discouraged from worshiping in the mosque because they "distract" men from their spiritual pursuit because women stimulate men's sexual urges rests on sham premise. Islam is a religion of reform and self-control. The covenant has established strict guidelines and boundaries over the believer's behavior both in private and in public.

> For men and women who surrender unto Allah, for men and women who believe, for men and women who are devout, for men and women who speak the truth, for men and women who persevere in righteousness, for men and women who are humble, for men and women who are charitable, for

men and women who fast and deny themselves, for men and women who guard their chastity, for men and women who remember Allah much, for them Allah has forgiveness and a great reward.

Say to the Believing men that they should lower their gaze and guard their modesty: That will make for greater purity for them: And Allah is acquainted with all that they do.

And say to the Believing women that they should lower their gaze and guard their modesty; that they should not display their adornments except what is ordinarily obvious, That they should draw a veil over their bosom and not display their adornments (Except to the immediate family) And that they should not strike their feet in order to draw attention to their hidden adornments.

And O you Believers! (Men and women) Turn you all together Toward Allah that ye may prosper. The believer's men and women are protectors one of another; they enjoin what is just and forbid what is evil; They observe regular prayers, practice regular charity, and obey Allah and His messenger. On them will Allah pour His mercy, for Allah is exalted in power, wise.

O you who believe! Guard your souls, If you follow (right) guidance, No hurt can come to you from those who stray; The goal of you all is to Allah, It is He who will show you the truth of all that ye do.

This *ayah* of the Koran has defined the boundaries of behavior for both men and women for all times to come. It tells men and women to lower their gaze in modesty. Could it be clearer? And then Allah tells both men and women:

- *You Believers! Turn you all together toward Allah that you may prosper.* (And this could only occur in prayer in a place of prostration.)

- *The believer's men and women are protectors one of another* (meaning that men and women work as team to protect their common spiritual and earthly interests).

- *They enjoin what is just and forbid what is evil* (a clear indication that men and women together promote a just and a moral community).

- *They observe regular prayers, practice regular charity, and obey Allah and His messenger.* (Again, Allah urges both men and women to establish regular salat, practice regular charity, and obey Allah's covenant as given to the blessed prophet in the Koran.)

- *On them will Allah pour His mercy, for Allah is exalted in power, wise.* (The believers who turn to Allah together in prayer, work to protect one another, promote a just and a moral society, establish regular prayer, give in charity, and obey Allah's covenant will bathe in Allah's mercy.)

The innate self of man, the *nafs*, has the ability to perform good and evil. Life is a chain of emotions, intentions, and actions. *Taqwa* of Allah drives away the temptations and cravings from man's *nafs*. Only Satan's temptations will lead a man to *Fahasha* and fulfillment of his lust. Every being is responsible for his own emotions, intentions, and actions. Every man has been bequeathed self-control over his own *nafs*. Life is but a trial of one's deeds on which men will be judged for their own actions. And women, likewise, will be judged for their own. The argument that men lose self-control over their lust in public places assumes that Muslim men have no more control over their animal instincts than a dog or a donkey. Through such reasoning, men abdicate moral responsibility for their own actions and behavior.

Men must assume responsibility for their own emotions, intentions, and actions. The Taliban and Wahhabi solution to manipulate the environment to make women fade away behind brick walls and veils, to keep men's erectile responses in check, raises important questions about men's control over their *nafs*. What does this say about men's capacity to take full responsibility for their own spirituality and actions? To what understanding of humanity are the men entitled to control the houses of worship?

> The Believers, men and women, are protectors one of another: they enjoin what is just and forbid what is evil: they observe regular prayers, practice regular charity, and obey Allah and His apostle. On them will Allah pour His mercy: for Allah is exalted in Power, Wise. (12)

To every man and to every woman, Allah has bestowed equal rights to freedom, faith, life, intellect, property, education, and freedom of speech and action, enjoining what is right and forbidding what is wrong.

5. Betrayal of the Covenant: Wealth

For some Muslims, craving for wealth and gold has replaced their covenant with Allah. Gold has become their god. The Koran says:

> Crave not those things of what Allah has bestowed His gifts more freely on some than others, men are assigned what they earn and women that they earn.

Allah created the earth and then bestowed on man His favor to extract sustenance from it. He also created the sun, moon, and stars to create a just equilibrium and harmony in the universe. The sun provides energy for the growth, sustenance, and well-being of humans, plants, and animals. Gradually, man began to extract more than his personal needs from the earth; and the boom of economics, trade, and commerce started, creating cycle imbalance, disharmony, wars, poverty, and injustice throughout the globe. This disharmony caused by greed not only blemished the humans, but the animal life also suffered by disappearance of species. Pollution and contamination of the environment resulted from the race to accumulate and hoard the world's wealth in a few hands. Man, disobeyed Allah's universal laws and covenant.

According to the Koran, economics, and the observance of the moral code of Allah's covenant go hand in hand, and they cannot be separated from each other.

> Glory to the Lord of the heavens and the earth, the Lord supreme! Exalted is He from all that they ascribe to Him.
>
> So, leave them to talk nonsense and amuse themselves until they meet that Day of theirs, that they have been promised.
>
> It is He who is Allah in heaven and Allah on earth; and He is the Wise, the Knower.
>
> And blessed is He, whose is the kingdom of the heavens and the earth, and all that is between them: with Him is the knowledge of the Hour: and to Him shall ye return.
>
> And those whom they invoke besides Allah have no power of intercession, except those who bear witness to the truth and are aware.

Sama in the Koran signifies the universe and *ardh* man's domain on the earth pertaining to his social and economic world. Allah is the Lord of the heavens and the earth and what is in between. The divine laws under which the universe functions so meticulously and smoothly should also apply to the economic life of man so that he might achieve a balanced, predictable, equitable, and just financial life. *Sama* is the source of Allah's benevolence to humanity and of His universal laws that govern human subsistence and sustenance on the earth. *Ardh* is controlling man's economic life in this world. Allah's kingdom over the heavens and the earth sustains man's economic life and directly affects man's conduct and his obedience to Allah's covenant.

Ayahs in Sura An-Nahl are explicit. Allah created the heavens and the earth for just ends, to bring peace, harmony, equilibrium, and justice to the universe. He is Allah the One, Lord of the creation. He sends water from the heavens for sustenance of life on the earth—humans, plants, and animals. Allah sends sunshine to the earth to provide warmth and light to sustain human, plant, and animal life. Allah fashioned moon and stars to create equilibrium in the universe, every object in its intended place revolving in its fixed orbit in perfect harmony and balance. Allah knows the secrets and mysteries of the heavens and the earth, the so-called sciences, and the knowledge of particles, elements, cells, mitochondria, chromosomes, gravity, and black holes, only an infinitesimal portion of which he revealed to man, yet man is arrogant and boastful.

Allah says to the believers, "Squander not your wealth among yourselves in egotism and conceit: Let there be trade and traffic amongst you with mutual goodwill nor kill or destroy yourselves: for verily Allah hath been Most Merciful to you. If any do that in rancor and injustice, soon shall we cast them into the fire: and easy it is for Allah? If you abstain from all the odious and the forbidden, Allah shall expel out of you all evil in you and admit you to a Gate of great honor.

"And crave not those things of what Allah has bestowed His gifts more freely on some than others, men are assigned what they earn and women that they earn. But ask Allah of His bounty. Surely Allah is knower of everything."

Land and the resources of life belong to Allah, who bestowed it to man and woman, His regents on the earth. The covenant expects man to tend Allah's garden for all His creatures, men and beasts, as well as conserve its resources for the future generations. Whatever is left over beyond one's needs should go to meet the necessities of the rest of humanity, starting with one's *qurba*, near and dear, and then the community, followed by the surrounding communities. The land does not belong to kings, states, governments, tribal chiefs, military, aristocracy, timars, or *iqtas*. Land cannot be owned by individuals or families nor inherited. Land belongs to Allah for the use of His creatures.

In return for all of Allah's favors, Allah commands the following:

- Justice (*'adl*). Justice, fairness, honesty, integrity, and evenhanded dealings are a prerequisite of every Muslim's conduct when dealing with others whether socially or in business transactions.
- Doing what is good or what is beautiful (*ihsan*). This attribute includes every positive quality such as goodness, beauty, and harmony. Human beings have an obligation to do what is wholesome and beautiful in their relationship with Allah and His creatures.
- Providing for those near to you (*qurba*) and kith and kin. Help them with wealth, kindness, compassion, humanity, and sympathy.

- Rejecting *Fahasha*, all evil deeds, lies, false testimony, fornication, selfishness, ingratitude, greed, and false belief.
- Fulfilling the covenant of Allah. Whosoever does beautiful and righteous deeds will be given new life and rewarded with greater wages by Allah.

> Allah commands justice, the doing of good, and liberality to kith and kin, and He forbids all shameful deeds, and injustice and rebellion: He instructs you, that ye may receive admonition.

> Fulfill the Covenant of Allah when ye have entered into it and break not your covenant after ye have confirmed it, indeed you have made Allah your surety; for Allah knows all that you do. (Koran 16:90–91)

> Whoever works righteousness, man, or woman, and has Faith, verily, to him will we give a new Life, a life that is good and pure, and we will bestow on such their reward according to the best of their actions. (Koran 16:97)

Tawhid, the main pillar of Islam, signifies that man's economic life depends wholly on Allah's laws of the universe and that their relationship to those who believe is through the obedience to His covenant. Allah maintains in the Koran that there is no creature on the earth whose sustenance is not provided by Allah.

> No creature moves on earth that Allah does not nourish. He knows its essential nature and its varying forms; every detail has its place in the obvious plan. (Koran 11:6)

How are the people in need provided for their sustenance and daily needs? All wealth belongs to Allah, who bestows it on some people more than others. This wealth is given in trust, whereby the possessor is obliged to give the surplus to Allah's cause, to his kin, to the widows and orphans, and to the needy first in his community and then in other communities around him. Wealth is to be shared so that no single individual of the *ummah*, or indeed in the world, should go hungry or be without education and shelter.

> It is not righteousness that ye turn your faces towards East or West; but it is righteousness to believe in Allah and the Last Day, and the Angels, and the Book, and the Messengers; to spend of your substance, out of love for Him, for your kin, for orphans, for the needy, for the wayfarer, for those who ask, and for the ransom of slaves; to be steadfast in prayer, and practice regular charity, to fulfill the covenants which you have made; and to be firm and patient, in pain (or suffering) and adversity, and throughout all periods of panic. Such are the people of truth, the God-fearing. (Koran 2:17)

> And when they are told, "Spend you of (the bounties) with which Allah has provided you," The Unbelievers say to those who believe: "Shall we then feed those whom, if Allah had so willed, He would have fed, Himself? Ye are in nothing but manifest error. (Koran 36:47)

> Alms are for the poor and the needy, and those employed to administer the funds; for those whose hearts have been (recently) reconciled (to the truth); for those in bondage and in debt; in the cause of Allah; and for the wayfarer: (thus is it) ordained by Allah, and Allah is full of knowledge and wisdom. (At-Tawbah 9:60, Koran)

In the above two verses, the clear indication is that man is given bounty by Allah. In return, his obligation is to distribute the surplus, after his needs have been met, to the needy. The Koran specifies that the charities *be* disbursed among the *fuqara* (the poor who ask), *al-masakin* (the poor and the needy who do not ask), and zakat administrators (those who spread the light of Islam to those inclined, for the freedom of those in bondage, those in debt, for the cause of Allah, and for the wayfarer who treads the path in Allah's service).

In the covenant, the individual surrenders to Allah his life and belongings in return for His guidance, a place in paradise in the hereafter, and peace with prosperity in this world. Every believer, according to his or her covenant with Allah, has the obligation to extend the benefits that Allah has provided him or her to those who have not received the same benefits. Such acts of generosity will be rewarded by Allah with a place in *Jannat* (place of peace and plenty) in the afterlife. Life of *Jannat* is to be attained in this world also, provided the compact with Allah is adhered to. The believer is Allah's instrument who will fulfill His promise to Adam that

> none will remain without food or clothes and none will suffer from heat or thirst. (Koran 20:118)

In the verses below, Allah has promised those who believe and obey His covenant that, as reward for their acts of charity, He will double the harvest of their labors, forgive their sins, and provide them of His bounties, nor shall they have fear nor grieve. Fear and grief arise from misfortunes, which cause anxiety and depression. Allah's promise, therefore, is to safeguard the believers from misfortunes.

And to those devouring usury, Allah will deprive all blessings. Obeying Allah's covenant provides *Jannat* in the hereafter and a life of *Jannat*, peace, and plenty in this world. It also brings balance, harmony, and stability to the economic life of the world in that it meets the necessities of each person and eliminates unnecessary suffering.

> O you who believe! Do no render in vain your charity by reminders of your generosity or by injury, like him who spends his wealth to be seen of men, but he does not believe

in Allah or in the Last Day. His likeness is the likeness of a smooth rock on which is a little soil; on it falls heavy rain, which leaves it bare. They will not be able to do anything with what they have earned. And Allah does not guide the disbelieving people.

And the likeness of those who spend their substance, seeking to please Allah and to strengthen their souls, is as a garden, high and fertile; heavy rain falls on it but makes it yield a double increase of harvest, and if it receives not heavy rain, light moisture suffices it. And Allah is seer of what you do. (Al-Baqarah 2:264–65, Koran)

Each basic community owns the land in its surrounds, tilled and administered by the community as a whole for the well-being of the community in justice and harmony according to the covenant of Allah. The Islamic economic system is based on capitalism in the production of wealth and socialism in its expenditure, with the difference being individuals are free and able to make wealth but are responsible for the needs of their kith and kin and their neighbor. The state has little role in the welfare system. The land owned by the community may be assigned to individuals or may be tilled communally for the mutual benefit of the whole community, producing food and paying for schools, hospitals, roadways, municipal services, and so on. The community is meant to be self-sufficient economically for all its needs and responsible for the welfare of every individual for his nutrition, clothing, shelter, health, schooling, and old-age provision.

6. Betrayal of the Covenant: The Un-Islamic International Monetary System

Proliferation of wealth through creation of fiat money in the twentieth century and the creation of capital through lending money on interest has corrupted the Muslim communities and their governments. In the Islamic system, money is based on the value of labor needed to produce a commodity, and this money is only a medium of exchange, a way of defining the value of an item but in itself has no value and therefore should not give rise to more money by earning interest through deposit in a bank or loaning it to someone else. The human endeavor, initiative, and risk involved in a productive venture are much more important than the money used to finance it. Money deposited in a bank, or hoarded, is potential capital rather than capital. Money becomes capital only when it is invested in a venture. Accordingly, money loaned to a business as a loan is regarded as a debt of the business, and it is not capital; as such, it is not entitled to any return, such as interest.

Muslims are encouraged to spend (purchase necessities or spend in the way of Allah) or invest their money and are discouraged from keeping their money idle. Hoarding money is unacceptable. Introduction of the Western monetary system in the Muslim countries has corrupted Islamic trade and commerce as well as the Islamic way of life. Giving of zakat and other charities recreates and circulates the total wealth within the community over a period of forty years. Every rich man is a boon to society as he circulates his wealth within his community. In Islam, there should be no billionaires as the dissipation of mandatory zakat will deplete the cycle of acquisition. Yet there are billionaires in the Arabian Peninsula.

Cult of money and acquisition: The cult of money and acquisition is very secretive. Allah's grace and bounty showers the earth to nurture the whole of His creation. There is enough in His grace to feed, shelter, clothe, educate, and nurture humanity and protect the rest of Allah's creation. Fewer than five hundred of the world's richest men control 5 percent of the world's wealth. Five percent of mankind has positioned itself to deprive 95 percent of humanity and the rest of Allah's creation from this beneficence. Their nets positioned under the tree of life catch most of the fruit before it falls to the earth to benefit the rest of Allah's creatures.

The cult of money, the *Mutaffifeen* control the world's economy through deceit, force, and subterfuge. Fewer than five thousand families, who all know one another, hold on to most of the world's wealth. Through a secret network of corporations, secret societies, religious cults, and international organizations, they control the natural resources of this world, and they plan to keep it that way. Through their minions in political, religious, financial, academic, military, and intelligence service organizations, they control the world's affairs to suit their own plan of control. They control the world's finest real estate and hoard gold. In today's world, such wealth is dormant, but it is held as a hedge in the future control of the world. The power play of the *Mutaffifeen* lies in the following.

1. Usury: The total debt of the governments and the peoples of the world far exceeds the total ownership of the wealth by the people. The *Mutaffifeen* bankers have indebted the world by creating paper money out of nothing and then lending it out to governments and people, who will never be able to escape the debt cycle as, in the bigger picture, there is never enough wealth in the world to pay back the principal and interest. Thus, governments and people will never be able to pay off the debt and will continue to pay the interest in perpetuity. With increasing debt, interest payment continues to rise to thousands and billions of dollars every year. All that money ends up in a few hands that control the governments in a very subtle, secretive way. The governments and the people of the world today are indebted to the tune of over one hundred trillion dollars. In other words, goods and services worth the nominal value of one hundred trillion dollars have changed hands with the help of "make-believe printed paper money" borrowed from a group of men who do not "own" the money lent.

Private owners of central banks issue the fake notes that run the world's economy. These *Mutaffifeen* receive an estimated five trillion dollars for their services every year in what is commonly called "interest payment." Through secret organizations, the *Mutaffifeen* artificially create crisis to scare citizens and governments. A powerful image of an enemy with the infinite ability of destruction and doom is created through the media and politics. The presidents and politicians are then seen rushing around the world, trying to stop the terrorists from destroying just and innocent civilizations.

The 9/11 implosion was created to cause chaos, fear, and uncertainty among the citizens. After creating such catastrophic crisis, the instruments of the secret societies the circle of evil strike. The blueprint for the creation of Pax Americana, drawn up by a group of people working within the Pentagon on behalf of the *Mutaffifeen*, was brought out in a timely fashion, pushing for the American occupation of Afghanistan and Iraq. The blueprint written in September 2000 was based on an earlier document recommending maintaining American bases in Saudi Arabia and Kuwait to keep American control over Arab oil. The minions of the *Mutaffifeen* were already discussing "going after Iran and Syria" after war in Afghanistan and Iraq.

Wars are planned by the *Mutaffifeen* to facilitate borrowing by the governments. Within a few months, the *Mutaffifeen* have indebted the Americans and the British governments by $550 billion. This is addition to the previously incurred debt of estimated $28 trillion owed by the Americans and the British. This debt will never be paid back. Nevertheless, Americans and the British people will continue to pay $550 billion dollars in interest year after year in perpetuity. In lieu of this debt, the American and the British soldiery, naval forces, secret services, and diplomats will continue to be beholden to the *Mutaffifeen*. They will be used to prod, convince, and bully the rest of the world into accepting ever-evolving schemes of deceit and extortion. Whether the Americans and the British people like it or not, they will be forced to do the devil's dirty work for the coming century.

With this amount of debt and budgetary deficit, the United States was at the verge of bankruptcy when three airplanes mysteriously crashed into the Twin Towers and the Pentagon on the eleventh of September 2001. There was compelling evidence that those in authority were aware of the impending attack on the American targets yet did nothing to stop them. The American Airlines flight 77 flew with great precision and dropped 7,000 feet in 2½ minutes, flying so low, taking utility poles, and clipping trees to its target, the Pentagon, while traveling at 530 miles per hour. This high-precision flight could not have been executed by desert Arabs or Afghans who had only flown Cessna or Piper Cherokee propeller planes in flight schools. Some of these pilots allegedly had not even mastered "touch and go" procedures. The pilots and the crew on board were all able bodied and strong and could not have been cowed down by hijackers brandishing mere box cutters. Surely, some of the passengers would have resisted.

There is little doubt that the 9/11 episodes was a well-orchestrated, well-planned, and technically high-precision job undertaken by skilled people in collaboration with those within the aviation authority, the air force, the FBI, the immigration department, and a centralized group of planners with international intelligence connections. Who did it? The answer lies in the fact about who benefited from this tragedy.

Three days after the World Trade Center attack, Congress approved a $410 billion spending bill. Half the money went to military spending, $15 billion to bail out the airline industry, $100 billion for New York City cleanup, $87 billion to Iraq and the Afghan War, and another $750 million for lost revenue to New York City. The Federal Reserve loaned another $100 billion to the insurance companies. That made $412 billion of debt.

This money is to be paid by the American people to the Federal Reserve bank, which in turn is owned by private banks. The private banks do not owe allegiance to anyone but to their own greed and avarice. The interest on this money amounting to $10 billion annually is owed in perpetuity at the current 2½% interest compounded daily. The Americans pay additional $370 billion in interest on their national debt to the same bankers annually in perpetuity. It is thus clear that a group of people benefit from wars and catastrophes; they create in secrecy, in intricate coordination with other secret groups to promote such tragedies.

Three secret societies—the Council on Foreign Relations, the Bilderberg Group, and the Trilateral Commission—rule the United States and influence the international and financial policies of the Americas, Europe, and to some extent the whole world. The Americans are under the impression that they elect their president democratically, who in turn runs the government according to the people's wishes. Nothing could be farther from the truth.

The Council on Foreign Relations has approximately three thousand members who join the council only by invitation by a corps of unnamed, faceless people. Although the members meet regularly, the planning and decision-making is the function of a super secretive inner circle that compartmentalizes the information provided to the members. Each member is only told what he essentially needs to know as part of his function. Only the inner circle is aware of the whole picture.

The Council of Foreign Relations picks presidential candidates for both the Republicans and the Democrats years ahead of the election. The candidates nurtured in the philosophy of the CFR are obedient to its dictates. The CFR then backs both the candidates through its mastery of the media and with money and organization, which they control. The news media is totally under the control of the secret societies, and the people are only told what the CFR wants them to know. The elections take the air of a highly publicized rooster fight with emotions running high for and against each candidate. On the morning of his victory, the winning candidate is presented by the CFR with the list of the names of his cabinet. The cabinet carries out the policies of the CFR. Almost all the people in the cabinet are chosen from among its three thousand members.

2. Trade: Since the end of the Cold War, the United States and the European Union has launched a trade war against the poor economies of the world. To be precise, it is the continuation of the colonial war on the assets of the poor nations when Europe launched its naval and maritime fleets on the shores of Africa and Asia in the seventeenth century. This war was interrupted for about forty years when there was no free trade and when the economies of the two rival groups were disconnected. Within each rival block, economies interacted through foreign aid in a competition for the hearts and minds of the Third World. There was at that time more give than take by the rival superpowers of the opposing powers.

This new trade war is being launched not by the poor economies that have suffered during the last three hundred years but by the countries that have reaped all the benefits of trade over the centuries due to an unequal trade and deceit. When the rich nations continue to squeeze every unfair advantage out of a trading system that has been shown to be unfair over the last three centuries, the world will plunge into a deep economic depression, chaos, and anarchy. The poor suffer more from economic depressions, a suffering they have become used to. The rich, although cushioned by their wealth, suffer in political repercussions, wars, and terror.

The believer and every citizen of the world seeking fairness, justice, and equality for all should be aware of these facts. For trading economies to be fair and beneficial to all, the trade among them has to be

1. free of ideology and politics,
2. equal and fair in terms of trade,
3. about global full employment and equality of wages,
4. about neutral gold, or commodity currency, to be used as the exchange medium of trade.

Countries generate wealth by the utilization of the skills of their manpower in production of their mineral, industrial, and agricultural products and services. Surplus trade produces the capital for domestic and social development. Because of "dollar hegemony," all foreign investment money of the developing nations goes to the export sector where US dollars can be earned. The dollar trade surpluses go to hold large dollar reserves to support the exchange rate of their currencies. The Third World economies cannot use their surplus trade earnings for domestic development and social programs because they are forced to use their huge dollar reserves to support the value of their currencies.

Exports of manufactured goods by low wage developing countries in the last thirty years have increased from 25 percent in 1965 to 75 percent, while the agricultural exports from developing country have fallen from 50 percent to less than 10 percent. Many developing countries have gained relatively little from the increase in the manufactured goods trade, where most of the profit is sucked up by the foreign capital. For instance, for a shirt manufactured in Bangladesh for Walmart, $1 goes to Bangladesh, $4 in expenses, and $20 to the foreign capital. The key cause of most unemployment in all developing countries is the trade-related collapse of agriculture, exacerbated by massive government subsidies provided to farmers in the USA and the European Union. The collapse of agriculture in developing countries means collapse of the whole economy.

Purchasing power parity measures the disconnection between exchange rates and local prices. For a dollar investor to earn the same interest rate in a foreign economy with a purchasing power parity of four, for example, between the US dollar and the Chinese yuan, the local wages in that country have to be four times (75 percent) lower than the US wages. However, the law of one price says that identical goods should sell for the same price in two separate markets when there are no transportation costs and differential taxes applied in those markets. Nevertheless, the law of one price does not apply to labor. Foreign capital producers seek to manufacture their goods in the lowest-wage locations and sell their goods in the highest-price markets. This is the incentive of outsourcing. The cross-border "one price" applies only to certain products such as oil. Thus, in economies like China, Pakistan, or Bangladesh with a purchase power parity of four, a rise in oil prices will cost four times more in other goods than in the USA or European Union. The larger the purchase power parity between the local currency and the dollar, the more severe is the tyranny of dollar hegemony on forcing down the wage differentials.

The Bretton Woods Conference at the end of the Second World War established the US dollar, at that time a solid currency backed by most of the world's gold, as a benchmark currency for financing international trade, with all other currencies pegged to it at fixed rates that changed only infrequently. The fixed exchange rate was designed to keep trading nations *honest* and to prevent them from running perpetual trade deficits. The Bretton Woods Agreement was conceived when cross-border flow of funds was not considered necessary or desirable for financing world trade. Not a single Muslim state was invited to participate in this conference. Since 1971, the dollar has changed from gold-backed currency to a *global reserve monetary instrument* that the United States can produce by fiat. The United States had frittered away all its gold reserves in twenty-five years after the Second World War by incurring both current account and fiscal deficits. First, it exhausted its gold and then incurred a debt that stands at seven and a half trillion dollars today. This debt is financed with fiat money.

1. World trade under the dollar hegemony is a game in which the USA prints paper dollars, and the rest of the world produces the real goods that the US *make-believe* paper money can buy.

2. The world's interlinked economies, through global trade, compete in exports to capture the needed fiat dollars to service their dollar-dominated foreign debts and to accumulate enough dollar reserves to sustain the exchange

value of their domestic currencies in foreign exchange markets.

3. To prevent the speculative and manipulative attacks on their currencies, the world's central banks must acquire and hold dollar reserves in sufficient amounts to counteract market pressure on their currencies in circulation. The higher the market pressure to devalue a particular currency, the more dollar reserves its central banks must hold. This provides a built-in support for a strong dollar that, in turn, forces all central banks to acquire and hold more dollar reserves, making it stronger.

4. Critical commodities, mostly oil, are denominated in dollars because only dollars can buy oil. This is the price the USA extracted from oil-producing countries for US tolerance of oil-producing cartel since 1973. This has caused an unprecedented growth of dollars in circulation around the world. This US capital-account surplus, in turn, finances the US trade deficit of two billion dollars per day. Moreover, any asset—regardless of its location in the world—that is denominated in dollars is a US asset in essence. When oil is denominated in dollars, the USA essentially owns the world's oil for free. Sixty percent of the world's currency reserves are denominated in dollars; therefore, they constitute an American asset. The dollar is a fiat currency, printed from paper and ink at almost no cost to the Americans. And the more the paper money the USA prints, the higher the price of US assets will rise.

5. Compelling developing economies to trade to accumulate surplus in US dollars subjects these economies to perpetual low wages, weak domestic consumption, and reduced investment for development projects.

The USA can print dollars at will and with impunity. The dollar is fiat money that is not backed by gold, US productivity, or US export prowess. The whole world's total gross national product is thirty trillion dollars. The US gross national product amounts to about ten trillion dollars measured in US currency. The United States government has frittered away all its gold reserves and other assets. Consequently, it has been forced to borrow from the rest of the world thirty-three trillion dollars to maintain its style of living and governance. And the people of the United States have to borrow another thirty-three trillion dollars to maintain their style of living. The Americans owe to themselves and to the rest of the world more than the value of the whole world's gross wealth. In other words, according to conventional wisdom, the US economy is bankrupt and should have gone into receivership years ago and treated in the same manner as Egypt and the Ottoman Empire in the late nineteenth century, when trustees were appointed to supervise their treasuries.

The US dollar is bankrupt and is incapable of being used as the world's trading currency. However, the dollar is backed by US military power. Any threat to the US hegemony and to the dollar hegemony is swiftly dealt with, with the might of the world's only superpower. The US military budget has gone up from $310 billion in 2001 to $738 billion in 2020. The US trade and fiscal deficit stands at over 6 percent of its GDP, and its military budget is 4 percent of GDP. In other words, the US trading partners are forced to subsidize one and a half times the annual cost of the US military, which in turn systemically undermines the world peace and stability.

In plain language, robbery and gangsterism controls the world through force and deceit. It is through propaganda, force, and fraudulent international institutions; the world has been duped into believing that the worthless US dollar is gold. While the deception lasts, the house of cards will stand. The slaves that prop the shaky walls of the house of cards are the Arab petrodollars, the thriving Chinese export trade, the drug trade, and the long-suffering third world poor. Once the people of the world recognize the dupery, the present world order will collapse on itself, and the world will be rid of the tyranny of the dollar hegemony, colonialism, and the one-thousand-year-old crusade against Islam. Unfortunately, the world will fall into turmoil and instability until a new system arises from the ashes of the old one.

During the 1991 presidential election campaign, Bill Clinton and his Democrats produced figures that revealed the obscene fact that 1 percent of Americans owned 40 percent of the wealth of the United States. They also said that if you eliminated home ownership and only counted businesses, factories, and office buildings, then the top 1 percent owned 90 percent of all the commercial wealth of the United States. Moreover, the top 10 percent, they said, owned 99 percent of the wealth.[65]

A corps of several thousand determined families among the top 1 percent of the American treasure holders forms the *patrician class*, akin to the old Roman aristocracy. Under the facade of democracy, the common folk (the *plebeians*) live under the illusion that they run the American administrations, elected by them every four years. In fact, the elections are farcical. The fact is that secret councils of the patricians determine the candidates who will run for presidency and, subsequently, the members of the president's cabinet and their government's fiscal and foreign policies.

The corps of patricians of old money, European money, and the new Jewish money determine the financial stakes around the

---

[65] Henry C. K. Liu, "US Dollar Hegemony Has Got to Go," *Asia Times*, April 11, 2002.

world and control the world's oil, minerals, agriculture, trade, and commerce. In fact, these few thousand patrician families of immense wealth control the president, armed forces, intelligence services of the United States, Federal Reserve bank, and other institutions of the government; and through them, they influence the policies of international organizations such as the United Nations, IMF, the World Bank, WTO, and the NATO. They determine when to send their legions and *praetorian guards* (the marines) to the outlying posts to conquer and plunder new lands and bring back gold, oil, minerals, and other wealth. While 1 percent of the US population, the filthy rich patricians, drain 90 percent of North America's wealth into their coffers, the common folk—brainwashed with patriotism and propaganda—live under the illusion of belonging to God's chosen people, in a land of opportunity justice, truth, milk, and honey. With their wits dimmed by the daily barrage of falsified images by the news media and by their government, the plebeians—90 percent of the common Americans—willingly pay the perpetual interest on the debt of *forty trillion dollars* accumulated by their patrician class in their quest for the world's wealth.

The world's total gross national product amounts to thirty trillion dollars. Fewer than eight hundred European and American men own and control three trillion dollars' worth of this wealth. In other words, eight hundred men from the Western world control ten percent of the world's wealth. With wealth comes the control of the world's economies.

3. Usury and Hoarding of Wealth. *Devour not usury, doubled and multiplied; be in taqwa of Allah (fear Allah) that ye may prosper.* Forbidden is the practice of usury to the Muslims. Forbidden is also making money from money. Money, in its present form, is only a medium of exchange, a way of defining the value of an item but in itself has no value and therefore should not give rise to more money by earning interest through deposit in a bank or loaning it to someone else. The human endeavor, initiative, and risk involved in a productive venture are much more important than the money used to finance it. Money deposited in a bank, or hoarded, is potential capital rather than capital. Money becomes capital only when it is invested in a venture. Accordingly, money loaned to a business as a loan is regarded as a debt of the business, and it is not capital. As such it is not entitled to any return, such as interest. Muslims are encouraged to spend (purchase necessities or spend in the way of Allah) or invest their money and are discouraged from keeping their money idle. Hoarding money is unacceptable. Allah's commandments in His covenant with the believers in the following three *ayahs* exhort:

a. *Muslims to spend after their needs are met in charity,*
b. *devour not in usury and*
c. *hoard not gold and silver.*

They ask thee how much they are to spend (in charity); say: "What is beyond your needs." Thus, doth Allah make clear to you His Signs: in order that ye may consider. (Koran 2:222)

Allah will deprive usury of all blessing but will give increase for deeds of charity; for He loves not creatures ungrateful and wicked. (Koran 2:275–76)

And there are those who hoard gold and silver and spend it not in the Way of Allah: announce unto them a most grievous penalty. (Al-A'raf 9:34)

Ghrar: *Uncertainty, risk, or speculation is forbidden.* Any transaction entered into should be free from uncertainty, risk, and speculation. The parties cannot predetermine a granted profit, and this does not allow an undertaking from the borrower or the customer to repay the borrowed principal, plus an amount to consider inflation. Therefore, options and futures are regarded as un-Islamic; so are foreign exchange transactions because rates are determined by interest differentials.

An Islamic government is forbidden to lend or borrow money from institutions—such as international banks, the World Bank, or the International Monetary Fund—on interest as both usury and interest are expressly forbidden. Banking based on fiat money is also forbidden. The value of money is diluted by the creation of new money out of nothing; the property rights of savers and those who have been promised future payments, such as pensioners, are violated. This is stealing. The trappings of money system and banking have been compared to that of a cult; only those who profit from it understand its inner workings. They work hard to keep it that way. The central banks print notes adorned with signatures, seals, and pictures of a president or that of a queen; counterfeiters are severely punished. Governments pay their expenses with them; populations are forced to accept them; they are printed like newspaper in vast quantity—representing an equal worth to all the treasures of this world, all the resources above and under the ground, all the assets of populations, and their work and labor—to fabricate every item that has ever been manufactured. Yet these notes cost nothing to make. In truth, this has been the greatest hoax, the worst most crime against humanity, a swindle of proportions never seen by humanity before.

As we have found, the Koran forbids usury, gambling, speculation, and hoarding of gold and silver. The Koran advocates trade, spending on good things in life and on the kith and kin, and providing wealth in the cause of Allah.

7. Betrayal of the Covenant: The Modern Economic System Is Entirely Alien to the Teachings of the Koran

The Dar es Salaam has slid downhill, submerged into the quicksand of make-believe economy. Every successful businessperson and trader is forced to operate in the sinful pagan system of economy. Here is the solution for a successful economic system as laid down in the covenant of the Koran:

1. Elimination of usury and interest in Dar es Salaam.

2. Elimination of fiat money and elimination of banking based on money created out of nothing with a printing press. There will be no more lending of nine times of the bank deposit to create capital and wealth. It is a fraudulent Western practice based on trickery. Such a practice constitutes institutionalized theft, supported by states and international institutions.

3. Creation of a unitary currency for the united Islamic state— gold dinars and silver dirhams based on the measures established by Umar ibn al-Khattab, the second caliph. A currency bureau, an arm of the state of Dar es Salaam, will supervise the minting and circulation of the currency.

4. Dar es Salaam's trading relations with the rest of the world involving drastic changes. All commodities utilized within the state will be produced within the country, and the *ummah* will be independent on foreign trading systems. The commodities for export—oil, minerals, raw and manufactured goods—will be sold against gold and in gold-based currency. Fiat currency, paper, and printed money will be abolished unless it is backed by gold.

5. Labor of every human in the Islamic state measured in a standardized index per hour worked. This index will

be uniform for every worker around the world. Pricing of commodities in international trade will be based on this index of equal value for the human labor internationally.

The Koran says:

⬦ Those that spend of their goods in charity by night and by day, in secret and in public, have their reward with their Lord: on them shall be no fear, nor shall they grieve.

⬦ Those who devour usury will not stand except stands the one whom the Satan by his touch has driven to madness. That is because they say: "Trade is like usury," but Allah hath permitted trade and forbidden usury. Those who after receiving direction from their Lord, desist, shall be pardoned for the past; their case is for Allah to judge; but those who repeat (the offence) are Companions of the Fire; they will abide therein (forever).

⬦ Allah will deprive usury of all blessing but will give increase for deeds of charity; for He does not love ungrateful and wicked creatures. (Al-Baqarah 2:274–76, Koran)

⬦ Those who believe and perform wholesome deeds, establish regular prayers and regular charity have rewards with their Lord. On them shall be no fear, nor shall they grieve.

⬦ Fear Allah and give up what remains of your demand for usury, if you are indeed believers. If you, do it not, take notice of war from Allah and His Messenger: but if you turn back, you will still have your capital sums.

⬦ Deal not unjustly, and ye shall not be dealt with unjustly.

⬦ If the debtor is in a difficulty, grant him time until it is easy for him to repay. But if ye remit it by way of charity, that is best for you. (Al-Baqarah 2:277–80, Koran)

◇ Devour not usury, doubled, and multiplied; be in taqwa of Allah (fear Allah) that ye may prosper.

◇ Fear the Fire, which is prepared for those who reject Faith; and obey Allah and the Messenger; that ye may obtain mercy.

◇ Be quick in the race for forgiveness from your Lord, and for a Garden whose measurement is that of the heavens and of the earth, prepared for the righteous.

◇ Those who give freely whether in prosperity, or in adversity; those who restrain anger, and pardon all humans; for Allah loves those who do beautiful deeds (*Al-muhsinun*). (Ali 'Imran 3:130–34, Koran)

◇ There are indeed many among the priests and clerics who in falsehood devour the substance of men and hinder them from the way of Allah. And there are those who bury gold and silver and spend it not in the way of Allah: announce unto them a most grievous penalty.

◇ On the Day when heat will be produced out of that wealth in the fire of Hell, and with it will be branded their foreheads, their flanks, and their backs, "This is the treasure which you buried for yourselves: taste then, the treasures which you buried!" (At-Tawbah 9:34–35, Koran)

8. Betrayal of the Covenant of Allah: Ignorance of the Covenant and Knowledge of Allah

When the Muslims forget Allah, fail in their knowledge of Allah's word, and ignore their covenant with Allah, they suffer the consequences.

> When you are told to make room in the assemblies, spread out and make room: ample room will Allah provide for you. And when ye are told to rise up, for prayers, *Jihad* or other good deeds rise up: Allah will exalt in rank those of you who

> believe and who have been granted Knowledge. And Allah is well acquainted with all you do. (Al-Mujadilah 58:11, Koran)

> He who taught (the use of) the Pen, Taught man that which he knew not. (Al-'Alaq 96:4–5, Koran)

> Is one who worships devoutly during the hours of the night prostrating himself or standing (in adoration), who takes heed of the Hereafter, and who places his hope in the Mercy of his Lord, (like one who does not)? Say: "Are those equal, those who know and those who do not know? It is those who are endued with understanding that receive admonition. (Az-Zumar 39:9, Koran)

All knowledge comes to humans through their openness to God. Humans accept the concept of God as the Creator of everything that is. He wills, and it is. He is beyond human comprehension, and His divine systems do not conform to the human concepts, creed, and dogma. Allah, God the Creator, created the galaxies, worlds, stars, sun, moon, little atoms, protons, neutrons, and tiny particles, which show the complexity of His genius. Allah, the Lord of creation, sends water from the heavens for sustenance of life on the earth. Allah directs sunshine to the earth to provide warmth and light to sustain, human, plant, and animal life. Allah formed the sun, moon, and stars to create equilibrium in the universe, every object in its intended place revolving in its fixed orbit in perfect harmony and balance. Allah created the secrets and mysteries of the heavens and the earth, the so-called sciences, and the knowledge of particles, elements, cells, mitochondria, chromosomes, gravity, and black holes, only a minute portion of which he revealed to man.

Allah clearly provided humans a mind to wonder at Allah's infinitesimal wisdom. Yet man is conceited and arrogant to believe that God is driven by man-created creed, testament, dogma, Sunna, and Sharia. Allah does not require a shrine, temple, *shakan*, tent, or talisman to live in. His presence is everywhere. He is present in the smallest particle (*nuqta*) and in the greatest expanse. He is accessible to each and every object that He has created. Every object obeys Allah's will except for man. Man has been given a free will. The covenant of Koran presents us with the scope of the freedom of choice that the humans have in doing that is wholesome and beautiful or what is corrupt and ugly. The human's role among the creation distinguishes right activity, right thought, and right intention from their opposites. It reminds us of how the scales of Allah's justice, the two hands of Allah—His mercy and His wrath—are reflected in the human domain, where people have been appointed Allah's vicegerents. Deeds of goodness and wholesomeness are associated with mercy, paradise, and the beautiful. Evil and corruption is rewarded with wrath, hell, and the ugly.

Allah the Divine is open to the most miniscule of beings. From the vastest of the expanse to the minutest of the particle, there is a connection with Allah, the Cherisher and Nourisher of the universe. Within this communion of the divine with the creation passes the Spirit of Allah into His creatures. The human lays his heart and mind open to Allah in submission to receive His Spirit and guidance.

In the space and the emptiness of the universe, there flow currents and whispers of wind and energy. These winds of silence, light, and sound carry the divine whisper of Allah, and in this sound is Allah's knowledge. This knowledge descends into the believer's receptive heart in peace, silence, and tranquility. When the angels and the Spirit descend with Allah's guidance, the eyes perceive the most beautiful divine light, the ears hear the softest tinkle of the bell, the nose smells the fragrance of a thousand gardens, and the skin feels the most tranquil of the gentle breeze. When this happens, the soul has seen nirvana. This is the knowledge of Allah. And this is the knowledge of certainty.

Allah sent thousands of prophets to mankind to teach humanity precepts and knowledge of His straight path of unity, truth, and goodness. Over thousands of years, these precepts and principles spread around the world through civilizations till mankind, as a whole, began to comprehend the knowledge of one universal God, the Creator of every particle and every being in the whole universe. Man listened and occasionally or frequently regressed into his inherent paganism, greed, selfishness, and egotism. Allah bestowed on man a vicegerency on the earth, a mind, a free will, and a covenant. Allah then announced that there were to be no more prophets. The era of prophecy had ended. The human, in stages, had received the knowledge required by man to live in submission to Allah's will (*islam*) in peace and harmony on the earth, have faith in the divine Master (*iman*), and perform wholesome and beautiful deeds (*ihsan*) in accordance with the divine laws, which were sent down as a guidance to every human community to a life of truth justice, goodness, and peace. Such knowledge consisted of the following.

Unity: There is one absolute Being from which all stems the universe of galaxies, and all the living things in the universe are all connected to one another and cannot be separated from that absolute Being. Everything alive—humans, animals, plants, and microorganisms—are created by the absolute Being, all nurtured with the same organic matter, all breathing the same air; and in turn, their physical self disintegrates to the same elements, which then return to the earth and the universe. In this cycle of creation and disintegration, the only permanence is of the Real, the absolute Being. All else is an illusion and a mirage. One moment humans are flesh and blood; in the next, they dust blown away by the wind. Nothing is left behind—no riches, no honor, no ego, and no pride. What is left, however, is an account of your deeds, on which one day you will be judged. Deeds of goodness and wholesomeness are rewarded with mercy, paradise, and the beautiful. Evil and corruption is rewarded with wrath, hell, and the ugly.

Mind: The human is bestowed with a mind and a free will. The mind has the ability to perceive ideas and knowledge from the divine and from the signs of Allah. The whisper of the divine, the rustle of the wind, the light of God (*nur*), the fragrance of God's creation, and the sensation of the divine touch all inspire the human mind with an endless stream of ideas and knowledge. Man has been granted the ability to process his thoughts and given knowledge with a free will.

The verse of the light encompasses the totality of the knowledge and guidance that God sent to man through His prophets. The pagan in man confused God's message and instead began to worship the messenger. With the end of the era of prophecy, man has the freedom to open his heart to the light of Allah and to learn to recognize the presence of God within himself in his own heart.

> Allah is the Light of the heavens and the earth. The parable of His Light is as if there were a Niche and within it a Lamp: the Lamp enclosed in Glass; the glass as it were a brilliant star: lit from a blessed Tree, an Olive, neither of the East nor of the West, whose Oil is well-nigh luminous, though fire scarce touched it: Light upon Light! Allah guides whom He will to His Light: Allah sets forth Parables for men, and Allah is the font of all Knowledge, and knows all things. Lit is such a light in houses, which Allah hath permitted to be raised to honor and celebrate His name. In them He is glorified in the mornings and in the evenings, over and over again. (An-Nur 24:35–36)

The parable of divine light is the foundation of the belief in one universal God for the whole of mankind. Allah is the light of the heavens and the earth that bestows life, grace, and mercy on His creatures. Allah loves His creation, and His *nur* is ever luminous in the hearts and minds of those who love Him, place their trust in Him, and open their heart and soul in submission to Him. In the hearts and the minds laid open to Allah in submission is a niche in which the light, the Spirit, and the knowledge of Allah ever glow. Such is the glow and the luminescence of the divine light, Spirit, and wisdom; it shines with the brilliance of a star—a star that is lit from divine wisdom, the tree of knowledge, and the knowledge of Allah's signs. For those who believe, Allah is within, and the believer is aglow with Allah's radiance—light upon light, light seen from the heavens and the earth. The dwellings in which Allah is glorified in the morning and in the evening over and over again are aglow with Allah's light and mercy.

Allah has granted knowledge and wisdom of *furqan* and *taqwa* to the believers who have opened their hearts and minds to Him. Man has been granted the freedom of choice in doing what is wholesome and beautiful or what is corrupt and ugly. It is only man, among the creation, who has been given the knowledge to distinguish right activity, right thought, and right intention from their opposites. This knowledge reminds the human of the scales of Allah's justice; the two hands of Allah, His mercy and His wrath, are reflected in the human domain, where people have been appointed Allah's vicegerents. Deeds of goodness and wholesomeness are associated with mercy, paradise, and what is beautiful. Evil and corruption is rewarded with wrath, hell, and what is ugly.

The fundamental knowledge is the knowledge of certainty (*ilm al-yaqin*, Koran 102:5).

The lure of wealth enthralls you.

Until you reach the graves.

But aye, then shall you know.

Again, aye then in the end shall you know.

Nay, were you to know with the knowledge of certainty?

You shall surly see the hellfire!

Surely you shall see it with the eye of certainty.

Then, shall you be questioned that Day about the pleasures (of wealth). (Koran 102:1–8)

This type of certainty results from human capacity for logic and reasoning and the appraisal of Allah's presence in the world, Allah's signs. The knowledge of certainty is rational and discursive, a point that the Koran acknowledges when it admonishes human beings to

Say: "Travel through the earth and see how Allah did originate creation; so will Allah produce a later creation: for Allah has power over all things. (Al-Ankabut 29:20, Koran)

It is He who gives life and death, and to Him (is due) the alternation of Night and Day: will ye not then understand? (Al-Mu'minun 23:80, Koran)

Over time and under the influence of contemplation and spiritual practice, the knowledge of certainty may be transformed into a higher form of knowledge of Allah, which the Koran calls the eye of certainty (*ain al-yaqin*, Koran 102:7). This knowledge is acquired by spiritual intellect, which believers in the east locate metaphorically in the heart. Once the heart and the mind are open to Allah in submission, they form the niche in which glows the divine light, the Spirit, and the wisdom of Allah in man.

Once opened, the heart receives knowledge as a type of divine light or illumination (*nur*), which leads the believer toward the remembrance of Allah. Just as with the knowledge of certainty (*ilm al-yaqin*) and with the eye of certainty (*ain al-yaqin*), the believer sees Allah's existence through His presence in this world. With the eye of certainty, what leads the believer to the knowledge of Allah are the arguments to be understood not by the rational intellect but by theophanic appearances (*bayyinat*) that strip away the veils of worldly phenomenon to reveal the divine reality underneath. The third and most advanced type of knowledge builds on the transcendent nature of knowledge itself. The highest level of consciousness is called the "truth of certainty" (*haqq al-yaqin*).

> But truly Revelation is a cause of sorrow for the Unbelievers.
> But verily it is Truth of assured certainty. So, glorify the name
> of thy Lord Most High. (Al-Haqqah 69:50–52, Koran)

This multidimensional conception of knowledge comprehends a reality that lies hidden within the unique world yet can be revealed by the human mind and the vision of the spiritual intellect through the signs of Allah that are present in the world itself. In the Koran, Allah calls on humanity:

> So I do call to witness what you see

> And what you see not,

> This is a Message sent down from the Lord of the Worlds.

But verily it is Truth of assured certainty. (Al-Haqqah 69:38–39, 43, 51, Koran)

9. The Covenant of Allah: The Roll of Islam in the Twenty-First Century

The miracle of the twenty-first century is that, in spite of warfare, turmoil, and *fitnah*, Islam is the fastest-spreading religion in the world. Three large regions of spiritual osmosis and spiritual regeneration are in India, sub-Saharan Africa, and the Euro-Christian world of Americas and Europe. The Koran is the most recited book every day in the world. Islam continues to influence other beliefs toward the belief in one universal God. There are now more believers in one universal God among Jews, Christians, Hindus, Buddhists, and other religions than at the time of the blessed *nabi*.

The foremost requirement for the Muslims in the twenty-first century lies not in empty slogans for Islam but in exemplary conduct in silence by the believers in their path of Allah. The reality of Islam lies in good intentions and beautiful deeds rather empty words and hypocrisy. The blessed *nabi* came with the message of peace and love in the world rather than a message of war and bloodshed. When Islam advances, the world gains tranquility, love, and knowledge. With the roll of true Islam, there is truth, honesty, justice, equality, and prosperity for all. The precepts of the covenant of Allah ensure human dignity, equality, justice, consultative government, a state where there is realization of lawful benefits to people, prevention of harm, removal of hardship, and education of individuals by inculcating in them self-discipline, patience, restraint, and respect for rights of others. It is a system under which there is restitution of all wrongs and imbalances in society. These things do not occur when the Muslims live in a daze of self, delusion, and hypocrisy. Injustice, *fitnah*, treachery, falsehood, and harm to people occur when they ignore that Allah's grace and mercy lies in obeying Allah's covenant. When one and a half billion people of Islam ignore Allah's commandments, they bring on themselves *fitnah* and oppression of the *Munafiqeen*. Living in self-delusion, lethargy, and inaction bring on *fitnah* and oppression. Allah helps those who help themselves. When people choose to live in disunity, disharmony, and subjugation, they have no hope. Hope is in Allah and in His covenant.

The Koran was sent to every human. Those who believe in it have mandate to have a complete knowledge of its precepts and act on them. It is not enough to recite the Koran in a parrot fashion and not understand its contents. This is not Islam.

The answer to this universal problem is to recite the Koran in a vernacular language for understanding and in Arabic for devotion. Over a period, the believer will achieve full, in-depth understanding of the Koran and the covenant of Allah. The same should apply to daily prayers. The believer should speak to Allah in his native tongue from his heart and in Arabic in congregation. Over a short period, the whole of the non-Arab Islamic world will achieve full understanding of Islam. The congregation prayers as well as the *adhan* in countries like India should be conducted in Hindi and in other native languages. This will bring understanding of Islam to one billion Hindus. Islam will become the native religion in India and over time extinguish all prejudice, discrimination, and hostility of the natives. Allah will then become the universal and personal God of every Hindu rather than hundreds of mythological gods created by centuries of ignorance, illusion, and un enlightenment.

The Arabic word *islam* means to resign or submit oneself. In religious terminology, it means submission or surrender of oneself to

Allah or to Allah's will. Allah is the only true reality, and everything else in the universe is dependent on Him for its reality and existence. Since Allah created the universe, all things in it are, as a result, totally dependent on Him and thus are totally "submissive" to Allah. Allah, being the Creator of all things, is the *Rabb*, the Sustainer of the whole creation. Thus, God the Creator is the universal God.

The Koranic notion of religious belief (*iman*) as dependent on knowledge is actualized in practice in the term *islam*. The term *islam* signifies the idea of surrender or submission. The type of surrender Islam requires is a deliberate, conscious, and rational act made by a person who knows with both intellectual certainty and spiritual vision that Allah, who is the subject of Koranic discourse, is the reality. The Muslim (fem. *Muslimah*) is "one who submits" to the divine truth and whose relationship with God is governed by *taqwa*, the consciousness of humankind's responsibility toward its creator.

However, consciousness of God alone is not sufficient to make a person a Muslim. Neither is it enough to be merely born a Muslim or to be raised in an Islamic cultural context. The concept of *taqwa* implies that the believer has the added responsibility of acting in a way that is in accordance with three types of knowledge: *ilm al-yaqin, ain al-yaqin*, and *haqq al-yaqin* (knowledge of certainty, eye of certainty, and truth of certainty). The believer must endeavor at all times to maintain himself in a constant state of submission to Allah.

> Trusting in the divine mercy of his Divine Master, yet fearing Allah's wrath, the slave of Allah walks the road of life with careful steps, making his actions deliberate so that he will not stray from the straight path that Allah laid out for him. It is an all-encompassing and highly personal type of commitment that has little in

common with academic understanding of Islam as a civilization or a cultural system.[66]

The universality of religious experience is an important premise of the Koran's argument against profane or secular life. This universalism has never been more important than it is in the present, when majority of the believers do not speak Arabic. Such transcendence of culture is necessary for the Koran, as the vehicle of the word of God, to overcome linguistic and cultural differences and express itself in a metalanguage that can be understood even when its original Arabic is translated into a non-Semitic language such as English, Mandarin, Turkish, Farsi, Urdu, or Hindi. Most humans, whatever their experiences and cultural background, think in similar ways and have similar wants and needs. The Koran seeks to establish a common foundation for belief that is based on such shared perceptions and experiences. Over and over again, the Koran reminds the reader to think about the truths that lie behind the familiar or mundane things of the world, such as signs of Allah in nature, the practical value of virtue, and the cross-cultural validity of moral principles. The Koran, therefore, appeals to both reason and experience in determining the criterion for distinguishing between truth and falsehood.

Iman: Faith of Islam is based on certain knowledge, which is both a liberation and a limitation. It is liberation in the sense that certainty of divine reality allows the human spirit to expand inward, outward, and upward so that consciousness becomes three dimensional. Nevertheless, it is also a limitation because with the knowledge of Allah comes a concomitant awareness of the limits and responsibility

---

[66] Vincent Cornell, "Fruit of Tree of Knowledge," in *Oxford History of Islam*, ed. John L. Esposito (Oxford University Press).

imposed on a person as a created being. Unlike a secular humanist, a true Muslim believer who submits to Allah cannot delude himself by claiming that he is the sole author of his destiny as he knows that a person's fate is routinely controlled by factors beyond his control.

Ihsan: The third dimension of *din* is *ihsan*. The word *ihsan* is derived from the word *husn* that designates the quality of being good, beautiful, virtuous, pleasing, harmonious, or wholesome. The word *ihsan* is a verb that means to establish or to perform what is good and beautiful. The Koran employs the word *ihsan* and its active particle *muhsin* (the one who does what is beautiful and good) in seventy verses. The Koran often designates Allah as the One who does what is beautiful, and *al-Muhsin* is one of Allah's divine names. Allah's beautiful work is the creation of the universe of galaxies, stars, sun, and moon, all in their ordained orbits destined in their paths by His mysterious forces. All are shining and luminescent with Allah's blessed light (*nur*), providing life and vigor to billions of His creatures so that they may acknowledge and the praise their Creator, who made this beautiful and wholesome universe.

The Koran ascribes the love of Allah in about fifteen verses. One of the emotions most closely associated with *ihsan* is *hubb*. To have *ihsan* is to do what is beautiful. According to the Koran in five verses, Allah loves those who have *ihsan* because by doing what is beautiful, they themselves have developed beautiful character traits and are worthy of Allah's love. In every Koranic verse where Allah is said to love something, the object is of this love are human beings, not the human species but those human beings whose traits and activities are beautiful.

The phrase *amilu al saalihaat* (to do good, to perform wholesome deeds) refers to those who persist in striving to set things right, who restore harmony, peace, and balance. The other acts of good works recognized in the covenant of the Koran are showing humility, being generous and charitable, being truthful, seeking knowledge and wisdom, being kind, being peaceful, loving others, and performing beautiful deeds.

The thirty-seven commandments of Allah comprise the thirty-seven steps or pillars that embrace the essence of the believer's faith. The synthesis of the three dimensions of *din* (religion)—*islam, iman,* and *ihsan*—is what links the true believer to the divine through total submission and faith in the reality of the Creator, in addition to performance of virtuous and wholesome acts of devotion and worship of the Sublime and wholesome deeds in the service of the Creator and His creation. The type of surrender Islam requires is a deliberate, conscious, and rational act made by a person who knows with both intellectual certainty and spiritual vision that Allah is the reality. The believer's relationship with God is governed by *taqwa,* the consciousness of humankind's responsibility toward its Creator.

The believer, upon his submission to Allah's will and mercy, enters into a covenant with Him, portrayed as a mutual understanding in which Allah proposes a system of regulations for the guidance of humans. This guidance is presented in the form of commandments to be accepted and implemented by people. Allah then promises what He will do in the event of man's willingness to abide by these commands and when he regulates his life according to them. The concept of the promise is clearly conditional on human obedience. The covenant of the Koran symbolizes the relationship between Allah and the human; the human becomes His steward, vicegerent, or custodian on the earth through submission and obedience to His will (*islam*) as expressed in His commands and is able to take advantage of Allah's promises and favors. Allah addresses those who believe in Him in seventy-five verses of the Koran, giving them guidance and advice and a promise of rewards in this world and the hereafter. Those who do not believe in Him—the infidels, the *kafirun*—are promised a place in hellfire forever. A similar punishment is promised to those who submit to Allah according to their word but not in their deeds. Such people are the hypocrites or the *Munafiqeen*.

The concept of the covenant also symbolizes the relationship between humans and the rest of His creation. They all share one Allah, one set of guidance and commandments, the same submission and obedience to Him, and the same set of expectations in accordance with His promises. They all can, therefore, trust one another since they all have similar obligations and expectations. In view of the Koran, humans, communities, nations, and civilizations will continue in harmony and peace so long as they continue to fulfill Allah's covenant.

CHAPTER FIVE

TWELVE STEPS TO FREEDOM

In Islam, life is a chain link of intention and action.

1. Submission to Allah is in tawhid, which is the proclamation of the unity of the believer with Allah and the communion of believers in one *ummah* under the grace and mercy of Allah. This proclamation of unity is in every call to prayer (*adhan*) from sunrise to sunset around the world each day. And in this communion, Allah declares,

> Your real friends are Allah, His Messenger and the Fellowship of Believers, those who establish regular prayers and regular charity. And they bow down humbly in worship. As to those who turn for friendship to Allah, His Messenger, and the fellowship of Believers, it is the Fellowship of Allah that must certainly triumph.

This unity is ordained by Allah. To enforce this unity of the *ummah*, each Believer must determine his intention with an action. This action is to show the power and the resolve of the *ummah* to those opposed to the unity of Islam, the *Munafiqeen* and the *kafireen*. Each believer will raise the standard of the *ummah* over their home, their mosque, and every institution everywhere in the world. This standard is the crescent and the star of Islam over the blue-sky background of the world and the universe of Allah. This is the standard of the Dar es Salaam. This standard represents tawhid and the precepts of the covenant of Allah that ensure human dignity, equality, justice, consultative government, a state where there is realization of lawful benefits to people, prevention of harm, removal of hardship, and education of every individual by inculcating in him self-discipline, patience, restraint, and respect for rights of others. It is a standard under which there is restitution of all wrongs and imbalances in society, Muslim and non-Muslim.

2. Each believer will act to ensure that his government, his leaders, the media, the universities, all Islamic organizations, and political parties declare the political unity of all Muslim states by the of twenty-seventh April 2034, the 125th anniversary of the forced abdication of the last genuine caliph, Abdul Hamid.

3. One and a half billion believers have the power and resolve to physically remove the rulers who oppose the unity of the *ummah*. The believers will peacefully march through the palaces and the offices of such rulers and remove from there all vestiges of *fitnah*, treachery, and oppression.

4. One and a half billion believers have the power and resolve to physically remove all Western and foreign military bases and intelligence services from all the lands of Islam. The believers will peacefully march through the bases and remove from there all vestiges of *fitnah*, treachery, and oppression.

Opposition to such eviction will meet several thousand remotely controlled, explosive-laden aerial, terrestrial, and maritime vehicles that will vaporize the power of the circle of evil and their agents from the land of Islam.

5. All pacts, treaties, and agreements, whether covert or open, signed by Muslim rulers with the Western powers have been extinguished with the invasion of Afghanistan and Iraq. Therefore, all such treaties are void.

6. The organization of Islamic states, the Dar es Salaam, will coordinate the following:

  • Establish a unified rapid deployment mobile expeditionary force under one command with troops from all Islamic states to defend from any *fitnah* and aggression every inch of the land of Islam. The force will comprise of 1,000,000 armored troops, 500 frontline aircraft, and naval fleets in all Muslim waters. They will defend the vulnerable lands and oceans of Islam including the Persian Gulf, Palestine, the Suez Canal, North and Eastern Africa, the Red and the Black Sea, the Indian Ocean, the Mediterranean and Indonesia.

  • Establish, train, and arm a volunteer mobile commando force of 12 million *Mujahideen* men and women organized in 1,200 independent and self-sufficient units with their own armored, air force, and marine units. Their loyalty will be to the precepts of the covenant of Allah and the Dar es Salaam.

7. A unified foreign policy will be established for all Islamic lands under a single unified organization. All treaties and pacts signed by individual states will automatically be extinguished. Relations and agreements with the rest of the

world will be renegotiated considering the contemporary circumstances.

8. A unified currency supported by gold will be established. No fiat money will be accepted in trade. Usury will be abolished, and banking and trade reorganized.

9. The Dar es Salaam, the Islamic union, will exit the Western-driven United Nations and its subsidiary organizations till the formation of a new world organization based on justice, peace and equality rather than power and riches. This world organization will represent the people of the world rather than nations. It will be run by the people for the well-being of the people of the world.

10. The Dar es Salaam will exit the World Bank, the International Monetary Fund, the World Trade Organization, and the Breton Woods Agreement. New agreements will be negotiated with the European, American, Chinese, Hindu, and African groups on the basis of equality, peace and justice for all the people of the world.

11. In the twenty-first century, most humans individually believe in one God, one Creator. They are communally prevented from acting on such a belief by organized religions and their priestly organizations. The covenant of Allah calls for goodness and charity for all mankind. To open this inclusive faith to mankind, some changes are required in our daily life. The daily congregational prayers should be in the local language so that Islam becomes a faith of each native community. Every mosque and Sufi *dargah* will organize and set up a kitchen for daily free meal for the indigent to introduce them to Allah's benevolence.

12. Within one year of the renewal of Islam's world order, reorganization of the structure of the Dar es Salaam's governance will take place. In Islam, there are no rulers, no priests, and no politicians. Every believer has inherited the Koran and the law and is the guardian and the executor of the law. In Allah's Dar es Salaam, men constitute 750,000,000 individuals of the *ummah*, and the women constitute the other 750,000,000; between them, they form one solid, united *ummah*. Together in partnership, men and women have produced the progeny of Adam to carry out the divine and omnipotent will of Allah. The Koran addresses all believers, both men and women, together:

> And you Believers (men and women)! Turn you all together towards Allah, that ye may attain bliss.

The Dar es Salaam constitutes the following territories of the *ummah:* Afghanistan, Albania, Algeria, Bahrain, Bangladesh, Benin, Bosnia, Brunei, Burkina Faso, Cameroon, Chad, Chechnya, Comoros, Djibouti, Egypt, Ethiopia, East Turkistan, Gabon, Gambia, Guinea, Guinea-Bissau, Guyana, Indonesia, Iran, Ivory Coast, Iraq, Jordan, Kashmir, Kazakhstan, Kosovo, Kuwait, Kyrgyzstan, Lebanon, Libya, Malaysia, Maldives, Mali, Mauritania, Morocco, Mindanao, Mozambique, Niger, Nigeria, Oman, Pakistan, Palestine, Qatar, Saudi Arabia, Senegal, Sierra Leone, Somalia, Sudan, Suriname, Syria, Tajikistan, Tanzania, Togo, Tunisia, Turkey, Turkmenistan, Uganda, United Arab Emirates, Uzbekistan, and Yemen. Other Muslim domains within the boundaries of Russia, China, India, Serbia, and Macedonia will have an extraterritorial association with the Dar es Salaam through their large Muslim populations. Every Muslim, whether residing in or outside the bounds of the Dar es Salaam, is a member of the *ummah* and has the right and the obligation to the citizenship of the Dar es Salaam. Equally, every non-Muslim residing within the bounds of the Dar es Salaam who has sworn allegiance to the state will have the same citizenship rights and obligations, as well as all freedoms prescribed by the Koran to the Muslims, in short absolute and complete equality (Document of Yathrib).

CHAPTER SIX

ELECTORAL COLLEGE OF THE *UMMAH*

At the grassroots level, the *ummah* has been—through divine guidance—a democratic society governing itself justly in consultation and consensus through its intrinsic resources. Historically, however, it was denied the means of a participatory democratic system of government at higher levels by ongoing upheavals in their lands caused by marauding armies in search of power and booty. The democratic and humane social system, at the basic level, could not be transformed into a viable democratic political order of consultation and consensus at the governing level because of the tribal, feudal, and sultanic, monarchial order of the ruling classes.

For over one thousand years, the rulers and their governments were cut off from the people. Troops and civil servants came from the tribal formations, the slaves, and the priestly classes. Land and revenue-bearing estates were allocated to the military commanders and revenue agents, and the people were merely sharecroppers. Such un-Koranic feudalism has continued to exist in all Islamic lands. Allah has proclaimed a code of conduct for the Muslim *ummah* in His covenant in the Koran. Without fulfilling the whole covenant of Allah, all acts of submission, faith, and of worship become meaningless and of little consequence.

The Ummah

Verily this brotherhood of yours is a single brotherhood,
and I am your Lord and Cherisher:
Therefore, serve me and no other,
And hold fast, all together the Rope
Which Allah stretches out for you and be not divided amongst yourselves.
And remember with gratitude Allah's favor on you:
For you were enemies and He joined your hearts in love,
So that by His Grace, you became brethren.
Let there arise out of you a band of people
Inviting to all that is good, enjoining what is
right, and forbidding what is wrong.
Be not like those who are divided amongst
themselves and fall into disputations
After receiving clear signs
For them is a dreadful penalty.
Ye are the best of the peoples evolved for mankind,
Enjoining what is right, forbidding what is wrong,
And believing in Allah.
Thus have we made of you an Ummah of the center, that you are witness?
Over other nations, and the Messenger a witness over yourselves.
Whoever submits his whole self to Allah, and
does wholesome and good deeds,
Has grasped indeed the most trustworthy handhold,
And with Allah rests the end
And decision of all affairs.

Allah is the Sovereign of the universe. The sovereignty of the Dar es Salaam rests with the Muslim *ummah*, it being the aggregate of individual believers, who do the bidding of Allah. For the aggregate to believe in and to comply with the divine commandments, the individual has to be reformed and taught his responsibilities as a member of a divinely ordained, indivisible brotherhood.

The responsibilities of the individual believer are as follows:

- Each citizen should understand and act upon the precepts of the covenant of Allah that ensure human dignity, equality, justice, consultative government, a state where there is realization of lawful benefits to people, prevention of harm, removal of hardship, and education of every individual by inculcating in him self-discipline, patience, restraint, and respect for rights of others. It is a standard under which there is restitution of all wrongs and imbalances in society, Muslim, and non-Muslim.
- The believer is responsible for his own conduct in spiritual and worldly matters as commanded by Allah.
- The believers are accountable to their kith and kin, their neighbors, and the community.
- Their duty includes solidarity, prosperity, intellectual enlightenment, liberty, justice, and the unity of the *ummah*.
- Their individual responsibility is to invite all to what is good, to enjoin what is right, and to forbid what is evil.
- The believer has the added responsibility to ensure that his *ulil amri* receives proper advice and acts in consultation and that all decisions regarding the din and the *ummah* are made in consensus.
- The believer has the responsibility to take steps to stop corruption, mismanagement and abuse of authority amongst the state functionaries employed on his behalf.

Insignificant raindrops fall on parched land singly and disappear forever; however, the same raindrops coalesce in strength to form little streams and then little rivulets and then join together to become mighty rivers flowing further, dropping into powerful and majestic waterfalls, yet again joining together with other rivers, lakes, and more hill torrents, to end up in mighty oceans ever increasing in size, in length, in depth, and in power yet at all times obedient to the will of Allah. Similarly, an insignificant man without faith is like a drop of water on parched land. Yet the same man, a believer, strengthened by his covenant with Allah, joins others with the covenant to form a little community that, again, with other communities in unity with Allah form a single united *ummah* of all the Muslims around the world, a powerful, united people witnessing over other nations, with Allah and His prophet witnessing over them.

Ummah el Nuqta

The fundamental unit of the *ummah* is the *ummah el nuqta*, consisting of about one thousand adults over the age of fifteen years, comprising about five hundred families of a neighborhood. This unit—an autonomous, self-help neighborhood—is administered in consultation and with consensus from within the *nuqta* by the community itself. The community will ensure the well-being of each member of this unit in matters of nutrition, spiritual and worldly education, health, housing, clean water, waste disposal, social planning, and development. The community will ensure that none of their members go without food, shelter, health care, and education.

    a. The *ummah el nuqta* will select/elect from among themselves by mutual consultation and consensus an *ulil amri*, a *sheikh al nuqta*, and a committee of four members (*mushirs*), two men and two women, to administer the affairs of the *nuqta* every two years for a tenure of four years. The *sheikh al nuqta* will run the affairs of the community and will act as the chair of the committee. The *sheikh al nuqta* will run the day-to-day affairs of the community with the help of his committee and an ongoing consultation with the community, and all decisions must be reached in consensus with the community. The *sheikh al nuqta* may be a man or a woman in accord with the community's will. The *mushirs* will also represent their community on various administrative boards related to education, health, transport, and municipal affairs and in matters of interest to the community at the next level of administration, the *ummah el Haraf.*

b. The *sheikh al nuqta* will be responsible for civic discipline and law and order within the community. He will mediate any disputes and will act as a magistrate at the community level. The community will police itself without interference from outside, except at the request of the committee.

c. Each *nuqta* will aim for the highest possible standard of public health, education, health care, housing, and nutrition for its members. It will promote universal literacy within a short period of four years, to be achieved with maximum effort on the part of each member to assist another. Such mutual assistance will also be carried out in matters of education, health, trade, business, and housing and in every other matter of civic and social concern within the community.

d. The community will also appoint an imam for a designated period, whose appointment may or may not be renewed according to the community's will. The imam will provide spiritual guidance to those seeking it, as well as religious services to the community.

e. As with the sheikh and the *mushirs*, the tenure of the imam will depend on his character, ability, and performance.

f. The provincial government will provide funding for the administration of *ummah el nuqta*. Community welfare and developmental projects will be funded from the zakat and *sadqah* contributions and the government funds.

Individual families, cooperative associations, and women's groups within the *nuqta* will be able to utilize their dormant and nonproductive wealth to create industry, jobs, and productivity within their community. It is estimated that an average couple in the Middle East owns one hundred grams of gold ornaments, with the rich owning several kilograms of gold, while the poor owns just a few grams; nevertheless, the average amounts to about a hundred grams per couple. The *nuqta* community (500 families × 100 g = 50 kg) will have access to 50 kg of gold for investment, converting a dormant hoard into a personal and community asset.

Ummah el Haraf

One hundred *nuqta* communities will get together and authorize the next level of administration, the *ummah el Haraf*, which will run the rural communities comprising about one hundred thousand adults or twenty-five thousand families. Some communities may merge where geographic or ethnic interests dictate so. One *mushirs* from the *ummah el nuqta* will represent his or her community on the *ummah el Haraf* executive council, and another representative will sit on the *ummah el haraf* planning committee to chart out the future course of the communities. In urban areas and cities, similar arrangements will constitute a city municipality executive council and planning council. The two *mushirs* from the *ummah el nuqta* will represent their community in the two *ummah el Haraf* councils. Care will be taken to balance the membership of the councils to maintain gender equality. The *mushirs* sitting on the executive and the planning committees of the *ummah el Haraf* will, in consultation with their communities, select the *sheikh el Haraf* from among themselves as the head. The sheikh will also chair both the executive and the planning councils.

a. The *mushirs* will, along with experts in their fields, sit on various committees dealing with hospitals, schools, highways, finance, police, water, garbage disposal, planning, business, commerce, and so on. Recognizing the sovereignty of the *ummah*, the sheikh and the *mushirs* will consult the community before coming to any decision. The decision-making will, of necessity, be slow and will require the assent of the community. The planning council will look at the needs of the community years ahead and will also act as the lawmakers in tune with the laws of Allah and act as a check on the executive. The executive council will run the day-to-day affairs of the *ummah el haraf* and execute the decisions and planning of the planning council. A council of the *sheikhs el nuqta* will ensure that none of the councils and their functionaries abuse their authority nor misappropriate public assets.

b. The *ummah el Haraf* is an autonomous body acting in a role assigned to it by the *ummahs el nuqta* and *ummahs el Haraf* enshrined in the constitution.

c. The communities of *ummah el Haraf*, consisting of twenty-five thousand families, will in consultation and in consensus select from among themselves one able person of impeccable character, ability, and experience every two years for a four-year term to represent their interests at the provincial and national levels.

d. A council of ten *sheikhs el Haraf* from ten *ummahs el Haraf*, ten representatives of the *sheikh el nuqta* from these communities, ten representatives of the *mushirs* of these communities, and twenty-five representatives of various organizations, guilds, ulema, professions, universities, and so on will constitute a *majlis-e-ijma*, which will act as the consultative body acting as the eyes, ears, and voice of an adult population of one million people of the region. It will compose of an equal number of men and women representatives. Each *majlis-e-ijma* will select two of their members to sit on the national and vilayet *ijma councils* to coordinate the national consensus on policy matters, which will be binding on the executive.

e. This *majlis-e-ijma* will, an ongoing basis, consult the communities in their area in matters of mutual interest and arrive at a consensus of opinion on that matter. And continuingly, it will liaise with their *naibs* on the *majlis-e-wataniya*, *majlis-e-villayats*, provincial and national executives, ministries of these governments, and officials and functionaries of these two levels of the government.

f. The *majlis-e-ijma* will, every two years, assign their ten selected representatives (the *naibs*) a responsibility on one of the following task forces assigned by the constitution to the *ummah el Haraf*:

i. The lower house of the national legislature, the *majlis-e-Wataniya*
ii. The provincial legislature, the *majlis-e-Villayats*
iii. The national executive
iv. The provincial executive
v. The planning council, formulating the strategies and the policies concerning the nation in all spheres such as defense, foreign policy, fiscal matters, trade and commerce, population, education, health issues, Sharia and legal matters, transport, ports, cultural affairs, agriculture, mining, industry, civic planning, scientific research, and so on, delineating the course of the country in the short and long terms.
vi. The security commission (*majlis-e-Naazir*), a watchdog and oversight bureau watching unobtrusively all the functions of the national and provincial governments, the government ministries and agencies, the intelligence services, the armed forces, the law enforcement agencies, and the courts.

The *naibs*, as a body, will create and strengthen institutions based on Koranic democratic principles that the sovereignty of the *ummah* and the Dar es Salaam devolves from the individual believer to a collective repository of executive sovereignty of the whole *ummah* as a trust from Allah. The people entrusted with authority to administer the *ummah*'s affairs by contract are the *wakil* and the servants of the *ummah* and not the masters or the rulers. The legislative, executive, policy and planning, and security institutions will in clear and no uncertain terms derive their authority from individual believers, collectively from the *ummah*, as prescribed by the Koran. This authority will be passed from below upward through the *mushirs* and the *naibs*.

The *majlis-e-ijma* in the middle is the eyes, ears, voice, and conscience of the *ummah*. It will—in consultation with the community and the institutions of the legislature, the executive, the policy and planning bureau, and the security council—develop a consensus of opinion and formulate the policies and agenda for the government to act on. The Muslim society has always been democratic and will, for the first time, universally have a democratic government with solid legislative and executive institutions. The authority will, in effect, devolve from the common man and woman believer at the grassroots to ascend through their appointed representatives to the head of the state and his executive. The governance will function like a pyramid, with the people forming the solid foundation and, at the apex, the government resting on the secure and firm institutional structure.

Political Structure: Based on Consultation and Consensus at the Grassroots

The political structure will be without political parties. Every citizen of the Dar-es-Salaam will be responsible to maintain an untrammeled democratic system through the election or appointment of only of *six* public officials.

1. Two *mushirs*, one man and one woman, to be appointed by a thousand adults of the *nuqta* community from among themselves for a four-year term every two years. The community will find people of faith; of impeccable character,

record of accomplishment, and ability; and particularly of honesty from among themselves. It will, in consultation and consensus, choose or elect the officials from a short list of people forwarded by various citizen groups. *Emphasis will be on the citizens' choice rather than self-recommendation and self-aggrandizement by individuals.*

2. The *sheikh el nuqta*, man or a woman, to be selected by the *nuqta* community for a four-year term from among people of impeccable character and proven ability.

3. One *naib*, a man and a woman to be elected alternatively every two years for a four-year term by the aggregate of ten *nuqta* communities, the *ummah el Haraf*, constituting one hundred thousand adults.

4. A *Raiis*, a man or a woman, will be elected by universal suffrage for a four-year term to run the administration of the vilayet as the chief executive.

5. An *emir* or a *caliph*. The whole adult population of the *ummah* from around the world will, for a six-year term, elect an emir or a caliph, the chief executive of the Dar es Salaam, from a list of people prepared by the national council of the *majlis-e-ijma* in consultation with all major organizations and ordinary citizens. The candidate nominated for this position should be of impeccable reputation and character, administrative ability, and communication and interpersonal skills. He should be a *momin*, having submitted to the absolute will of Allah, with his actions and relationship with Him being governed by *taqwa* of Allah. The emir or the caliph should act in accordance with the three types of knowledge: *ilm al-yaqin, ain al-yaqin,* and *haqq al-yaqin* (knowledge of certitude, eye of certitude, and truth of certitude). He should be known to be in a state

of constant submission, *taqwa* of Allah. The caliph should be a natural leader, leading through example, piety, and humility through the guidance of his covenant with Allah. The caliph will guide and administer but will not rule. He and his family will have no privileges other than those defined by his office. The caliph will carry no titles or honors other than those pertaining to his office.

6. A council of the states composed of the *Raiis* of every state or his deputy will form the upper house of the *majlis-e-Wataniya* to protect the rights of each state.

7. There will be no obvious opposition party in the *majlis-e-Villayats* or in the *majlis-e-Wataniya* as in the Western democracies. The Islamic system has a built-in check and balance system within the framework of consultation and consensus at all levels of the government. The *majlis-e-ijma* and its national and state councils as well as the policy and planning councils are, at all times, open to the special interest and lobby groups to present their viewpoint. The security council and the *majlis-e-ijma* will unobtrusively oversee the conduct of the governments and their functionaries, putting an end to any irregularities before they take root and become entrenched.

Ummah el Villayat

The autonomous Muslim states that exist today will become the autonomous vilayets of the Dar es Salaam. All Muslim countries that function today as independent states will amalgamate into one united country, the Dar es Salaam. The population will form one united *ummah*, the *ummah wast* as proclaimed by Allah in the Koran, and their present rulers will cease to exercise every form of authority. Their authority will revert to the *ummah* as commanded by Allah. The sixty or so countries will become vilayets—states that will unite to form the Dar es Salaam, with autonomy to run their own affairs internally in the fields of health, education, agriculture, irrigation, highways, law and order, forestry, fisheries, municipalities, industry, internal trade, and commerce.

a. The states or the vilayets will be totally autonomous in the internal affairs as described above.

b. The legislative assembly, the *majlis-e-Villayats*, will have authority to enact legislation in accordance to the tenets of the covenant of the Koran. It will also act as watchdog over the executive. The *naibs* appointed by the *ummah el Haraf* will constitute the *majlis*, will derive their authority from the *ummah el Haraf*, and will act in consultation and in consensus with *ummah el Haraf* and the *majlis-e-ijma* of their district in the best interests of the nation.

c. The head of the executive, the *Raiis*, and his deputy will be elected directly by the *ummah el Villayat* in consultation and in the consensus from a number of people recommended by the council of *majlis-e-ijma* of the vilayet for a four-year term.

d. The *Raiis* will administer with the help of a cabinet of his selection from the *naibs* and other experts approved by the *majlis-e-Villayats* for a four-year period.

e. A policy and planning bureau composing of *naibs* and experts in their fields will on an ongoing basis formulate alternate policies in every sphere of the jurisdiction of the vilayet. The policies will be discussed by the legislature and the executive in an open forum of the legislature; modified, accepted, or rejected by the *majlis* and the executive; and then implemented by the executive.

f. Task forces composing of the representative *naibs* and experts in various fields will research and collect information to advise various ministries on policy matters concerning their subject. Various interest groups will be invited for their opinions on the subject matter, and their advice and interest should be given due consideration in formulating a policy.

g. The *Raiis* will derive his authority from the *ummah* and will act according to Allah's covenant and with the consent and the consensus of the *ummah* through the *majlis-e ijma*, *majlis-e-Villayats*, policy and planning council, and various interest groups.

h. All citizens of any race, caste, creed, religion, gender, age, and wealth shall stand equal in the eyes of the law, same as in the eyes of Allah. There shall be no elite in the state, and no one shall use a title or a name to show superiority over other beings. All titles bestowed, inherited, or self-assumed shall extinguish.

i. The services of every person to the *ummah* and to the nation given selflessly will be recognized to be as such, and no person shall have precedence in recognition of such services in the form of land grant or with funds from the public treasury, which are not available to other citizens.

j. For the purposes of law and citizenship, any person declaring his submission to Allah and His covenant is a believer and a Muslim. For the purposes of the state, there will be no sects, and the rights of all citizens, Muslim and non-Muslim, will be protected.

Ummah el Dar es Salaam: Ummah Wast

The Dar es Salaam is the composite political entity representing the home of every member of the *ummah* around the world. It is an amorphous landmass in which every home and place of worship of the believer is included. The state of Dar es Salaam will nurture every human under the commandments of Allah's covenant. In the Dar es Salaam, every human—man and woman, from the highest to the lowest, from the first to the last—shall have equal, unimpeded, and unquestionable right to liberty; right to practice his faith in accordance with his beliefs as, in Islam, there is no compulsion in matters of religion; right to life, which means intellectual, physical, and emotional well-being; right to safeguard one's property; right to intellectual endeavors, acquisition of knowledge, and education; right to earn a living; and right to free speech and action to enjoin good and forbid evil. In enjoying these freedoms, the individual will ensure that his activities do not impinge on the rights and freedom of others.

Every believer inherited the Koran, the covenant of Allah, the *din*, and the Dar es Salaam after his or her submission to Allah. When the blessed prophet passed away, the Koran and the *din* were bequeathed to every believer. This custodianship of the Koran, the covenant, and the *din* rests with every believer individually until the last day. In the Dar es Salaam, individual believers collectively and temporarily bestow this custodianship to a person of their choice for a defined period with conditions; in return, that individual is to exercise authority to manage the affairs of the Islamic state. While this authority may be bestowed, it can also be withdrawn if that individual fails to exercise his charge to the satisfaction of the majority of believers. During the period of discharge of his duties, this appointee will be called the caliph.

At the top of the pyramidal hierarchy of the *ummah*, the head of state and the successor to the temporal power of the blessed prophet of Allah is the caliph, appointed to office by universal suffrage by every adult believer for a period of six years. The national council of *majlis-e-ijma* and other organizations will nominate suitable candidates after consultation with citizens. Those nominated for the position of caliph will be presented to the people by the *majlis-e-ijma*. For this position, there will be no electioneering and no self-recommendation. The lessons of schism and disunity of Islam caused by Mu'awiyah's seizure of the caliphate in the sixty-sixth year of hijra will not be forgotten.

Ten *naibs* or deputies elected by the composite of fifty *haraf* communities every two years will be assigned to serve on the following bodies for a four-year term:

1. *Majlis-e-Wataniya* (national parliament).
2. *Majlis-e-Villayats* (provincial parliament).
3. National executive.
4. Provincial executive.
5. The planning councils formulating strategies and policies concerning the nation in all spheres such as defense, foreign policy, trade and commerce, fiscal matters, population, education, agriculture, health issues, Sharia and legal matters, transport, ports, cultural affairs, mining, civic planning, scientific research, security, and intelligence, and so on. This committee will plan the possible course for the nation in the short and the long terms.
6. The security commission (*majlis-e-Naazir*), a watchdog and an oversight bureau watching unobtrusively all functions of the provincial and national governments, the government

ministries and agencies, the intelligence services, the armed forces, the law enforcement forces, and the courts. One member will represent their *Haraf* community on the advisory committee of the caliph and the *Raiis*. These members' services will be allocated to various subcommittees as required by the needs of the day.

7.   One member appointed to the *ijma council*. The function of this council will be to consult with the *ummah* and assess the degree of consensus on various issues in the public domain. The committee's function will also include education of the public opinion by providing true and honest information on the state matters of concern to the citizens. The Dar es Salaam's modus operandi shall be based on truth and trust as advocated by the covenant of Allah. These *Haraf* community representatives will represent the public consensus on issues under consideration to their assigned committees, commissions, and the *majlis*. These ten members from their communities will be the best education tools to enlighten their communities on the workings of an Islamic system of governance based on Allah's covenant. Honest two-way communication from the base to the apex of the pyramid of governance and vice versa will smash any barriers of misunderstanding between the levels of administration and the people. This web of communication will unify the *ummah*. Rules, laws, and conduct of governance based on the thirty-seven commandments of the covenant of Allah will drive away Satan and humans controlled by him. These ten representatives of *Haraf* communities, representing a population of five million, will meet regularly with the citizen groups to deal with their questions and problems in a formal,

documented manner and find the solutions to the questions from the officialdom of the state.

The *nuqta* communities of one thousand adults, totaling a population of about twenty-five hundred, will be the basic community of the Dar es Salaam. This community holds the executive sovereignty of the Dar es Salaam. Six hundred thousand such autonomous communities form the basis of consultation and consensus of decision-making in all issues relating to the Dar es Salaam, where the democratic control over the nation begins at the grass roots and disseminates all the way to the top.

The believer's covenant with Allah reforms the individual by setting him or her to Allah's straight path. Similarly, reformed individuals in the community reinforce one another's resolve and actions in accordance with the straight path. Every believer when reciting *shahadah* in the daily prayer also pledges obedience to the covenant of Allah:

> Verily those who pledge their allegiance unto you (O Muhammad), pledge it unto none but Allah; the Hand of Allah is over their hands. Thereafter whosoever breaks his Covenant does so to the harm of his own soul, and whosoever fulfils his Covenant with Allah, Allah will grant him an immense Reward. (Al-Fath 48:10, Koran)

The actions of believers reflect their faith and total submission to Allah—the only Deity; the Knower of the hidden and the manifest; the Rahman and the Rahim; the Sovereign; the Pure; the Hallowed, Serene, and Perfect; the Protector; the Almighty; the Supreme; the Creator; the Most High; the Most Great. Allah sent the blessed Muhammad and His other blessed messengers as witnesses to mankind, bearing glad tidings that Allah is the only reality and that everything else is dependent on Allah. Allah revealed the divine message, the Koran, to Blessed Prophet Muhammad as guidance and a covenant to humankind. Those who obey the covenant and Allah as guidance and hold on to Allah receive His grace, mercy, benevolence, and protection. The believers have Allah's presence in mind at all times. And all their actions are with the awareness that Allah is with them; though they may not see Him, He sees them.

The believers of Allah pledge to

1. serve Allah's creation—human, animal, plant, the earth, and the atmosphere—with generous, beautiful, and *righteous* deeds and provide their kin, neighbors, community, and those in need with sustenance from their means and wealth.
2. be just and truthful.
3. shun shameful deeds, *Fahasha*.
4. be united within the *ummah*.
5. seek protection of Allah the *Waliy* and reject Jews, Christians, and the infidels as their *awliya*, protectors.
6. fight in Allah's cause and fight injustice, unbelief in Allah, *fitnah*, and tyranny until there is no more *fitnah*, treachery, and oppression and justice prevails altogether everywhere.
7. forbid murder and not to take life, which Allah has made life sacred.
8. not betray the trust of Allah and His prophet with theft, deception, fraud, corruption, and dishonesty.
9. not devour usury nor hoard wealth.
10. be good, kind, and caring to their parents.
11. not kill or deprive you children because of poverty (abortion and murder).

12. treat one another in kindness and on the basis of equality and justice.

13. not crave those things of what Allah has bestowed His gifts more freely on some than others, with men being assigned what they earn and women what they earn.

14. be just and stand firmly for justice and truth as witness to Allah and always speak the truth, always dealing justly so that he shall not be dealt with unjustly.

15. invite others to what is good and right and forbid what is wrong.

16. avoid suspicion, which leads to sin.

17. not ridicule other believers.

18. avoid secret counsels, which are inspired by Satan.

19. intoxicants, gambling, carrion, blood, flesh of swine, and any food on which a name other than that of Allah has been invoked.

20. not prohibit and make unlawful the good things that Allah has made lawful and to commit no excess.

21. respect other people's privacy and enter not their houses without first asking permission.

On ninth day of *Zul-hajj* in the tenth year of hijra, Allah in His mercy proclaimed to the humankind through His blessed messenger that,.

- Allah had perfected the din of the believers, bestowed on them His blessings, and decreed Islam as the *din* of believers.
- In Sura Al-Kahf, Allah proclaims, "We have explained in detail in this Qur'an, for the benefit of mankind every kind of similitude, but man is in most things contentious."

- In Taha, it says, "So we have made the Qur'an easy in your own tongue that with it you may give glad tidings to the righteous and warnings to people given to contention."

- In Ad-Dukhan, it says, "Ha Mim. By the Book that makes matters lucid; We revealed it during blessed night, verily we are always warning against Evil. Therein is proclaimed every wise decree, by command from Our Presence, for we are ever sending Revelations, as a Mercy from Your Lord, for He is the Hearer and the Knower."

- In these suras, Allah proclaims that His message to mankind in the Koran "is perfect, detailed, easy and lucid." Accordingly, Allah's *din* is not to be tampered by humans at any time. After that day, any additions, and alterations to the *din* of the believers are a man-made innovation.

POSTSCRIPT
FATE OF TREASON

Talat Pasha, Enver Pasha, and Cemal Pasha formed the triumvirate that seized the Ottoman government and led the Ottoman Empire into the First World War, which essentially a war of Christians against Christians fought for the control of wealth and trade of Europe and the world. Neither the people of the empire nor the cabinet, parliament, or the army had been informed of the decision to go to war. They were the tools of the German emperor and had no interest in the welfare of their own people. Germany lost the war, and as a result, the Turks were badly defeated. Mustafa Kemal abandoned Syria, Iraq, and Arabia, leaving the Islamic nation to the mercy of the British and the French. Talat Pasha, Enver Pasha, and Cemal Pasha abandoned the field and made a run for their lives. Syria, Iraq, and Arabia were captured by the British, the French, and their Arab tools. What was once a united empire was divided into Azerbaijan, Turkey, Syria, Lebanon, Iraq, Saudi Arabia, Yemen, Oman, Kuwait, Aden, and the Trucial States by the Turks, the British, and the French in the name of Turkish and Arab nationalism under the control of Western tools.

What Was the Fate of the Traitors to Islam and Allah's Covenant?

In July 1919, a Turkish court-martial investigating the conduct of the government during the war period condemned the three—Talat Pasha, Enver Pasha, and Cemal Pasha—to death. At the time the sentence was pronounced, Talat had already fled to Germany, in which country Enver Pasha and Cemal had also taken refuge. Enver had since returned to Turkey and joined the nationalists.

Talat Pasha: An unsuccessful attempt to assassinate Talat was made in Constantinople early in 1915, at which time he was seriously wounded by the would-be murderer's bullet. Talat Pasha, former grand vizier of Turkey and one of the three leaders of the Young Turk movement, was murdered in Berlin on March 15, 1921, in an act of revenge by an Armenian assassin. He was walking in a street in a western suburb with his wife when a young man who had been following overtook them and, tapping Talat on the shoulder, pretended to claim acquaintance with him. Then drawing a revolver, the man shot Talat through the head and with a second shot wounded the wife. Talat fell to the pavement and was killed instantly. He had been on the run in fear for his life. He had been living as a fugitive under assumed names, first in Switzerland and later in Germany. He evidently feared the fate that had now overtaken him, for he had frequently changed his address in Berlin and, at the time of his death, was living at a pension in the West End.

Cemal Pasha: The fall of Jerusalem in December 1917 sent Cemal back to Constantinople, where he remained in office until the collapse of the Young Turk administration in October 1918. He subsequently fled Constantinople along with other ministers aboard a German ship. Cemal thereafter served as liaison officer in talks between the newly established Soviet Union and the postwar Turkish government. He also spent a brief period acting as a military adviser to Afghanistan. He was murdered by Armenian assassins at Tbilisi on July 21, 1922.

Enver Pasha: Enver died on August 4, 1922, in hiding near Baljuan, in present-day Republic of Tajikistan, of a wound that he sustained while fleeing from Russian cavalry. The ambitions and treachery of this forty-one-year-old soldier and adventurer led to the overthrow of the authority of the Ottoman sultan. As a tool of the German monarch, his actions resulted in the defeat and dismemberment of the Ottoman Empire and enslavement of the Muslims for over hundred years.

Sharif Hussein of Mecca: In June 1916, supported by Abdullah, Faisal, and his other sons, Sharif Hussein proclaimed the Arab Revolt against the sultan and the caliph of the Ottoman Empire. For Hussein and sons, it was an act of treason—treason against their religion, treason against their people, and treason against his sovereign to whom they had sworn allegiance and loyalty. Faisal, who was a serving officer in the Ottoman Army, deserted his post in Syria to join the revolt. The revolt proved to be a dud. Hussein, it turned out, had no following at all. Muslims did not respond to his call nor did the Arabs. Under his banner, or rather the one that a British official designed for him, those who rallied under him were closer to one thousand rather than one hundred thousand, and they were Bedouin tribesmen and not soldiers. And those who did join were bribed with British gold.

Faisal's camel corps presented a pretense that Syria was liberated by the Arabs themselves. In fact, there were a million British Indian troops fighting in the Middle East in 1918 and only thirty-five hundred Husseini troops, and on the face of it was a British war of conquest over the Arabs and not a war of liberation for them. The

British, on May 9, 1916, in a secret convention, had already promised Arab Syria to the French (Sykes-Picot Agreement) and on November 2, 1917, in the Balfour Declaration, gave away Arab Palestine to the Jews. The Lawrence-Hussein-sons puppet show was being cleverly orchestrated from London. Each one of the players understood their role and the reward for their part except Hussein and sons. The ambiguous language, willful face-to-face lies, secret agreements, double dealings, deception, flattery, and bribery as a skill and art had become the trademark of English diplomacy over the previous one hundred years. The Arabs and the Bedouin had their own share of guile and cunningness; they were, however, no match for the Anglos as the next one hundred years would reveal. And the Arab leaders never learned.

After the war, Sharif Hussein—the commoner from Istanbul—declared himself the king of Hejaz and the caliph of Islam. The Muslim world ridiculed the king. The British had no further use for him and dropped him like a dirty rag. Angry with the British for their deception, Hussein sank into deep depression. He abdicated his pretend throne in favor of his son Ali. Ali, in turn, was driven out from Mecca by Ibn Sa'ud with the British help in 1925.

As a compensation for his loyalty and services, the British granted Hussein a villa in Cyprus and a pension. For his treasonable services against Islam, this caliph of Islam and a gallant servant of the British was elevated to the rank of a Knight of the Grand Cross in the Most Honorable Order of the Bath by the English sovereign. Hussein died a broken man in 1933.

Faisal ibn Hussein: Faisal deserted his post in the Ottoman Army and a seat in the Turkish Senate to join the revolt against the Ottomans. The English, in their duplicity, had promised parts of Syria to the Arabs, the French, and the Jews. The English proclaimed Faisal the king of Syria on March 8, 1920. The French chased him out of Damascus on July 27, 1920, with English connivance. The English, unable to control the restive population of Iraq in need of a willing sheikh for hire, selected Faisal as a good pliable tool to control Iraq. Faisal was proclaimed king of the British protectorate of Mesopotamia on August 21, 1921. He ruled over Iraq as the nominal ruler under the British protection and guidance till his death of heart disease in Bern, Switzerland, on September 8, 1933. Till the end, he hung on to his puppet strings. For his loyalty to the British Crown, this son of the pretender to the caliphate was awarded the title of the rank of a Knight of the Grand Cross in the Most Honorable Order of the Bath, three months before he died.

Faisal was installed king of an artificial country in which different clans had enjoyed historic rights. In 1922, the Kurdish leader Mahmood declared an independent Kurdistan as had been originally envisioned by the Paris Peace treaties of 1919. Originally Britain's choice to govern in the Sulaymaniyah region, Mahmood had fallen out with the British in 1919 and had been captured but later pardoned. His second revolt in 1922 came at a time when Turkey was pressing hard its claims to Mosul. The British, with the complicity of Faisal, responded by suppressing the revolt in 1924. Under Faisal's sovereignty, the British Royal Air Force bombed the Iraqi villages, tribes, and crops repeatedly for over two and a half years. The British aircraft used poison and mustard gas to put down the peoples fight for independence.

At the time Britain was creating the throne for Faisal, Kurdistan was deeply divided. Kirkuk and Arbil demanded separate governorates and opposed the Arab rule of Iraq. Nevertheless, faced with potential for continuing revolts, Faisal's government agreed not to appoint Arab officials in Kurdish provinces.

In 1925, a major Kurdish uprising inside Turkey led by Sheikh Sa'd had repercussions in Iraqi Kurdistan, but violence did not break out again until 1927. In the meantime, Kurdish leaders had been increasingly frustrated by their powerlessness in Parliament, where Arabs dominated. In 1927, a new uprising was led by Sheikh Ahmad Barzani, the uncle of the present head of the Kurdistan Democratic Party in Iraq, Mas'ud Barzani. Sheikh Ahmad had been ruling his own area pretty much without government interference, and as control from Baghdad increased, so did his resistance. His revolt continued until 1932, when he surrendered to Turkish troops rather than to Arabs in Baghdad. In the meantime, a massacre in Sulaymaniyah in 1930 had helped cement the rise of Kurdish nationalism.

In 1933, in Faisal's last year on the throne, the Iraqi government clashed with the Assyrian minority, and the Iraqi Army carried out a full-scale massacre of Assyrians in the north, many of whom had already been driven out of Turkey. Faisal was succeeded by his son King Ghazi, a playboy of sorts, and reputed to be a homosexual.

In 1934 and 1935, there were tribal uprisings along the middle Euphrates, some of them quite serious. A new Kurdish uprising occurred in August of 1935, and soon after this, the Yezidis—a small, syncretistic, isolated sect living in northern Iraq—also rose. Further uprisings occurred in the Basra area in 1935 and 1936.

In October 1936, Gen. Bakr Sidqi—the army commander— staged a coup. This was the first military coup in the modern Arab world (though it had Ottoman and Iranian models in the early twentieth century to emulate). Sidqi, of Kurdish origin but not a Kurdish nationalist, had been commander of the northern region army units during several of the revolts and made his name putting down the Assyrian "troubles"; in alliance with the so-called Ahali Group political faction, he took power, and King Ghazi accepted the coup. By now, the army was a central player in politics. Nuri as-Said would play a key role in the years that followed, usually as the British puppet.

In 1939, young king Ghazi was unexpectedly killed in an automobile accident. Some believe that he was murdered. There was a deliberate cover-up of circumstances leading to Ghazi's death. The speculation was that Nuri as-Said and the English collaborated in Ghazi's murder. Ghazi's son, Faysal, became king as Faysal II; but as he was only four years old, regency was established under Emir 'Abd al-Ilah, a cousin on the Hashemite side and also a maternal uncle of the young king.

Azza, the daughter of Faisal ibn Hussein and the granddaughter of Hussein ibn Ali, the pretender to the caliphate, renounced Islam in 1936 to marry a Greek hotel waiter.

Faysal II: The last British puppet on the Iraqi throne was murdered by army mutineers on July 14, 1958, bringing an inglorious end to the dynasty of treason and treachery.

Nuri as-Said: The pillar of British rule in Iraq was recognized by the people of Baghdad while on the run in a woman's garb. He was captured by the people and slaughtered. In July 1958, as tensions and mass demonstrations against the regime mounted, a military group known as the Free Officers overthrew Britain's venal political agents, the Hashemite monarchy of Faysal II and the government of Prime Minister Nuri as-Said, in a military coup. The royal family and Nuri were assassinated. Such was the loathing for Nuri that his naked body was dragged ignominiously through the streets of Baghdad until it was reduced to a pulp. Forty years of brutal exploitation and political repression by the British and their Hashemite collaborators had come to an end.

Abdullah ibn Hussein: He was appointed an emir as an instrument of British policy to help moderate and dampen the Palestinian opposition to the Jewish settlement in Palestine. Sir Herbert Samuel was appointed the high commissioner to direct Abdullah in this direction. At the Cairo conference, Lawrence summed up the British position by declaring, "It will be preferable to use Transjordan as a safety valve, by appointing a ruler who would bring pressure to bear, to check anti Zionism[67]." The West used Abdullah to undermine Arab efforts against Israel in 1948. Abdullah secretly met Zionist leaders from 1922 onward, merely a year after the creation of Transjordan. These meetings continued during the Palestinian disturbances in 1932 and 1936. The amity between the two conspiring sides was so total that, in a meeting, Abdullah and the Jewish envoy discussed ways of eliminating the mufti of Jerusalem, the leader of Palestinians, and the enemy of both sides[68]. He secretly conspired with Chaim Weizmann for the partition of Palestine in 1947. Abdullah was murdered in the Al-Aqsa Mosque in July 1951 by a nationalist Palestinian.

Hussein: Abdullah's grandson started his secret contacts with the Israeli leaders in 1957, and by 1963, regular meetings[69] with the leaders became a regular occurrence. In 1963, Hussein made secret visit to Tel Aviv. In the period preceding 1967, Hussein performed several treasonable acts, which were openly anti-Arab. In response to the creation of PLO, which wanted to replace him as the Palestinian representative, Hussein's[70] intelligence service provided the names and location of the Palestinian fighters infiltrating and battling the Israelis.

---

[67] Dann, *Great Powers*, 94.

[68] Shlaim, *Partition*, 203.

[69] Raviv and Melman, *Every Spy*, 213.

[70] Black and Morris, *Secret War*, 238.

Hussein did not stop here. His intelligence service also provided Israeli's information about other Arab countries.[71]

From 1970 onward, there were several secret meetings between Hussein and the Israeli defense minister Moshe Dayan and with Israeli prime minister Golda Meir.[72] This extensive period of secret Jordanian Israeli cooperation produced the most treasonable act of Hussein's life, informing Israel of the impending Egyptian-Syrian attack of October 1973.[73]

Hussein ibn Talal narrowly escaped several assassination attempts. Throughout their long career of treason and treachery to Islam, the descendants of Sharif Hussein boasted of their holy prophetic bloodline. In Islam, the only thing that a believer requires is Allah's hand over his hand. Respect of the bloodline is the old relic from the days of priesthood of gods bequeathed on Islam through the pagan Quraish. Remember Abu Jahl? He was of the same bloodline as the blessed prophet, yet he had been condemned in the Koran to the posterity.

Of the seven members of the Hashemite clan who became kings, Hussein ibn Talal was the only one who escaped assassination or eviction from his throne. Hussein ibn Ali, Ali ibn Hussein, Faisal ibn Hussein, and Talal ibn Abdullah were forced to abandon their throne and kingdom. Faisal had the good fortune to gain another kingdom. Ghazi, Faysal II, and Abdullah were murdered by their subjects. Treachery and glory carry their price.

Anwar Sadat: Sadat forgot his own roots and began to take advice and comfort from Kissinger and the Israeli lobby in Washington. Against the advice of his closest advisers and leaders

---

[71] Raviv and Melman, *Every Spy*, 214.

[72] Heikal, *Secret Channels*, 310.

[73] Black and Morris, *Secret War*, 265.

of other Arab countries, Sadat offered himself as a servant and a tool the circle of evil, the *Yahudi-Salibi* confederation. He made a trip to Israel and addressed the Knesset, the Israeli parliament. Under the American tutelage and patronage, he abandoned his Arab allies, negotiated, and signed a peace treaty with many secret appendices with Israel at the expense of the Palestinians and Syrians and Muslims in general. As a consequence, all Palestine and the Golan Heights are under Israeli occupation. The Arabs are disunited and in disarray. Sadat sold out Egyptian sovereignty, the Islamic nation, and the Islamic holy places in Jerusalem for three billion dollars a year. He took Jews and Christians as *awliya* and willfully disobeyed the covenant that every Muslim, if he was a believer, has pledged to obey. He also disobeyed the provisions of the covenant of Yathrib and the prophet's teaching:

> Just as the bond to Allah is indivisible, all the believers shall stand behind the commitment of the least of them. All believers are bonded one to another to the exclusion of other men. This Pax Islamica is one and indivisible. No believer shall enter a separate peace without all other believers whenever there is fighting in the cause of God but will do so only on the basis of equality and justice to all others.

Puffed by the stature the Americans gave Anwar Sadat, he began to behave like a pharaoh. This son of an impoverished petty official began to live in opulence. He moved from palace to palace. He also loved to be saluted by thousands of parading soldiers. During a military parade in Cairo in 1981, Lt. Khaled Istambouli of the Egyptian Army, along with accomplices, jumped out of an armored vehicle opposite the presidential dais and sprayed the dais with hundreds of bullets with their automatic weapons. instantly killing Anwar Sadat, the modern pharaoh.

Gen. Pervez Musharraf: No person in Islam has the knowledge, power, or authority to declare himself to be the arbiter of the fate of the *ummah* nor its state. Those who do so in their arrogance and ignorance take on themselves the prerogatives of Allah. And this is *shirk*, and Allah has ordained the fate of those who defy Him.

There have been several attempts on the life of Musharraf. Since then, he has led a life of a prisoner in his own gilded cage in Dubai, on the run from a death sentence in Pakistan. What fate awaits him; Allah only knows. Knowledge of the fate of his fellow traitors foreshadows sad forebodings for him.

APPENDIX

adalah: One capable of adjudication.

'adl: Justice.

ad-deen: Commitment, obligation, responsibility, pledge, promise, oath, contract, compact, covenant, pact, and treaty agreement.

ahd: Commitment, obligation, responsibility, pledge, promise, oath, contract, compact, covenant, pact, and treaty agreement.

ahkam: Legal verdict, judgment, permissible.

ain al-yaqin: Eye of certainty.

ardh: The earth, man's domain.

amanah: Trust.

amilu: Deeds.

aql: Intellect, human reasoning.

awliya: Friends and protectors.

ayah: Verses of the Koran.

ayan: Local notables.

babas: Sufi holy men.

batil: Falsehood, untruth, opposite of *haqq.*

beys: Local notables.

bhakti: Sanskrit: love and attachment to God.

burka: Head-to-foot garment worn by some women in the Middle East and South Asia.

covenant: Commitment, obligation, responsibility, pledge, promise, oath, contract, compact, pact, and treaty agreement.

Dar es Salaam: The abode of peace; the land of Islam.

darar: Hardship.

din: Total belief system based on the practice of total submission to God's will, accompanied by acts of beautiful deeds that endeavor to set things right and restore harmony, peace and balance. A synthesis of *islam*, *iman*, and *ihsan*.

devshirme **class:** Ottoman custom of taking young slaves from among the Slavic peoples for use in bureaucracy and as loyal officers in the army.

dhikr: Remembrance of Allah.

dynameis: Greek: divine "powers."

ehad: Hebrew: one. Equivalent of Arabic *ahad*.

Enuma elish: The Babylonian epic of creation.

Fahasha: Shameful, indecent; sexual misconduct.

faqih: Jurist.

fasiq: Impostor.

fasiqun: Rebellious transgressors.

fatwa: A religious edict; decree in matters of religious law.

fay: Income from the captured territories.

fiqh: Science of jurisprudence.

fuqara: Those who ask or beg.

furqan: Criterion to judge between right and wrong.

ghazzu: Tribal raids of pre-Islamic times, practiced by the likes of Ibn Sa'ud.

goyim: Hebrew, Yiddish: a pejorative term for non-Jews, used in Talmud, Jewish literature, and speech Hadith; a story; saying and deeds of the prophet.

Hadith: collection of stories (of the prophet's sayings and actions).

hajj: Pilgrimage to Mecca.

halal: That which is permitted.

Haleem: Magnanimous.

Hanafi: Followers of the school of jurisprudence of Abu Hanifah.

Hanbali: Followers of the school of jurisprudence of Imam Hanbal.

haqq: Absolute truth.

haqq al-yaqin: Truth of Certainty.

haraj: Harm.

haram: Unlawful; illegal.

harramma: Unlawful.

hasana: Beautiful, wholesome, good.

hubb: Love.

hukm: Command; edict.

husn: Good, beautiful, wholesome.

husna: Beautiful, good.

ihram: Precincts of Kaaba; in the state of piety and dress for the *hajj.*

ihsan: Doing good and wholesome deeds.

ijma: Mutual consultation.

ijtihad: Capacity to find answers to the dilemmas of the community.

Ikhwan: Brothers.

ilm al akhlaq: Knowledge of conduct of the faith.

ilm al kalam: Knowledge of dogmatic theology; knowledge of reason or rational investigation.

ilm al-yaqin: Knowledge of certainty.

ilm ladduni: Knowledge from Allah.

iman: Faith of Islam; second dimension of Islam.

imam: A person who leads the congregation prayers. In Shiite Islam, a descendant of the prophet who is looked on as the leader of the community.

imitatio dei: Latin: imitation of God.

insan: Mankind, humankind, humans.

iqtas: Land grants in lieu of services.

Islah: Establishing wholesomeness, reform.

islam: A voluntary submission to the will of Allah.

Isr: A firm covenant, compact, or contract that if one does not fulfill becomes liable for punishment.

Jannat: Paradise. Garden of eternity.

Jannat adn: Gardens of eternity.

Jammaa: Community of Muslims.

jihad: Struggle to the utmost; striving to purify oneself; struggle against oppression and tyranny.

jum'ah: Friday (prayers).

kafir: The nonbelievers; infidel, pagan, ungrateful.

kafirun: The plural of *kafir.*

kafireen: The plural of *kafir.*

kavod: Hebrew: glory of divine presence.

khanqahs: Sufi hospices.

Kharijites: Seceders, those who disaffiliate.

kufr: The act of disbelief in Allah; ingratitude.

ma'ashiyyat: Economics.

madrassas: Religious schools.

madhab: Fraternity or school of jurisprudence.

madhahib: Plural of *madhab.*

ma'eeshat: Life of hardship; economic hardship.

masha'ikhs: Leaders of fraternities of jurisprudence.

mawla: Protector and helper.

millet: Autonomous religious communities in the Ottoman Empire.

mihnah: Inquisition.

mithaq: Tie of relationship between two parties.

mitzvoth: Hebrew: commandments.

mufsidun: Worker of corruption.

muhsin: Performer of wholesome deeds.

mufti: A jurist and scholar of Islamic law.

malaika: Angels.

Munafiqeen: Hypocrites, truth concealers.

Munkar: Wrong.

mushrikun: Unbelievers.

mushirs: Advisers, representatives.

Mutaffifeen: Purveyors of fraud.

muttaqeen: One with *taqwa*; a true believer.

nabi: The one who is given the divine revelation. It does not mean "prophet." *Prophet* is a Jewish and Christian terminology that means "clairvoyant or a forecaster of events."

nirvana: Sanskrit: the sense of ecstasy or dread in the presence of a reality.

nur: Allah's blessed light.

padishah: An Iranian and Indian title of a king.

pasha: High-ranking official in the Ottoman Empire.

Qarmatian: a Sufi sect organized around khankahs and religious communities.

qutb: An imaginary divine axis representing justice.

Rabb: Lord.

Rahamat: Divine mercy.

Rahim: Most merciful.

Rahman: Most gracious.

rashidun: Righteous.

rasul, rasool: The one who receives a revelation and then communicates it to others. "Messenger" is a mistranslation of *rasul*. The *rasul* knows and understands the revelation and, on the basis of this knowledge, communicates this word of Allah.

471

reava: Flocks; Turkish subjects.

şabr: Patience, fortitude.

şābir: Patient one.

şabbār: Patience.

şābara: Plural for the ones who are patient.

Sahaba: Companions of the Prophet.

salat: Contact prayers; prayers that require standing, bowing, and kneeling to Allah in submission.

salihat: Wholesome.

sama: The heavens; the sky.

shakan: Hebrew: to set up a tent.

Shakoor: Appreciative

Sura: Chapter.

tabi'un: Governors.

Taslim: Last part of the salat prayer asking for blessings on the people on the left and the right.

tapulu: Lands given to the military in lieu of services.

taqwa **of Allah:** Awareness of Allah's presence.

timars: Endowment of estates in lieu of military service.

Tawhid: Unity of Allah.

ulema: Scholars of Islam; those knowledgeable in Islamic law.

ulil amri minkum: A person appointed to administer affairs of a community.

ummah wast: The middle nation; the nation given to moderation.

ummah: Islamic community; the nation of the Muslims.

ummah el nuqta: *Nuqta* is a dot. Thus, the *ummah el nuqta* forms the lowest level or the basic community in a democracy.

waqf: Endowment

wakil: Representative.

yashmak: Veil; a head-to-toe garment worn by some Muslim women.

zalimun: Evildoers.

zakat: Mandatory charity; cleansing of oneself.

Page Break

ABOUT THE AUTHOR

Dr. Munawar Sabir was born in Kenya, then a British colony. He received his education in Kenya, Pakistan, England, and Canada. As a product of Muslim and secular heritages of Africa, Asia, Europe, and North America, he has gone back to delve deep into his original heritage of the *din* and the Koran.

Dr. Munawar Sabir has written six books on contemporary Islam, the covenant of the Koran, and the historical events that have shaped the current state of Islamic societies. These books are the culmination of over forty years of observation, study, and research on Islam and the sociopolitical development of Islamic societies in relation to their fulfillment of the covenant of Allah.

Munawar Sabir is a fellow of the Royal College of Physicians and Surgeons of Canada. He has practiced medicine in Britain and Canada for over fifty-eight years and has published scientific papers on neurological disorders of the musculoskeletal system.

In this book, Dr. Munawar Sabir argues that the Koran is a living, vibrant communion between Allah and His creatures. The lines of thought and the step-by-step guidance laid out by Allah for the individual believer fourteen hundred years ago continue to vitalize the community of believers as it did in the course of early Islam's belief, thought, and history. The sense of the word read, recited, and explained by the scholars of Islam has remained anchored to the meaning given to it by the *masha'ikhs* of the schools of jurisprudence at the time of the Umayyad and the Abbasid caliphates of the Middle Ages. The Quran is forever. The religion that passes as Islam today—that is, the Islam of the masses, the scholars, and the ruling classes both of the Shia and the Sunni—is the fossilized version of the Islam of the Middle Ages. Its facade, however dilapidated, is there, but the spirit is essentially medieval. It is not the Islam of the Koran, nor it is the Islam of the blessed *nabi*.

It is essential that each Believer connect with Allah. Koran, Allah's word, is the primary source of the believers' spiritual well-being. Recitation of the Koran imparts peace, tranquility, and closeness to Allah and also renews the believers vow to obey Allah's covenant. All believers memorize some parts of the Koran, particularly Sura Al-Fatihah and certain other verses to recite the salat. The salat is the daily renewal of the Koran in the believer, a daily rejuvenation of his or her covenant with Allah and communion with Him.

The blessed *Nabi* said, "*Iman is* knowledge in the heart, a voicing with the tongue and activity with the limbs." The term *heart*, often used in the Koran, refers to a specific faculty or a spiritual organ that provides the humans *intellect* and *rationality*. Therefore, *iman* in effect means confidence in the Reality and truth of things and commitment to act on the basis of the truth that they know. Thus, *iman* (faith) involves words and actions on the basis of that knowledge.

Koran is Allah's speech to the believers, and it is the foundation of everything Islamic. Thus, the humans connect with Allah by speaking to Him. The believer speaks to Allah through daily salat and supplication, *du'a*. The words are accompanied by action of the body, symbolizing subservience, respect, and humility. The salat consists of cyclic movements of standing in humility in the presence of Allah, bowing down to Him, going down in prostration in the Lord's presence, sitting in humility, reciting verses from the Koran, and praising Allah. Recitation of the Koran serves to embody it within the person reciting salat.

Allah is light (*nur*), and His word (the Koran) is His luminosity. To embody the Koran through faith and practice is to become transformed by this divine light that permeates through the believer in his closeness Allah has bestowed the human with a mind and free will. The mind has the ability to perceive ideas and knowledge from the divine and from the signs of Allah. The whisper of the divine, the rustle of the wind, the light of God (*nur*), the fragrance of God's creation, and the sensation of the divine touch all inspire the human mind with an endless stream of ideas and knowledge. Man has been granted knowledge and the ability to process his thoughts with free will.

The verse of the light encompasses the totality of the knowledge and guidance that Allah sent to the human through His prophets. The pagan in the human confused God's message and instead began to worship the messenger. With the end of the era of prophecy, man has the freedom to open his heart to the light of Allah and to learn to recognize the presence of Allah within himself, in his own heart.

> Allah is the Light of the heavens and the earth. The parable of His Light is as if there were a Niche and within it a Lamp: the Lamp enclosed in Glass; the glass as it was a brilliant star: lit from a blessed Tree, an Olive, neither of the East nor of the West, whose Oil is well-nigh luminous, though fire scarce touched it: Light upon Light! Allah guides whom He will to His Light: Allah sets forth Parables for men, and Allah is the font of all Knowledge, and knows all things. Lit is such a light in houses, which Allah hath permitted to be raised to honor and celebrate His name. In them He is glorified in the

mornings and in the evenings, over and over again. (An-Nur
24:35–36, Koran)

The parable of divine light is the fundamental belief in one universal God for the whole humankind. Allah is the light of the heavens and the earth that bestows life, grace, and mercy on His creatures. Allah loves His creation, and His *nur* is ever luminous in the hearts of those who love Him, place their trust in Him, and open their heart and soul in submission to Him. In the hearts and minds laid open to Allah in submission is a niche in which glows the light, Spirit, and knowledge of Allah. Such is the glow and the luminescence of the divine light, Spirit, and wisdom; it shines with the brilliance of a star—a star that is lit from divine wisdom, the tree of knowledge, and the knowledge of Allah's signs. For those who believe, Allah is within, and the believer is aglow with Allah's brilliance—light upon light, light seen from the heavens and the earth. The dwellings in which Allah is glorified in the morning and in the evening over and over again are aglow with Allah's light and mercy.

Allah has granted knowledge and wisdom of *furqan* and *taqwa* to the believers who have opened their hearts and minds to Him. Man has been granted the freedom of choice in doing what is wholesome and beautiful or what is corrupt and ugly. It is only man among the creation who has been given the knowledge to distinguish right activity, right thought, and right intention from their opposites. This knowledge reminds the human of the scales of Allah's justice; the two hands of Allah—His mercy and His wrath—are reflected in the human domain, where people have been appointed Allah's vicegerents. Deeds of goodness and wholesomeness are associated with mercy, paradise, and what is beautiful. Evil and corruption is rewarded with wrath, hell, and what is ugly.

It is in the Koran that the Muslims will find the answers to their search. The remedy to the ills of modern-day Islamic world lies in the pages of the holy book in the step-by-step guidance of Allah.

Printed in the United States
by Baker & Taylor Publisher Services